Lecture Notes in Computer Science   **11419**

Commenced Publication in 1973
Founding and Former Series Editors:
Gerhard Goos, Juris Hartmanis, and Jan van Leeuwen

More information about this series at http://www.springer.com/series/7411

David Choffnes · Marinho Barcellos (Eds.)

Passive and Active Measurement

20th International Conference, PAM 2019
Puerto Varas, Chile, March 27–29, 2019
Proceedings

 Springer

Editors
David Choffnes
Northeastern University
Boston, MA, USA

Marinho Barcellos
Federal University of Rio Grande do Sul
Porto Alegre, Rio Grande do Sul, Brazil

ISSN 0302-9743   ISSN 1611-3349   (electronic)
Lecture Notes in Computer Science
ISBN 978-3-030-15985-6   ISBN 978-3-030-15986-3   (eBook)
https://doi.org/10.1007/978-3-030-15986-3

Library of Congress Control Number: 2019934742

LNCS Sublibrary: SL5 – Computer Communication Networks and Telecommunications

This Springer imprint is published by the registered company Springer Nature Switzerland AG
The registered company address is: Gewerbestrasse 11, 6330 Cham, Switzerland

Preface

Welcome to the proceedings of the 20th edition of the Passive and Active Measurements (PAM) Conference! This year's conference marked two important milestones. First, the conference took place during March 27–29 in Puerto Varas, Chile—the southernmost location for any international networking conference to date. Second, this was PAM's 20th anniversary, a testament to the rich, vibrant, and thriving network measurement research community that continues to make PAM one of the top publication venues in our field.

We are pleased to present 20 papers that cover a wide range of important networking measurement and analysis topics from low layers of the network stack up to applications, using measurements at scales large and small, and covering important aspects of the network ecosystem such as routing, DNS, privacy, security, and performance. We received 75 submissions from 197 authors in nearly 100 institutions and 19 countries. The 39 members of the Technical Program Committee (TPC) were tasked with providing well-reasoned, substantiated, and constructive reviews to determine the set of papers that would appear in this year's program. Each submission was assigned at least three reviewers, with a few papers receiving additional reviews in cases where additional viewpoints or expert opinions were needed. After the review phase, the chairs led an online discussion for each paper that received at least one positive review, with a particular focus on identifying the strengths of the submissions instead of focusing only on flaws. We were particularly happy with the quality of reviews and discussions from our TPC, and are excited by the 20 papers that they selected. Please join us in extending our gratitude to the TPC members for their hard work.

We would also like to thank several members of the Organizing Committee, who helped make the conference a successful event. This includes the general chairs, Javier Bustos and Fabián Bustamante, who managed the arrangements on site, the publicity chair, Pedro Casas, and Steve Uhlig for his experience and advice. Last, we thank all of the authors and attendees who make PAM such an interesting and important conference for two decades running, and we look forward to seeing what the next 20 years of PAM will bring!

March 2019

David Choffnes
Marinho Barcellos

Organization

General Chairs

Javier Bustos   NIC Labs, University of Chile, Chile
Fabián Bustamante   Northwestern University, USA

Program Chairs

David Choffnes   Northeastern University, USA
Marinho Barcellos   Federal University of Rio Grande do Sul, Brazil

Web Chair

Mara José Vilches   NIC Labs, University of Chile, Chile

Registration Chair

Ivana Bachmann   NIC Labs, University of Chile, Chile

Publicity Chair

Pedro Casas   AIT, Austria

Steering Committee

Fabio Ricciato   University of Salento, Italy
George Riley   Georgia Institute of Technology, USA
Ian Graham   Endace, New Zealand
Neil Spring   University of Maryland, USA
Nevil Brownlee   The University of Auckland, New Zealand
Nina Taft   Google, USA
Matthew Roughan   University of Adelaide, Australia
Rocky K. C. Chang   The Hong Kong Polytechnic University, SAR China
Yong Liu   New York University, USA
Xenofontas Dimitropoulos   University of Crete, Greece
Mohamed Ali (Dali) Kaafar   Data61, CSIRO, Australia

Program Committee

Alberto Dainotti	CAIDA, UC San Diego, USA
Amogh Dhamdhere	CAIDA, UC San Diego, USA
Andrew Moore	University of Cambridge, UK
Anja Feldmann	MPI Informatik, Germany
Anna Sperotto	University of Twente, The Netherlands
Aruna Balasubramanian	Stony Brook, USA
Cristel Pelsser	University of Strasbourg, France
David Choffnes	Northeastern University, USA
Eduardo Grampn	UDeLaR, Uruguay
Fabian Bustamante	Northwestern University, USA
Georgios Smaragdakis	MIT/TU Berlin, Germany
Hassan Asghar	Data61, CSIRO, Australia
Ignacio Castro	Queen Mary University of London, UK
Italo Cunha	Federal University of Minas Gerais, Brazil
Javier Bustos	University of Chile, Chile
Jelena Mirkovic	ISI/USC, USA
Justine Sherry	CMU, USA
Kensuke Fukuda	National Institute of Informatics, Japan
Marco Mellia	Politecnico di Torino, Italy
Maria Papadopouli	FORTH, University of Crete, Greece
Marinho Barcellos	Federal University of Rio Grande do Sul, Brazil
Mark Allman	ICSI, USA
Matthew Luckie	University of Waikato, New Zealand
Narseo Vallina-Rodriguez	IMDEA Networks/ICSI, USA
Oliver Hohlfeld	RWTH Aachen, Germany
Philipp Richter	MIT, USA
Quirin Scheitle	TUM, Germany
Ralph Holz	University of Sydney, Australia
Ramakrishna Padmanabhan	University of Maryland, USA
Ramakrishnan Durairajan	University of Oregon, USA
Robert Beverly	Naval Postgraduate School, USA
Sara Ayoubi	Inria, France
Steve Uhlig	Queen Mary University of London, UK
Steven Bauer	MIT, USA
Taejoong Chung	RIT, USA
Theo Benson	Brown University, USA
Thomas Karagiannakis	MSR, UK
Xenofontas Dimitropoulos	FORTH and ETH Zurich, Greece/Switzerland
Youngseok Lee	Chungnam National University, South Korea

Sponsors

Verizon Digital Media Services
Comcast
NIC Chile Research Labs
Akamai

Contents

Mobile Networks

Leveraging Context-Triggered Measurements to Characterize LTE Handover Performance

Shichang Xu[(✉)], Ashkan Nikravesh, and Z. Morley Mao

University of Michigan, Ann Arbor, USA
{xsc,ashnik,zmao}@umich.edu

Abstract. In cellular networks, handover plays a vital role in supporting mobility and connectivity. Traditionally, handovers in a cellular network focus on maintaining continuous connectivity for legacy voice calls. However, there is a poor understanding of how today's handover strategies impact the network performance, especially for applications that require reliable Internet connectivity.

In this work, using a newly designed context-triggered measurement framework, we carry out the first comprehensive measurement study in LTE networks on how handover decisions implemented by carriers impact network layer performance. We find that the interruption in connectivity during handover is minimal, but in 43% of cases the end-to-end throughput degrades after the handover. The cause is that the deployed handover policy uses statically configured signal strength threshold as the key factor to decide handover and focuses on improving signal strength which by itself is an imperfect metric for performance. We propose that handover decision strategies trigger handover based on predicted performance considering factors such as cell load along with application preference.

1 Introduction

Mobile devices rely on cellular networks to get network access to support data services. Since the coverage of each cell[1] is limited, handover between cells is essential for ensuring continuous connectivity and mobility. In addition, when the device is in the coverage of multiple cells, a proper policy should handover the mobile device to a cell that provides good performance.

There has been little work to understand how the deployed cellular network handover policies affects network layer performance in the wild. Specifically, questions such as what is the interruption in the network during handover and whether network performance consistently improves after handover are not well understood. In this paper, we perform the first large-scale study of handovers in LTE network using crowd-sourced measurements of over 200 users across three major carriers for the purpose of evaluating the performance implications of

---

[1] Each cellular base station has one or more set of antennas and it communicates with the mobile devices in one or more sectors called cells each of which has a unique ID [7].

© Springer Nature Switzerland AG 2019
D. Choffnes and M. Barcellos (Eds.): PAM 2019, LNCS 11419, pp. 3–17, 2019.
https://doi.org/10.1007/978-3-030-15986-3_1

existing handover algorithms and policies. Performing measurements to capture transient handover events efficiently is challenging. To address such challenges, we develop a novel context-triggered measurement framework that dynamically initiates performance measurements of interest only when handover is likely to occur to reduce the measurement overhead.

Based on our measurement results, we identified fundamental limitations in the current design and deployment of handover algorithms: the use of static configurations on signal strength difference with neighboring cells and a lack of awareness of network performance. As a consequence, in 43% of cases the throughput degrades after the handover. By analyzing physical layer information in LTE network, we found that the cause of the performance degradation is that target cells have higher load and allocate less physical resources.

Our findings help motivate the need for handover algorithms based on network performance considering both signal strength and cell load. The measurement also shows the opportunity to improve the handover decision (Sect. 4): (a) currently handovers do not occur only when devices experience poor signal strength, indicating that the time of handover could be potentially changed without risk of link failures; (b) the dense deployment of cells provides more than one candidate target cell the device could be potentially handed over to in many cases.

We summarize the main contribution of our work below.

– We designed a context-triggered measurement framework to support lightweight and accurate handover measurements. Using this setup, we collected 5 months' data from 200 users across three major cellular carriers in the U.S. to investigate performance impact of handover in LTE network.
– Using cross-layer analysis to incorporate radio link layer visibility with our data collector, we found that the current deployed handover policy relies on statically configured thresholds on signal strength. It focuses on improving signal strength and leads to potential performance degradation after the handover.
– We found that the interruption caused by intra-LTE handover is usually minimal. However, the median performance improvement after the handover is close to 0 in metrics including latency, throughput and jitter. The current handover algorithms do not appear to optimize performance.
– We identified that the performance degradation after handover is caused by higher load in the target cell and less allocated physical resources to the devices. We proposed cells predict performance after handover based on signal strength and cell load information and make handover decisions based on performance.

2   Background and Related Work

In this section, we first provide some background on handovers (Sect. 2.1). The related terminologies are summarized in Table 1. Then we summarize related works (Sect. 2.2).

Table 1. Related terminologies in LTE network

Terminology	Definition
Reference Signal Received Power (RSRP)	The average power received from the reference signals. It is a metric of the downlink signal strength
Physical Resource Block (PRB)	The basic unit of allocation of resources to the UE
Event A3	The signal strength of neighbor cell becomes better than the serving cell by a *relative* threshold value

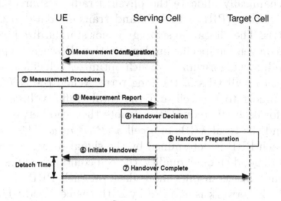

Fig. 1. The general handover procedure in a LTE network

2.1 LTE Handover and Data Transmission Procedure

Handovers within LTE networks are initiated by the cells and they can maintain ongoing network connections. We first define some basic terminology. *Serving cell* is the cell a user equipment (UE) is currently connected to. *Target cell* becomes the serving cell after the handover. We also refer to the original serving cell after the handover completes as the *source cell*.

As Fig. 1 shows, to help decide when to trigger handover, the mobile device measures radio signal strength of both the serving cell and neighbor cells periodically. A commonly used metric of signal strength is *Reference Signal Received Power* (RSRP), *i.e.,* the average power received from the reference signals of the cell. The serving cell sends the *measurement configuration* to the device to specify when measurement results should be reported back. Depending on the measurement configurations, the *measurement reports* can be either event-triggered or periodical. Event-triggered reports are sent only when the link quality satisfies certain conditions. From previous work, a common trigger for intra-LTE handover is *event A3* [8,11], where the signal strength of neighbor cell becomes better than the serving cell by a relative threshold value. Based on factors including measurement reports and load information, the serving cell makes decisions on handover [13]. The actual handover decision algorithm depends on the implementation at eNodeB or LTE base-station. After the source cell determines to perform a handover for a UE, it conducts a negotiation with the target cell to ensure enough resource at the target cell. Then it sends a message to the UE to initiate the handover. The UE disconnects with the source cell and connects to the target cell. After it successfully connects to the target cell, it notifies the target cell of the completion of the handover. These signaling messages between the cell and the UE are exchanged using radio resource control (RRC) protocol.

To understand how the network layer performance is determined by the lower layer in LTE network, we also briefly describe the data transmission procedure in the physical layer. Wireless communication requires radio spectrum resources. In LTE, cells dynamically allocate the physical radio resources in the unit of *physical resource blocks* (PRBs) to UEs and transmit data to the UEs using the allocated PRBs. The allocation strategy is not standardized in the specification and depends on vendor-specific implementation. However, typically cells use proportional scheduling algorithm [7], which optimizes cell efficiency while maintaining fairness across all UEs in the long term. When the *cell load* increases, i.e. more UEs connect to the cell and the total traffic volume increases, the allocated PRBs for each UE reduce. We denote the ratio between the allocated PRBs to a UE and the total PRBs of a cell as *PRB ratio*. The number of bytes transmitted by each PRB is determined by the signal strength, i.e., with strong signal strength and good channel quality, the cell could use coding schemes with high efficiency and thus transmits more data on each PRB. In summary, the performance in LTE network is affected by both the cell load which determines the PRB allocation and the signal strength which determines the transmission efficiency.

2.2 Related Work

The problem of handover in cellular networks has attracted significant attention in both academia and industry. However, there is little work on understanding the performance impact of handover decisions in operational LTE network.

Previous work measured intra-LTE handovers using simulation [8,9] and testbeds [13,22] to understand the performance of applications during handover. Our work differs in that we measured the handover performance in the wild. Recent work [14,16,19,23] study persistent handover loops caused by misconfigurations. We also identify such misconfigurations for a few cells in the wild but find they are not dominant. Our focus is to characterize the interruption caused by handover regardless of handover loops and compare the network performance before and after handover to understand the performance implications of deployed handover policies. Some other work [4,12,20,21] studied handovers between different technologies, e.g. 3G and 4G. Our work studies handover between different cells in LTE network.

3   Methodology

To understand the impact of handover on performance in the wild, we crowd-source our measurement using a context-triggered measurement framework.

3.1   On-Device Measurement Support

We combine passive monitoring with active measurements to study handover with minimal measurement overhead.

Passive Monitoring. We keep track of device context including network type, signal strength and location. Through a novel use of the built-in diagnostic interface from Qualcomm communication chips, we also collect (1) lower layer RRC layer information including measurement configurations and handover messages and (2) physical layer information including PRB allocations. Our lower-layer message collection builds upon SnoopSnitch [2] which is an open-source Android app aimed to detect attacks such as fake base station using data from the Diagnostic Interface. The collector requires root privilege and reads the raw radio messages from the character device /dev/diag when DIAG_CHAR option is activated in Android kernel. The collector also collects fine-grained signal strength information from the diagnostic interface every 40 ms, while the signal strength information from Android API updates only every two to three seconds. We are one of the first to crowd-source LTE radio-link layer messages.

Active Measurement. To understand how handover impacts network performance, we use the Mobilyzer measurement library [18], a principled mobile network measurement platform, to measure network performance. We issue ping, TCP throughput, and UDP burst measurements to capture network characteristics using metrics including latency, throughput, jitter, packet loss.

Compared with passive monitoring, active measurements consume data resources and can cause significant impact on battery life. As data and battery resources are scarce on mobile devices, we need to capture performance during handover events efficiently. Towards this goal, we develop a context-triggered framework to trigger measurements only when a handover is predicted to occur in the near future.

Context-Triggered Measurement Framework. In general, deciding when to issue measurements is a challenging task. If we simply perform measurements periodically, the interval is difficult to configure. A small interval leads to large amount of unnecessary measurements that fail to capture interesting phenomena, wasting valuable data and battery resources on the device; while a large interval can miss the phenomena we are interested in.

One approach to solving this problem is to trigger measurements [3] based on context that specifies the conditions of interest. We estimate the likelihood of observing relevant events based on the device context and trigger measurements only when the probability of capturing desired events is high. This helps reduce unnecessary measurements while capturing more events of interest.

We design a context-triggered measurement framework atop Mobilyzer [18]. We send the devices measurement tasks with specific context requirements. The devices keep monitoring related context and trigger measurements once the context conditions are met. Note that different contexts contain different information with different cost. Even querying the same context with different granularity requirement has different cost implications. These considerations motivate our design of supporting a multi-level triggering procedure. At the first level, we monitor a context with the lowest cost. If the context indicates that the possibility of desired event occurrence is high, we monitor another context with higher cost or the same context with higher accuracy. This can be done with multiple layers until we reach high confidence that the event will occur. There is certainly a trade-off from using many levels to reduce measurement overhead but at the cost of introducing delay in capturing the event of interest which could lead to fewer events captured. We argue that the number of levels need to be adjusted depending on the type of events and the overhead of triggering at each level.

We apply this framework to understand the performance impact of handovers. Based on the passively collected lower layer messages, we find that LTE handovers usually happen when a cell with a stronger signal strength than the connected cell is discovered for a mobile user (Sect. 4). We implement the framework as follows. We first use sensors to detect user movement, as the power consumption of movement detection sensors such as accelerometers is only 5 mW for an active device. Once we detect that the user is moving, we start to read fine-grained signal strength data from the diagnostic interface, which consumes around 200 mW. If the neighbor cell signal strength is stronger than the serving cell, a ping, throughput or udp burst measurement is triggered, consuming more than 1500 mW to activate the radio [10].

To evaluate the effectiveness of the framework, we run simulation on all traces collected from PhoneLab deployment [5] as explained later. Figure 2 compares the overhead and accuracy of measurements with and without context triggered framework. $T = x$ means the measurement are triggered when the signal strength of neighbor cell is stronger than the serving cell by the threshold of x dBm. $P = y$ denotes periodic measurement every y minutes. We calculate the overhead as the average number of measurements for identified handovers, and accuracy as the percentage of measurements that capture handovers. As shown, our framework can reduce the overhead to 1% while increasing the accuracy by 10 times. In the actual deployment, labeled as "Real" in Fig. 2, we use $T = 0$. Compared to the simulation results, the real deployment has a slightly lower overhead and accuracy, because we imposed constraints on the resource usage of active measurements to reduce impact on user experiences.

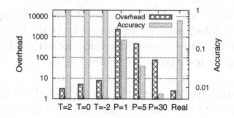

Fig. 2. Context-triggered measurement improves efficiency and accuracy of measurements for intra-LTE handovers (PhoneLab). ($T = x$: triggered measurement using x dBm threshold. $P = y$: periodic measurement every y min).

3.2   Crowd-Sourced Measurement

PhoneLab Deployment. PhoneLab [5] is a smartphone testbed located at the University at Buffalo with more than 200 participants. Each participant receives a Nexus 5 device running Android Lollipop with unlimited Sprint data plan. Developers can deploy experiments on the devices by modifying the Android system.

To understand handover policies and performance impacts, we add a system service called *HandoverTrackerService* in Android system. This service monitors context information of the device and triggers active measurements. The lower layer information and measurement results are uploaded to servers. At the beginning of deployment, we keep collecting lower layer messages and perform active measurement periodically to avoid bias in the collected data. After analyzing the data and understanding when handover is triggered, we update the deployment and leverage the context-triggered measurement framework to reduce the measurement overhead.

To guarantee minimal influence of active measurements on user experience, heavy-weight measurements such as throughput are performed only when the screen is off and users are not interacting with the device. To control the power consumption of issued active measurements, we build an energy model for all measurements, and stop all measurements when the power consumption reaches 10% of total battery resources after the device is unplugged from the power source. We also enforce a limit on the daily data usage generated by the active measurements.

We deploy the measurement system on PhoneLab testbed and collect a dataset PHONELAB for 5 months from January 2016 to May 2016[2]. In total we observe 8403 cells and 283,556 intra-LTE handover events. For active measurements, we collect 49,594 throughput measurements, 159,210 ping measurements and 50,409 UDP burst measurements.

---

[2] We confirm the inferred handover policy from PHONELAB are still current with the newer MobileInsight dataset as described later in Sect. 4.

Local Deployment. We also deploy our measurement setup to 20 local users with unlimited AT&T data plans. We install an app called *HandoverTrackerApp* on their devices. The app collects the same information as *HandoverTrackerService* in PhoneLab deployment. We also collect data from a local device with T-Mobile service.

Both the crowd-sourced measurements and local deployment were IRB approved. The descriptions of the experiment and collected data are presented to the participants and they have the option to opt-out the experiment data collection.

MobileInsight Dataset. MobileInsight dataset [1] is a publicly available dataset containing lower layer cellular messages[3] collected from more than 8 US/Chinese network carriers spanning 3 years from year 2015 to 2018 using the tool MobileInsight [15]. The types of lower layer information collected by MobileInsight is similar to our data collection deployed on PhoneLab.

4   Handover Policy Inference

In LTE networks, the cells make decisions on when to initiate handovers. The handover decision process is not standardized in the 3GPP specification and is left to be defined using carriers' network configurations. To infer handover trigger policies in practice, we implement an RRC stack emulator that keeps track of the current device information, such as RRC connected state, connected cell ID, measurement configurations, and processes handover related messages. We feed RRC messages from each device to the emulator and output information including recent measurement reports and corresponding measurement configurations when processing handover initialization commands.

We first characterize the deployment of the cells and analyze how many cells the device usually observes from the signal strength measurements of neighboring cells in the PhoneLab dataset. We find that in 77.4% of cases the device observes at least one neighboring cell. In 41.9% of cases, the devices observe multiple neighboring cells. These neighboring cells can be of good signal strength. Among all the measurements, in 18.5% of cases, there is at least 1 neighbor cell with RSRP no worse than 5 dBm lower than the serving cell. This indicates that carriers deploy cells densely to ensure connectivity and the potential chances of performing handovers between cells are high.

We find a strong correlation between measurement reports sent from the UE to the cell (shown in Fig. 1) and handover events observed on the UE. As illustrated in Fig. 3, 95.4% of handovers in Sprint occur within 100 ms after the measurement report is sent. If we consider a measurement report helps *trigger* the handover when a handover occurs within 500 ms after a measurement report is sent, for all carriers studied, more than 99.4% of handovers are triggered by measurement reports, as shown in Table 2. Such close timing proximity implies potential causality.

---

[3] The MobileInsight dataset does not have active measurements on network performance.

Table 2. Overall statistics of handovers.

Carriers	Sprint	T-Mobile	AT&T
Handovers triggered from events	99.84%	100%	99.40%
Handovers triggered from event A3	98.39%	89.51%	94.41%
Event A3 triggering handovers	91.87%	88.73%	87.58%
Handover count	283,556	286	330
Handover-involved cell count	6,304	33	45

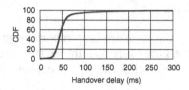

Fig. 3. Measured delay from the last measurement report to the time when handover starts (Sprint).

We find the majority type of measurement reports that triggers handovers is event A3. Event A3 indicates that $signal_{neighbor} - signal_{serving} > threshold$. 98.39% of all handovers in Sprint network are triggered by event A3 reports. On the other hand, event A3 measurement reports have a high success rate of triggering handover. In Sprint network, for 91.9% of event A3 reports, the cell initiates a handover within 500 ms. For 98.1% of event A3 reports, the cell initiates a handover within 2 s. One reason why some reports fail to trigger handovers is that the device releases the RRC connection or the data collector stops collecting data before the handover occurs.

We find for each pair of cells, the threshold value of event A3 that triggers handover is statically configured and does not change over a long period. In the Sprint network, for the pairs of cells that have more than 100 handovers, 10.4% always set the threshold to 2 dBm and 2.9% always set it to 4 dBm. The other cells used the threshold of 2 dBm at the first 2 months of our data collection period and then changed to 4 dBm. The threshold of event A3 can affect how often handover happens. A lower threshold can be met more easily, thus encouraging more frequent handovers.

To understand whether handovers occur mostly for devices experiencing poor signal strength, we plot the distribution of the serving cell's RSRP values right before handovers in Fig. 4. As shown, there is no direct relationship between current serving cell signal strength and handover occurrence. Handover occurs even when serving cell signal strength is already strong. For AT&T and Sprint, more than 20% of handovers happen when serving RSRP is stronger than −100 dBm. This is due to the fact that most of the handover events are triggered by event A3 using the relative signal strength threshold.

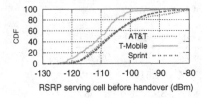

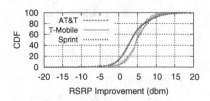

Fig. 4. RSRP of serving cell before the handover. Despite strong signal strength, handovers still occur.

Fig. 5. In 90% of cases, signal strength improves after intra-LTE handover.

From the definition of the measurement report events, we know that handovers triggered by event A3 are likely to improve the signal strength of the UE. This is confirmed by Fig. 5, showing the signal strength improvement after the handover.

We also validate our observation using the MobileInsight dataset. Among the 4873 observed handover events in the dataset, 86.5% are triggered by event A3 measurement reports. For 99.1% of the cell pairs, the A3 threshold value triggering handover is fixed. This confirms similar handover policies are used across time across different carriers. We next study the performance implications of such handover policies.

5 Performance Impact of Handover

We characterize the disruption during handover and the performance change after handover.

5.1 Performance Disruption During Handover

Due to the underlying physical radio layer transmission mechanism, during intra-LTE handovers, the device has to disconnect from the currently connected cell before connecting to the target cell, thus introducing a period during which the device is detached from the network preventing any data exchange. This unavoidably generates an interruption to ongoing traffic during handover. In intra-LTE handovers, the detach time is defined as the interval from the time when the device receives handover initialization message from the source cell and the time when the device successfully connects to the target cell.

To maintain good user experience during handover, the detach time needs to be kept low. In our observation, the detach time of successful handovers is within 35 ms, which is quite minimal. However, handovers can fail due to various reasons such as insufficient radio resources in the target cell. When a handover fails, detach time can increase dramatically. If the UE fails to connect to the target cell, the UE aborts the handover process and initiates connection re-establishment procedure with the source cell instead, which increase the detach time up to 775 ms from our observations. Moreover, in some cases, the

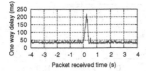 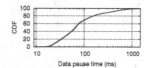 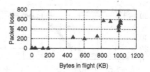

Fig. 6. An example of data pause caused by handover. 0 is the time when the handover occurs (Sprint).

Fig. 7. Data pause in UDP burst measurement during handover (Sprint)

Fig. 8. TCP packet loss during handover due to limited buffer size in source cell for lossless handovers (AT&T)

re-establishment request is rejected by the source cell, and the UE is forced to release the connection and establish a new connection. This can further increase the detach time to 2.7 s. The handover failure rate observed in Sprint is 0.18%.

Low detach time does not necessarily mean low impact on application-layer traffic. After the UE connects to the target cell, it may not resume data transmission from the new cell immediately. We use UDP burst measurement to characterize the *data pause time* during handover. Figure 6 shows an example of UDP measurement results. After the handover, the first few packets are delayed for about 200 ms. As Fig. 7 shows, the median data pause time is 66 ms, which increases traffic jitter and may degrade real-time applications such as VoIP.

We examine packet losses during handover. During the handover, some data may be buffered in the source cell if the device is receiving data. Depending on how such data is handled, intra-LTE handovers can be categorized as *seamless*, which discards all data in the PDCP retransmission queue in the source cell, or *lossless* which forwards such data to the target cell. Recent work [17] shows that seamless handover is better in terms of goodput while lossless handover is better in terms of latency. We find that all cells in Sprint network use lossless handover, as no packet loss is found after the handover.

In AT&T network, we found three cells drop packets when there are handovers between them. In order to understand the underlying cause of this phenomena, we carry a Nexus 5 device that keeps downloading data from a local server while moving in the coverage area of these three cells. Server throughput is throttled at different values using the *tc* tool. All tcpdump traces from both the server and the client are captured.

Figure 8 shows bytes in flight right before the handover and the corresponding number of lost packets during the handover. We find that the number of lost packets has a strong correlation with the number of bytes in flight. We infer that there is a buffer in the cell that buffers packets during the data transmission between the server and the device. When a handover happens between the source cell and the target cell, the source cell tries to forward packets in the buffer to the target cell. However, during handover, the device cannot receive packets from the source cell in time, thus the number of accumulated packets at the cell may exceed the buffer size. In that case, the source cell has to drop packets during the handover.

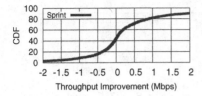

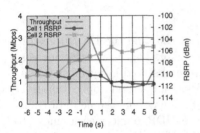

Fig. 9. Throughput improvement after handover (Sprint).

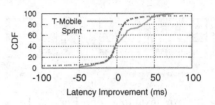

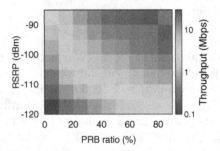

Fig. 10. Latency improvement after handover (Sprint).

Fig. 11. An example of performance degradation after handover even through signal strength gets improved (Sprint). At time 0, a handover occurs from Cell1 to Cell2.

Fig. 12. The performance depends on both signal strength and allocated PRB (Sprint).

We infer the cause of this unusual behavior of these three cells during handover is the poor configuration of their buffer size. From the experiment results, the buffer size of these cells is between 250 KB to 400 KB. For normal TCP connections, the small buffer size does not cause packet loss due to the flow control in TCP. However, during handover, the small buffer size can easily lead packets loss, further degrading the performance of handover. In the worst case of our experiment, the duration of retransmission for the lost packets is 2.27 s, which can greatly degrade user experiences.

5.2   Performance Change After Handover

One desirable goal of handover is to improve performance after switching to a new cell. We analyze the data to compare performance before and after the handover.

We filter out the throughput measurements that include handovers and calculate the average throughput value in the 5 s before the handover occurs and the average value in the 5 s after the handover. As shown in Fig. 9, we find that the throughput does not improve consistently after the handover. In 43% of cases, the throughput decreases after the handover. Similar to throughput, neither latency (Fig. 10) nor jitter improves consistently based on the ping and UDP

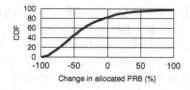

Fig. 13. The performance degradation is associated with higher cell load and less allocated PRBs (Sprint).

burst measurements. The median improvement is close to 0 for all these metrics. The current handover algorithms do not appear to optimize performance.

As mentioned in Sect. 4, the currently deployed handover decisions of all the carriers use signal strength as one of the key metrics and focus on improving signal strength after the handover. However, signal strength is an imperfect metric for performance, as performance also depends on other factors such as allocated PRBs determined by the cell load [6]. We calculate the throughput values each second using the crowd-sourced data and associate them with the RSRP and obtained PRB ratio. As shown in Fig. 12, the achieved throughput is determined by the PRB ratio as well.

Figure 11 shows an example where signal strength increases after the handover, but the performance degrades. To confirm the root cause of such performance degradation, we look into the change in allocated PRBs after handover for the cases where throughput decreases. As shown in Fig. 13, in most of such cases the allocated PRBs of the UE decreases after the handover, indicating that the target cell has a higher load.

Instead of making handover decisions simply based on signal strength, we propose that each cell maintains a 2-dimensional performance map from signal strength value ranges and load value ranges to performance ranges including throughput, loss rate, and delay. The performance values are updated by passively monitoring ongoing traffic at the cell. The cells exchange the performance information of the UE and UE's perceived signal strength of the potential target cell with its neighbors and trigger handover only if there is significantly enough performance improvements. The type of performance metric to be considered depends on user traffic demand inferred from its traffic types.

6   Conclusion

Handovers are essential for maintaining connectivity as users move with their devices. With the introduction of small cells in the incoming 5G network, handovers will become more frequent and critical. In this paper, we conduct the first comprehensive empirical study to investigate the decision strategies of intra-LTE handover in the wild and analyze their impact on performance. Our study examines currently deployed decision policies by carriers and sheds light on opportunities for improving the handover decision process with respect to application performance.

Our analysis shows that the policies enforced by carriers are not optimized in terms of performance. The key factor to decide handover is signal strength, and the handover trigger thresholds are found to be statically configured. We discover that the performance can degrade after the handover. We propose that the handover decision should depend on performance information predicted using both signal strength and cell load information.

Acknowledgements. This work is partially supported by NSF under the grants CCF-1628991 and CNS-1629763.

References

1. MobileInsight Data Sharing. http://www.mobileinsight.net/data.html
2. SnoopSnitch. https://opensource.srlabs.de/projects/snoopsnitch
3. Allman, M., Paxson, V.: A reactive measurement framework. In: Claypool, M., Uhlig, S. (eds.) PAM 2008. LNCS, vol. 4979, pp. 92–101. Springer, Heidelberg (2008). https://doi.org/10.1007/978-3-540-79232-1_10
4. Balachandran, A., et al.: Modeling web quality-of-experience on cellular networks. In: Proceedings of the 20th Annual International Conference on Mobile Computing and Networking, pp. 213–224. ACM (2014)
5. University of Buffalo: PhoneLab: A Smartphone Platform Testbed. https://www.phone-lab.org/
6. Chakraborty, A., Navda, V., Padmanabhan, V.N., Ramjee, R.: LoadSense: passively estimating cellular load. In: 2014 Sixth International Conference on Communication Systems and Networks (COMSNETS), pp. 1–3. IEEE (2014)
7. Cox, C.: An Introduction to LTE: LTE, LTE-Advanced, SAE and 4G Mobile Communications. Wiley, Hoboken (2012)
8. Dimou, K., et al.: Handover within 3GPP LTE: design principles and performance. In: 2009 IEEE 70th Vehicular Technology Conference Fall (VTC 2009-Fall), pp. 1–5. IEEE (2009)
9. Herman, B., Petrov, D., Puttonen, J., Kurjenniemi, J.: A3-based measurements and handover model for NS-3 LTE. In: The Third International Conference on Mobile Services, Resources, and Users (MOBILITY 2013), pp. 20–23 (2013)
10. Huang, J., Qian, F., Gerber, A., Mao, Z.M., Sen, S., Spatscheck, O.: A close examination of performance and power characteristics of 4G LTE networks. In: Proceedings of the 10th International Conference on Mobile Systems, Applications, and Services, pp. 225–238. ACM (2012)
11. Jansen, T., Balan, I., Turk, J., Moerman, I., Kurner, T.: Handover parameter optimization in LTE self-organizing networks. In: 2010 IEEE 72nd Vehicular Technology Conference Fall (VTC 2010-Fall), pp. 1–5. IEEE (2010)
12. Javed, U., Han, D., Caceres, R., Pang, J., Seshan, S., Varshavsky, A.: Predicting handoffs in 3G networks. In: Proceedings of the 3rd ACM SOSP Workshop on Networking, Systems, and Applications on Mobile Handhelds, p. 8. ACM (2011)
13. Kantola, R.: Performance of handover in long term evolution. Ph.D. thesis, Aalto University (2011)
14. Li, Y., Deng, H., Li, J., Peng, C., Lu, S.: Instability in distributed mobility management: revisiting configuration management in 3G/4G mobile networks. In: Proceedings of the 2016 ACM SIGMETRICS International Conference on Measurement and Modeling of Computer Science, pp. 261–272. ACM (2016)

15. Li, Y., Peng, C., Yuan, Z., Li, J., Deng, H., Wang, T.: MobileInsight: extracting and analyzing cellular network information on smartphones. In: MobiCom, pp. 202–215 (2016)

16. Li, Y., Xu, J., Peng, C., Lu, S.: A first look at unstable mobility management in cellular networks. In: Proceedings of the 17th International Workshop on Mobile Computing Systems and Applications, pp. 15–20. ACM (2016)

17. Nguyen, B., et al.: Towards understanding TCP performance on LTE/EPC mobile networks. In: Proceedings of All Things Cellular Workshop (2014)

18. Nikravesh, A., Yao, H., Xu, S., Choffnes, D., Mao, Z.M.: Mobilyzer: an open plat-form for controllable mobile network measurements. In: Proceedings of MobiSys (2015)

19. Peng, C., Li, Y.: Demystify undesired handoff in cellular networks. In: 2016 25th International Conference on Computer Communication and Networks (ICCCN), pp. 1–9. IEEE (2016)

20. Shafiq, M.Z., Erman, J., Ji, L., Liu, A.X., Pang, J., Wang, J.: Understanding the impact of network dynamics on mobile video user engagement. In: The 2014 ACM International Conference on Measurement and Codeling of Computer Systems, pp. 367–379. ACM (2014)

21. Tu, G.H., Peng, C., Wang, H., Li, C.Y., Lu, S.: How voice calls affect data in opera-tional LTE networks. In: Proceedings of the 19th Annual International Conference on Mobile Computing and Networking, pp. 87–98. ACM (2013)

22. Zhang, L., Okamawari, T., Fujii, T.: Performance evaluation of TCP and UDP during LTE handover. In: 2012 IEEE Wireless Communications and Networking Conference (WCNC), pp. 1993–1997. IEEE (2012)

23. Zhao, X., Ma, H., Jin, Y., Yao, J.: Measuring instability of mobility management in cellular networks. IEEE Netw. (2018)

Measuring Web Quality of Experience
in Cellular Networks

Alemnew Sheferaw Asrese[1(✉)], Ermias Andargie Walelgne[1], Vaibhav Bajpai[2],
Andra Lutu[4], Özgü Alay[3], and Jörg Ott[2]

[1] Aalto University, Espoo, Finland
alemnew.asrese@aalto.fi
[2] Technische Universität München, Munich, Germany
[3] Simula Metropolitan, Oslo, Norway
[4] Telefonica Research, Barcelona, Spain

Abstract. Measuring and understanding the end-user browsing Quality of Experience (QoE) is crucial to Mobile Network Operators (MNOs) to retain their customers and increase revenue. MNOs often use traffic traces to detect the bottlenecks and study their end-users experience. Recent studies show that Above The Fold (ATF) time better approximates the user browsing QoE compared to traditional metrics such as Page Load Time (PLT). This work focuses on developing a methodology to measure the web browsing QoE over operational Mobile Broadband (MBB) networks. We implemented a web performance measurement tool WebLAR (it stands for Web Latency And Rendering) that measures web Quality of Service (QoS) such as TCP connect time, and Time To First Byte (TTFB) and web QoE metrics including PLT and ATF time. We deployed WebLAR on 128 MONROE (a European-wide mobile measurement platform) nodes, and conducted two weeks long (May and July 2018) web measurement campaign towards eight websites from six operational MBB networks. The result shows that, in the median case, the TCP connect time and TTFB in Long Term Evolution (LTE) networks are, respectively, 160% and 30% longer than fixed-line networks. The DNS lookup time and TCP connect time of the websites varies significantly across MNOs. Most of the websites do not show a significant difference in PLT and ATF time across operators. However, Yahoo shows longer ATF time in Norwegian operators than that of the Swedish operators. Moreover, user mobility has a small impact on the ATF time of the websites. Furthermore, the website design should be taken into consideration when approximating the ATF time.

1 Introduction

Recent studies show that mobile data traffic is increasing exponentially, and web browsing is amongst the dominant applications on MBB networks [13]. The dependency on MBB networks and the widespread availability of LTE is boosting user expectations towards fast, reliable, and pervasive connectivity. The users make the MNOs responsible for the shortcomings in the mobile experience [5].

© Springer Nature Switzerland AG 2019
D. Choffnes and M. Barcellos (Eds.): PAM 2019, LNCS 11419, pp. 18–33, 2019.
https://doi.org/10.1007/978-3-030-15986-3_2

This demand pushes the MNOs to further enhance the capabilities of the mobile networks for emerging applications. One of the challenging use cases for MBB networks is the mobility scenario [28], for example, browsing the web while commuting in a high-speed train. Thus, for MNOs, it is paramount to understand the end-user browsing experience while using their network [16]. Users are mostly concerned with the fulfillment of the quality expectation rather than the level of the QoS metrics like throughput.

There have been a number of previous efforts (Sect. 4) to measure and understand the performance of MBB networks. NetRadar [34,37], SamKnows broadband measurement [12], Meteor [32] are some of the tools that have been developed to measure the QoS metrics from MBB network. These tools either aim at measuring the metrics related to QoS or do not indicate how the metrics are used to measure the QoE. Moreover, web performance and QoE have been well studied [3,9,13,14,19,25–27,33]. Nonetheless, most of the studies that investigated mobile web QoE are either from lab experiments or do not cover a wide range of metrics to approximate the end-user browsing experience. As a result, our understanding of web QoE on operational MNOs is limited. Mainly, this is because of two reasons: (1) the lack of large-scale measurements that investigate the application level metrics in operational MBB networks, and (2) the mapping of the network QoS to objective application QoS metrics and then to the subjective QoE, has not been well validated for mobile networks.

Our first contribution in this work (Sect. 2) is the design and development of *WebLAR* [7], a lightweight tool for measuring the end-user web experience over operational MNOs. The measurement tool can be deployed at scale and captures web latency and QoE metrics at different layers such as the DNS lookup time, TCP connect time, PLT, and the ATF time. The ATF time is the time required to show the content in the browsers' current viewport [15]. The authors in [9,25] used two different approaches to approximate the ATF time in fixed-line networks. Asrese *et al.* [9] used a pixel-wise comparison of the changes in the browser's viewport to approximate the ATF time. They capture a series of screenshots of the webpage loading process and compare the pixel difference between consecutive screenshots with a three seconds threshold. When there is no change observed for three seconds, the webpage is considered as rendered completely. The ATF time is the difference between the starting time of the webpage loading process and the time where the last pixel change is observed. Hora *et al.* [25] used the browsers timing information to approximate the ATF time. They consider that the ATF time is the integral of the downloading time of the main HTML file, scripts, stylesheets and the images located in the above-the-fold area. By adopting the methods from the existing work [9,25], we designed WebLAR to approximate the ATF time in operational MNOs. In addition, WebLAR captures network and device level metadata information such as the radio access technology, the GPS locations, CPU and memory usage in the device. Different confounding factors such as the device affect the QoE. In this work, we build a baseline view by using MONROE, a platform that can be used for performing measurements in a more controlled setting.

The second contribution of this work (Sect. 3) are the insights derived from the dataset collected using WebLAR. We deployed WebLAR on MONROE [6], a Europe-wide experimental platform for MBB network measurement. We measured the performance of eight popular websites from 128 stationary and mobile MONROE nodes distributed across Norway and Sweden. In our measurement campaign, measuring a larger set of websites was not possible because of data quota limitation. So, we picked eight websites (Appendix A) that are popular in Norway and Sweden. The result from our analysis shows that there is a difference in DNS lookup time, and TCP connect time of the websites across different MNOs. For most of the websites, there is no significant difference in PLT and ATF time across the operators. However, we also observed a big variation in ATF time of Yahoo between MNOs across different countries. That is, Yahoo has longer ATF time in the Norwegian MNOs. Moreover, we observed that user mobility does not have a significant effect on the web QoE.

The applicability of the aforementioned approaches [9,25] to approximate the ATF time have not been validated for webpages that have different design style. That is, one approach may work better for certain types of webpages but may not work well for others. Using the dataset collected using WebLAR, we showed that the website design should be taken into consideration while using the browser timing information and the pixel-wise comparison approaches to approximate the ATF time (Sect. 3.3). We also showed that for the pixel-wise comparison approach three seconds threshold is sufficient to determine when the content in the above-the-fold area of the webpage is stabilized. To encourage reproducibility [11], we open source the tool [7], and release the collected dataset along with the Jupyter notebooks [10] that were used for parsing and analysing the results.

2   Experiment Design

We begin by presenting our methodology (Sect. 2.1) to approximate the ATF time of websites. We provide details on the design, the experimental workflow (Sect. 2.2), and the implementation aspects (Sect. 2.3) of WebLAR required for its deployment on the MONROE platform.

2.1   Methodology

The contents in the *above-the-fold* area of the webpage (that is, the content within the current viewport of the browser) are the key parts of the webpage for the user to judge whether or not the page has downloaded and rendered. As such, the time at which the contents in the above-the-fold area stop changing and reach the final state is one objective metric to approximate the user QoE [15]. We refer to this as ATF time. One way to approximate the ATF time is by monitoring the pixel changes in the visible part of the webpage and detecting when it stabilizes [9]. Another method is approximating by using the performance timing information that the browsers provide [25]. Browsers provide

APIs to retrieve performance and navigation time information of the websites. The two approaches have their limitations. The webpage may not stabilize due to different reasons; for example, it may contain animating contents. As such, it might be difficult to detect when the webpage stabilizes. This makes it harder to approximate the ATF time using the pixel-wise approach. Conversely, in some cases it is difficult to identify the exact location of some types of objects. This is one of the challenges in approximating the ATF time using the browser's timing API. Thus, one approach could better approximate ATF time for certain types of websites, while the other approach may underestimate or overestimate it.

Recent studies [9, 25] have developed tools to estimate the ATF time in fixed-line networks. We take this forward by designing and developing WebLAR that measures the web QoE in cellular networks by combining both approaches. WebLAR can approximate the ATF time using both the pixel-wise comparison [9] and using the browser performance timing information [25]. Unlike [9], where the measurement system approximates the ATF time by downloading all the web objects at the measurement nodes and pushing them to a centralized server location for processing, we approximate the ATF time at the MONROE nodes themselves. For simplicity of notations, we refer the ATF time approximated using this method as ATF_p time. Hora *et al.* [25] developed a Google Chrome extension to approximate the ATF time, which requires user interaction. Since the mobile version of Google Chrome does not support extensions (at least without using additional tools), it is not possible to use the browser timing information to approximate the ATF time in mobile devices. To close this gap, WebLAR approximates the ATF time in measurement probes that mimic mobile devices. We refer the ATF time approximated using this approach as ATF_b time. Moreover, using the browsers timing API, WebLAR also records metrics such as the DNS lookup time, TCP connect time, TTFB, and PLT. The browser API also enables us to get the web complexity metrics [22] including the number and the size of objects of the webpages. WebLAR also captures metadata information about the network conditions at the measurement nodes (e.g., MBB coverage profiles, signal strength) and other information that describe the user's mobility (e.g., GPS coordinates) and other events like CPU and memory usage.

2.2   Experiment Workflow

Figure 1 shows the sequence of operations of WebLAR experiment in MONROE measurement platform. The MONROE measurement platform provides a web interface where the users can submit their custom experiment (#1 in Figure). The MONROE back-end service then schedules (#2) the submitted user experiments to the selected nodes. It also starts the execution of the test according to the parameters that the user provided through the web interface. Once a node receives the commands for executing an experiment, it checks whether the `docker` container that contains the test is available locally. Otherwise, it fetches the `docker` container from a remote repository. Then the node starts the container with the parameters given in the MONROE web interface.

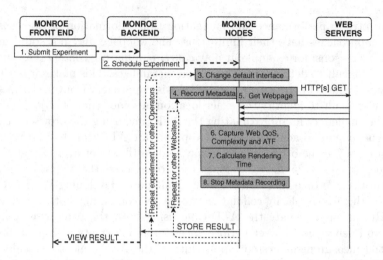

Fig. 1. Sequence diagram of the experiment using WebLAR tool in MONROE measurement platform.

When the container begins running the WebLAR experiment, WebLAR starts by checking the available network interfaces that have cellular connectivity and changes the default gateway (#3) to one of the available interfaces to fetch the webpages. Then, the node immediately starts capturing the metadata information and simultaneously runs the Google Chrome browser (version 62) using Chromedriver (version 2.33) (#4 and #5). The Google Chrome browser starts in Incognito and maximized mode and with no-sandbox option. The browser issues HTTP[S] GET request to the given URL. When the browser starts downloading the webpage a video of the browsing session progress is captured for 30 s. Moreover, we capture the web QoS and complexity metrics of the webpage (#6) by using the browser timing information. At the same time, the ATF time is approximated using the timing information retrieved using the browser API. Once the browsing session is completed the recorded video is converted into a series of screenshots (bitmap images) in every 100 ms interval and the ATF time is calculated by comparing the pixel changes within the consecutive screenshots (#7). Then we stop capturing the metadata (#8) and send the results annotated with the metadata to the MONROE back-end. In one experiment submission, the steps from #3 to #8 may repeat depending on the number of cellular connectivity that the node has and the number of the webpages that the user wishes to measure. Finally, the user can retrieve the results from the MONROE back-end and can do analysis.

2.3   Implementation

The Pixel-Wise Comparison Approach: We designed a Java program that records a video (10 frames per second) of the browsing session on a predefined screen size. Then by using `ffmpeg` [23], the video is converted into bitmap images in 100 ms interval. `imagemagic` [1] is used to compare the pixel difference between consecutive images. Then we utilise a `python` script [9] to determine the ATF_p time from the pixel differences. The ATF_p time is the point where there are no more pixel changes in consecutive X screenshots (*i.e.*, X/10 s threshold). A study [21] in 2016 shows the average PLT in 4G connection is 14 s. The study shows that more than half of the mobile users abandon the sites that take longer than three seconds to load. The study revealed that 75% of the mobile sites take longer than ten seconds to load. In the WebLAR experiment, we set three thresholds (3, 10 and 14 s) for declaring whether or not the webpage stabilizes. Hence, the ATF_p time is approximated with different webpage stabilizing thresholds.

Browser Heuristic-Based Approach: We used the Google Chrome browser API and utilized the performance timing information to approximate ATF_b time using the browser's heuristic. First we detect all the resources of the website and their location on the webpage. Then, to approximate the ATF_b time, we integrate the download time of the images (that are located in the ATF area), javascript files, cascaded style sheet files, and the root document that contains the DOM structure of the webpage. Moreover, using the browser API, the QoS metrics such as the DNS lookup time, TCP connect time, TTFB, the DOM load time and PLT are captured. The web complexity metrics such as number and size of resources are also extracted using the API. We wrote a javascript implementation to approximate the ATF_b time and integrated it within the Java program used to approximate the ATF_p time.

3 Analysis

We begin by presenting the dataset (Sect. 3.1) we collected after deploying WebLAR on the MONROE platform. We present the analysis using this dataset, focussing on IP path lengths (Sect. 3.2), web latency and QoE (Sect. 3.3) and specifically QoE under mobility (Sect. 3.4) conditions.

3.1 Dataset

We ran the WebLAR experiment for two weeks (May 19–26, 2018 and July 2–9, 2018) in 128 MONROE nodes located in Norway and Sweden. The nodes are equipped with one or two SIM cards with 4G connectivity. Nine of the nodes deployed in Norway are connected with a Swedish operator roaming [29] in Norway. Our measurement campaign covers a total of six operators. During the campaign, nodes are set to fetch specific pages of eight popular websites (Appendix A). The WebLAR experiment execute every six hours. In the rest of this paper, we refer to the websites with the name of their base URL. We performed pre-processing to prune out results where the experiment failed to report values of all metrics (e.g., due to browser timeout settings) leaving us with ~18K data points.

3.2 IP Path Lengths

We began by analysing the IP paths towards the measured websites. WebLAR uses `traceroute` to measure the IP path length and the round trip time towards the websites. To study the IP path length and the latency difference in LTE and fixed-line networks, we ran WebLAR on 29 MONROE nodes in Italy, Norway, Spain, and Sweden. Figure 2(1) shows the IP path length towards selected websites in fixed-line and LTE networks from 29 MONROE nodes. The result shows that in the median case, the IP path length in LTE and fixed-line network is similar.

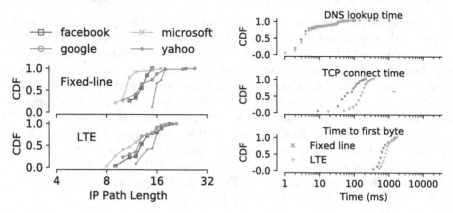

Fig. 2. The distribution of (1) IP path length and (2) web QoS metrics from fixed-line and LTE broadband networks as observed from selected 29 nodes.

3.3 Web Latency and QoE

Figure 2(2) shows the latency towards the websites from fixed-line and LTE networks from 29 MONROE nodes. We observe that there is no significant difference in the DNS lookup time and PLT (not shown) of the websites from fixed-line and LTE network. However, the TCP connect time and TTFB of the websites are shorter in fixed-line network. For instance, in the median case, in LTE network the TCP connect time, and TTFB are respectively, 160% and 30% longer than that observed in fixed-line networks. Due to security reason, the browser timing API gives the same value for the start and end of the TCP connect and DNS lookup time for cross-origin resources. That is, unless the user explicitly allows the server to share these values, by default the TCP connect time and DNS lookup time is 0 for the cross-origin resources [30]. As a result, three websites (Google, Microsoft, and Yahoo) report 0 for these metrics. The discussion of the DNS lookup time and TCP connect time does not include these three websites.

Figure 3(1) shows the latency of the websites under different MNOs. Note, the Norwegian and Swedish operators are labeled with NO_o and SE_o, respectively, where $o \in \{1, 2, 3\}$. SE_r refers to a Swedish operator roaming in Norway. The result shows the MNOs have different performance in terms of DNS lookup time (ranges from 35 ms to 60 ms, in the median case) and TCP connect time (ranges from 100 ms to 200 ms, in the median). One of the causes for the variation in the DNS lookup time across the MNOs could be attributed to the presence of cached DNS entries [36]. The result also shows that, the difference in TTFB and PLT of the websites across different MNOs is not high (*i.e.*, in the median case, only 200 ms to 600 ms difference in PLT). We applied Kolmogorov - Smirnov test to investigate the significance of the difference in PLT across MNOs. In most of the cases, we found a smaller p-value (below 0.05) between the PLT of the websites across MNOs. This confirms that there is a difference in PLT of the websites across MNOs. We also found a higher p-value between PLT across MNOs within the same country (*e.g.*, 0.46 between NO_2 and NO_2, 0.4 between SE_1 and SE_3). This observation indicates that MNOs within the same country exhibit similar PLT towards these websites. The result also shows that there is up to 1 s improvement in the PLT compared with a previous [21] observations.

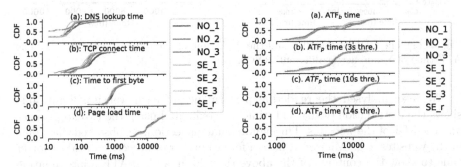

Fig. 3. The distribution of (1) DNS lookup time, TCP connect time, TTFB, and PLT and (2) ATF time as approximated using the two approaches.

Figure 3(2) shows the distribution of the ATF time towards websites across different MNOs as approximated using the two approaches. Figure 3 (2, top) shows the approximated ATF_b time. The long tails of the distribution in this result is due to Facebook and BBC, which have higher number of objects and overlapping images in the above-the-fold area. Figure 3 (2, bottom 3) show the ATF_p with three, ten and 14 s threshold, respectively. From the result, we can see that in the median case, the ATF_b is shorter than the ATF_p time with three seconds threshold. This indicates that three seconds is a sufficient threshold to declare whether the website has stabilized or not. As such, going forward, we only consider three seconds threshold for approximating the ATF time using the pixel-wise comparison approach. The difference in the ATF time of the websites across most of the MNOs is small (*i.e.*, in the median case, the difference is 100 ms to 300 ms). However, we notice that the difference in ATF time between SE_r and the other MNOs is large (*i.e.*, in the median case, ATF_b time can be

up to 400 ms and ATF_p time can be up to 4200 ms). By applying a Kolmogorov
- Smirnov test, we found a smaller p-value (below 0.05) between the ATF_b time
of the different MNOs. This confirms that there is a difference between ATF_b
times across MNOs. Only the ATF_b time of websites between SE_1 and SE_3
shows a p-value of 0.75, highlighting similar QoE between the two MNOs.

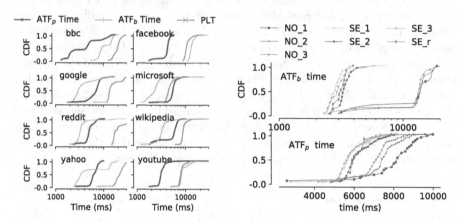

Fig. 4. (1) The CDF of the PLT and the ATF time of the different websites. (2) The
ATF time of Yahoo across different MNOs.

We also analysed the rendering performance of each website. Figure 4(1)
shows the distribution of the ATF time approximated using the two approaches
and the PLT of the websites. Through manual inspection, we observed that some
of the websites, e.g., Microsoft, have a fewer number of objects and take shorter
time to show the contents of the above-the-fold area. The ATF approximation
using both approaches confirms this. On the contrary, websites like Facebook
have multiple objects located in the above-the-fold area (confirmed through manual inspection). The objects may overlap each other where some of the objects
may not be visible in the front unless the user takes further action (e.g., clicking
the sliding button). In such cases, the browser heuristic based ATF time approximation overestimates the ATF time. Hence, for these kinds of websites, the ATF
time approximation based on the browser heuristic does not better represent the
end user experience. That is, the missing or delay in the download of those over-
lapped objects do not have effect in the visual change of the websites. Therefore,
for the websites that have overlapping objects in the above-the-fold area, the
ATF time needs to be approximated in a different way. For instance, Fig. 4(1)
shows that the ATF_p time of Facebook is below half of its PLT, which is much
shorter than its ATF_b time. This shows that the pixel-wise comparison approach
of ATF time approximation is better for websites that have overlapping contents.
However, approximating the ATF time using the pixel-wise comparison approach
may also overestimate the ATF time for some websites. For instance, Microsoft
has fewer images in the above-the-fold area, and the ATF_b time is short. However, the visual look of the webpage seems to be manipulated by using css and

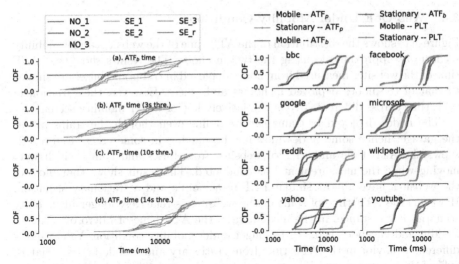

Fig. 5. The distribution: (1) the ATF time of the websites under mobility condition across different operators, and (2) The ATF time and PLT of the websites under different mobility conditions.

javascripts and have animating contents. As a result, the pixel-wise comparison approach yields longer ATF time for this website. Therefore, the design of the website can have an impact on the two ATF time approximation methods. Furthermore, due to the design pattern adopted by some websites, the objects are fetched asynchronously and the TCP connection may not be closed. As such, the javascript onLoad event may fire before all the objects are fetched. In such cases, the ATF_b time is longer than that of the PLT.

Figure 4(1) also shows that the ATF time of BBC, Yahoo and Wikipedia exhibits a bimodal distribution. We investigated this aspect further by observing the ATF time of these websites from different operators. For instance, Fig. 4(2) shows the distribution of the ATF time of Yahoo across the different MNOs approximated using the two approaches. The result reveals that in the Norwegian MNOs, Yahoo takes longer to show the contents in the above-the-fold area. As such, the bimodal distribution of ATF time is due to the difference observed in the operators across different country. The impact of the longer download time of the objects in the above-the-fold area is reflected in the ATF_p time of the websites. For the other two websites we see a difference across the operators. That is, the bimodal distribution happens in all operators. Figure 4(2) and 3(1) also show that the Swedish operator roaming in Norway has a similar QoE with the native Swedish operator. As such, the home-routed roaming [29] configuration does not have much impact on the QoE when the user travels relatively small distances (*i.e.*, between Norway and Sweden).

3.4   Web QoE Under Mobility Conditions

Figure 5(1) shows the distribution of the ATF time of the websites under mobility scenario as approximated using the two methods. The results show that ATF time of the websites measured from nodes deployed in trains and buses are similar to that of the nodes deployed in homes and offices. However, the variation in ATF time across different MNOs is relatively higher under mobility scenario.

The nodes deployed in trains can be online even though the trains are at the garage; hence some nodes may not be moving in some cases. Figure 5(2) shows the ATF time and PLT of websites from buses and trains which were moving while the measurement was conducted. The result shows that most of the websites have almost similar PLT in a mobile and a stationary situation. However, the ATF time of some of the websites is relatively longer in mobility scenario. For instance, in the median case, the ATF time of Microsoft, Yahoo, Reddit, and Facebook is 0.3 to 1 s longer under mobility condition. Yahoo shows different behavior in the ATF time from stationary and mobile nodes. That is, 60% of the measurements from the mobiles nodes, and 40% of the measurements from the stationary nodes show a drastic change (more than 7 s difference) of the ATF time. To understand the causes for this drastic change we analyzed the ATF time of this website at each operator. We found that in the Norwegian operators Yahoo takes longer time to show the contents in the above-the-fold area. One of the causes for this could be the IP path length between the operators and the Yahoo content server. Using a `traceroute` measurement we analyzed the IP path lengths that the nodes traverse to reach the web servers from different locations. We observed that the nodes hosted in Norwegian operators traverse up to 20 IP hops to reach the Yahoo web server. Instead, other Swedish operators take a maximum of 16 IP hopes to reach Yahoo's web server.

4   Related Work

The web has been well studied. Various web QoE measurement tools and methodologies are available [8,9,25,35]. Most of these tools focus on fixed-line networks. For instance, Varvello *et al.* [35] designed *eyeorg*, a platform for crowd-sourcing web QoE measurements. The platform shows a video of the page loading progress to provide a consistent view to all the participants regardless of their network connections and device configurations. Unlike *eyeorg*, our measurement tool does not require user interaction to evaluate the web QoE, rather it uses different approaches to approximate the web QoE. Cechet *et al.* [18] designed mBenchLab that measure web QoE in smartphones and tablets by accessing cloud hosted web service. They measured the performance of few popular websites and identify the QoE issues observing the PLT, the traditional web QoE metric. Casas *et al.* [17] studied the QoE provisioning of popular mobile applications using subjective laboratory tests with end-device through passive measurement. They also studied QoE from feedback obtained in operational MNOs using crowd-sourcing. They showed the impact of access bandwidth and latency on QoE of different services including web browsing on Google Chrome.

Balachandran *et al.* [13] proposed a machine learning approach to infer the web QoE metrics from the network traces, and studied the impact of network characteristics on the web QoE. They showed that the web QoE is more sensitive for the inter-radio technology handover. Improving the signal to noise ratio, decreasing the load and the handover can improve the QoE. Ahmad *et al.* [4] analyzed call-detail records and studied WAP support for popular websites in developing regions. Nejati *et al.* [31] built a testbed that allows comparing the low-level page load activities in mobile and non-mobile browsers. They showed that computational activities are the main bottlenecks for mobile browsers, which indicates that browser optimizations are necessary to improve the mobile web QoE. Dasari *et al.* [20] studied the impact of device performance on mobile Internet QoE. Their study revealed that web applications are more sensitive for low-end hardware devices compared to video applications.

Meteor [32] is a measurement tool which determines the speed of the network and estimates the experience that the user can expect while using selected popular applications given their connection requirements. The methodology used by Meteor is not open aside from the high-level explanation of the system. It is not clear how the expected experience is computed and which performance metrics are used for a given application. Perhaps, it is based on QoS metrics like throughput and latency test, which may not be the only factors that affect the performance of different application [20]. Unlike Meteor, we measure different metrics at the network and application level, e.g., TTFB, PLT, as well as ATF time at the browser which is more important from the user perspective. WebPageTest [2] and Google Lighthouse [24] are other tools designed to assess the web performance from different locations using different network and device types. These tools measure PLT, SpeedIndex, TTFB, time to visually complete (TTVC), first contentful paint (FCP), first meaningful paint (FMP), time to interactive (TTI), and last visual change metrics. WebLAR measures the ATF time, but it does not measure SpeedIndex, TTVC, TTI, and FCP yet. SpeedIndex [3] is a metric proposed by Google to measure the visual completeness of a webpage. It can be approximated either by capturing video of the webpage download progress or by using the paint events exposed by Webkit. We make WebLAR publicly available [7] and invite the measurement community for contributions to help improve this tool.

5   Conclusions

We presented the design and implementation of WebLAR – a measurement tool that measures web latency and QoE in the cellular network. We applied ATF time as the metric to approximate the end-user experience. We followed two different approaches to approximate the ATF time: pixel-wise comparison and the browser heuristics. We deployed WebLAR on the MONROE platform for two weeks. The results show that the DNS lookup time and PLT of the selected websites have similar performance in LTE and fixed-line networks. However, the TCP connect time and TTFB of the websites are longer in LTE networks. Moreover, the DNS lookup time and TCP connect time of the websites varies across

MNOs. For most of the websites, PLT, and ATF time do not have a significant difference across operators. We observed that mobility has small impact on the ATF time of the websites. We also showed that the design of the website should be taken into account when using two approaches to approximate the ATF time.

Limitations and Future Work: We only measured eight websites in this study and did not perform a subjective QoE evaluation. We also did not consider the impact of device capabilities on the web QoE since our measurement nodes were homogenous. In the future, we plan to extend WebLAR to capture other metrics such as RUM SpeedIndex, TTI, first contentful paint and also evaluate the ATF time using different screen sizes.

Appendix A   List and Category of Measured Webpages

The websites are selected from different categories such as social media, news websites, and WIKI pages. Moreover, while selecting these websites, the design of the websites (from simple to media-rich complex webpages) and the purpose of the websites are taken into consideration. Furthermore, for each website we selected a specific webpage that does not require user interaction to show meaningful contents to the user.

- News websites
  - http://www.bbc.com
  - https://news.google.com
- Wiki websites
  - https://en.wikipedia.org/wiki/Alan_Turing
  - https://www.reddit.com
- Social media websites
  - https://www.youtube.com
  - https://www.facebook.com/places/Things-to-do-in-Paris-France/110774245616525
- General websites
  - https://www.microsoft.com
  - https://www.yahoo.com.

Appendix B   Additional Observations

Although not specific to mobility scenario, Fig. 5(2) also shows that PLT can under- or over-estimate the web QoE. For instance, for Facebook, the `onLoad` event fires before all the necessary web objects in the above-the-fold area are downloaded. For these types of websites the PLT underestimates the user QoE. On the other hand, for websites like Yahoo and Reddit, the ATF is shorter compared with PLT time, which overestimates the user QoE.

References

1. ImageMagick: tool to create, edit, compose, or convert bitmap images. https://imagemagick.org. Accessed 12 Oct 2018
2. WebPageTest. https://www.webpagetest.org. Accessed 09 Jan 2019
3. WebPagetest Metrics: SpeedIndex. https://sites.google.com/a/webpagetest.org/docs/using-webpagetest/metrics/speed-index. Accessed 15 Oct 2018
4. Ahmad, S., Haamid, A.L., Qazi, Z.A., Zhou, Z., Benson, T., Qazi, I.A.: A view from the other side: understanding mobile phone characteristics in the developing world. In: ACM IMC (2016). http://dl.acm.org/citation.cfm?id=2987470
5. Akamai White Paper: Measuring Real Customer Experiences over Mobile Networks. https://www.akamai.com/jp/ja/multimedia/documents/white-paper/measuring-real-customer-experiences-over-mobile-networks-report.pdf. Accessed 12 Oct 2017
6. Alay, Ö., et al.: Experience: an open platform for experimentation with commercial mobile broadband networks. In: ACM MobiCom (2017). https://doi.org/10.1145/3117811.3117812
7. Asrese, A.S.: WebLAR: A Web Performance Measurement Tool (2019). https://github.com/alemnew/weblar
8. Asrese, A.S., Eravuchira, S.J., Bajpai, V., Sarolahti, P., Ott, J.: Measuring web latency and rendering performance: method, tools & longitudinal dataset. IEEE Trans. Netw. Serv. Manag. (2019, to appear)
9. Asrese, A.S., Sarolahti, P., Boye, M., Ott, J.: WePR: a tool for automated web performance measurement. In: IEEE Globecom Workshops (2016). https://doi.org/10.1109/GLOCOMW.2016.7849082
10. Asrese, A.S., Walelgne, E., Bajpai, V., Lutu, A., Alay, Ö., Ott, J.: Measuring web quality of experience in cellular networks (dataset) (2019). https://github.com/alemnew/2019-pam-weblar
11. Bajpai, V., Kühlewind, M., Ott, J., Schönwälder, J., Sperotto, A., Trammell, B.: Challenges with reproducibility. In: SIGCOMM Reproducibility Workshop, pp. 1–4 (2017). https://doi.org/10.1145/3097766.3097767
12. Bajpai, V., Schönwälder, J.: A survey on internet performance measurement platforms and related standardization efforts. IEEE Commun. Surv. Tutor. **17**(3), 1313–1341 (2015). https://doi.org/10.1109/COMST.2015.2418435
13. Balachandran, A., et al.: Modeling web quality-of-experience on cellular networks. In: ACM MobiCom (2014). https://doi.org/10.1145/2639108.2639137
14. Barakovic, S., Skorin-Kapov, L.: Multidimensional modelling of quality of experience for mobile web browsing. Comput. Hum. Behav. **50**, 314–332 (2015). https://doi.org/10.1016/j.chb.2015.03.071
15. Brutlag, J., Abrams, Z., Meenan, P.: Above the Fold Time: Measuring Web Page Performance Visually. https://conferences.oreilly.com/velocity/velocity-mar2011/public/schedule/detail/18692
16. Cao, Y., Nejati, J., Wajahat, M., Balasubramanian, A., Gandhi, A.: Deconstructing the energy consumption of the mobile page load. Proc. ACM Meas. Anal. Comput. Syst. **1**(1), 6 (2017). https://doi.org/10.1145/3084443
17. Casas, P., Seufert, M., Wamser, F., Gardlo, B., Sackl, A., Schatz, R.: Next to you: monitoring quality of experience in cellular networks from the end-devices. IEEE Trans. Netw. Serv. Manag. **13**(2), 181–196 (2016). https://doi.org/10.1109/TNSM.2016.2537645

18. Cecchet, E., Sims, R., He, X., Shenoy, P.J.: mBenchLab: measuring QoE of Web applications using mobile devices. In: International Symposium on Quality of Service, IWQoS (2013). https://doi.org/10.1109/IWQoS.2013.6550259
19. Chen, Q.A., et al.: QoE doctor: diagnosing mobile app QoE with automated UI control and cross-layer analysis. In: ACM Internet Measurement Conference (2014). https://doi.org/10.1145/2663716.2663726
20. Dasari, M., Vargas, S., Bhattacharya, A., Balasubramanian, A., Das, S.R., Ferdman, M.: Impact of device performance on mobile internet QoE. In: Internet Measurement Conference, pp. 1–7 (2018). https://doi.org/10.1145/3278532.3278533
21. DoubleClick: The Need for Mobile Speed: Better User Experiences, Greater Publisher Revenue. https://goo.gl/R4Lmfh. Accessed 26 Feb 2018
22. Eravuchira, S.J., Bajpai, V., Schönwälder, J., Crawford, S.: Measuring web similarity from dual-stacked hosts. In: Conference on Network and Service Management, pp. 181–187 (2016). https://doi.org/10.1109/CNSM.2016.7818415
23. FFmpeg: FFmpeg: a complete, cross-platform solution to record, convert and stream audio and video. https://ffmpeg.org. Accessed 12 Oct 2018
24. Google: Lighthouse: an open-source, automated tool for improving the quality of web pages. https://developers.google.com/web/tools/lighthouse. Accessed 09 Jan 2019
25. da Hora, D.N., Asrese, A.S., Christophides, V., Teixeira, R., Rossi, D.: Narrowing the gap between QoS metrics and Web QoE using above-the-fold metrics. In: Beverly, R., Smaragdakis, G., Feldmann, A. (eds.) PAM 2018. LNCS, vol. 10771, pp. 31–43. Springer, Cham (2018). https://doi.org/10.1007/978-3-319-76481-8_3
26. Hosek, J., et al.: Mobile web QoE study for smartphones. In: IEEE GLOBECOM Workshop (2013). https://doi.org/10.1109/GLOCOMW.2013.6825149
27. Hoßfeld, T., Metzger, F., Rossi, D.: Speed index: relating the industrial standard for user perceived web performance to web QoE. In: IEEE International Conference on Quality of Multimedia Experience (2018). https://doi.org/10.1109/QoMEX.2018.8463430
28. Li, L., et al.: A longitudinal measurement study of TCP performance and behavior in 3G/4G networks over high speed rails. IEEE/ACM Trans. Netw. **25**(4), 2195–2208 (2017). https://doi.org/10.1109/TNET.2017.2689824
29. Mandalari, A.M., et al.: Experience: implications of roaming in Europe. In: MOBICOM, pp. 179–189 (2018). https://doi.org/10.1145/3241539.3241577
30. Mozilla: Using the Resource Timing API. https://developer.mozilla.org/en-US/docs/Web/API/Resource_Timing_API/Using_the_Resource_Timing_API. Accessed 24 May 2018
31. Nejati, J., Balasubramanian, A.: An in-depth study of mobile browser performance. In: Conference on World Wide Web, pp. 1305–1315 (2016). https://doi.org/10.1145/2872427.2883014
32. OpenSignal: Meteor. https://meteor.opensignal.com. Accessed 12 May 2017
33. Sackl, A., Casas, P., Schatz, R., Janowski, L., Irmer, R.: Quantifying the impact of network bandwidth fluctuations and outages on Web QoE. In: IEEE International Workshop on Quality of Multimedia Experience (2015). https://doi.org/10.1109/QoMEX.2015.7148078
34. Sonntag, S., Manner, J., Schulte, L.: Netradar - measuring the wireless world. In: IEEE International Symposium and Workshops on Modeling and Optimization in Mobile, Ad Hoc and Wireless Networks (2013). http://ieeexplore.ieee.org/document/6576402/

35. Varvello, M., Blackburn, J., Naylor, D., Papagiannaki, K.: EYEORG: a platform for crowdsourcing web quality of experience measurements. In: ACM Conference on emerging Networking EXperiments and Technologies (2016). https://doi.org/10.1145/2999572.2999590

36. Walelgne, E.A., Kim, S., Bajpai, V., Neumeier, S., Manner, J., Ott, J.: Factors affecting performance of web flows in cellular networks. In: IFIP Networking (2018)

37. Walelgne, E.A., Manner, J., Bajpai, V., Ott, J.: Analyzing throughput and stability in cellular networks. In: IEEE/IFIP Network Operations and Management Symposium, pp. 1–9 (2018). https://doi.org/10.1109/NOMS.2018.8406261

Realtime Mobile Bandwidth Prediction Using LSTM Neural Network

Lifan Mei[1(✉)], Runchen Hu[1], Houwei Cao[2], Yong Liu[1], Zifa Han[3],
Feng Li[3], and Jin Li[3]

[1] ECE, New York University, New York City, NY 11201, USA
{lifan,rh2619,yongliu}@nyu.edu
[2] CS, New York Institute of Technology, New York City, NY 10023, USA
hcao02@nyit.edu
[3] Huawei Technologies, Nanjing, China
{hanzifa,frank.lifeng,mark.lijin}@huawei.com

Abstract. With the popularity of mobile access Internet and the higher bandwidth demand of mobile applications, user Quality of Experience (QoE) is particularly important. For bandwidth and delay sensitive applications, such as Video on Demand (VoD), Realtime Video Call, Games, etc., if the future bandwidth can be estimated in advance, it will greatly improve the user QoE. In this paper, we study realtime mobile bandwidth prediction in various mobile networking scenarios, such as subway and bus rides along different routes. The main method used is Long Short Term Memory (LSTM) recurrent neural network. In specific scenarios, LSTM achieves significant accuracy improvements over the state-of-the-art prediction algorithms, such as Recursive Least Squares (RLS). We further analyze the bandwidth patterns in different mobility scenarios using Multi-Scale Entropy (MSE) and discuss its connections to the achieved accuracy.

Keywords: Bandwidth prediction · Long Short Term Memory · Multi-Scale Entropy · Bandwidth measurement

1 Introduction

We have witnessed the tremendous growth of mobile traffic in the recent years. Users are increasingly spending more time on mobile apps and consuming more content on their mobile devices. The growth trend is expected to accelerate in the foreseeable future with the introduction of 5G wireless access and new media-rich applications, such as Virtual Reality and Augmented Reality. However, one main challenge for mobile app developers and content providers is the high volatility of mobile wireless connections. The physical channel quality of a mobile user is constantly affected by interference generated by other users, his/her own mobility, and signal blockages from static and dynamic blockers [8,9]. The bandwidth available for a mobile session is ultimately determined by the adaptations cross

D. Choffnes and M. Barcellos (Eds.): PAM 2019, LNCS 11419, pp. 34–47, 2019.
https://doi.org/10.1007/978-3-030-15986-3_3

the protocol stack, ranging from adaptive coding and modulation at PHY layer, cellular scheduling at data link layer, hand-overs between base stations, to TCP congestion control, etc. For many mobile apps involving user interactivity and/or multimedia content, e.g., gaming, conferencing and video streaming, it is critical to accurately estimate the available bandwidth in realtime to deliver a high quality of user Quality-of-Experience (QoE). In the example of video streaming, many recent algorithms on Dynamic Adaptive Streaming over Http (DASH) optimize the video rate selection for incoming video chunks based on the predicted TCP throughput in a future time window of several seconds [5,11,15]. To cope with the unavoidable TCP throughput prediction errors, one has to be conservative in video rate selection and resort to long video buffering to absorb the mismatch between the predicted and actual TCP throughput. Both degrade user video streaming QoE. Interactive video conferencing has much tighter delay constraint than streaming. To avoid self-congestion, the available bandwidth on cellular link has to be accurately estimated in realtime, which is used to guide the realtime video coding and transmission strategies [10,16]. Bandwidth overestimate will lead to long end-to-end video delay or freezing, bandwidth underestimate will lead to unnecessarily poor perceptual video quality. Again, accurate realtime bandwidth prediction is crucial for delivering good conferencing experience, especially in mobile networking scenarios.

In this paper, we study realtime mobile bandwidth prediction using Long Short Term Memory (LSTM) [1] recurrent neural network. Recent advances in Deep Learning have demonstrated that Recurrent Neural Networks (RNN) are powerful tools for sequence modeling and can learn temporal patterns in sequential data. RNNs have been widely used in Natural Language Processing (NLP), speech recognition and time series processing [17,18]. There are rich structures in realtime mobile network bandwidth evolution, due to user mobility patterns, wireless signal propagation laws, physical blockage models, and the well-defined behaviors of network protocols. This presents abundant opportunities for developing LSTM-based realtime mobile bandwidth estimation. The main idea is to offline train LSTM RNN models that capture the temporal patterns in various mobile networking scenarios. The trained LSTM RNN models will be used online to predict in realtime the network bandwidth within a short future time window. Specifically, we investigate the following research questions:

1. *How much prediction accuracy improvement can LSTM deep learning models bring over the conventional statistical prediction models?*
2. *How predictable is realtime bandwidth at different prediction intervals under different mobility scenarios? Is the LSTM prediction accuracy dependent on specific mobility scenarios?*
3. *Should one train a separate LSTM model for each mobility scenario, or train a universal LSTM model that can be used in different scenarios?*

Towards answering these questions, we made the following contributions:

- We conducted a mobile bandwidth measurement campaign to collect consecutive bandwidth traces in New York City. Our traces cover different transportation methods along different routes at different time of day[1].
- We developed LSTM models for realtime one-second ahead and multi-second ahead bandwidth predictions. Through extensive experiments on our own dataset and the HSDPA dataset [7], we demonstrated that LSTM significantly outperforms the existing realtime bandwidth prediction algorithms.
- We systematically evaluated the sensitivity of LSTM models to different mobility scenarios by comparing the performance of *per-scenario, cross-scenario* and *universal* predictions. Using Multi-Scale Entropy (MSE) analysis, we studied the connection between prediction accuracy and bandwidth regularity at different time scales. MSE also provides us with guidelines to explore cross-scenario bandwidth prediction.

The rest of the paper is organized as the following. The related work on realtime bandwidth prediction is reviewed in Sect. 2. We formally define the realtime bandwidth prediction problem and introduce our LSTM based prediction models in Sect. 3. The performance of LSTM models is evaluated by public dataset and our own dataset in Sect. 4. We conduct Multi-Scale Entropy analysis on our collected bandwidth traces and analyze the prediction accuracy in Sect. 5. The paper is concluded with future work in Sect. 6.

2   Related Work

Realtime bandwidth prediction has been a challenging problem for the networking community. Simple history-based TCP throughput estimation algorithm was proposed in [12]. Authors of [13] proposed to train a Support Vector Regress (SVR) model [14] to predict TCP throughput based on the measured packet loss rate, packet delay and the size of file to be transmitted. In the context of DASH video streaming, in [11], we adopted prediction algorithm in [12] to guide realtime chunk rate selection, and used a customized SVR model similar to [13] for DASH server selection. Authors of [20] and [15] used the Harmonic Mean of TCP throughput for downloading the previous five chunks as the TCP throughput prediction for downloading the next chunk. In [5], authors developed Hidden Markov Model (HMM) for bandwidth prediction. HMM model is parameterized by history bandwidth, and HMM state transition is used to infer future bandwidth. In the context of video conferencing, in [16], a cellular link is modeled as a single-server queue driven by a doubly-stochastic service process. Bandwidth available for a user is measured by the packet arrival dispersion at the receiver end, and future bandwidth prediction is generated by probabilistic inference based on the single-server queue model. In [10], we used an adaptive

---

[1] The collected NYU Metropolitan Mobile Bandwidth Trace Dataset (NYU-METS), is publicly available at https://github.com/NYU-METS/Main.

filter, Recursive Least Squared (RLS), to make realtime bandwidth prediction. We showed that RLS achieves good prediction accuracy on volatile cellular links. Based on the accurate bandwidth prediction, they proposed a new video conferencing system that can deliver higher video rate and lower video delay than Facetime in side-by-side comparisons.

All the previous predictors are based on the conventional statistical or machine learning models and generate predictions based on short bandwidth history. Different from the conventional models, LSTM deep learning models are more flexible and can be trained by large datasets to better capture the long-term and short-term temporal structures in bandwidth time series. A recent work on Deep Reinforcement Learning (DRL) based DASH [19] takes historical bandwidth samples as part of the input state vector for DRL to directly generate video chunk rate selection. DRL based DASH achieves better performance and robustness than the traditional DASH. While DRL-DASH implicitly mines the temporal structure in bandwidth, there is no direct/explicit training and validation optimized for bandwidth prediction.

3 LSTM Based Realtime Bandwidth Prediction

3.1 Realtime Bandwidth Prediction Problem

Let $x(t)$ be the bandwidth available for a user at time t. Given some bandwidth measurement frequency, one can obtain a discrete-time series of $\{x(t), t = 1, 2, \cdots .\}$. The realtime bandwidth prediction problem at time t is to estimate the bandwidth available for a user at some future time instant $x(t+\tau)$ given all the observed bandwidth measurements so far, i.e.,

$$\hat{x}(t+\tau) = \mathbf{f}\left(\{x(k), k = 1, 2, \cdots, t\}\right). \tag{1}$$

There are many ways to build the estimation function $\mathbf{f}(\cdot)$, ranging from simple history-repeat, i.e., $\hat{x}(t+\tau) = x(t)$, Exponential Weighted Moving Average (EWMA), $\hat{x}(t+1) = (1-\alpha)\hat{x}(t) + \alpha x(t)$, Harmonic Mean, $\hat{x}(t+\tau) = h/\sum_{k=0}^{h-1} 1/x(t-k)$, etc., to more sophisticated signal processing approaches, such as Kalman filter [6] and Recursive Least Squares (RLS) [3]. In [10], we used RLS for realtime bandwidth prediction. By assuming $\hat{x}(t+1) = \sum_{k=0}^{h-1} \omega(k)x(t-k)$, RLS recursively finds the coefficients ω that minimizes a weighted linear least squares cost function.

In the bandwidth prediction part of [10], it was shown that RLS achieves better accuracy than other averaging and signal processing algorithms, such as Least Mean Square and EWMA etc.

3.2 LSTM-Based Prediction Model

While all those methods use history measurements to generate bandwidth prediction, they did not fully explore the temporal patterns in realtime bandwidth evolution for more accurate prediction. Meanwhile, LSTM network has recently

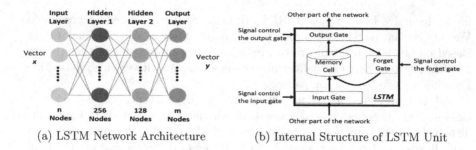

(a) LSTM Network Architecture   (b) Internal Structure of LSTM Unit

Fig. 1. LSTM network for realtime bandwidth prediction

emerged as a powerful tool for exploring temporal structures in sequential data. As illustrated in Fig. 1a, a LSTM network consists of layers of LSTM units.

As illustrated in Fig. 1b, a common LSTM unit is composed of a cell, an input gate, an output gate and a forget gate. The cell is responsible for "memorizing" values over arbitrary time intervals; hence the word "memory" in LSTM. Each of the three gates can be thought of as a "conventional" artificial neuron, as in a multi-layer (or feed-forward) neural network: they compute an activation (using an activation function) of a weighted sum. Intuitively, they can be considered as regulators of the flow of values going through the connections between the LSTM units; hence the denotation "gate". There are connections between these gates and the cell. Detailed LSTM reviews can be found in [1,2].

The input to our LSTM bandwidth prediction network is the recent bandwidth measurements, i.e, $\mathbf{x} = [x(t), x(t-1), \cdots, x(t-n+1)] \in R^n$, the output is the predicted bandwidth in a future time window $\mathbf{y} = [\hat{x}(t+1), x(t+2), \cdots, x(t+m)] \in R^m$. Note that since LSTM network adaptively keeps "memory", the bandwidth prediction for time window $(t, t+m]$ is not only directly determined by the recent bandwidth history in $(t-n, t]$, but also indirectly affected by bandwidth history before $t-n$ through the memory cells. This gives LSTM more flexibility in capturing long-term bandwidth evolution trends than the traditional signal processing and averaging approaches working on a moving history window. Following the architecture in Fig. 1a, we build a LSTM network with one input Layer, one output layer and two hidden layers, each with 256 and 128 LSTM units respectively[2]. Given the LSTM architecture, the mapping from input $\mathbf{x}$ to output $\mathbf{y}$ is parameterized by all the parameters in the LSTM network, denoted as θ, which are obtained by minimizing the loss function in training.

Since we study realtime bandwidth prediction for a range of mobile networking scenarios, one option is to train a separate LSTM network for each scenario, that is using bandwidth data collected from scenario i to train a LSTM network with parameters $\theta^{(i)}$, and then use it to predict bandwidth for scenario i, i.e.,

---

[2] We also tried a LSTM network with 256 and 256 nodes, and a LSTM network with 128 and 128 nodes. The performance difference is not significant. The results presented in this paper is based on the 256 + 128 LSTM network.

$$\textbf{per-scenario:} \qquad \hat{\mathbf{y}}^{(i)} = \textbf{LSTM}\left(\mathbf{x}^{(i)}, \theta^{(i)}\right), \quad \forall i. \tag{2}$$

Another option is to train one universal LSTM network with parameters $\theta^{(0)}$ using all data collected from all scenarios, and hope the trained universal LSTM model can be used to predict bandwidth in all scenarios, i.e.,

$$\textbf{universal:} \qquad \hat{\mathbf{y}}^{(i)} = \textbf{LSTM}\left(\mathbf{x}^{(i)}, \theta^{(0)}\right), \quad \forall i. \tag{3}$$

The third option is to train a LSTM network using data from scenario i, then use it to predict bandwidth in scenario j.

$$\textbf{cross-scenario:} \qquad \hat{\mathbf{y}}^{(j)} = \textbf{LSTM}\left(\mathbf{x}^{(j)}, \theta^{(i)}\right), \quad i \neq j. \tag{4}$$

To generate training samples, we use a sliding-window based approach. For example, to predict the bandwidth in the next second ($m = 1$) based on the bandwidth measurements in the previous five seconds ($n = 5$), in the training, we use every consecutive six bandwidth measurements as one training data point. The first five seconds bandwidth form the input vector, and the sixth second bandwidth is the output label. Likewise, for the general multiple seconds prediction, i.e., predicting the future bandwidth for the next m seconds based on the previous n seconds bandwidth, we use every consecutive $n + m$ bandwidth measurements as one data point. The first n measurements form the input vector, and the last m measurements form an output label vector.

4   Data Collection and Performance Evaluation

4.1   Datasets

It is critical to train and test LSTM models using large representative bandwidth datasets. We first used the HSDPA [7] dataset from the University of Oslo. It consists of cellular bandwidth traces collected on different transportation methods, including Train, Tram, Ferry, Car, Bus and Metro. For each trace, it recorded the bandwidth and location every 1,000 ms, and the duration for each trace ranges from 500 to 1,000 s. However, we later found that the bandwidth traces are too short for MSE analysis. We also collected long bandwidth traces in New York City MTA bus and subway by ourselves. Figure 2 shows some sample routes for our bandwidth collection, including Subway 7 Train, Subway Q Train, Bus B57 and B62. On each route, we conducted multiple experiments at different time of day. For each experiment, we connect a LTE mobile phone with unlimited data plan to a remote server in our lab. We run $iPerf$ and record TCP throughput every 1,000 ms. All the bandwidth samples are logged on the server side. The duration of each trace ranges from 10,000 to 20,000 s. It took us four months to complete the first batch of data. We are continuing this measurement campaign and keep adding new traces to our NYU-METS Dataset for future research.

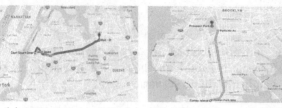

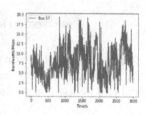

| (a) MTA Subway 7 Train | (b) MTA Subway Q Train | (c) Bus 57 Raw Trace |

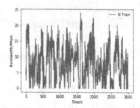

| (d) MTA Bus 57 | (e) MTA Bus 62 | (f) Q Train Raw Trace |

Fig. 2. New York City self-measured bandwidth

Table 1. Evaluation results on NYU-METS traces

	7A Train	7B Train	Bus 57	Bus 62	N Train
Testset Average	6.39	4.76	10.04	2.55	8.98
RLS RMSE	2.57	2.19	2.59	0.87	3.04
RLS MAE	1.69	1.49	1.72	0.66	2.11
Harmonic RMSE	2.98	2.60	2.79	0.94	3.36
Harmonic MAE	1.86	1.68	1.78	0.70	2.26
LSTM RMSE	**2.26**	**2.05**	**2.32**	**0.72**	**2.81**
LSTM MAE	**1.49**	**1.41**	**1.54**	**0.55**	**1.90**
RLS RMSE Error Ratio	40.3%	46.0%	25.8%	34.2%	33.8%
RLS MAE Error Ratio	26.5%	31.3%	17.1%	26.1%	23.5%
HAR RMSE Error Ratio	46.6%	54.6%	27.8%	37.0%	37.4%
HAR MAE Error Ratio	29.1%	35.4%	17.7%	27.4%	25.2%
LSTM RMSE Error Ratio	35.3%	43.1%	23.1%	28.2%	31.3%
LSTM MAE Error Ratio	23.3%	29.6%	15.3%	21.4%	21.2%
Relative RMSE Impro over RLS	**14.0%**	**6.7%**	**11.8%**	**21.2%**	**8.2%**
Relative MAE Impro over RLS	**13.6%**	**5.9%**	**11.9%**	**21.6%**	**11.0%**
Relative RMSE Impro over Harmonic	**31.8%**	**26.7%**	**20.4%**	**31.1%**	**19.5%**
Relative MAE Impro over Harmonic	**24.9%**	**19.7%**	**15.8%**	**27.7%**	**18.9%**

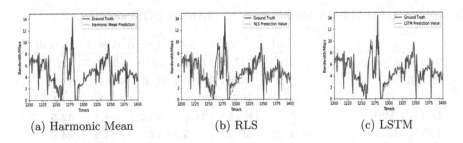

(a) Harmonic Mean   (b) RLS   (c) LSTM

Fig. 3. Harmonic Mean, RLS and LSTM predictions on Subway 7 Train

4.2   Next-Second Prediction

For the next-second prediction, the dimension of LSTM output is $m = 1$, and we pick LSTM input dimension of $n = 5$ for evaluation. Figure 3 visually compares the predicted values from Harmonic Mean, RLS and LSTM with the ground truth for a trace collected on NYC Subway 7 Train. For LSTM training, we use Adam optimizer [21] with default parameters (including learning rate, beta, etc) in training. 80% of the trace is used for training, the rest 20% is used for testing. We manually adjust dropout and epoch based on the performance of model.

We use the *Root Mean Square Error (RMSE)* and *Mean Absolute Error (MAE)* between the predicted bandwidth and the ground truth as the main accuracy measures. The complete prediction result of the three algorithms on our NYU-METS Dataset is reported in Table 1. (LSTM runs in the *per-scenario* mode). The unit is *Mbps*. LSTM has the lowest RMSE and MAE cross all mobility scenarios. The average accuracy improvement of LSTM over RLS and Harmonic Mean in RMSE are 12.4% and 25.9% respectively, for MAE, these are 12.8% and 21.4% respectively. Since Harmonic Mean performs much worse than the other two, in the following, we only compare LSTM with RLS.

Table 2 compares the accuracy of per-scenario LSTM with RLS on the HSDPA dataset. The unit for the numbers is *kbps*. LSTM still outperforms RLS in all mobility scenarios. The Relative Improvement of LSTM over RLS are around 14.1% and 13.9% for RMSE and MAE respectively. For HSDPA dataset, we also trained a *universal* LSTM model by using all traces from different transportation scenarios, including Bus, Tram, Train, Metro and Car, then test its accuracy on individual transportation scenarios. However, it is performance is inferior to the corresponding per-scenario models. For some scenarios, its performance is even worse than RLS. Due to the space limit, we don't report the detailed statistics here. We defer the discussion on *cross-scenario* prediction to the next section, and defer universal prediction to future investigation.

Table 2. HSDPA traces evaluation result of LSTM and RLS

	Ferry	FerryB	Tram	TramB	Metro	MetroB
Testset Average	248.4	217.6	118.8	133.4	96.0	119.7
RLS RMSE	71.3	88.9	35.3	35.6	34.2	35.5
RLS MAE	53.1	58.5	25.5	26.6	25.8	26.9
LSTM RMSE	**60.8**	**80.4**	**31.5**	**30.2**	**29.2**	**32.5**
LSTM MAE	**45.6**	**50.1**	**23.3**	**22.3**	**23.2**	**24.3**
RLS RMSE Error Ratio	28.7%	40.9%	29.8%	26.7%	35.7%	29.7%
RLS MAE Error Ratio	21.4%	19.7%	21.5%	19.9%	26.7%	22.5%
LSTM RMSE Error Ratio	24.5%	37.0%	26.6%	22.6%	30.4%	27.1%
LSTM MAE Error Ratio	18.4%	16.8%	19.6%	16.7%	24.3%	20.3%
Relative RMSE Impro	**17.3%**	**10.6%**	**12.2%**	**17.8%**	**17.4%**	**9.3%**
Relative MAE Impro	**16.5%**	**16.9%**	**9.5%**	**19.3%**	**11.0%**	**10.6%**

4.3 Multi-second Prediction

We now study the prediction accuracy for longer time intervals. For LSTM model, we fix the input vector dimension to be $n = 10$, and vary the output vector dimension m from 2 to 5. In other words, LSTM network takes as input the bandwidth vector in the previous ten seconds to predict bandwidth for up to five seconds ahead. For each combination of n and m, we train a different LSTM model, denoted as $LSTM(n, m)$. Note that, at time t, a $LSTM(n, m)$ model can generate bandwidth predictions for $t + i$, $1 \le i \le m$. To make RLS generate prediction i seconds ahead, we simply update RLS parameters by using bandwidth of i seconds ahead, instead of the next second, as the targeted output.

Table 3. Prediction RMSE on RLS and LSTM

	1st sec	2nd sec	3rd sec	4th sec	5th sec
RLS	2.57	2.88	3.16	3.53	3.76
$LSTM(10, 1)$	**2.26**	–	–	–	–
$LSTM(10, 2)$	2.27	**2.66**	–	–	–
$LSTM(10, 3)$	2.29	2.68	**2.96**	–	–
$LSTM(10, 4)$	2.33	2.69	2.97	**3.21**	–
$LSTM(10, 5)$	2.40	2.71	2.98	3.22	**3.40**
Improvement over RLS	**13.7%**	**8.2%**	**6.8%**	**9.9%**	**10.6%**

Table 3 compares the prediction accuracy of different LSTM models and RLS on the NYC Subway 7 Train trace. The RMSE value unit is *Mbps*. Not coincidentally, all LSTM models outperform RLS at all prediction intervals. In the

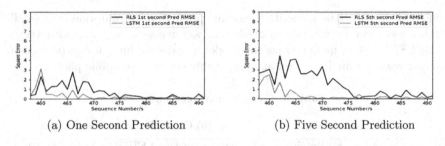

(a) One Second Prediction   (b) Five Second Prediction

Fig. 4. RLS vs LSTM multi-second prediction

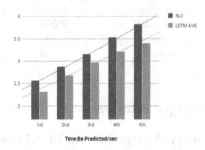

Fig. 5. Impact of prediction interval on LSTM and RLS

representative results, the best prediction accuracy for interval i is achieved by $LSTM(10, i)$, marked in bold fonts. Theoretically, $LSTM(n, m)$ model is trained to minimize the prediction errors for all intervals from 1 to m. Consequently, the prediction error at interval $m_1 < m$ will be larger than those of $LSTM(n, m_2)$ models ($m_1 \leq m_2 < m$). Figures 4a and b illustrate sample prediction error evolution of RLS and LSTM for one second and five second intervals. Y-axis is the square error between prediction value and ground truth. It is visually clear that LSTM RMSE is lower than RLS most of the time. The accuracy improvement of LSTM is more prominent for the five second prediction interval. Figure 5 compares the average RMSE for all LSTM models with RLS at different prediction intervals. Both RMSEs increase as the prediction interval increases. The slope for LSTM increase is 0.270, while that for RLS is 0.302. This suggests that not only LSTM is more accurate than RLS at individual prediction intervals, LSTM's accuracy decays slower than RLS as the interval increases.

4.4   Computation Overhead

To validate the feasibility of offline training and online prediction, we report the computation overhead of our LSTM models. Our CPU Configuration is: 4th Gen Intel Core i5-4210U (1.70 GHz 1600 MHz 3 MB). Neural Network Structure: Hidden Layer 1 & 2 have 256 and 128 nodes respectively. The training and running overhead detail is presented in Table 4. Even though the offline training time is long, once the training is done, the trained model can be used for realtime prediction. As shown in Table 4b, the online prediction consumption is so small. It takes less than six seconds to predict 12,500 five seconds bandwidth vector in the $LSTM(10, 5)$ model. Once the model is trained offline, it can be used to generate realtime prediction on any reasonably configured mobile phone.

Table 4. Computation consumption

(a) Offline Training

Trainsize	Batchsize = 2	Batchsize = 4
13,000	120s/epoch	62s/epoch
10,000	95s/epoch	50s/epoch
5,000	49s/epoch	26s/epoch
3,000	35s/epoch	14s/epoch
1,000	11s/epoch	6s/epoch

(b) Online Running Consumption

Prediction Size	$LSTM(10, 1)$	$LSTM(10, 5)$
12,500	4,953ms	5,706ms
5,000	2,396ms	2,590ms
2,500	1,191ms	1,239ms
500	266ms	386ms
50	38ms	53ms

5   Multi-Scale Entropy Analysis

5.1   Prediction Accuracy Analysis Using Multi-Scale Entropy

The predictability of a time series is determined by its complexity and the temporal correlation at different time scales. The traditional entropy measure can be used to quantify the randomness of a signal: the higher the entropy, the more random thus less predictable. However, the traditional entropy measure cannot model the signal complexity and temporal correlation at different time scales. Recently, *Multi-Scale Entropy (MSE)* [4] has been proposed to measure the complexity of physical and physiologic time series. Given a discrete time series $\{x(i), 1 \leq i \leq N\}$, a coarse-grained time series $\{y^{(s)}(j)\}$ can be constructed at scale factor of $s \geq 1$:

$$y^{(s)}(j) \triangleq \frac{1}{s} \sum_{i=(j-1)s+1}^{js} x(i), 1 \leq j \leq N/s.$$

Then the entropy measure of $\mathbf{x}$ at time scale s can be calculated as the entropy of $\mathbf{y}^{(s)}$:

$$H^{(s)}(\mathbf{x}) \triangleq H(\mathbf{y}^{(s)}) = -E[\log p(\mathbf{y}^{(s)})], \tag{5}$$

where $p(\mathbf{y}^{(s)})$ is the probability density of the constructed signal at scale s. By varying s, one can examine the complexity/regularity of $\mathbf{x}$ at different time scales. The Multi-Scale Entropy curve $H^{(s)}(\mathbf{x})$ also reveals the temporal correlation structures of the time series [4].

We apply MSE to study the predictability of network bandwidth under different mobile networking scenarios. MSE can represent the regularity patterns of each scenario. Given a set of scales $\mathcal{S} = [s_0, s_1, \cdots, s_m]$, we generate a MSE vector for scenario i as $MSE_i \triangleq [H^{(s)}(\mathbf{x_i}), s \in \mathcal{S}]$, where $\mathbf{x_i}$ is bandwidth trace from scenario i. MSE_i can be used to analyze the per-scenario prediction accuracy for scenario i, as defined in (2). Additionally, by comparing MSE_i and

MSE_j, we can also study the feasibility of cross-scenario prediction between scenarios i and j, as defined in (4). More specifically, we measure the MSE similarity between scenarios i and j as the weighted sum of the correlation coefficient and Euclidean distance between MSE_i and MSE_j. We will demonstrate the connection between MSE and prediction accuracy of both per-scenario and *cross-scenario* predictions next.

5.2 MSE Analysis of NYC MTA Traces

We apply MSE analysis to bandwidth from every scenario in New York City MTA traces. Figure 6a and b plot the raw bandwidth traces for two sample traces. They present different variability at different scenarios. Figure 6c shows the results of Multi-Scale Entropy for five sample traces. The scale is from 1 to 15. According to the [4], to make the MSE analysis valid, the sequence should be at least 1,000 points at each scale. From the result of Fig. 6c, we find that same routes share similar MSE patterns. For example, 7A Train and 7B Train traces were both collected from 7 train but on different days. From the curves of Bus 57 and Bus 62, we find that even though the transportation methods are the same, due to different routes, the MSE patterns can be very different. Table 5a shows the *cross-scenario* prediction accuracy in RMSE. Each row is for a model trained using data from some mobility scenario, each column is the prediction accuracy for the testset from some mobility scenario. For example, Row 3 & Column 1 shows that the LSTM model trained by Bus 57 data can achieve RMSE of 2.276 when predicting bandwidth for 7A Train testset.

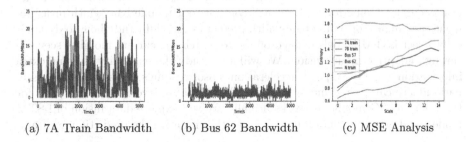

(a) 7A Train Bandwidth   (b) Bus 62 Bandwidth   (c) MSE Analysis

Fig. 6. Multi-Scale Entropy of different mobility scenarios

Table 5. Multi-Scale Entropy analysis

(a) Cross-scenario Prediction RMSE

	7A	7B	B57	B62	N
7A Model	**2.257**	2.060	2.475	0.746	2.837
7B Model	2.267	**2.052**	2.369	0.749	2.817
B57 Model	2.276	2.096	**2.320**	0.754	2.830
B62 Model	2.762	2.205	3.278	**0.719**	3.423
N Model	2.259	2.091	2.382	0.770	**2.808**

(b) MSE Similarity

	7A	7B	B57	B62	N
7A	-	1.223	1.176	1.021	1.106
7B	1.221	-	1.121	1.044	1.080
B57	1.166	1.118	-	1.029	1.123
B62	0.630	0.696	0.665	-	0.690
N	0.984	0.964	1.038	0.907	-

Table 5b shows the MSE similarity between different mobility scenarios. Table 6 reports for each scenario i the correlation between its MSE similarity with other scenarios and the accuracy of *cross-scenario* prediction using models trained for other scenarios. Close to -1 correlations suggest that higher MSE similarity leads to higher accuracy (lower RMSE). Multi-Scale Entropy analysis provides a good measure to explore the possibility of *cross-scenario* prediction, which can be very beneficial for mobility scenarios with limited available data for training Deep learning models.

Table 6. Correlation between MSE similarity and cross-scenario prediction accuracy

	7A Train	7B Train	Bus 57	Bus 62	N Train
Correlation value	−0.916	−0.943	−0.945	−0.937	−0.994

6   Conclusion

In this paper, we studied realtime mobile bandwidth prediction. We developed LSTM recurrent neural network models to capture the rich temporal structures in mobile bandwidth traces for accurate prediction. In both next-second and multi-second predictions, LSTM outperforms other state-of-the-art prediction algorithms, such as RLS and Harmonic Mean. Using Multi-Scale Entropy analysis, we investigated the connection between MSE and *cross-scenario* prediction accuracy. Going forward, we will continue our mobile bandwidth measurement campaign. For online bandwidth prediction, we will study how to dynamically select LSTM models trained offline to match the current mobility scenario through adaptive model fusion. We will also study the feasibility of using extra information, e.g. GPS, speed/acceleration sensor readings, to assist mobility scenario identification and model selection. We will also develop LSTM models for the emerging 5G mobile networks. Finally, we will explore data fusion of LSTM models and other prediction models to further improve the prediction accuracy.

References

1. Gers, F.A., Schmidhuber, J., Cummins, F.: Learning to forget: continual prediction with LSTM, pp. 850–855 (1999)
2. Sundermeyer, M., Schlüter, R., Ney, H.: LSTM neural networks for language modeling. In: Thirteenth Annual Conference of the International Speech Communication Association (2012)
3. Haykin, S.S.: Adaptive Filter Theory. Pearson Education India, Delhi (2008)
4. Costa, M., Goldberger, A.L., Peng, C.K.: Multiscale entropy analysis of complex physiologic time series. Phys. Rev. Lett. **89**(6), 068102 (2002)

5. Yi, S., et al.: CS2P: improving video bitrate selection and adaptation with data-driven throughput prediction. In: Proceedings of the 2016 ACM SIGCOMM Conference, pp. 272–285. ACM (2016)
6. Brown, R.G., Hwang, P.Y.C.: Introduction to Random Signals and Applied Kalman Filtering, vol. 3. Wiley, New York (1992)
7. HSDPA. http://home.ifi.uio.no/paalh/dataset/hsdpa-tcp-logs/
8. Bai, T., Vaze, R., Heath, R.W.: Analysis of blockage effects on urban cellular networks. IEEE Trans. Wirel. Commun. **13**(9), 5070–5083 (2014)
9. Bai, T., Vaze, R., Heath, R.W.: Using random shape theory to model blockage in random cellular networks. In: 2012 International Conference on Signal Processing and Communications (SPCOM), pp. 1–5. IEEE (2012)
10. Eymen, K., Liu, Y., Wang, Y., Shi, Y., Gu, C., Lyu, J.: Real-time bandwidth prediction and rate adaptation for video calls over cellular networks. In: Proceedings of the 7th International Conference on Multimedia Systems, p. 12. ACM (2016)
11. Guibin, T., Liu, Y.: Towards agile and smooth video adaptation in dynamic HTTP streaming. In: Proceedings of the 8th International Conference on Emerging Networking Experiments and Technologies, pp. 109–120. ACM (2012)
12. He, Q., Dovrolis, C., Ammar, M.H.: On the predictability of large transfer TCP throughput. In: Proceedings of ACM SIGCOMM (2005)
13. Mirza, M., Sommers, J., Barford, P., Zhu, X.: A machine learning approach to TCP throughput prediction. In: ACM SIGMETRICS (2007)
14. Smola, A.J., Schölkopf, B.: A tutorial on support vector regression. Stat. Comput. **14**(3), 199–222 (2004)
15. Yin, X., Jindal, A., Sekar, V., Sinopoli, B.: A control-theoretic approach for dynamic adaptive video streaming over HTTP. In: ACM SIGCOMM Computer Communication Review, vol. 45, no. 4, pp. 325–338. ACM (2015)
16. Winstein, K., Sivaraman, A., Balakrishnan, H.: Stochastic forecasts achieve high throughput and low delay over cellular networks. In: NSDI, vol. 1, no. 1, pp. 2–3 (2013)
17. Cho, K., et al.: Learning phrase representations using RNN encoder-decoder for statistical machine translation. arXiv preprint arXiv:1406.1078 (2014)
18. Hinton, G., et al.: Deep neural networks for acoustic modeling in speech recognition: the shared views of four research groups. IEEE Sig. Process. Mag. **29**(6), 82–97 (2012)
19. Mao, H., Netravali, R., Alizadeh, M.: Neural adaptive video streaming with pensieve. In: Proceedings of the Conference of the ACM Special Interest Group on Data Communication, pp. 197–210. ACM (2017)
20. Jiang, J., Sekar, V., Zhang, H.: Improving fairness, efficiency, and stability in HTTP-based adaptive video streaming with festive. IEEE/ACM Trans. Netwo. (TON) **22**(1), 326–340 (2014)
21. Kingma, D.P., Ba, J.: Adam: a method for stochastic optimization. arXiv preprint arXiv:1412.6980 (2014)

Measurement at Internet Scale

Hidden Treasures – Recycling Large-Scale Internet Measurements to Study the Internet's Control Plane

Jan Rüth[(⊠)], Torsten Zimmermann, and Oliver Hohlfeld

RWTH Aachen University, Aachen, Germany
{rueth,zimmermann,hohlfeld}@comsys.rwth-aachen.de
https://icmp.netray.io

Abstract. Internet-wide scans are a common active measurement app-roach to study the Internet, e.g., studying security properties or protocol adoption. They involve probing large address ranges (IPv4 or parts of IPv6) for specific ports or protocols. Besides their primary use for prob-ing (e.g., studying protocol adoption), we show that—at the same time—they provide valuable insights into the Internet control plane informed by ICMP responses to these probes—a currently unexplored secondary use. We collect one week of ICMP responses (637.50M messages) to sev-eral Internet-wide ZMap scans covering multiple TCP and UDP ports as well as DNS-based scans covering >50% of the domain name space. This perspective enables us to study the Internet's control plane as a by-product of Internet measurements. We receive ICMP messages from ~171M different IPs in roughly 53K different autonomous systems. Addi-tionally, we uncover multiple control plane problems, e.g., we detect a plethora of outdated and misconfigured routers and uncover the presence of large-scale persistent routing loops in IPv4.

1 Introduction

Internet scans are a valuable and thus widely used approach to understand and track the evolution of the Internet as one of the most complex systems ever created by humans. They are widely applied in different fields, including net-working and security research: e.g., to find vulnerable systems [9], to measure the liveness of IP addresses [3], or to measure the deployability of new proto-cols, features [11], or their evolution [33]. Advances in scanning methodologies enabled probing the entire IPv4 address space for a single port within minutes or hours, depending on the available bandwidth and configured scan rate (see tools such as ZMap [10] or MASSCAN [18]). Thereby, regular scans of the entire IPv4 address space have become feasible, e.g., providing an insightful perspective into protocol evolution (see e.g., QUIC [31]). This line of scan-based works has cre-ated a rich body of contributions with valuable insights into Internet structure and evolution. These works have in common that they focus on one particular feature or protocol as their objective to study (*primary use*).

© Springer Nature Switzerland AG 2019
D. Choffnes and M. Barcellos (Eds.): PAM 2019, LNCS 11419, pp. 51–67, 2019.
https://doi.org/10.1007/978-3-030-15986-3_4

Table 1. Weekly scan schedule fueling our dataset, DNS-based scans use our own resolver infrastructure. For IPv4-wide scans, we utilize ZMap.

	Mon	Tue	Wed	Thu	Fri	Sat	Sun
Source	DNS						
Protocols & Ports	TCP/443, gQUIC/443						
Source	Alexa	1% IPv4	IPv4				
Protocols & Ports	TCP/80, TCP/443	TCP/80, TCP/443	TCP/80	iQUIC/443	gQUIC/443	TCP/443	

In this work, we argue that Internet-wide scans have a less explored *secondary use* to study the Internet control plane while scanning for their primary use, e.g., to detect routing loops while *primarily* probing for QUIC-capable servers. That is, we study Internet control plane responses sent via ICMP as response to non-ICMP probe packets (e.g., QUIC) and show that Internet-wide scans are a hidden treasure in that they produce a rich ICMP dataset that is currently neglected, e.g., to uncover network problems. The interesting aspect is that these ICMP-responses are a valuable secondary use that is generated as by-product of any Internet-wide scan. They thus enable to study the Internet control plane (e.g., to detect routing loops) without requiring dedicated scans (as performed a decade ago [20,36]) that would increase the scanning footprint.

Our observations on the Internet's control plane are fueled by regular ZMap scans of the IPv4 address space for multiple TCP and UDP ports as well as DNS-based scans of top lists and zone files for mainly TLS, HTTP/2, and QUIC. We evaluate one full week of ICMP responses to multi-protocol Internet-scans covering the entire IPv4 address space and >50% of the domain name space(base domains).

Our contributions are as follows:

- We propose to use Internet-wide scans to study the Internet control plane via ICMP response, e.g., to detect routing loops or misconfigurations.
- Within our one week observation period, we collect ∼637.50M ICMP messages which we make available at [22].
- We shed light on how Internet-scans trigger ICMP responses across the Internet.
- Our data shows a plethora of misconfigured systems e.g., sending ICMP redirects across the Internet or producing deprecated source quench messages.
- We find many networks and hosts to be unreachable, our scans uncover large sets of unreachable address space due to routing loops.
- We provide a growing ICMP dataset at https://icmp.netray.io.

Structure. The next section (Sect. 2) starts by providing an overview of our ICMP dataset. Following this, we dive into our dataset and dissect it (Sect. 3). Driven by our findings, we inspect unreachable hosts due to routing loops and quantifies their presence in today's Internet (Sect. 4). Finally, we discuss related works (Sect. 5) and conclude the paper (Sect. 6).

2   Scan Infrastructure and Dataset

Infrastructure. Our scans are sourced by two different modes, on the one hand, we use the ZMap [10] port scanner on multiple machines to perform different scans over the course of a week, and on the other hand, we continuously probe >50% of the DNS space. Table 1 summarized our weekly scan schedule, we did not specifically create these scans and this schedule for this paper, it is the result of ongoing research efforts.

These scans typically involve scanning TCP/80 for TCP initial window configurations [30] or TCP fast open support. Further, we investigate TCP/443 for HTTP/2-support [37] and TLS, additionally, we scan on UDP 443 for Google QUIC (gQUIC) [31] and IETF-QUIC (iQUIC). Our DNS-based scans are fueled by using our own resolvers to resolve various record types for domains listed in zone files of multiple TLDs (e.g., .com, .net, .org), which can be obtained from the registries, and we use A-records to investigate TLS, HTTP/2, and gQUIC. All of our scans including the DNS resolutions originate from a dedicated subnet. To collect all ICMP traffic that is directed towards these hosts, we install a mirror port at their uplink switch and filter it to only contain ICMP traffic that belongs to our measurement network. Since we perform no measurements that generate ICMP messages themselves, we exclude those sent from our host (only ping responses) leaving us with only incoming ICMP traffic.

Dataset. We base our observations on one full week in September 2018. In this week we received 169 GB resp. ~637.50M ICMPv4[1] messages (excluding those explicitly triggered in Sect. 4). ICMP messages follow the structure shown in Fig. 1, they are fundamentally made up of a type field and, to further specify a subtype, a code field, and depending on their value additional information may follow.

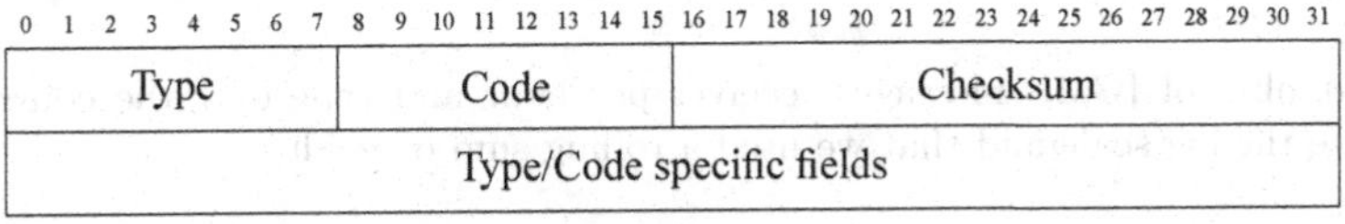

```
0  1  2  3  4  5  6  7  8  9  10 11 12 13 14 15 16 17 18 19 20 21 22 23 24 25 26 27 28 29 30 31
```

Type	Code	Checksum
Type/Code specific fields		

Fig. 1. ICMP header structure. Type and this type's sub type (code) determine message contents, e.g., often packets triggering the ICMP message are quoted.

---

[1] Please note that we do not have a fully IPv6-capable measurement infrastructure and thus focus on IPv4 only.

Table 2. ICMP types with their occurrence frequency in our dataset. Ordered by frequency.

Type	Count	Uniq. IP	Uniq. AS		Type	Count	Uniq. IP	Uniq. AS
Dest. Unreach.	476.68M	170.30M	52.92K		EchoReply	6.08K	301	58
TimeExceeded	139.53M	455.13K	18.40K		Other	1.48K	606	43
Redirect	18.12M	243.25K	2.29K		TimestampReq.	73	9	6
EchoRequest	3.12M	10.64K	861		Param.Problem	20	16	9
SourceQuench	46.18K	2.65K	364		Addr.MaskReq.	4	1	1

3   Study of ICMP Responses

To begin our investigations, we first summarize the ICMP responses to our scans by looking at the distribution of ICMP message types and their frequency of occurrence in Table 2. We observe 75 different ICMP type/code combinations during our observation period with significantly different occurrence frequencies. While we mostly receive standardized ICMP messages, we also receive some messages for which we could not find a standard, summarized as *Other* in Table 2, on which we do not further focus in this paper. The table lists the total count of these messages as well as the number of unique source IPs (router/end-host IPs) that generated the messages and number of ASes they are contained in. Over the course of the week, we run different scans. Notably, on Sundays and Mondays (see Table 1), no IPv4-wide ZMap scans are performed.

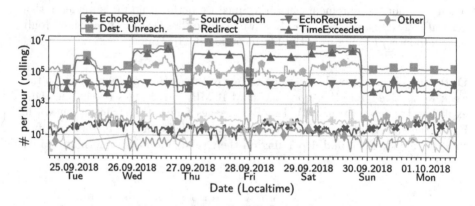

Fig. 2. Number of ICMP messages receiver per hour and type over the course of a week. Note the log scale and that we used a rolling sum over 1 h.

Figure 2 thus puts the data from Table 2 into a temporal context showing the rolling sum over 1 h intervals of the major ICMP types. We observe that the ICMP traffic varies over the course of the week, e.g., echo requests are rather static, other types like destination unreachable mainly follow our ZMap scan schedule.

Quoted IP Packet. Apart from the different ICMP types, many ICMP messages contain parts of the packet that caused the creation of the messages. We further inspect these quoted IPv4 packets within the ICMP messages. From all received ICMP messages, 99.5% are supposed to contain IP packets (according to the RFCs), of these only 0.07% cannot be decoded, e.g., because there is simply not enough data or these are no IPv4 packets. Of the decodable packets, we find 180.25M unique source IP/payload length combinations, 76% are longer than 40 bytes, i.e., enough to inspect IP and TCP headers when no options are used[2], 24% are exactly 28 byte long, so just enough to inspect the transport ports. Thus, when no options are used, the chances are high that ICMP messages received by an ICMP receiver can be demultiplexed to the respective application process. This extends the finding in [26] that showed a prevalence of 28 byte responses for TCP `traceroutes`. Next, we focus on the destination address field within the quoted IP header. These should correspond to addresses which are targeted by our scanners. Interestingly, from all ICMP messages, we find over 1.06M messages with destination IPs that are in reserved address space, i.e., unallocated or private addresses (e.g., 192.168.0.0/24). Since all our scanners explicitly blacklist these IP addresses, we believe that these messages are produced behind network address translations (NATs). We next use the contained source addresses to understand the relation to our measurements.

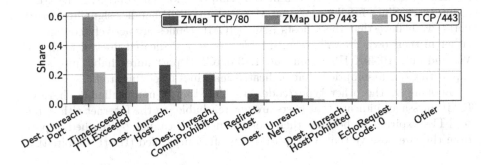

Fig. 3. ICMP messages triggered by ZMap and DNS-based scans.

Takeaway. *ICMP traffic shows a temporal correlation to measurement traffic, most messages indicate unreachability. In our collected dataset, quoted IP packets typically contain enough information to inspect everything up to the end of the TCP header. Further, a substantial number of messages seems to be generated behind NATs allowing to peek into private address spaces.*

3.1 Responses to Individual Measurements

Since we perform a variety of different measurements independent of this study, our first investigation is how different measurements affect the generation of

---

[2] To reduce the capture size, our packet capture caps packets at 98 byte allowing no further investigation, we find 67% having the maximum capture size.

ICMP traffic. To this end, we compare two ZMap scans and a purely DNS-based scan. For the ZMap scans, we focus on one that enumerates reachable TCP port 80 (HTTP) and UDP port 443 (QUIC) hosts, for DNS, we use a scan that probes for HTTP/2 support via TCP port 443. We are able to clearly tie the ICMP messages to the different scans via IPs and ports either from the quoted IP message or from IP itself.

Figure 3 shows the distribution of ICMP types *and* codes (top 8) that we receive for the respective scans. As already indicated by Table 2, we receive a large amount of destination unreachable messages. However, depending on the scan, their amount and share greatly vary, especially when looking at the respective code. For example, unreachable ports are very common for our UDP-based ZMap scan, however, in comparison, the TCP-based ZMap scan shows only a small fraction of unreachable ports. This is no surprise as TCP should reply with a RST-packet if a port is unreachable and does typically not generate ICMP messages. In contrast, there is no such mechanism in UDP, even through something comparable to TCP's RST exists in QUIC. However, QUIC is implemented in user-space, thus when the kernel cannot demultiplex a packet to a socket it must resort to issuing an ICMP unreachable message. Looking at our DNS-based scan, we still find that more than 20% of the ICMP messages signal unreachability through ICMP in contrast to TCP RSTs, something that, e.g., the default ZMap TCP-SYN scan module simply ignores in contrast to its UDP counterpart. Since in all major operating systems TCP handles signaling closed ports, we believe that these hosts issuing ICMP replies are actively configured either in their own firewalls (e.g., iptables) or in a dedicated firewall to do so. We find only 16.49K IPs issuing *all* 1.13M ICMP port unreachable messages, supporting our assumption that dedicated machines filter this traffic.

Looking at the other types/codes, we find that a non-negligible share of ICMP messages indicate that hosts are not reachable via the Internet either due to TTLs expiring or because their host or network cannot be reached. Apart from this, we observe that TCP port 443 is often firewalled (HostProhibited).

Takeaway. *Depending on the protocol and port, we get different feedback from the Internet's control plane. Our findings indicate that, e.g., ICMP port unreachable messages should not be ignored for TCP-based scans as is currently the case.*

3.2   ICMP Echos

ICMP echo requests (Type: 8) are the typical `ping` to which an echo reply is sent. RFC792 defines only a single code point, i.e., code $= 0$ which represents "no code", still we observe some non-standard code points. Some security scanners use non-standard code points for operating system fingerprinting, e.g., a standard Linux will echo the requested code point in its reply. Still, pings to our measurement infrastructure seem quite common, for code $= 0$, we find 10.57K unique IPs out of 840 autonomous systems (ASes). It seems that our scanning activities trigger systems to perform ping measurements towards us, yet, we do not know their actual purpose. We suspect that this could be caused by intrusion detection systems (IDSs) that monitor the liveness of our hosts.

Echo Replies. Since our hosts do not perform echo requests, we were surprised to find echo replies in our dataset. We observe different code points with different frequencies but overall we find over a couple of thousand of these replies. To investigate what causes these seemingly orphaned messages, we inspect their destinations. Since our measurements are identifiable either by IP or additionally by weekday, we associate messages to measurements. We find most echo replies are with code = 3 (except for 5 messages), all 5.75K of these echos are destined to our DNS resolvers and originate from only 86 IP addresses in 2 Chinese ASes. While many ICMP packets contain IP quotations, echo replies typically do not, they usually mirror data contained in the echo request. Yet, we still find IP packets together with DNS query *responses* that are destined to our resolver. Thus, it seems that the packets are generated on the reverse path, however, they are not sent back to the source (DNS server) but they are forwarded to the destination (us). Inspecting the source IP within the IP fragments, we find IP addresses from the same two ASes, as it turns out the 88 ICMP source IPs all respond to DNS queries which hints at their use as a DNS server cluster. Yet, we were unable to manually trigger these ICMP reply packets when trying to send DNS requests to these IPs, we only observed that DNS requests were always answered by two separate packets from the same IP, however, with different DNS answers. Further, the packets seem to stem from different IP stacks (significantly different TTLs, use of IP ID or not, don't fragment bit set or not). While the different stack fingerprints could be the result of middleboxes altering the IP headers, the general pattern that we observe hints at DNS spoofing.

3.3 Source Quench

ICMP Source Quench (SQ) messages (Type: 4, Code: 0) were a precursor of today's ECN mechanism, used to signal congestion at end-hosts and routers. The original idea (RFC792 [28]) was that a router should signal congestion by sending SQ messages to the sources that cause the congestion. In turn, these hosts should react, e.g., by reducing their packet rate. However, research [12] found that SQ is ineffective in e.g., establishing fairness and IETF has deprecated SQ-generation in 1995 [2] and SQ-processing in 2012 in general [17]. Major operating systems ignore SQ-messages for TCP at least since 2005 to counter blind throughput-reduction attacks [16]. Further, [13] claims that SQ is rarely used because it consumes bandwidth in times of congestion.

In our traces, we observe 2.65K unique IPs located in 364 ASes issuing SQ messages, despite the deprecation. Out of these IPs, 34.42% are located in only 5 ASes. Moreover, 609 IPs that generate SQ messages were directly contacted by our measurement infrastructure, i.e., are the original destination of the request causing this SQ message (according to the IPv4 header contained within the ICMP message). Among the remaining SQ messages, we find a few messages where the original destination and the source of the SQ messages are located in ASes of different operators, i.e., possible transit networks. Exemplarily, we observe that IPs located in AS1668 (AOL Transit Data Network) and AS7018 (AT&T) issued SQ messages when IPs located in AS8452 (Telecom Egypt) were contacted. As a final step, we see that 53 destination IPs in our measurements trigger the generation of SQ messages and are also contained in A-records of our DNS data that we collect. Out of these 53 IPs, 22 IPs generated the SQ messages themselves, i.e., no on-path intermediary caused the creation of this message.

In addition, we checked how vendors implement or handle this feature. Cisco removed the SQ feature from their IOS system after Version 12 in the early 2000s [5]. Hewlett Packard's cluster management system (Serviceguard) generated SQ messages due to a software bug in a read queue, which was fixed by a patch in 2010 [21]. In their router configuration manual (September 2017), Nokia also marks SQ messages as deprecated [27]. Although we cannot identify devices and their operating system version in our measurements, we assume that some devices are not updated to a current version or are following a configuration that enables them to generate SQ messages. This is not forbidden per se but given that ICMP SQ creation was deprecated over 20 years ago, our findings highlight that removing features from the Internet is a long term endeavor.

3.4   Redirect

ICMP redirect messages (Type: 5), are sent by gateways/routers to signal routes to hosts. While [15] finds networks which require redirect messages to be architected sub-optimally in the first place, RFC1812 [2] states that a router *must not* generate redirect messages unless three properties are fulfilled: *(i)* The packet is being forwarded out the same physical interface that it was received from, *(ii)*, the IP source address in the packet is on the same logical IP (sub)network as the next-hop IP address, and *(iii)*, the packet does not contain an IP source route option. Similar checks [4] are used by receiving hosts to check the validity of the message (e.g., redirected gateway and issuing router must be on the same network).

Since none of the 18.12M redirect messages originate from our network, the routers generating them either violate rule *(ii)* or some obscure address translation is in place on their networks. In our data, we even find roughly 2.7K unique redirects to private address space. Within our dataset, we observed 105.78K network redirects and 18.01M host redirects. Network redirects are problematic since no netmask is specified and it is up to the receiving router to interpret this correctly. For this reason, RFC1812 [2] demands that routers *must not* send this type. We find that the network redirects originate from 238 different ASes affecting nearly 19k different destinations of which less than 20 are mapped in any of our DNS data. Yet, all these ASes thus contain questionable router configurations that are outdated at least since 1995. Similarly, we find that the much larger fraction of host redirects originate from 2.20K ASes that affected over 400k destinations of which we find roughly 900 mapped in our DNS data. This suggests that a substantial number of end-systems are connected via sub-optimally architected or misconfigured networks.

Table 3. ICMP messages received indicating some form of unreachability with known type and code ordered by frequency.

Type	Code	Count	Type	Code	Count
Dest. Unreach.	Port	256.72M	Dest. Unreach.	Frag.Needed	26.66K
TimeExceeded	TTLExceeded	139.52M		NetProhibited	26.28K
Dest. Unreach.	Host	107.15M	TimeExceeded	Frag.Reassembly	7.31K
	CommProhibited	71.70M	Dest. Unreach.	HostUnknown	336
	HostProhibited	23.07M		NetTOS	25
	Net	17.94M		NetUnknown	6
	Protocol	51.04K		SourceIsolated	2

3.5 Unreachable Hosts

Reachability is a fundamental requirement to establish any means of communication. Given that Table 2 lists 476.68M destination unreachable messages this looks troublesome at first. Yet, not all unreachability is bad, e.g., firewalls actively protect infrastructure from unpermitted access, i.e., when iptables *rejects* a packet (in contrast to simply dropping it) it generates an ICMP response. By default, a port unreachable message (Type: 3, Code: 3) is produced but other types can be manually specified by the network operator. Our scans in themselves certainly trigger a certain amount of firewalls or some IDSs. In contrast, when a path is too long and the IP TTL reaches zero, routers typically generate an ICMP TTL exceeded message indicating that the destination is not reachable but this time due to the network's structure. Similarly, ICMP destination unreachable messages for host unreachable (Type: 3, Code: 1) should indicate that there is currently simply no path to a host, e.g., because it is not connected or the link is down. Table 3 summarizes the unreachability that we observe in our dataset.

As already indicated in Sect. 3.1, our UDP-based ZMap scans have the highest share of port unreachable messages putting them at the top. We inspect the origin of the messages and the actual destination that our scans targeted to see if the end-hosts generate the messages or an intermediate firewall. It seems that 96% of the messages are indeed generated by end-hosts or machines that can answer on their behalf (NATs).

Host and Network. Unreachable hosts and networks codes are used to give hints that currently no path is available and the RFCs explicitly note that this may be due to a transient state and that such a message is not proof of unreachability. To check for transient states, we compare the unreachable hosts on Thursday with those on Friday in our ZMap (both UDP 443) scan and additionally with the same scan (Thursday) one week later (captured separately from our initial dataset) and investigate if hosts become reachable that were unreachable before or vice versa.

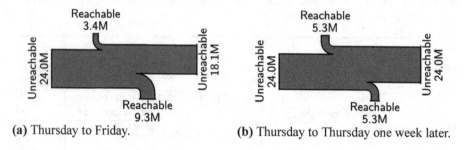

(a) Thursday to Friday.   **(b)** Thursday to Thursday one week later.

Fig. 4. Different scans (left to right of each plot) trigger different amount of host unreachable messages. (a) Compares the changes within one day. (b) Within one week.

Figure 4 visualizes the change between these two days (a) and within one week (b) for host unreachable messages. We can see that within two days, the majority of hosts remain unreachable, a small number of hosts that were previously *reachable*[3] become unreachable, similarly, previously unreachable hosts become reachable. Looking at the changes within a full week, we observe that the total amount of unreachable hosts stays the same, however, roughly the same amount of previously reachable host become unreachable and vice versa. To dig into these once unreachable and then reachable hosts, we inspect to which AS they belong finding that 82% of all hosts are from the same ASes. A possible explanation might be that while our observations seem to indicate a change, the ICMP message generation is subject to rate-limiting [19]. Thus there might be routers that generated unreachable messages on Thursday for a certain host, however, this router could be subject to rate-limiting on Friday for the same host or the week after leading to a false impression of reachability and continuity, still, a substantial number of hosts remain unreachable. Another possibility is that some hosts are only up at certain times of the day leading to differences in the reachability.

Time Exceeded. Similar to host unreachability, Time Exceeded messages (Type:11) indicate unreachability but due to network issues. Either the Fragment Reassembly (Code: 1) time was exceeded, i.e., the time that IP datagrams are buffered until they can be reassembled when IP fragmentation happens, or the TTL runs out (Code: 0), i.e., the path length exceeds the sender-defined limit. For the former, we find some thousand messages but they stem from only 30 ASes, since many of our scans use small packets, fragmentation is unlikely in

---

[3] With reachable we actually mean *not unreachable*, i.e., we do not get ICMP unreachable messages, which must not mean that this host was reached by the scan.

the first place. Yet, for example, the UDP ZMap scans use roughly 1300 byte per packet which is in the range of typical [7] MTUs when fragmentation could occur. Since the default ZMap functions to create IP packets (which we use) do not set the *don't fragment bit*, only some of our measurements trigger the 26.66K *fragmentation needed and DF set* ICMP messages (see Table 3). However, over time, these ICMP messages could give valuable insights into path MTU in the Internet.

TTL Exceeded messages have the second largest occurrence (139.52M) within our dataset. They were produced in 18.40K different ASes covering 35.5M different destinations that our scans tried to reach of which ~32K are again present in A-records of our DNS data and are thus unreachable. We inspect the TTL field of the quoted IP packets that triggered the ICMP messages to see if the TTL was actually zero when the message was generated. To do so, we first generate all unique pairs of router IP and TTL values and then count the different TTLs observed. Out of these, 97% of the TTLs show a value of one, followed by ~2.4% with a zero, we expect these two, since a router should drop a $TTL = 0$ or, depending on the internal pipeline, also $TTL = 1$, when the packet is to be forwarded. Nevertheless, we also find larger TTLs, 2, 3, 4, 5, and 6 directly follow in frequency, yet, we also find some instances of over 200 or even 255. The very large TTLs could hint at middleboxes or routers rewriting the TTL when they generate the message to hide their actual hop count. The lower numbers could be indicators for MPLS networks. By default, e.g., Cisco [6] and Juniper [24] routers copy the IP TTL to the MPLS TTL on ingress and also decrement the IP TTL within the MPLS network. It is possible to separate IP TTL and MPLS TTL and there are heated discussions whether one should hide the MPLS network from traceroutes or not which has also been subject of investigations [8]. Thus packets expiring within an MPLS network will still trigger an ICMP TTL exceeded, however, the quoted IP packet will have the TTL value they had at the MPLS ingress router, thus, if the IP TTL is still copied at ingress a traceroute could still reason about an MPLS network.

Since we were surprised to see this many TTL exceeded messages across all scanner types (see Sect. 3.1), we checked our scanners to see which TTL they were actually using to see if our setup simply has too small values. All our ZMap-based scanners initialize the TTL field with its maximum of 255 possible hops, all scanners building on top of the transport layer interfaces, in contrast, use the current Linux default of 64 hops as also recommended in RFC1700 [29]. Given that we are at least on the recommended hop count, this leaves us with three possibilities, *(i)* the current recommendation of 64 is too low to reach these hosts, *(ii)* there are middleboxes modifying the TTL to a much lower value, or, *(iii)* there are routing loops on the path to these hosts. After shortly summarizing our findings, we continue by exploring the latter.

3.6 Summary

As the previous sections have shown, our Internet-wide scans produce an insightful *secondary* dataset of ICMP responses. Driven by these messages, we identified a potential DNS spoofer, found that long deprecated source quench messages are still generated in today's Internet and that ICMP redirects are sent across different administrative domains pointing to several outdated and misconfigured networks. Without crafting a dedicated dataset, our scans enable us to study Internet reachability and we believe that longitudinal studies offer a way to deal with the challenge of ICMP rate-limiting.

4   Routing Loops

Routing loops are an undesirable control plane misconfiguration that render destination networks unreachable and that challenge a link's load [35]. In essence, IP's TTL protects the Internet from indefinitely looping packets and thus ICMP TTL messages inform the sender that a router dropped a packet after exceeding the allowed number of router hops (TTL). While the potential for routing loops is known, only a few studies investigated their presence a decade ago [20,36], current information on the presence and prevalence is missing. Therefore, we study routing loops on the basis of ICMP TTL exceeded messages triggered by our scans. We further argue that routing loops can be frequently investigated as a by-product of Internet-wide scans that are regularly conducted for different purposes.

4.1   Methodology: Detecting Loops

ICMP TTL exceeded messages are not necessarily caused by loops, also overly large paths or middleboxes could trigger these messages. To investigate whether or not an actual loop is present, we perform `traceroutes` for the original destinations (in the quoted IP) of the ICMP TTL exceeded messages. Since our traceroutes are subject to ICMP rate-limiting, especially when packets start to loop, we customize traceroute. Our traceroute slows down its sending rate when detecting an already seen IP address (loop indicator), otherwise, it follows the design of *Paris traceroute* [1] reusing flow identifiers for each hop to trigger the same forwarding behavior in ECMP-like load balancers.

Since the traceroutes can still be noisy due to hosts that do not generate ICMP at all or are still subject to rate-limiting, especially when also other traffic flows into a loop, we put strong demands on our loop. For each hop on the path that does not generate a reply, we assign a new unique label, all others are simply labeled by the answering IP. From this list of labels, we create a directed graph connecting each label-induced node to its successor and on this path we compute all elementary cycles using [23]. On an elementary cycle, no node appears twice except that the first and last node are the same. Then, on each of these possible cycles we inspect the node with the highest degree, and if this node's degree is larger than 5^4, we mark this traceroute as having a loop. This will yield

---

[4] This is basically a precaution against bad load balancers traded against the required TTL.

loops as long as at least one router in the loop generated ICMP TTL exceeded messages, which we found to work reasonably well when traceroute pauses the packet generation for at least 500 ms when observing an already seen IP address. Thus in a loop of two routers, we will send each router a packet roughly every second.

4.2   Routing Loops in the Wild

We seed our traceroutes by ICMP TTL exceeded messages generated from our Internet-wide scans[5]. Since we get way too many TTL exceeded messages to traceroute them all without generating substantial rate-limiting, we restrict us to a single traceroute for each unique /24 subnet within 30-min intervals. Thus for two TTL exceeded messages for a destination from the same /24 subnet, we only perform a single traceroute if the messages arrive within 30 min.

For our assessment of routing loops, we investigate TTL exceeded messages in the last week of August 2018. To avoid rate-limiting we also limit our traceroutes that we perform in parallel; generating all traceroutes for this single week took us until the end of September 2018. While this skews our data, it enables us to reason about the persistence of these loops since every 30 min the same /24 could be scheduled for a rescan. In total, we performed ~27M traceroutes to ~612K different /24 subnets from 28K ASes, of these, 439K subnets from 19.8K ASes are unreachable due to a loop. We further inspect how many loops are present and if loops are only within a single AS or whether loops cross AS borders and are thus potentially on a peering link. To do so, we count the number of distinct loops and ASes involved in the loops and find 167K different loops in 13.9K ASes. Of these loops, 136K have IPs for all routers involved in the loop, thus allowing an in-depth inspection. Looking at the ASes involved, we find that 13% (17.7K) already cover all different ASes paths involved (i.e., we replaced each IP by the respective AS), of these 4.8K cross AS boundaries. The top three ASes involved in the loops are AS171 (Cogent) a Tier-1, AS9498 (BHARTI Airtel Ltd.), an Indian ISP, and AS3549 (Level 3), again a Tier-1.

Persistence. To investigate the persistence, we restrict our view to traceroutes that were performed two weeks after the initial TTL exceeded message was triggered by our Internet-wide scans. In contrast to our previous observation, loops from roughly 150 ASes disappear, yet, we still find 4.6K loops crossing AS borders, in total still rendering 404K subnets unreachable. Thus, most loops seem to persist and are not resolved.

Loops at our Upstream ISP. Within our data, we also found loops in the AS of our upstream ISP. We contacted the ISP about our findings which they were able to confirm. Since many of the loops are outside of their administrative domain even though they manage the address space, they were still able to give

---

[5] Our dataset excludes TTL exceeded messages generated by these traceroutes.

us more details on a loop that they were able to fix. For one loop, they found that the first router had a static route for our tested destination towards its next hop, yet, the next hop had no specific forwarding information for this destination and thus used its default gateway, which however was the previous router with the static route thus causing the loop.

Takeaway. *Routing loops seem to persist in large parts of the Internet, challenging the question if the address space cut off by the loops is in use after all or if there are other routers that would be taken from different vantage points. We believe routing loops have a huge potential for causing congestion when exploited and thus a persistent monitoring seeded by large-scale Internet measurements that informs operators could be a long-term attempt to reduce routing loops.*

5   Related Work

Our work relates to approaches analyzing ICMP traffic and its generation in general, as well as approaches that focus on particular studies built upon ICMP, e.g., path/topology discovery and routing loops. In the following, we discuss similarities and differences to our work but we remark that the body of works building on top of ICMP is far larger but conceptually differ in that they do not analyze ICMP as a by-product.

Bano et al. [3] also use ZMap and capture *all* (cross-layer) responses to probe traffic to infer IP liveness but run specific measurements to generate this traffic, we believe that our dataset could be used to perform a similar analysis. Malone et al. [26] analyze the correctness of ICMP quotations. They base their analysis on a dataset obtained via `tcptraceroute` in 2005, targeting around 84K web servers. While most of the reported messages are of type ICMP time exceeded, they also find around 100 source quench messages, which were already deprecated then. As we have shown, by looking at the ICMP responses to Internet-wide scans, we are able to update their findings on a regular basis without having to craft a dedicated dataset. Guo et al. [19] present FADER, an approach to detect the presence of ICMP rate-limiting in measurement traces. While we did not focus on rate-limiting, we found indicators for rate-limiting. We believe that longitudinal studies seeded by Internet-wide scans can, in the long run, help to overcome limited visibility due to rate-limiting.

In 2002, Hengartner et al. [20] have characterized and analyzed the presence of routing loops in a Tier-1 ISP backbone trace. Xia et al. [35,36] have further tracerouted over 9M IP addresses to find routing loops in 2005. Transient routing loops have also been subject to investigation [34] and they are well studied [14,32]. Lone et al. [25] investigate routing loops in CAIDA data to study source address validation but do not focus on their prevalence in the Internet, further, in contrast to using the CAIDA dataset that actively runs traceroutes against all /24, we utilize indications from ongoing measurement data to investigate loops. While these works show that routing loops are a known problematic misconfiguration, their presence in the Internet has not been analyzed for over

10 years. By recycling Internet-wide scans, we can seed such investigations and enable persistent monitoring of this phenomenon showing that routing loops are still a problem today.

6   Conclusion

In this paper, we used ICMP responses triggered by large-scale Internet measurements to study how the Internet's control plane reacts to these measurements. Thereby, we found that these responses are hidden treasures that are typically neglected but offer great insights into the configuration of Internet-connected systems. Our analyses of different ICMP responses led us to many misconfigured routers, e.g., sending ICMP redirects across the Internet, or outdated systems, e.g., generating long-deprecated source quench messages. Further, our analysis showed a large and nuanced degree of unreachability in the Internet. More specifically, our scans hint at the existence of routing loops, which we found to persist in large parts of the Internet. We hope that these ICMP by-products are analyzed by more researchers when performing large-scale measurements and that the regular nature of these scans will enable persistent monitoring of the Internet's control plane and that, especially when brought to the attention of operators, misconfigurations can be fixed. To this end, we make our dataset publicly available at [22].

Acknowledgments. Funded by the Excellence Initiative of the German federal and state governments, as well as by the German Research Foundation (DFG) as part of project B1 within the Collaborative Research Center (CRC) 1053—MAKI. We would like to thank the network operators at RWTH Aachen University, especially Jens Hektor and Bernd Kohler as well as RWTH's research data management team.

References

1. Augustin, B., et al.: Avoiding traceroute anomalies with Paris traceroute. In: ACM IMC (2006)
2. Baker, F.: Requirements for IP Version 4 Routers. RFC 1812, RFC Editor (1995)
3. Bano, S., et al.: Scanning the internet for liveness. SIGCOMM CCR **48**(2), 2–9 (2018)
4. Braden, R.: Requirements for Internet Hosts - Communication Layers. RFC 1122, RFC Editor (1989)
5. Cisco: IP Routing Frequently Asked Questions. https://www.cisco.com/c/en/us/support/docs/ip/border-gateway-protocol-bgp/28745-44.html#qa5
6. Cisco Systems, Inc.: Cisco IOS XR MPLS: mpls ip-ttl-propagate (2014). https://www.cisco.com/c/en/us/td/docs/routers/xr12000/software/xr12k_r4-1/mpls/command/reference/b_mpls_cr41xr12k/b_mpls_cr41xr12k_chapter_010.html#wp28648 46713
7. Custura, A., Fairhurst, G., Learmonth, I.: Exploring usable Path MTU in the Internet. In: IFIP Network Traffic Measurement and Analysis Conference (2018)
8. Donnet, B., Luckie, M., Mérindol, P., Pansiot, J.-J.: Revealing MPLS Tunnels obscured from traceroute. SIGCOMM CCR **42**(2), 87–93 (2012)

9. Durumeric, Z., et al.: The matter of heartbleed. In: ACM IMC (2014)
10. Durumeric, Z., Wustrow, E., Halderman, J.A.: ZMap: fast internet-wide scanning and its security applications. In: USENIX Security (2013)
11. Edeline, K., Kühlewind, M., Trammell, B., Donnet, B.: copycat: Testing differential treatment of new transport protocols in the wild. In: Proceedings of the Applied Networking Research Workshop (ANRW) (2017)
12. Finn, G.G.: A connectionless congestion control algorithm. SIGCOMM CCR **19**(5), 12–31 (1989)
13. Floyd, S.: TCP and explicit congestion notification. SIGCOMM CCR **24**(5), 8–23 (1994)
14. Francois, P., Bonaventure, O.: Avoiding transient loops during the convergence of link-state routing protocols. IEEE/ACM Trans. Netw. **15**, 1280–1292 (2007)
15. Gill, S.: ICMP redirects are ba'ad, mkay? Technical report, Team Cymru Inc. (2002)
16. Gont, F.: ICMP Attacks Against TCP. RFC 5927, RFC Editor (2010)
17. Gont, F.: Deprecation of ICMP Source Quench Messages. RFC 6633, RFC Editor (2012)
18. Graham, R.: MASSCAN: Mass IP Port Scanner (2018). https://github.com/robertdavidgraham/masscan
19. Guo, H., Heidemann, J.: Detecting ICMP rate limiting in the internet. In: Beverly, R., Smaragdakis, G., Feldmann, A. (eds.) PAM 2018. LNCS, vol. 10771, pp. 3–17. Springer, Cham (2018). https://doi.org/10.1007/978-3-319-76481-8_1
20. Hengartner, U., Moon, S., Mortier, R., Diot, C.: Detection and analysis of routing loops in packet traces. In: ACM SIGCOMM Workshop on Internet Measurement (2002)
21. Hewlett Packard: HP-UX - Serviceguard A.11.19 on HP-UX 11.31: Source Quench Seen for Every IPMON Ping. https://support.hpe.com/hpsc/doc/public/display?docId=emr_na-c02190964
22. Rüth, J., Zimmermann, T., Hohlfeld, O.: ICMP Dataset and Tools (2018). https://icmp.netray.io
23. Johnson, D.: Finding all the elementary circuits of a directed graph. SIAM J. Comput. **4**(1), 77–84 (1975)
24. Juniper Networks, Inc.: no-propagate-ttl - TechLibrary - Juniper Networks (2017). https://www.juniper.net/documentation/en_US/junos/topics/reference/configuration-statement/no-propagate-ttl-edit-protocols-mpls.html
25. Lone, Q., Luckie, M., Korczyński, M., van Eeten, M.: Using loops observed in traceroute to infer the ability to spoof. In: Kaafar, M.A., Uhlig, S., Amann, J. (eds.) PAM 2017. LNCS, vol. 10176, pp. 229–241. Springer, Cham (2017). https://doi.org/10.1007/978-3-319-54328-4_17
26. Malone, D., Luckie, M.: Analysis of ICMP quotations. In: Uhlig, S., Papagiannaki, K., Bonaventure, O. (eds.) PAM 2007. LNCS, vol. 4427, pp. 228–232. Springer, Heidelberg (2007). https://doi.org/10.1007/978-3-540-71617-4_24
27. Nokia: Router Configuration Guide Release 15.0.R5. https://infoproducts.alcatel-lucent.com/cgi-bin/dbaccessfilename.cgi/3HE11976AAACTQZZA01_V1_7450%20ESS%207750%20SR%207950%20XRS%20and%20VSR%20Router%20Configuration%20Guide%20R15.0.R5.pdf
28. Postel, J.: Internet Control Message Protocol. RFC 792, RFC Editor (1981)
29. Reynolds, J., Postel, J.: Assigned Numbers. RFC 1700, RFC Editor (1994)
30. Rüth, J., Bormann, C., Hohlfeld, O.: Large-scale scanning of TCP's initial window. In: ACM IMC (2017)

31. Rüth, J., Poese, I., Dietzel, C., Hohlfeld, O.: A first look at QUIC in the wild. In: Beverly, R., Smaragdakis, G., Feldmann, A. (eds.) PAM 2018. LNCS, vol. 10771, pp. 255–268. Springer, Cham (2018). https://doi.org/10.1007/978-3-319-76481-8_19

32. Sridharan, A., Moon, S., Diot, C.: On the correlation between route dynamics and routing loops. In: ACM IMC (2003)

33. Varvello, M., Schomp, K., Naylor, D., Blackburn, J., Finamore, A., Papagiannaki, K.: Is the web HTTP/2 yet? In: Karagiannis, T., Dimitropoulos, X. (eds.) PAM 2016. LNCS, vol. 9631, pp. 218–232. Springer, Cham (2016). https://doi.org/10.1007/978-3-319-30505-9_17

34. Wang, F., Qiu, J., Gao, L., Wang, J.: On understanding transient interdomain routing failures (2009)

35. Xia, J., Gao, L., Fei, T.: Flooding attacks by exploiting persistent forwarding loops. In: ACM IMC (2005)

36. Xia, J., Gao, L., Fei, T.: A measurement study of persistent forwarding loops on the internet. Comput. Netw. **51**, 4780–4796 (2007)

37. Zimmermann, T., Rüth, J., Wolters, B., Hohlfeld, O.: How HTTP/2 pushes the web: an empirical study of HTTP/2 server push. In: IFIP Networking Conference (2017)

Caching the Internet: A View from a Global Multi-tenant CDN

Marcel Flores[(✉)] and Harkeerat Bedi

Verizon Digital Media Services, Los Angeles, USA
marcle.flores@verizondigitalmedia.com

Abstract. Commercial Content Delivery Networks (CDNs) employ a variety of caching policies to achieve fast and reliable delivery in multi-tenant environments with highly variable workloads. In this paper, we explore the efficacy of popular caching policies in a large-scale, global, multi-tenant CDN. We examine the client behaviors observed in a network of over 125 high-capacity Points of Presence (PoPs). Using production data from the Edgecast CDN, we show that for such a large-scale and diverse use case, simpler caching policies dominate. We find that LRU offers the best compromise between hit-rate and disk I/O, providing 60% fewer writes than FIFO, while maintaining high hit-rates. We further observe that at disk sizes used in a large-scale CDN, LRU performs on par with complex polices like S4LRU. We further examine deterministic and probabilistic cache admission policies and quantify their trade-offs between hit-rate and origin traffic. Moreover, we explore the behavior of caches at multiple layers of the CDN and provide recommendations to reduce connections passing through the system's load balancers by approximately 50%.

1 Introduction

Content Delivery Networks (CDNs) provide a core piece of modern Internet infrastructure [16,39]. They handle immense volumes of traffic flowing between end users and content providers. To facilitate this transmission, while reducing end-user latency, CDNs employ complex caching systems which include numerous optimizations to improve performance and operational efficiency. Many such systems are purpose-built for specific application workloads or physical constraints, allowing for solutions that are tailor-made to their needs [4,22,38]. While highly effective in context, they are designed to manage well-defined and homogeneous workloads, granting the operators greater knowledge and control.

Unfortunately, many purpose-built approaches do not apply in multi-tenant environments where the operating characteristics are a function of the behavior of end users (*i.e.*, user request patterns), the behavior of content providers (*i.e.* customer churn, origin behavior), and the content served. These factors result in wide variability of request behaviors in both geography and time, potentially limiting the effectiveness of many specialized techniques.

In this study, we examine the behavior of the Edgecast CDN, a global multi-tenant CDN, exploring the variations observed in request patterns and file access

© Springer Nature Switzerland AG 2019
D. Choffnes and M. Barcellos (Eds.): PAM 2019, LNCS 11419, pp. 68–81, 2019.
https://doi.org/10.1007/978-3-030-15986-3_5

behaviors through the use of a *cache emulator*. We consider caching at multiple tiers in a CDN: disk cache (on the order of terabytes) and a load balancer cache (on the order of gigabytes). In each tier, we explore the trade-offs inherent in their operating constraints. We investigate the individual and combined impacts of cache admission (*i.e.*, which objects are cached) and eviction (*i.e.*, which objects to remove) policies.

We find that relatively simple and easy to manage approaches, such as Least-Recently-Used (LRU), provide similar performance to more complex techniques (S4LRU) and are able to improve disk reads by 60% versus simpler techniques, such as First-In-First-Out (FIFO). At the load balancer level, we are able to serve nearly 50% of requests from cache employing probabilistic admission and FIFO with just 1 GB. The view from a global commercial network allows us insight at a scale that provides meaningful and realistic analysis of the behavior of web caching in the wild. This represents a step towards managing the complexities of multi-tenant environments, as many CDN and service providers must do.

We present an overview of related work and previous examinations of cache behavior in Sect. 2. In Sect. 3 we examine the behaviors of production workloads and explore how they drive our intuitions on caching behavior. In Sect. 4 we present an overview of our test environment and provide an evaluation of the various caching methodologies in Sect. 5. We explore the further potential for improvement in the systems in Sect. 6. Finally, we conclude in Sect. 7.

2   Related Work

Cache management techniques have a significant history in computer systems [11, 24, 26, 32, 33]. However, many of these systems focus on the particular case of page caching. Web-caching systems have examined traditional web object behavior, exploring cacheability if objects follow zipf and zipf-like distributions [8, 21], and stretched exponential distributions [20]. Others have explored emergent behaviors that arise from caching on the web [9, 12, 13, 23, 37]. Our work builds its intuitions from many of these works, in particular in the applicability of FIFO and LRU in the context of large PoPs with large disks and a diverse set of clients. We further note that in the context of a commercial CDN, the traffic is self-selected for cacheability, as those with cacheable content are most likely to purchase commercial CDN services.

A number of high performance caches have been developed for both web objects [1, 3] and generic objects [2, 17]. Numerous proposals have explored extensions to these systems, with an eye towards making them more efficient for particular workloads [7, 15]. While effective in context, many of these systems and modifications are unusable in generic caching systems, in particular for large scale deployments that cannot readily change core caching technologies.

Other studies have examined the structure, performance and behaviors of CDNs [18, 25, 29]. Further studies have examined the nature of specific request behaviors, including flash crowds [27, 40] and social networks [35]. Google proposed a system for debugging the performance of their CDN with WhyHigh [30].

In [34] and [19], the authors examine a large university trace and examine the potential cache performance for CDNs and traditional web delivery. In [36], the authors characterized the workloads of a CDN and examined its cache performance, proposing an approach called *content-aware caching*. Here, we explore the cache behaviors of content-agnostic policies that are available in production, and develop an understanding of cache interactions in the CDN.

Finally, a number of purpose built systems have been designed to deal with large scale and complex cache workflows. For example Facebook's photo caching systems [5,22,38]. While similar, these systems are designed for managing internal systems, rather than external customer needs. AdaptSize [6] uses Markov chains to learn client request pattern shifts. Other systems such as Google's Janus [4] are designed to optimize workflows for FLASH storage. However, their system requires manual intervention, which is untenable in commercial CDN settings. Fundamentally, the final back-end origins are operated by third parties and the workloads are highly variable based on both end-user (access) and customer (server side) behaviors. These constraints alter the levels of performance that are acceptable and the needs of each level of the cache.

3 Overview of a Global CDN

This study is based on the Edgecast CDN, which features a global deployment of Points-of-Presence (PoPs) around the world. The considered network consists of PoPs that are well connected to the Internet, as the network aggressively peers when possible, resulting in a network of over 3000 global interconnections which provide a total network capacity of over 50 Tbps. The CDN further employs Anycast routing for replica selection, which means that the traffic which arrives at a PoP may depend on the underlying network.

We note that contrary to some other approaches to rapidly delivering content to end-users [10,14], the model studied here focuses on the construction of *super-*PoPs. These PoPs consist of a large number of servers, usually on the order of hundreds, providing significant resources at each location. These super Pops are then placed in locations with good network connectivity, providing low latency access to large Internet Exchanges (IX) and other peering opportunities. Since each PoP is equipped with significant compute and storage capacities, PoPs can process significant traffic load before they must reach out to other caches.

Importantly, the CDN is a multi-tenant environment. Unlike many purpose-built platforms [4,22,38], it must respond to a large variety of content, from large software updates to streaming video, to images on a web-page. This combination of behaviors means that the entire global network must be flexible to changing behaviors and needs from customers. Indeed, we demonstrate that many of the fundamental characteristics do change, making static analysis difficult. We must further exercise care in the impact different approaches may have on individual customers, and in particular, if the approaches may result in pathological behaviors for some customers but not others (*e.g.* never caching a particular customers content). This constraint drives the use of techniques that can be easily assessed and which have intuitive and clear behavior.

3.1 Diversity in Accessed Content

Here, we provide some background on the nature of the CDN traffic profile. As noted in previous work [6], the CDN caches ultimately handle traffic from a highly diverse set of sources, which include many larger-scale traffic patterns, individual client access behaviors, file types, and file sizes. We aim to provide an intuitive understanding of what kind of traffic arrives at each PoP, which will ultimately determine the policies that work best in these caching systems.

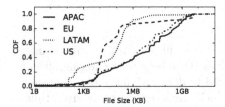

Fig. 1. Requested file sizes from a geographically distributed set of regions (over 24 h).

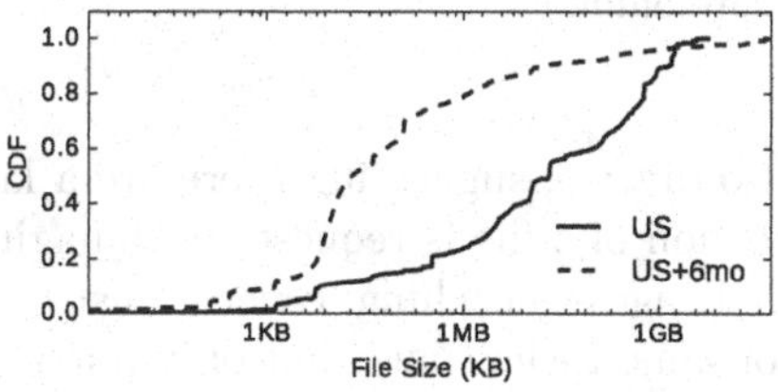

Fig. 2. Distribution of requested file sizes within the US, 6 months apart.

Figure 1 shows the distribution of the request file sizes from 4 regions around the world: APAC indicates a sample from a PoP in India, EU in Europe, US in the United States, and LATAM in South America. First, we see that the spread of request sizes at each region is quite high, with 10% of files about 1 KB at nearly all locations on the low end, and with 90th percentiles as high as 1 GB in APAC and the US. Second, the behavior across PoPs is diverse, with median request sizes that vary from 10 s of kilobytes (EU, LATAM) to 10 s of megabytes (US, APAC). This variation reveals the patterns that these caching system must be prepared to deal with: there are no fixed distributions in the sizes of responses across locations.

Figure 2 shows that these differences are not limited to the geographic domain. Here we examine 24 h of log traces taken from the same PoP 6 months apart (both on matching weekdays). The median requested file size decreases from 24 MB to 14 KB. This high variation over time indicates that even at the same server in the same PoP we may see large variations.

These changes are an effect of the following attributes observed from the perspective of a multi-tenant CDN: (a) the busiest customers vary from region to region and shift over time, (b) content profiles of customers also change over time, impacting the overall cache contents (c) routine CDN traffic management efforts shift traffic across PoPs. However, in all cases, per PoP configurations must remain generic and able to handle such diversity of traffic behaviors.

The situation is further complicated by variations in the nature of requests. Figure 3 shows a scatter plot of the bytes delivered over file sizes for all requests seen on a single server in the US over a 24 h period. Along the diagonal are files for which the entire file is delivered. However, the area above the diagonal is

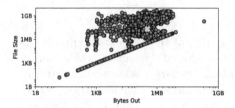
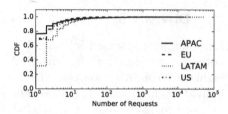

Fig. 3. Bytes requested vs. file size cached on CDN (red "x" shows median). (Color figure online)

Fig. 4. File request distribution. We observe high variation across regions.

also diverse, suggesting there are a large number of files for which only a small portion of a file is requested. Managing both of these behaviors adds significant challenges to caching: caches must be prepared to deal with large files that may consume cache space, but only portions of which are accessed at any given time. We further see this same type of spread over multiple regions, suggesting this variation is commonplace.

Figure 4 shows the number of requests seen for each file for each of the geographically distributed PoPs. For the US, APAC, and EU, between 60 and 80% of files are only requested once. On the other hand, the most popular files are extremely popular, with some being requested orders of magnitude more. While the LATAM PoP saw a lower proportion of requests with a single request, the majority of files still saw a small number of requests. The variation in these distributions again hint at the importance of cache policy selection: many files are not well suited for caching and may waste cache space. Therefore we require a robust caching system that is not sensitive to the presence of such behaviors.

3.2 Similarities in Client Request Pattern

Next, we examine the popularity of objects over time. This will provide us with a sense of how objects in the cache are accessed. Figure 5 shows the number of hits for each object in the cache, binned by the last accessed time by the hour. Here

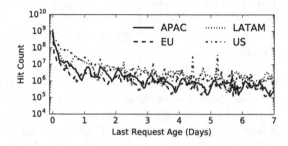

Fig. 5. Temporal hit-rate view of caches from various regions, which show a histogram of cache-hits binned by age. The popularity consistently decreases for all regions.

the x-axis is the last access age, indicating how many days prior to the snapshot the item was last accessed. Here we see that the most recently accessed content is indeed the most popular, by nearly three orders of magnitude. This follows our intuition about web content accesses and suggests that recency will likely be an important input into the caching systems. Furthermore, we see similar patterns across all geographic regions and long time scales, suggesting this behavior is common to different PoPs and time frames.

This access behavior indicates the importance of recency when considering any caching policy. Indeed, any policy that can keep the freshest objects in the cache will be able to serve the most requests. Furthermore, the consistency of this behavior, where we otherwise saw significant variations in request size and pattern, provides the foundation of our expectations in the subsequent section: recency based algorithms that are flexible to request type are likely to do well.

4 Cache Evaluation Framework

Our analysis is based on a *caching emulator* designed to facilitate the assessment of arbitrary cache policies[1]. In particular, it was designed to consume CDN cache server access logs and closely match the behavior of the production cache. The emulator also allows pre-population of its cache with contents of a production server and enables the tracking and statistics collection of cache data. We emphasize that this system *emulates* cache behaviors rather than estimating using a simple model: since the system relies on observed access logs, it behaves as a production implementation would (Fig. 6).

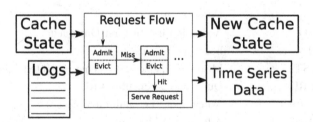

Fig. 6. Data flow diagram of the emulator. Each client request passes through a stack of arbitrarily configured caches.

The emulator models the flow of requests through a series of tiered caches. When a request is processed, it checks the first cache. If the object is present, the request is labeled a hit and the object is "returned" from that cache. Otherwise, it is labeled a miss and passed to the next layer. These layers can be other arbitrary caches or can be treated as an external origin. Each abstract cache layer is provided with admission and eviction policies. The admission policy

---

[1] Available at https://github.com/VerizonDigital/edgecast_caching_emulator.

determines which requested objects are cached at that level, and the eviction policy describes which objects to remove from the cache when it is full. Each layer tracks a relevant statistics: including the hit rate and the bytes written.

In this study, we consider 30 days of access logs from a set of cache servers from the geographic regions shown in the previous section. Each log entry represents a client request that was handled by a single server in a PoP. Each log entry contains the timestamp when the request was logged, the size of the requested asset, the status code returned from the back-end system (*i.e.* a cache hit or miss), the bytes delivered to the client (which will be less than the asset size in cases of range requests), as well as the url of the asset requested. This information allows us to conduct a thorough study on the behaviors observed directly in the trace, as well as enabling us to replay this traffic in the emulator. Doing so allows us to examine what-if scenarios in which we employ alternative cache policies and mechanisms on real-world access behaviors.

5   Evaluation

Here we provide an analysis of various caching techniques using the above framework. We explore the implementation of caching at: the disk (storage on the scale of terabytes), and at a load balancer (gigabytes). We examine each of these in the context of the constraints of the network described in Sect. 3. Table 1 provides an overview of the policies we examine along with a brief description.

Table 1. Cache policies examined in this study.

Policy	Type	Description
Eviction	FIFO	A simple First In First Out queue
	LRU	Least recently used
	COST	LRU based, size and recency weighted equally
	S4LRU	Quadruply segmented LRU [22]
	Infinite	No eviction (i.e., unlimited cache)
Admission	N-Hit	Admit on N^{th} request
	Probabilistic (Pr)	Admit with fixed probability
	Prob-Size (Pr.Size)	Admit with probability dependent on the file size [6]

We focus first on cache *eviction*, the process of determining which objects to remove from the cache when it becomes full. We begin with FIFO, as it's generally the simplest to implement and widely used in industry. Next, we examine LRU, as it is a robust and standard caching algorithm, and our analysis in the previous section suggests the asset request patterns have clear recency properties. We further examine a method similar to Greedy-Dual-Size [11] which computes an eviction *score* which grants equal weight to frequency and file size. Finally, we examine S4LRU, as it provides a relatively direct extension of LRU, and has been shown to perform well in other web-object caching environments [22].

In examining cache *admission*, we present an examination of N-Hit Caching, a bloom filter based approach that produces deterministic output and has been shown effective in industry [28,31]. We further examine a commonly considered alternative that admits objects with a fixed probability, and a methodology which uses a size-based probabilistic admission [6].

5.1 Cache Eviction

Here, we examine disk eviction policies: FIFO, LRU, COST, and S4LRU [22]. Here, FIFO presents the obvious simplest solution, followed closely by LRU. COST is a variant of LRU in which a *cost* is computed for each object that linearly weights file size and recency. The lowest scores (*i.e.* intuitively the largest and oldest files) are then evicted first. The final policy, S4LRU, consists of 4 LRU "queues". On a cache miss, an object is inserted into the first queue. On subsequent hits, it's promoted to the head of next queue. If it's in the final queue, it is simply moved to the head of that queue. Each queue then works as an independent LRU cache. When the object is evicted, it goes to the head of the previous queue. If that queue is the first, it is evicted entirely. This process essentially encodes frequency into an LRU-like structure. In all of the experiments in this section, we use the *default* admission policy, which admits all objects into the cache.

First, we examine the most straightforward metric: hit-rate. Indeed, the hit-rate is a fundamental measure of how well the cache is performing, and in many instances will correlate directly with the CDN's ability to respond with a low response time. Here, we consider the performance of the algorithms over various disk sizes: for each algorithm and disk size, we play back 7 days worth of cache accesses, accounting for the majority of the regular diurnal patterns[2]. We further consider the performance of an infinite cache, which represents the optimal hit rate without knowledge of the future.

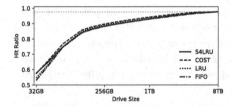
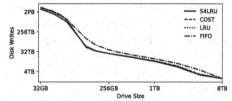

Fig. 7. Hit-rates of eviction algorithms. The horizontal line shows the hit-rate of an infinite cache.

Fig. 8. Disk writes for each eviction algorithm.

---

[2] We observed similar results when using the full 30 days of logs.

Figure 7 presents the results of these experiments. First, we note the obvious increase in hit rate as the disk increases in size: with a larger disk we are able to respond from the cache more often. We also note that the performance of the algorithms becomes more similar with a larger disk, suggesting that the marginal impact from our choice of algorithm is reduced. In particular, we note that at large enough disks, traditional LRU performs quite well, approaching the hit rate of the infinite cache of 97.5%. We see similar behavior from the byte-hit rate, but refrain from showing here due to space constraints.

The hit-rate alone, however, fails to show the whole picture: there are additional considerations when using each of these algorithms. In particular, the load induced via the write operations that must be performed, which may have an adverse effect on the underlying hardware (e.g. solid state disks). Next we examine the disk write behavior of each policy.

Figure 8 shows the total disk writes (log scale) achieved for each disk size. The disk size has a sizeable impact on the total volume of writes, with the smallest disks incurring total write costs on the order of petabytes, larger disks requiring only 10 s of terabytes. Beyond this, we see that FIFO performs consistently worse than the LRU-based approaches, uniformly requiring additional disk writes, about 60% more in the 4 TB case. High write volume puts greater load on the underlying hardware, straining its performance and reducing overall lifetimes. Content which has to be written out to disk must also be fetched externally, causing greater delay in the delivery to the end-user.

While all 4 algorithms appear to perform relatively well at large enough disks (within 1% above the 4 TB level), there are still potentially other costs, in particular additional disk writes, in the case of FIFO. Among the 3 LRU based policies, their similar performance makes vanilla LRU particularly appealing, as it is the least expensive in terms of complexity and management.

5.2   Cache Eviction with Selective Admission

Despite the generally good behavior of LRU, there are some behaviors in CDN web traffic which can poison attempts at maintaining a healthy cache with an eviction policy alone. In particular, we recall from Fig. 4 that many files are only requested a single time, creating pressure on the cache, and in particular the storage medium, for files that will *never* be accessed from the cache. However, we further recall that the most popular files were requested extremely frequently. We therefore also consider the use of a cache admission policy that can alleviate the underlying amount of writes a cache disk will need to do, reducing hardware load and overall cache churn.

First, we consider a bloom filter placed in front of the disk cache, implementing a technique we call *second hit caching* (2-Hit) [28,31,36]. The process is simple: on a miss, if the appropriate hash of a requested item is not in the bloom filter, it is added to the filter but not cached. If, on the other hand, it is in the bloom filter, the object is added to the cache. In this way we are able to avoid caching objects which are requested only a single time. Very popular items, however, are still quickly pulled into the disk cache, minimizing negative impact.

We further consider two alternative admission policies: a probabilistic admission which caches objects with a fixed probability of p (which we refer to as Pr.), and a size based probabilistic policy which admits objects of size bytes with probability $e^{\frac{-size}{c}}$ [6] (Pr.Size). In both cases, the intuition is that popular items will be requested frequently, increasing the likelihood that they make it into the disk cache. In the size based methodology, the system biases towards objects which are smaller than c, capturing the risk of allowing very large objects into the cache. In our evaluations we consider a range of values for p, from .25 to .75, and c, from 100 MB to 1 GB. In this section we further consider each of these three policies when combined with the 3 eviction policies described in the previous section on a 4 TB cache disk.

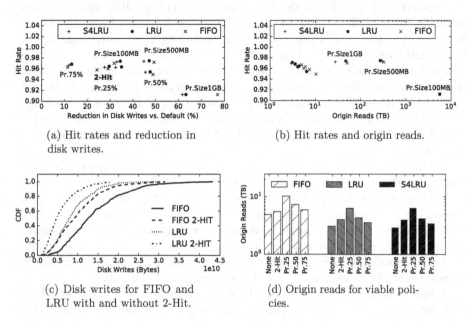

(a) Hit rates and reduction in disk writes.

(b) Hit rates and origin reads.

(c) Disk writes for FIFO and LRU with and without 2-Hit.

(d) Origin reads for viable policies.

Fig. 9. Impact on hit-rate, disk writes and origin reads by LRU, FIFO and S4LRU with selective admission: 2-Hit (N-hit, where N=2), Pr., and Pr.Size.

Figure 9a shows the hit rate achieved by each combination of policies and the relative improvement to disk writes (*i.e.* the percentage reduction in disk writes versus using no admission policy with the same eviction policy). The hit rates range from 92 to 97%. Furthermore, some of the policies, in particular the Pr.Size approaches, show *significant* reductions in disk writes. The smaller probabilistic and second hit showed modest improvements to disk writes, between 10 and 33%.

Figure 9b shows the impact on hit-rate versus the absolute origin reads (*i.e.* the bytes that had to be fetched from the customer origin). Here we see that the disk writes were an insufficient view: the Pr.Size methodologies significantly increased the bytes read from origin, rendering them unusable. This is the result of the largest objects never making it into cache, forcing them to always pull from origin. The probabilistic and 2-Hit policies had much more modest increases, between 12 and 30%, depending on the eviction policy.

Origin traffic is particularly sensitive in a CDN environment, as reducing origin traffic is one of the core purposes of the CDN itself. Furthermore, unlike purpose built or in-house solutions, origin traffic results in increased cost for a third party. On the other hand, ensuring a higher hit-rate provides end-users with improved latency. CDN operators much balance these trade-offs, hence, the use of an admission policy to control the load on the cache medium may make sense, but it must be done with extreme care, as it can undermine the CDNs efficacy, as seen in the Pr.Size case.

Figure 9c shows a CDF of the disk writes of FIFO and LRU, with and without 2-Hit (we exclude S4LRU and Prob. Admission from this figure for clarity, but note that they performed similarly to LRU and 2-Hit, correspondingly). Importantly, origin reads and disk writes differ when using a selective admission policy, since an object may be fetched from origin multiple times before it is written to disk. Even though FIFO showed promising improvements to disk writes when using an admission policy, the writes for FIFO were high enough that FIFO remains an outlier. In the median case, the over 30% improvement on disk write operations still left FIFO-2-Hit performing more write operations than LRU.

Figure 9d shows a closeup view of the absolute origin reads achieved by each viable algorithm grouped by eviction policy (*i.e.* excluding the Prob. size policies). First, we note that all three eviction policies exhibit similar impacts, confirming our previous findings that the eviction policy becomes less critical with large disks. The lowest probability admission, $p = .25$ also shows a significant increase in origin reads, due to the difficulty for any one item to make it into the cache. Finally, we see that 2-hit and $Pr.75$ show similar results, nearly in proportion to their difference in disk write savings seen in Fig. 9a.

While we have seen here that a probabilistic admission with a relatively high probability ($p = .75$) and 2-Hit perform similarly, we consider a final operation component: in many production settings, determinism can be extremely valuable. Specifically, when debugging and testing, it can often be important that the system behaves deterministically, providing consistent results, not just at scale, but for individual requests. This need makes 2-Hit an appealing method, despite its increase in complexity over purely probabilistic methods.

6   Load Balancer Cache

Next, we consider placing a cache in-front of the L7 load balancers. Specifically, in the above studies, we considered caches which were co-located with the caching servers. Here, we examine an arrangement where the cache sits *earlier* in the request processing. This creates the opportunity to manage traffic at it's first entry point inside of the PoP, eliminating significant amounts of intra-datacenter traffic, easing load on cache servers and intermediate appliances, further reducing request latency. This placement also demands that the caches be managed

Table 2. Hit/byte-hit rate achieved by the load balancer cache.

Method	Size	Hit-rate	Byte hit-rate
P. size 32 KB	1GB	.49	.05
P. size 16 MB		.44	.01
P. size 256 MB		.36	.03
P. size 32 KB	5GB	.50	.06
P. size 16 MB		.54	.03
P. size 256 MB		.44	.09

simply: i.e. they must sit ahead of much of the complex configuration logic that drives the true disk caches. Therefore, we stick to a bare-bones eviction policy, pursuing only FIFO systems with a Pr.Size admission policy, avoiding the need for bloom filters or other stored state.

Moreover, this placement means that our threshold for good performance is much different than more traditional components of the cache hierarchy. Specifically, very low cache hit rates do not necessarily mean that the cache is performing poorly: even a small reduction in hit rate reduces the load that must pass through the load balancer and land on the main caches. Even in the event of a cache miss, the request is still backed by the underlying cache server.

Table 2 presents the hit-rates and byte hit-rates seen for two possible cache sizes, 1 and 5 GB, and 3 size admission parameters, 32 KB, 16 MB, and 256 MB. The hit-ratios remain relatively steady, with roughly 50% of requests being serviced by the cache, excepting the smaller cache with large admission parameter. The byte hit-rates however are very low, showing that very few bytes are served from the cache, even when its size is increased to 5 GB. Despite this, it offers significant potential, as the measured hit rates would correspond to 50% of connections terminating at the load balancer.

7 Conclusion

We have presented a study of the caching behavior of a large scale, global, CDN. We explored the global accessed patterns observed by the CDN, examining both historical log behaviors and the contents of caches. While we saw significant variations in the access and request file size, fundamentally, the caches exhibited similar behaviors, with the newest objects being the most popular.

We further examined behaviors of cache evictions and admission policies, going from the bottom up: first considering a large disk cache alone, followed by more complex arrangements. In the disk cache we explored the trade off between complexity and performance, where we found that with large enough disks, relatively simple methods (LRU, in particular), function well, while avoiding the pitfalls of the simplest methods (FIFO). When considering admission policies, we again found simplicity dominated, as more complex methods had operational challenges and increased origin reads. We additionally explored how we could reduce connections to the L7 load-balancers significantly by introducing an in-memory cache earlier in the network. Ultimately, our findings provide a critical lesson in operational systems: robust and flexible approaches, like LRU, provide the best trade-off between performance and operational constraints.

References

1. Nginx http server. https://www.nginx.org
2. Redis key-value store. http://redis.io
3. Varnish http cache. https://www.varnish-cache.org
4. Albrecht, C., et al.: Janus: optimal flash provisioning for cloud storage workloads. In: Proceedings of the USENIX ATC 2013, pp. 91–102 (2013)
5. Atikoglu, B., Xu, Y., Frachtenberg, E., Jiang, S., Paleczny, M.: Workload analysis of a large-scale key-value store. In: Proceedings of the SIGMETRICS 2012, pp. 53–64 (2012)
6. Berger, D.S., Sitaraman, R.K., Harchol-Balter, M.: AdaptSize: orchestrating the hot object memory cache in a content delivery network. In: Proceedings of the USENIX NSDI 2017, pp. 483–498 (2017)
7. Blankstein, A., Sen, S., Freedman, M.J.: Hyperbolic caching: flexible caching for web applications. In: Proceedings of the (USENIX ATC 2017), pp. 499–511 (2017)
8. Breslau, L., Cao, P., Fan, L., Phillips, G., Shenker, S.: Web caching and Zipf-like distributions: evidence and implications. In: Proceedings of the INFOCOM 1999, vol. 1, pp. 126–134, March 1999
9. Cáceres, R., Douglis, F., Feldmann, A., Glass, G., Rabinovich, M.: Web proxy caching: the devil is in the details. In: Proceedings of the WISP 1998, pp. 11–15 (1998)
10. Calder, M., Fan, X., Hu, Z., Katz-Bassett, E., Heidemann, J., Govindan, R.: Mapping the expansion of Google's serving infrastructure. In: Proceedings of the IMC 2013, pp. 313–326 (2013)
11. Cao, P., Irani, S.: Cost-aware WWW proxy caching algorithms. In: Proceedings of the USITS 1997, p. 18 (1997)
12. Cao, P., Zhang, J., Beach, K.: Active cache: caching dynamic contents on the web. In: Proceedings of the Middleware 1998, pp. 373–388 (1998)
13. Chankhunthod, A., Danzig, P.B., Neerdaels, C., Schwartz, M.F., Worrell, K.J.: A hierarchical internet object cache. In: Proceedings of the USENIX ATC 1996, p. 13 (1996)
14. Chen, F., Sitaraman, R.K., Torres, M.: End-user mapping: next generation request routing for content delivery. In: Proceedings of the SIGCOMM 2015, pp. 167–181 (2015)
15. Cidon, A., Eisenman, A., Alizadeh, M., Katti, S.: Cliffhanger: scaling performance cliffs in web memory caches. In: Proceedings of the NSDI 2016, pp. 379–392 (2016)
16. Dilley, J., Maggs, B., Parikh, J., Prokop, H., Sitaraman, R., Weihl, B.: Globally distributed content delivery. IEEE Internet Comput. **6**, 50–58 (2002)
17. Fitzpatrick, B.: Distributed caching with memcached (2004)
18. Freedman, M.J.: Experiences with CoralCDN: a five-year operational view. In: Proceedings of the NSDI (2010)
19. Gummadi, K.P., Dunn, R.J., Saroiu, S., Gribble, S.D., Levy, H.M., Zahorjan, J.: Measurement, modeling, and analysis of a peer-to-peer file-sharing workload. In: Proceedings of the SOSP 2003, pp. 314–329 (2003)

20. Guo, L., Tan, E., Chen, S., Xiao, Z., Zhang, X.: The stretched exponential distribution of internet media access patterns. In: Proceedings of the PODC 2008, pp. 283–294 (2008)
21. Hasslinger, G., Ntougias, K., Hasslinger, F., Hohlfeld, O.: Performance evaluation for new web caching strategies combining LRU with score based object selection. In: Proceedings of the ITC 2016, pp. 322–330 (2016)
22. Huang, Q., Birman, K., van Renesse, R., Lloyd, W., Kumar, S., Li, H.C.: An analysis of Facebook photo caching. In: Proceedings of the SOSP 2013, pp. 167–181 (2013)
23. Ihm, S., Pai, V.S.: Towards understanding modern web traffic. In: Proceedings of the IMC 2011, pp. 295–312 (2011)
24. Jiang, S., Zhang, X.: LIRS: an efficient low inter-reference recency set replacement policy to improve buffer cache performance. In: Proceedings of the SIGMETRICS 2002, pp. 31–42 (2002)
25. Johnson, K., Carr, J., Day, M., Kaashoek, M.: The measured performance of content distribution networks. Comput. Commun. 24, 202–206 (2001)
26. Johnson, T., Shasha, D.: 2Q: a low overhead high performance buffer management replacement algorithm. In: Proceedings of the VLDB 1994, pp. 439–450 (1994)
27. Jung, J., Krishnamurthy, B., Rabinovich, M.: Flash crowds and denial of service attacks: characterization and implications for CDNs and web sites. In: Proceedings of the WWW 2002, pp. 293–304 (2002)
28. Khakpour, A., Peters, R.J.: Optimizing multi-hit caching for long tail content. Patent No. US8639780 B2, January 2014
29. Krishnamurthy, B., Wills, C., Zhang, Y.: On the use and performance of content distribution networks. In: Proceedings of the IMW 2001, pp. 169–182 (2001)
30. Krishnan, R., et al.: Moving beyond end-to-end path information to optimize CDN performance. In: Proceedings of the IMC 2009, pp. 190–201 (2009)
31. Maggs, B.M., Sitaraman, R.K.: Algorithmic nuggets in content delivery. SIGCOMM Comput. Commun. Rev. 45, 52–66 (2015)
32. Megiddo, N., Modha, D.S.: ARC: a self-tuning, low overhead replacement cache. In: Proceedings of the FAST 2003, pp. 115–130 (2003)
33. O'Neil, E.J., O'Neil, P.E., Weikum, G.: The LRU-K page replacement algorithm for database disk buffering. In: Proceedings of the SIGMOD 1993, pp. 297–306 (1993)
34. Saroiu, S., Gummadi, K.P., Dunn, R.J., Gribble, S.D., Levy, H.M.: An analysis of internet content delivery systems. In: Proceedings of the OSDI (2002)
35. Scellato, S., Mascolo, C., Musolesi, M., Crowcroft, J.: Track globally, deliver locally: improving content delivery networks by tracking geographic social cascades. In: Proceedings of the WWW 2011, pp. 457–466 (2011)
36. Shafiq, M.Z., Khakpour, A.R., Liu, A.X.: Characterizing caching workload of a large commercial content delivery network. In: Proceedings of INFOCOM 2016, pp. 1–9, April 2016
37. Shim, J., Scheuermann, P., Vingralek, R.: Proxy cache algorithms: design, implementation, and performance. IEEE Trans. Knowl. Data Eng. 11, 549–562 (1999)
38. Tang, L., Huang, Q., Lloyd, W., Kumar, S., Li, K.: RIPQ: advanced photo caching on flash for Facebook. In: Proceedings of the FAST 2015, pp. 373–386 (2015)
39. Wang, J.: A survey of web caching schemes for the internet. SIGCOMM Comput. Commun. Rev. 29, 36–46 (1999)
40. Wendell, P., Freedman, M.J.: Going viral: flash crowds in an open CDN. In: Proceedings of the IMC 2011, pp. 549–558 (2011)

Sundials in the Shade

An Internet-Wide Perspective on ICMP Timestamps

Erik C. Rye$^{(\boxtimes)}$ and Robert Beverly

Naval Postgraduate School, Monterey, CA, USA
rye@cmand.org, rbeverly@nps.edu

Abstract. ICMP timestamp request and response packets have been standardized for nearly 40 years, but have no modern practical application, having been superseded by NTP. However, ICMP timestamps are not deprecated, suggesting that while hosts must support them, little attention is paid to their implementation and use. In this work, we perform active measurements and find 2.2 million hosts on the Internet responding to ICMP timestamp requests from over 42,500 unique autonomous systems. We develop a methodology to classify timestamp responses, and find 13 distinct classes of behavior. Not only do these behaviors enable a new fingerprinting vector, some behaviors leak important information about the host e.g., OS, kernel version, and local timezone.

Keywords: Network · Time · ICMP · Fingerprinting · Security

1 Introduction

The Internet Control Message Protocol (ICMP) is part of the original Internet Protocol specification (ICMP is IP protocol number one), and has remained largely unchanged since RFC 792 [21]. Its primary function is to communicate error and diagnostic information; well-known uses today include ICMP echo to test for reachability (i.e., ping), ICMP time exceeded to report packet loops (i.e., traceroute), and ICMP port unreachable to communicate helpful information to the initiator of a transport-layer connection. Today, 27 ICMP types are defined by the IESG, 13 of which are deprecated [11].

Among the non-deprecated ICMP messages are timestamp (type 13) and timestamp reply (type 14). These messages, originally envisioned to support time synchronization and provide one-way delay measurements [19], contain three 32-bit time values that represent milliseconds (ms) since midnight UTC. Modern clock synchronization is now performed using the Network Time Protocol [18] and ICMP timestamps are generally regarded as a potential security vulnerability [20] as they can leak information about a remote host's clock. Indeed, Kohno et al. demonstrated in 2005 the potential to identify individual hosts by variations in their clock skew [12], while [6] and [4] show similar discriminating power when fingerprinting wireless devices.

D. Choffnes and M. Barcellos (Eds.): PAM 2019, LNCS 11419, pp. 82–98, 2019.
https://doi.org/10.1007/978-3-030-15986-3_6

```
 0  1  2  3  4  5  6  7  8  9 10 11 12 13 14 15 16 17 18 19 20 21 22 23 24 25 26 27 28 29 30 31
```

type=13/14	code=0	checksum		
id		sequence		
orig_ts				
recv_ts				
xmit_ts				

Fig. 1. ICMP timestamp message fields

In this work, we reassess the extent to which Internet hosts respond to ICMP timestamps. Despite no legitimate use for ICMP timestamps today, and best security practices that recommend blocking or disabling these timestamps, we receive timestamp responses from 2.2 million IPv4 hosts in 42,656 distinct autonomous systems (approximately 15% of the hosts queried) during a large-scale measurement campaign in September and October 2018. In addition to characterizing this unexpectedly large pool of responses, we seek to better understand *how* hosts respond. Rather than focusing on clock-skew fingerprinting, we instead make the following primary contributions:

1. The first Internet-wide survey of ICMP timestamp support and responsiveness.
2. A taxonomy of ICMP timestamp response behavior, and a methodology to classify responses.
3. Novel uses of ICMP timestamp responses, including fine-grained operating system fingerprinting and coarse geolocation.

2   Background and Related Work

Several TCP/IP protocols utilize timestamps, and significant prior work has examined TCP timestamps in the context of fingerprinting [12]. TCP timestamps have since been used to infer whether IPv4 and IPv6 server addresses map to the same physical machine in [2] and combined with clock skew to identify server "siblings" on a large scale in [24].

In contrast, this work focuses on ICMP timestamps. Although originally intended to support time synchronization [19], ICMP timestamps have no modern legitimate application use (having been superseded by NTP). Despite this, timestamps are not deprecated [11], suggesting that while hosts must support them, little attention is paid to their implementation and use.

Figure 1 depicts the structure of timestamp request (type 13) and response (type 14) ICMP messages. The 16-bit identifier and sequence values enable responses to be associated with requests. Three four-byte fields are defined: the *originate timestamp* (orig_ts), *receive timestamp* (recv_ts), and *transmit timestamp* (xmit_ts). Per RFC792 [21], timestamp fields encode milliseconds (ms) since UTC midnight unless the most significant bit is set, in which case the field may be a "non-standard" value. The originator of timestamp requests

should set the originate timestamp using her own clock; the value of the receive
and transmit fields for timestamp requests is not specified in the RFC.

To respond to an ICMP timestamp request, a host simply copies the request
packet, changes the ICMP type, and sets the receive and transmit time fields.
The receive time indicates when the request was received, while the transmit
time indicates when the reply was sent.

Several prior research works have explored ICMP timestamps, primarily for
fault diagnosis and fingerprinting. Anagnostakis et al. found in 2003 that 93%
of the approximately 400k routers they probed responded to ICMP timestamp
requests, and developed a tomography technique using ICMP timestamps to
measure per-link one-way network-internal delays [1]. Mahajan et al. leveraged
and expanded the use of ICMP timestamps to enable user-level Internet fault
and path diagnosis in [16].

Buchholz and Tjaden leveraged ICMP timestamps in the context of forensic
reconstruction and correlation [3]. Similar to our results, they find a wide variety
of clock behaviors. However, while they probe ~8,000 web servers, we perform
an Internet-wide survey including 2.2M hosts more than a decade later, and
demonstrate novel fingerprinting and geolocation uses of ICMP timestamps.

Finally, the nmap security scanner [15] uses ICMP timestamp requests, in
addition to other protocols, during host discovery for non-local networks in order
to circumvent firewalls and blocking. nmap sets the request originate timestamp
to zero by default, in violation of the standard [21] (though the user can manually specify a timestamp). Thus, ICMP timestamp requests with zero-valued
origination times provide a signature of nmap scanners searching for live hosts.
While nmap uses ICMP timestamps for liveness testing, it does not use them for
operating system detection as we do in this work.

To better understand the prevalence of ICMP timestamp scanners, we analyze 240 days of traffic arriving at a /17 network telescope. We observe a total
of 413,352 timestamp messages, 93% of which are timestamp requests. Only 33
requests contain a non-zero originate timestamp, suggesting that the remainder
(nearly 100%) are nmap scanners. The top 10 sources account for more than
86% of the requests we observe, indicating a relatively small number of active
Internet-wide scanners.

3   Behavioral Taxonomy

During initial probing, we found significant variety in timestamp responses. Not
only do structural differences exist in the implementation of [21] by timestamp-
responsive routers and end systems (e.g., little- vs big-endian), they also occur
relative to how the device counts time (e.g., milliseconds vs. seconds), the device's
reference point (e.g., UTC or local time), whether the reply is a function of
request parameters, and even whether the device is keeping time at all.

Table 1. ICMP timestamp classification fingerprints

Num	Class	Request	Response		
		cksum	orig_ts	recv_ts	xmit_ts
1	Normal	Valid	-	$\neq$ xmit_ts, $\neq 0$	$\neq 0$
2	Lazy	Valid	-	$=$ xmit_ts	$\neq 0$
3	Checksum-Lazy	Bad	-	-	-
4	Stuck	valid	-	const	const
5	Constant 0	Valid	-	0	0
6	Constant 1	Valid	-	1	1
7	Constant LE 1	Valid	-	$htonl(1)$	$htonl(1)$
8	Reflection	Valid	-	request$_{recv\_ts}$	request$_{xmit\_ts}$
9	Non-UTC	Valid	-	$> 2^{31} - 1$	$> 2^{31} - 1$
10	Timezone	Valid	-	$|recv\_ts - orig\_ts| \% \left(3.6 \times 10^{6}\right) < 200\,\text{ms}$	-
11	Little Endian	Valid	-	$|htonl(recv\_ts) - orig\_ts| < 200\,\text{ms}$	-
12	Linux $htons()$ Bug	Valid	-	$\% 2^{16} = 0$	$\% 2^{16} = 0$
13	Unknown	Valid	-	-	-

3.1 Timestamp Implementation Taxonomy

Table 1 provides an exhaustive taxonomy of the behaviors we observe; we term these the ICMP timestamp *classifications*. Note that this taxonomy concerns only the *implementation* of the timestamp response, rather than whether the responding host's timestamp values are correct.

- **Normal:** Conformant to [21]. Assuming more than one ms of processing time, the receive and transmit timestamps should be not equal, and both should be nonzero except at midnight UTC.
- **Lazy:** Performs a single time lookup and sets both receive and transmit timestamp fields to the same value. A review of current Linux and FreeBSD kernel source code reveals this common lazy implementation [10,13].
- **Checksum-Lazy:** Responds to timestamp requests even when the ICMP checksum is incorrect.
- **Stuck:** Returns the same value in the receive and transmit timestamp fields regardless of the input sent to it and time elapsed between probes.
- **Constant 0, 1, Little-Endian 1:** A strict subset of "stuck" that always returns a small constant value in the receive and transmit timestamp fields.
- **Reflection:** Copies the receive and transmit timestamp fields from the timestamp request into the corresponding fields of the reply message[1].
- **Non-UTC:** Receive and transmit timestamp values with the most significant bit set. As indicated in [21], network devices that are unable to provide a timestamp with respect to UTC midnight or in ms may use an alternate time source, provided that the high order bit is set.
- **Linux *htons()* Bug:** Certain versions of the Linux kernel (and Android) contain a flawed ICMP timestamp implementation where replies are truncated to a 16-bit value; see Appendix A for details.
- **Unknown:** Any reply not otherwise classified.

---

[1] We find no copying of originate timestamp into the reply's receive or transmit fields.

3.2   Timekeeping Behavior Taxonomy

We next categorize the types of timestamp responses we observe by what the host is measuring and what they are measuring in relation to.

- **Precision:** Timestamp reply fields should encode ms to be conformant, however some implementations encode seconds.
- **UTC reference:** Conformant to the RFC; receive and transmit timestamps encode ms since midnight UTC.
- **Timezone:** Replies with receive and transmit timestamps in ms relative to midnight in the device's local timezone, rather than UTC midnight.
- **Epoch reference:** Returned timestamps encode time in seconds relative to the Unix epoch time.
- **Little-Endian:** Receive and transmit timestamps containing a correct timestamp when viewed as little-endian four-byte integers.

4   Methodology

We develop `sundial`, a packet prober that implements the methodology described herein to elicit timestamp responses that permit behavioral classification. `sundial` is written in C and sends raw IP packets in order to set specific IP and ICMP header fields, while targets are randomized to distribute load. We have since ported `sundial` to a publicly available ZMap [8] module [22].

Our measurement survey consists of probing 14.5 million IPv4 addresses[2] of the August 7, 2018 ISI hitlist, which includes one address per routable /24 network [9]. We utilize two vantage points connected to large academic university networks named after their respective locations: "Boston" and "San Diego." Using `sundial`, we elicit ICMP timestamp replies from ∼2.2 million unique IPs.

This section first describes `sundial`'s messages and methodology, then our ground truth validation. We then discuss ethical concerns and precautions undertaken in this study.

4.1   sundial Messages

In order to generate and categorize each of the response behaviors, `sundial` transmits four distinct types of ICMP timestamp requests. Both of our vantage points have their time NTP-synchronized to stratum 2 or better servers. Thus time is "correct" on our prober relative to NTP error.

1. **Standard:** We fill the originate timestamp field with the correct ms from UTC midnight, zero the receive and transmit timestamp fields, and place the lower 32 bits of the MD5 hash of the destination IP address and originate timestamp into the identifier and sequence number fields. The hash permits detection of destinations or middleboxes that tamper with the originate timestamp, identifier, or sequence number.

---

[2] As IPv6 does not support timestamps in ICMPv6, we study IPv4 exclusively.

2. **Bad Clock:** We zero the receive and transmit fields of the request, choose an identifier and sequence number, and compute the MD5 hash of the destination IP address together with the identifier and sequence number. The lower 32 bits of the hash are placed in the originate timestamp. This hash again provides the capability to detect modification of the reply.

3. **Bad Checksum:** The correct time in ms since UTC midnight is placed in the originate field, the receive and transmit timestamps are set to zero, and the identifier and sequence number fields contain an encoding of the destination IP address along with the originate timestamp. We deliberately choose a random, incorrect checksum and place it into the ICMP timestamp request's checksum field. This timestamp message should appear corrupted to the destination, and a correct ICMP implementation should discard it.

4. **Duplicate Timestamp:** The receive and transmit timestamps are initialized to the originate timestamp value by the sender, setting all three timestamps to the same correct value. The destination IP address and originate timestamp are again encoded in the identifier and sequence number to detect modifications.

Many implementation behaviors in Sect. 3 can be inferred from the first, standard probe. For instance, the standard timestamp request can determine a normal, lazy, non-UTC and little-endian implementation. In order to classify a device as stuck, both the standard and duplicate timestamp requests are required. Two requests are needed in order to determine that the receive and transmit timestamps remain fixed over time, and the inclusion of the duplicate timestamp request ensures that the remote device is not simply echoing the values in the receive and transmit timestamp fields of the request. Similarly, timestamp reflectors can be detected using the standard and duplicate request responses.

The checksum-lazy behavior is detected via responses to the bad checksum request type. The Linux `htons()` bug behavior can be detected using the standard request and filtering for reply timestamps with the two lower bytes set to zero. In order to minimize the chance of false positives (i.e., the correct time in ms from UTC midnight is represented with the two lower bytes zeroed), we count only destinations that match this behavior in responses from both the standard and bad clock timestamp request types.

To detect the unit precision of the timestamp reply fields, we leverage the multiple requests sent to each target. Because we know the time at which requests are transmitted, we compare the time difference between the successive requests to a host and classify them based on the inferred time difference from the replies.

Finally, we classify responsive devices by the reference by which they maintain time. We find many remote machines that observe nonstandard reference times, but do not set the high order timestamp field bit. A common alternative timekeeping methodology is to track the number of ms elapsed since midnight local time. We detect local timezone timekeepers by comparing the receive and transmit timestamps to the originate timestamp in replies to the standard request. Receive and transmit timestamps that differ from our correct originate

Table 2. Ground truth classification of ICMP timestamp behaviors

OS	Behavior	Notes
Windows 7–10	Off by default	With Windows firewall off, lazy LE
Linux	Lazy	
Linux 3.18 (incl Android)	Lazy	htons() bug
Android kernel 3.10, 4.4+	Lazy	
BSD	Lazy	
OSX	Unresponsive	
iOS	Off by default	
Cisco IOS/IOS-XE	Lazy	MSB set if NTP disabled, unset if enabled
JunOS	Lazy	

timestamp by the number of ms for an existing timezone (within an allowable error discussed in Sect. 5.2) are determined to be keeping track of their local time.

Last, a small number of devices we encountered measured time relative to the Unix epoch. Epoch-relative timestamps are detected in two steps: first, we compare the epoch timestamp's date to the date in which we sent the request; if they match, we determine whether the number of seconds elapsed since UTC midnight in the reply is suitably close to the correct UTC time.

4.2 Ground Truth

To validate our inferences and understand the more general behavior of popular operating systems and devices, we run **sundial** against a variety of known systems; Table 2 lists their ICMP timestamp reply behavior.

Apple desktop and mobile operating systems, macOS and iOS, both do not respond to ICMP timestamp messages by default. Initially, we could not elicit any response from Microsoft Windows devices, until we disabled Windows Firewall. Once disabled, the Windows device responds with correct timestamps in little-endian byte order. This suggests that not only are timestamp-responsive devices with little-endian timestamp replies Windows, but it also worryingly indicates that its built-in firewall has been turned off by the administrator.

BSD and Linux devices respond with lazy timestamp replies, as their source code indicates they should. JunOS and Android respond like FreeBSD and Linux, on which they are based, respectively. Of note, we built the Linux 3.18 kernel, which has the htons() bug described in Sect. 6; it responded with the lower two bytes zeroed, as expected. This bug has made its way into Android, where we find devices running the 3.18 kernel exhibiting the same signature.

Cisco devices respond differently depending on whether they have enabled NTP. NTP is not enabled by default on IOS; the administrator must manually enable the protocol and configure the NTP servers to use. If NTP has not been enabled, we observe devices setting the most significant bit, presumably

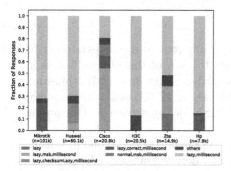

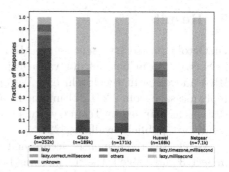

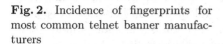

Fig. 2. Incidence of fingerprints for most common telnet banner manufacturers

Fig. 3. Incidence of fingerprints for most common CWMP scan manufacturers

to indicate that it is unsure whether the timestamp is accurate, and filling in a UTC-based timestamp with the remaining bits, according to its internal clock.

Telnet Banner and CWMP GET Ground Truth. To augment the ground truth we obtained from devices we were able to procure locally, we leveraged IPv4 Internet-wide Telnet banner- and CPE WAN Management Protocol (CWMP) parameter-grabbing scans from `scans.io` [23]. From October 3, 2018 scans, we search banners (Telnet) and GET requests (CWMP) for IP addresses associated with known manufacturer strings. We then probe these addresses with `sundial`.

Figure 2 displays the most common fingerprints for a subset of the manufacturers probed from `scans.io`'s Telnet banner-grab dataset, while Fig. 3 is the analogous CWMP plot. We note that non-homogeneous behavior within a manufacturer's plot may be due to several factors: different behaviors among devices of the same manufacturer, banner spoofing, IP address changes, and middleboxes between the source and destination. We provide further details regarding our use of the `scans.io` datasets in Appendix B.

4.3   Ethical Considerations

Internet-wide probing invariably raises ethical concerns. We therefore follow the recommended guidelines for good Internet citizenship provided in [8] to mitigate the potential impact of our probing. At a high-level, we only send ICMP packets, which are generally considered less abusive than e.g., TCP or UDP probes that may reach active application services. Further, our pseudo-random probing order is designed to distribute probes among networks in time so that they do not appear as attack traffic. Finally, we make an informative web page accessible via the IP address of our prober, along with instructions for opting-out. In this work, we did not receive any abuse reports or opt-out requests.

5   Results

On October 6, 2018, we sent four ICMP timestamp request messages as described in Sect. 4.1 from both of our vantage points to each of the 14.5 million target IPv4 addresses in the ISI hitlist. We obtained at least one ICMP timestamp reply message from 2,221,021 unique IP addresses in 42,656 distinct autonomous systems as mapped by Team Cymru's IP-to-ASN lookup service [5]. Our probing results are publicly available [22].

We classify the responses according to the implementation taxonomy outlined in Sect. 3 and Table 1, the timekeeping behavior detailed in Sect. 3.2, and the correctness of the timestamp reply according to Sect. 5.2. Tables 3 and 4 summarize our results in tabular form; note that the implementation behavior categories are not mutually exclusive, and the individual columns will sum to more than the total column, which is the number of unique responding IP addresses. We received replies from approximately 11,000 IP addresses whose computed MD5 hashes as described in Sect. 4.1 indicated tampering of the source IP address, originate timestamp, or id and sequence number fields; we discard these replies.

5.1   Macro Behavior

Lazy replies outnumber normal timestamp replies by a margin of over 50 to 1. Because we had assumed the normal reply type would be the most common, we investigated open-source operating systems' implementations of ICMP. In both the Linux and BSD implementations, the receive timestamp is filled in via a call to retrieve the current kernel time, after which this value is simply copied into the transmit timestamp field. Therefore, all BSD and Linux systems, and their derivatives, exhibit the lazy timestamp reply behavior.

Normal hosts can appear lazy if the receive and transmit timestamps are set within the same millisecond. This ambiguity can be resolved in part via multiple probes. For instance, Table 3 shows that only ~50% of responders classified as normal by one vantage are also marked normal by the other.

The majority (61%) of responding devices do not reply with timestamps within 200 ms of our NTP-synchronized reference clock, our empirically-derived correctness bound discussed in Sect. 5.2. Only ~40% of responding IP addresses fall into this category; notably, we detect smaller numbers devices with correct clocks incorrectly implementing the timestamp reply message standard. For example, across both vantage points we detect thousands of devices whose timestamps are correct when interpreted as a little-endian integer, rather than in network byte order. We discover one operating system that implements little-endian timestamps in Sect. 4.2. In another incorrect behavior that nevertheless indicates a correct clock, some devices respond with the correct timestamp and the most significant bit set – a behavior at odds with the specification [21] where the most significant bit indicates a timestamp either not in ms, or the host cannot provide a timestamp referenced to UTC midnight. In Sect. 4.2, we discuss an operating system that sets the most significant bit when its clock has not been synchronized with NTP.

Table 3. Timestamp reply implementation behaviors (values do not sum to total)

Category	Boston	Both	San Diego	Category	Boston	Both	San Diego
Normal	40,491	19,819	40,363	Stuck	855	849	873
Lazy	2,111,344	1,899,297	2,112,386	Constant 0	547	546	555
Checksum-Lazy	28,074	23,365	28,805	Constant 1	200	199	207
Non-UTC	249,454	211,755	249,932	Constant LE 1	22	19	23
Reflection	2,325	2,304	2,364	htons() Bug	1,499	665	1,536
Correct	850,787	803,314	850,133	Timezone	33,317	23,464	33,762
Correct LE	11,127	5,244	11,290	Unknown	38,495	11,865	32,956
Correct - MSB	1,048	386	973				
Total					2,194,180	1,934,172	2,189,524

Over 200,000 unique IPs (>10% of each vantage point's total) respond with the most significant bit set in the receive and transmit timestamps; those timestamps that are otherwise correct are but a small population of those we term Non-UTC due to the prescribed meaning of this bit in [21]. Some hosts and routers fall into this category due to the nature of their timestamp reply implementation – devices that mark the receive and transmit timestamps with little-endian timestamps will be classified as Non-UTC if the most significant bit of the lowest order byte is on, when the timestamp is viewed in network byte order. Others, as described above, turn on the Non-UTC bit if they have not synchronized with NTP.

Another major category of non-standard implementation behavior of ICMP timestamp replies are devices that report their timestamp relative to their local timezone. Whether devices are programmatically reporting their local time without human intervention, or whether administrator action is required to change the system time (from UTC to local time) in order to effect this classification is unclear. In either case, timezone timestamp replies allow us to coarsely geolocate the responding device. We delve deeper into this possibility in Sect. 5.4.

Finally, while most responding IP addresses are unsurprisingly classified as using milliseconds as their unit of measure, approximately 14–16% of IP addresses are not (see Table 4). In order to determine what units are being used in the timestamp, we subtract the time elapsed between the standard timestamp request and duplicate timestamp request, both of which contain correct originate timestamp fields. We then subtract the time elapsed according to the receive and transmit timestamps in the timestamp reply messages. If the difference of differences is less than 400 ms (two times 200 ms, the error margin for one reply) we conclude that the remote IP is counting in milliseconds. A similar calculation is done to find devices counting in seconds. Several of the behavioral categories outlined in Sect. 3.1 are included among the hosts with undefined timekeeping behavior – those whose clocks are stuck at a particular value and those that reflect the request's receive and transmit timestamps into the corresponding fields are two examples. Others may be filling the reply timestamps with random values.

Table 4. Timestamp reply timekeeping behaviors

Category	Boston	Both	San Diego
Millisecond	1,826,696	1,722,176	1,866,529
Second	47	37	68
Epoch	1	1	1
Unknown timekeeping	367,436	211,958	322,926
Total	2,194,180	1,934,172	2,189,524

5.2 Timestamp Correctness

In order to make a final classification – whether the remote host's clock is correct or incorrect – as well as to assist in making many of the classifications within our implementation and timekeeping taxonomies that require a correctness determination, we describe in this section our methodology for determining whether or not a receive or transmit timestamp is correct.

To account for clock drift and network delays, we aim to establish a margin of error relative to a correctly marked originate timestamp, and consider receive and transmit timestamps within that margin from the originate timestamp to be correct. To that end, we plot the probability density of the differences between the receive and originate timestamps from 2.2 million timestamp replies generated by sending a single standard timestamp request to each of 14.5 million IP addresses from the ISI hitlist [9] in Fig. 4.

Figure 4 clearly depicts a trough in the difference probability values around 200 ms, indicating that receive timestamps greater than 200 ms than the originate timestamp are less likely than those between zero and 200 ms. We reflect this margin about the y-axis, despite the trough occurring somewhat closer to the origin on the negative side. Therefore, we declare a timestamp correct if it is within our error margin of 200 ms of the originate timestamp.

5.3 Middlebox Influence

To investigate the origin of some of the behaviors observed in Sect. 3 for which we have no ground truth implementations, we use `tracebox` [7] to detect middleboxes. In particular, we chose for investigation hosts implementing the reflection, lazy with MSB set (but not counting milliseconds), and constant 0 behaviors, as we do not observe any of these fingerprints in our ground truth dataset, yet there exist nontrivial numbers of them in our Internet-wide dataset.

In order to determine whether a middlebox may be responsible for these behaviors for which we have no ground truth, we `tracebox` to a subset of 500 random IP addresses exhibiting them. For our purposes, we consider an IP address to be behind a middlebox if the last hop modifies fields beyond the standard IP TTL and checksum modifications, and DSCP and MPLS field alterations and extensions. Of 500 reflection IP addresses, only 44 showed evidence of being

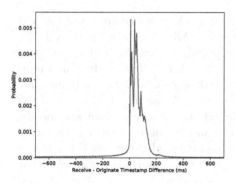

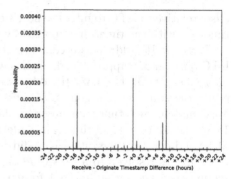

Fig. 4. Empirical `recv_ts`- `orig_ts` PMF

Fig. 5. Response error; note hourly peaks

behind a middlebox, suggesting that some operating systems implement the reflect behavior and that this is a less common middlebox modification. The lazy with MSB set (but non-ms counting) behavior, on the other hand, was inferred to be behind a middlebox in 333 out of 500 random IP addresses, suggesting it is most often middleboxes that are causing the lazy-MSB-set fingerprint. Finally, about half of the constant 0 IP addresses show middlebox tampering in `tracebox` runs, suggesting that this behavior is both an operating system implementation of timestamp replies as well as a middlebox modification scheme.

5.4 Geolocation

Figure 5 displays the probability distribution of response error, e.g., `recv_ts` − `orig_ts`, after correct replies have been removed from the set of standard request type responses. While there is a level of uniform randomness, we note the peaks at hour intervals. We surmise that these represent hosts that have correct time, but return a *timezone-relative* response (in violation of the standard [21] where responses should be relative to UTC). The origin of timezone-relative responses may be a non-conformant implementation. Alternatively, these responses may simply be an artifact of non-NTP synchronized machines where the administrator instead sets the localtime correctly, but incorrectly sets the timezone. In this case, the machine's notion of UTC is incorrect, but incorrect relative to the set timezone. Nevertheless, these timezone-relative responses effectively leak the host's timezone. We note the large spike in the +9 timezone, which covers Japan and South Korea; despite the use of `nmap`'s OS-detection feature, and examining web pages and TLS certificates where available, we could not definitively identify a specific device manufacturer or policy underpinning this effect.

To evaluate our ability to coarsely geolocate IP addresses reporting a timezone-relative timestamp, we begin with ∼34,000 IP addresses in this category obtained by sending a single probe to every hitlist IP from our Boston vantage. Using the reply timestamps, we compute the remote host's local timezone offset relative to UTC to infer the host's timezone. We then compare our inferred timezone with the timezone reported by the MaxMind GeoLite-2 database [17].

For each IP address, we compare the MaxMind timezone's standard time UTC-offset and, if applicable, daylight saving time UTC offset, to the timestamp-inferred offset. Of the 34,357 IP addresses tested, 32,085 (93%) correctly matched either the standard timezone UTC offset or daylight saving UTC offset, if the MaxMind-derived timezone observes daylight saving time. More specifically, 18,343 IP addresses had timestamp-inferred timezone offsets that matched their MaxMind-derived timezone, which did not observe daylight saving time. 11,188 IP addresses resolved to a MaxMind timezone, whose daylight saving time off-set matched the offset inferred from the timestamp. 2,554 IP addresses had timestamp-inferred UTC offsets that matched their MaxMind-derived standard time offset for timezones that do observe daylight saving time. Of the inferred UTC-offsets that were not correct, 1,641 did not match either the standard time offset derived from MaxMind, or the daylight saving time offset, if it existed, and 631 IP addresses did not resolve to a timezone in MaxMind's free database.

6   Conclusions and Future Work

We observe a wide variety of implementation behavior of the ICMP timestamp reply type, caused by timestamps' lack of a modern use but continued require-ment to be supported. In particular, we are able to uniquely fingerprint the behavior of several major operating systems and kernel versions, and geolocate Internet hosts to timezone accuracy with >90% success.

As future work, we intend to exhaustively scan and classify the IPv4 Internet, scan a subset with increased frequency over a sustained time period, and to do so many vantage points. We further plan to integrate the OS-detection capabilities we uncover in this work into nmap, and add tracebox functionality to sundial in order to better detect middlebox tampering with ICMP timestamp messages.

Acknowledgments. We thank Garrett Wollman, Ram Durairajan, and Dan Ander-sen for measurement infrastructure, our shepherd Rama Padmanabhan, and the anony-mous reviewers for insightful feedback. Views and conclusions are those of the authors and not necessarily those of the U.S. government.

Appendix A: Linux htons() Bug

While investigating the source code of open-source operating systems' imple-mentation of ICMP timestamps, we observed a flaw that allows fine-grained fingerprinting of the Linux kernel version 3.18. The specific bug that allows this fingerprinting was introduced in March 2016. An update to the Internet timestamp generating method in af_inet.c errantly truncated the 32-bit times-tamp to a 16-bit short via a call to the C library function htons() rather than htonl(). When this incorrect 16-bit value is placed into the 32-bit receive and transmit timestamp fields of a timestamp reply, it causes the lower two bytes to be zero and disables the responding machine's ability to generate a correct reply timestamp at any time other than midnight UTC. This presents a unique signature of devices running the Linux kernel built during this time period. In order to identify these devices on the Internet, we filter for ICMP timestamp replies containing receive and transmit timestamp values with zeros in the lower two bytes when viewed as a 32-bit big-endian integer. While devices that are correctly implementing ICMP timestamp replies will naturally reply with timestamps containing zeros in the lower two bytes every 65,536 milliseconds, the probability of multiple responses containing this signature drops rapidly as the number of probes sent increases.

Being derived directly from the Linux kernel, the 3.18 version of the Android kernel also includes the flawed `af_inet.c` implementation containing the same `htons()` truncation, allowing for ICMP timestamp fingerprinting of mobile devices as well.

While Linux 3.18 reached its end of life [14] in 2017, we observe hosts on the Internet whose signatures suggest this is the precise version of software they are currently running. Unfortunately, this presents an adversary with the opportunity to perform targeted attacks.

Appendix B: `scans.io` Ground Truth

We use Telnet and CWMP banners in public `scans.io` as a source of ground truth. It is possible to override the default text of these protocol banners, and recognize that this is a potential source of error. However, we examine the manufacturer counts in aggregate under the assumption that most manufacturer strings are legitimate. We believe it unlikely that users have modified their CWMP configuration on their customer premises equipment to return an incorrect manufacturer.

Parsing the Telnet and CWMP scans for strings containing the names of major network device manufacturers provided over two million unique IP addresses. Table 5 summarizes the results; note that for some manufacturers (e.g., Arris) approximately the same number of IPs were discovered through the Telnet scan as the CWMP scan, for others (e.g., Cisco and Huawei) CWMP provided an order of magnitude greater number of IPs, and still others (e.g., Mikrotik and Netgear) appeared in only one of the two protocol scans. Note that these numbers are not the number of timestamp-responsive IP addresses denoted by n in Figs. 2 and 3.

With the IP addresses we obtained for each manufacturer, we then run `sundial` to each set in order to elicit timestamp reply fingerprints and determine whether different manufacturers tend to exhibit unique reply behaviors. Figures 2 and 3 display the incidence of timestamp reply fingerprints for a subset of the manufacturers we probed, and provide some interesting results that we examine here in greater detail.

No manufacturer exhibits only a singular behavior. We attribute this variety within manufacturers to changes in their implementation of timestamp replies

Table 5. Unique IP addresses per manufacturer for each scan

Manufacturer	Telnet count	CWMP count
Arris	8,638	5,281
Cisco	29,135	1,298,761
H3C	80,445	-
HP	24,027	-
Huawei	170,710	2,377,079
Mikrotik	190,484	-
Netgear	-	17,723
Sercomm	-	899,492
Ubiquiti	598	-
Zhone	6,999	-
ZTE	17,972	560,177
Zyxel	5,902	-

over time, different implementations among different development or product groups working with different code bases, and the incorporation of outside implementations inherited through acquisitions and mergers.

Second, we are able to distinguish broad outlines of different manufacturers based on the incidence of reply fingerprints. In Fig. 2, we note that among the top six manufacturers, only Huawei had a significant number of associated IP addresses (~10%) that responded with the checksum-lazy behavior. More than half of the Cisco IP addresses from the Telnet scan exhibited the lazy behavior with the most significant bit set while counting milliseconds, a far greater proportion than any other manufacturer. Also noteworthy is that none of the manufacturers represented in the Telnet scan exhibits large numbers of correct replies. In our Telnet data, Mikrotik devices responded with a correct timestamp reply roughly 25% of the time, a higher incidence than any other manufacturer. This suggests that perhaps certain Mikrotik products have NTP enabled by default, allowing these devices to obtain correct time more readily than those that require administrator interaction. Our CWMP results in Fig. 3 demonstrate the ability to distinguish manufacturer behavior in certain cases as well, we note the >70% of Sercomm devices that exhibit only the lazy behavior, as well as Sercomm exhibiting the only timezone-relative timekeeping behavior among the CWMP manufacturers.

Finally, we note differences between the protocol scans among IP addresses that belong to the same manufacturer. Cisco, Huawei, and ZTE appear in both protocol results in appreciable numbers, and are represented in both figures in Sect. 4.2. Although Cisco devices obtained from the Telnet scan infrequently (~10%) respond with correct timestamps, in the CWMP data the proportion is nearly 40%. Huawei devices from the Telnet data are generally lazy responders that count in milliseconds, however, this same behavior occurs only half as frequently in the CWMP data. Further, the fingerprint consisting solely of the lazy behavior represents nearly a quarter of the CWMP Huawei devices, while it is insignificant in the Telnet Huawei data. While the differences between the Telnet and CWMP data are less pronounced for ZTE, they exist as well in the lack of appreciable numbers of ZTE devices setting the most significant bit in replies within the CWMP corpus.

Appendix C: Timezone-Relative Behavior

Figure 5 displays the probability mass function of the differences between the receive and originate timestamps for a sundial scan conducted on 9 September 2018 from the Boston vantage after responses with correct timestamps have been removed. Discernible peaks occur at many of the hourly intervals representing timezone-relative responders, rising above a base level of randomness. The hourly offsets in Fig. 5 may need to be normalized to the range of UTC timezone offsets, however. For example, depending on the originate timestamp value, a responding host's receive timestamp at a UTC offset of $+9$ may appear either nine hours ahead of the originate timestamp, or $15\,h$ behind, as $-15 \equiv 9(\bmod\ 24)$. In Fig. 5 we see large spikes at both $+9$ and $-15\,h$, but in reality these spikes represent the same timezone.

Table 6. Inferred UTC-offsets from timestamp replies

UTC offset	−12	−11	−10	−9	−8	−7	−6	−5	−4	−3.5	−3	−2	−1	1	2
Count	73	1	7	3	386	476	666	1,763	2,660	2	246	228	5	7,215	1,819
UTC offset	3	3.5	4	4.5	5	5.5	6	6.5	7	8	9	9.5	10	11	
Count	449	8	62	3	87	17	14	13	565	3,496	13,861	6	215	11	

We identify timezone-relative responses systematically by computing the local time in milliseconds for each of the UTC-offsets detailed in Table 6, given the originate timestamp contained in the timestamp response. We then compare each candidate local timezone's originate timestamp to the receive timestamp in the reply. If the candidate originate timestamp is within the 200 ms correctness bound established in Sect. 5.2, we classify the IP address as belonging to the timezone that produced the correct originate timestamp. Table 6 details the number of timezone-relative responders we identified during the 9 September sundial scan.

References

1. Anagnostakis, K.G., Greenwald, M., Ryger, R.S.: cing: Measuring network-internal delays using only existing infrastructure. In: Twenty-Second Annual Joint Conference of the IEEE Computer and Communications, vol. 3, pp. 2112–2121 (2003)

2. Beverly, R., Berger, A.: Server siblings: identifying shared IPv4/IPv6 infrastructure via active fingerprinting. In: Mirkovic, J., Liu, Y. (eds.) PAM 2015. LNCS, vol. 8995, pp. 149–161. Springer, Cham (2015). https://doi.org/10.1007/978-3-319-15509-8_12
3. Buchholz, F., Tjaden, B.: A brief study of time. Digit. Invest. **4**, 31–42 (2007)
4. Cristea, M., Groza, B.: Fingerprinting smartphones remotely via ICMP timestamps. IEEE Commun. Lett. **17**(6), 1081–1083 (2013)
5. Cymru, Team: IP to ASN mapping (2008). https://www.team-cymru.org/IP-ASN-mapping.html
6. Desmond, L.C.C., Yuan, C.C., Pheng, T.C., Lee, R.S.: Identifying unique devices through wireless fingerprinting. In: Proceedings of the First ACM Conference on Wireless Network Security, pp. 46–55 (2008)
7. Detal, G., Hesmans, B., Bonaventure, O., Vanaubel, Y., Donnet, B.: Revealing middlebox interference with tracebox. In: ACM SIGCOMM Internet Measurement Conference, pp. 1–8 (2013)
8. Durumeric, Z., Wustrow, E., Halderman, J.A.: ZMap: fast internet-wide scanning and its security applications. In: USENIX Security, pp. 605–620 (2013)
9. Fan, X., Heidemann, J.: Selecting representative IP addresses for Internet topology studies. In: ACM SIGCOMM Internet Measurement Conference, pp. 411–423 (2010)
10. FreeBSD: FreeBSD Kernel ICMP Code, SVN Head (2018). https://svnweb.freebsd.org/base/head/sys/netinet/ip_icmp.c?revision=336677
11. Internet Engineering Standards Group: Internet Control Message Protocol (ICMP) Parameters (2018). https://www.iana.org/assignments/icmp-parameters/icmp-parameters.xhtml
12. Kohno, T., Broido, A., Claffy, K.C.: Remote physical device fingerprinting. IEEE Trans. Dependable Secure Comput. **2**(2), 93–108 (2005)
13. Linux: Linux Kernel ICMP Code, Git Head (2018). https://github.com/torvalds/linux/blob/master/net/ipv4/icmp.c
14. Linux: The Linux Kernel Archives (2018). https://www.kernel.org/
15. Lyon, G.: Nmap Security Scanner. https://nmap.org
16. Mahajan, R., Spring, N., Wetherall, D., Anderson, T.: User-level internet path diagnosis. ACM SIGOPS Oper. Syst. Rev. **37**(5), 106–119 (2003)
17. MaxMind: GeoLite2 IP Geolocation Databases (2018). https://dev.maxmind.com/geoip/geoip2/geolite2/
18. Mills, D., Martin, J., Burbank, J., Kasch, W.: Network Time Protocol Version 4: Protocol and Algorithms Specification. RFC 5905 (Proposed Standard), June 2010. http://www.ietf.org/rfc/rfc5905.txt
19. Mills, D.: DCNET Internet Clock Service. RFC 778 (Historic), April 1981. http://www.ietf.org/rfc/rfc778.txt
20. MITRE: CVE-1999-0524. Available from MITRE, CVE-ID CVE-1999-0524, August 1999. http://cve.mitre.org/cgi-bin/cvename.cgi?name=CVE-1999-0524
21. Postel, J.: Internet Control Message Protocol. RFC 792 (INTERNET STANDARD), September 1981. http://www.ietf.org/rfc/rfc792.txt
22. Rye, E.C.: Sundial ICMP Timestamp Inference Tool (2019). https://www.cmand.org/sundial
23. Scans.io: Internet-Wide Scan Data Repository. https://scans.io
24. Scheitle, Q., Gasser, O., Rouhi, M., Carle, G.: Large-scale classification of IPv6-IPv4 siblings with variable clock skew. In: 2017 Network Traffic Measurement and Analysis Conference (TMA), pp. 1–9. IEEE (2017)

Measurement at Other Scales

Where on Earth Are the Best-50 Time Servers?

Yi Cao[✉] and Darryl Veitch

School of Electrical and Data Engineering, University of Technology Sydney,
Sydney, Australia
{Yi.Cao,Darryl.Veitch}@uts.edu.au

Abstract. We present a list of the Best-50 public IPv4 time servers by
mining a high-resolution dataset of Stratum-1 servers for Availability,
Stratum Constancy, Leap Performance, and Clock Error, broken down
by continent. We find that a server with ideal leap performance, high
availability, and low stratum variation is often clock error-free, but this
is no guarantee. We discuss the relevance and lifetime of our findings,
the scalability of our approach, and implications for load balancing and
server ranking.

Keywords: Leap second · NTP · Stratum-1 server ·
Network measurement · LI bits · UTC · Load balancing ·
Clock synchronization

1 Introduction

A high proportion of the global computer population achieves its time synchronization via public time servers accessed by the NTP protocol. Such servers are
hierarchical in that a *Stratum-s* (or S-s) timeserver itself synchronizes to a *Stratum s − 1* server. Anchoring the system are the *Stratum-1* time servers, which
have local access to reference hardware.

Clients rely on their server's notion of time, however, as we describe below,
server quality varies in important ways, often with no warning being delivered to
clients. It would clearly be of interest to map out server quality across the Internet, both for its own sake, and also to inform client server selection. However, it
is not immediately clear how this could be achieved at scale, and reliably, across
the latency noise of the Internet.

Recently the problem of server health monitoring has begun to receive attention, in particular regarding the small but critical Stratum-1 class. Techniques,
described in [5,18], have been developed for the unambiguous detection of errors
in server clock timestamps, even from vantage points where the path to the server
is both long in terms of Round Trip Time (RTT), and noisy. In [18], studying
around 100 servers, it was found that significant errors are not rare, being found
in a surprisingly high proportion of popular public servers, including many from
National Laboratories. Errors can be both large in magnitude (10's to 100's of

© Springer Nature Switzerland AG 2019
D. Choffnes and M. Barcellos (Eds.): PAM 2019, LNCS 11419, pp. 101–115, 2019.
https://doi.org/10.1007/978-3-030-15986-3_7

milliseconds and even beyond) and long lasting (from hours to days and even continuously over months), or both. In [17] a similar server set was analyzed with respect to their leap second performance, and recently [5], using a new and much larger data set, looked at both server clock error and protocol failures during the end-2016 leap second. In these servers, which include all those Stratum-1 servers employed in the widely used NTP Pool service [11], only 37.3% were found to perform adequately.

In this paper we mine the IPv4 data set, available at [4], used in [5]. We evaluate quality according to four dimensions: server Availability, behaviour surrounding a Leap Second (a stress test for both NTP protocol compliance and clock behaviour), Stratum Constancy, and finally, severity of server Clock Errors. We limit our list to 50 members, and within this group servers are not explicitly ranked. Instead, because of the importance to clients of the RTT to its server, a key factor in synchronization performance in practice (though not necessarily in theory, see [16]) due to its correlation with path asymmetry, congestion and loss, we structure our results in a per-continent then per-country breakdown.

There are a number of arguments for a 'Best-50'. One is for direct use by measurement specialists, in particular operators of measurement infrastructures [1,2,14], who require servers of both high availability and high accuracy. Another is to highlight the server health issue. Quantifying best practice increases awareness of ongoing problems, and provides the context (and an incentive) for efforts to improve the system and to track performance over time. A third goal is to explore concretely a number of quality metrics, and how they relate to actual, verifiable errors in server timing. Although there have been some papers surveying network timing performance [6–10], we believe this is the first attempt to accurately identify the best servers, using diverse metrics.

After providing background in Sect. 2 and an overview in Sect. 3, the main results are presented in Sect. 4. Section 5 discusses their significance, limitations, and implications for the definition and use of a server quality rank, with reference to load balancing services including NTP Pool. We conclude in Sect. 6.

2 Background

We summarize the experimental setup, data set and server list (see [5] for full details). We then summarize the operation of the NTP Pool service.

2.1 The Experiment

The experiment covered a 64 day period from Nov. 16 2016 to Feb. 2 2017, including the end-2016 leap second. For each server in a target server list in parallel, an independent instance of a request–response exchange daemon, using a per-server customized polling period as close to $\tau = 1\,$s as possible, was launched.

For an NTP packet i which successfully completes its round-trip from the client to server and back, a 4-tuple $stamp$ $\{T_{a,i}, T_{b,i}, T_{e,i}, T_{f,i}\}$ of timestamps is recorded. Here $T_{b,i}, T_{e,i}$ are the (incoming and outgoing respectively) UTC timestamps made by the server. These are extracted from the returning NTP packet header, along with the Leap Indicator (LI) bits and the server Stratum field. The timestamps $T_{a,i}, T_{f,i}$ are of passively tapped NTP packets, hardware timestamped using high performance Endace DAG 7.5G4 capture cards, whose hardware clocks are disciplined to a rubidium atomic clock, itself locked to a roof mounted GPS receiver. The error in the client side timestamps measurement is therefore sub-microsecond and is ignored here.

The IPv4 servers studied came from five sources:

Org: the public S-1 URL list maintained at *ntp.org*
Pool: S-1 servers participating in the NTP Pool Project
LBL: S-1 servers caught at the Lawrence Berkeley Laboratory border router
Au: the set of Australian public facing S-1 servers (plus 6 private)
Misc: miscellaneous servers of interest.

The servers which returned useful data, 459 in total, are broken down by source in Table 1 (the sets overlap). Of the AU servers, 6 are in fact private and will be excluded from the final results. Table 2 provides a geographical breakdown. The low values for AF, AN and SA reflect the immaturity of Internet timing infrastructure across these continents.

Table 1. Server source breakdown.

Population	Org	Pool	LBL	Au	Misc
#	197	258	257	14	10
%	43	56	56	3	2

Table 2. Continental breakdown of servers.

Population	AF	AN	AS	EU	NA	OC	SA
#	1	0	50	203	169	29	7
%	0.2	0	0.9	44.2	36.8	6.3	1.5

2.2 NTP Pool

The NTP Pool Project [11] provides a load balancing and convenient configuration service for millions of NTP clients, by supplying a set of URLs resolved via a tailored DNS server, to members of a pool of participating volunteer NTP servers of various strata.

Users can access at *pool.ntp.org* the complete worldwide pool, or subsets thereof at *#.pool.ntp.org*, where # is one of {0,1,2,3}. These subsets are influenced by client geo-location but otherwise random, and refresh every hour [12]. The full details of how server subsets are selected is not documented.

A degree of client-control is supported via *CONT.pool.ntp.org*: continental zone pools where CONT is one of {africa, antarctica, asia, europe, north-america, oceania, south-america}, and CY-coded country pools at *CY.pool.ntp.org*, and #. prefixed subsets of these [13].

For the pool associated to a given client at a particular time, the system uses DNS round robin to resolve URL queries to the IP address of a server in that pool. NTP Pool includes a monitoring system which queries the pool servers, scoring their performance based in NTP packet fields including {offset, stratum, LI, RTT, noresponse}. Servers are evaluated periodically and only those with a *score* above 10 are made available.

3 Server Characterization

We characterize servers according to the following four criteria or dimensions.

Availability. This simple but critical criterion is measured by the ratio of response packets received to request packets sent. This will underestimate the true availability, because of packet loss and reachability failure in the network.

Stratum Constancy. Possible stratum values range from $S = 0$ (unsynchronized), to $S = 1, 2 \ldots 16$. A Stratum-1 server may change stratum if its hardware reference has a problem, if the system has a reboot, or if its synchronization daemon/algorithm decides it would prefer an remote reference, and stratum values of 0, 2, 3 or even higher could result. We measure the 'Stratum-1 downtime' (S1Downtime) as the proportion of response packets which report a stratum other than 1. Values of S1Downtime close to zero suggest a well managed Stratum-1 server in a stable environment. We also record the list of all stratum values ever seen.

Leap Performance. Leap Second events are a stress test for servers, both in terms of the detailed clock performance (does it jump cleanly by exactly 1 second at exactly the right time, and nothing else?) and protocol compliance (does it set the LI bits in accordance with the standard?). This question was studied in detail for each server in the list in [5]. Here we classify servers according to a subset of the characterization defined there, as:
Ideal: no observed clock error linked to the leap second, ideal protocol behaviour;
Adequate: no clock error, compliant protocol behaviour;
Clock Good: no evidence of clock error about the leap,

where Ideal $\subset$ Adequate $\subset$ Clock Good $\subset$ All. For convenience, we add two more classes by set difference:

Clock Good Only (CGO): Clock-Good\Adequate;
Clock Not Good (CNG): All\Clock-Good.

Although leap seconds are rare, they occur regularly. If a server handles them poorly, the impact can be severe, for example taking weeks to jump, or never.

Clock Errors/Anomalies. Our approach is based on the methodology we pioneered in [18] for the remote detection and measurement of server errors. It uses baseline analysis of the RTT timeseries to identify changes in the 'Error'

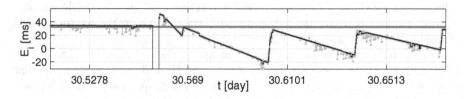

Fig. 1. Server errors cause $E(i)$ to deviate from its true underlying value (green line). (Color figure online)

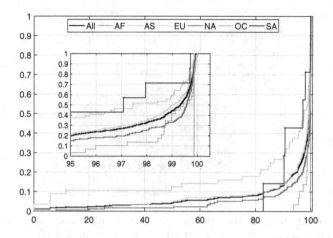

Fig. 2. CDF of Availability (in %) over all servers (black), and per-continent.

time series $E_i = (D_i^{\uparrow} - D_i^{\downarrow})/2$ due to server errors, rather than the alternatives of path routing changes and/or congestion. Here $D_i^{\uparrow} = T_{b,i} - T_{a,i}$ and $D_i^{\downarrow} = T_{f,i} - T_{e,i}$ are the empirical outgoing and incoming delays to the server. An example of a server error zone, beginning at around $t = 30.544$ days, is given in Fig. 1.

We have improved the methodology of [18] by (i) replacing non-linear filtering based congestion suppression (which can be fooled in certain circumstances) with strict RTT bounding, (ii) systematically recording not only error sizes but also the precise locations of all error zones, (iii) increasing the granularity of error frequency reporting: we classify servers according to the number of errors as: **G**ood: no errors; **R**are: less than one error per week; **C**ommon: more than one error per week, but not **H**igh; and **H**igh: continuous stretches of error covering at least 25% of the trace. In [18] **R** and **C** were combined into **R**.

Since the selection of error zones is performed manually (due to the need to disambiguate from complex routing, congestion and error scenarios), the detection process is very labor intensive. It is essential however for our purposes here where, unlike [18], we evaluate not only error presence and representative size but also how often the server is in error (see *Errtime* below).

3.1   Server Overview

We provide some context by examining the first three of the above dimensions over all servers.

Figure 2 shows the Cumulative Distribution Function (CDF) of availability for all servers. Availability is good overall, with 80% of servers having values exceeding 95%, and over half exceeding 99%. The per-continent results show lower availability for regions further from the testbed in Sydney, Oceania. This can be explained through a measurement bias due to higher loss rates over longer paths leading to lower apparent availability.

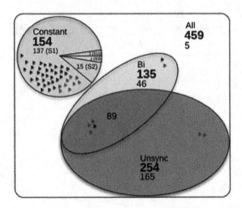

Fig. 3. Relationship between the Stratum classes. Symbols denote servers in the Best-50, red symbols denote those with server errors. (Color figure online)

The leap performance results over all servers appear in Table 3. Only 37% exhibit Adequate behavior, necessary to allow their clients to navigate a leap second without incident.

Table 3. Leap performance summary.

	All	CGO	CNG	Clock Good	Adequate	Ideal
#	459	134	154	305	171	36
%	100	29	34	66	37	8

Figure 3 provides a pertinent classification of servers according to strata. In the Constant class only one stratum value is ever seen (not always Stratum-1!), in Bi only two, and in Unsync at least one response carries Stratum-0. We see that 154 servers (34%) have constant strata, and the majority of the 305 that do not, 254 or 83%, announced themselves as unsynchronized at least once.

Overall 137 servers (30%) announce themselves as Stratum-1 in each and every response. This appears as a discrete mass of weight 0.3 at the origin in the S1Downtime CDF in Fig. 4, which shows that servers which are not Constant have a wide variety of S1Downtime values.

4   The Best-50 Servers

What we would ideally like is clear: to find servers that are always available, and that have no detectable clock errors. However, to determine the latter implies a prior detailed examination, which is too labour intensive using our server error methodology and tools to deal with 459 servers, each with up to 2 months of high resolution data, each with potentially a large number of errors.

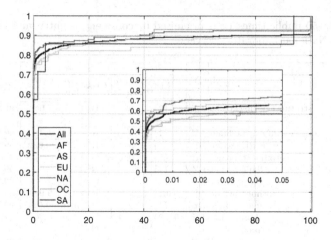

Fig. 4. CDF of S1Downtime (in %) over all servers (black), and per-continent.

Accordingly, our approach is to first assemble a list of ostensibly high quality servers using the dimensions of Availability and Stratum Constancy that are readily calculated, and Leap Performance, available from prior work, and to apply the Clock Error analysis on this much smaller number of servers, which moreover are likely to be simpler to analyse. In this way we approximate the ideal above in a scalable way (see Sect. 5), with a practically appropriate bias toward servers with stable management (high Stratum Constancy) and competent configuration and performance during high stress (Leap Performance).

More precisely we proceed as follows. For Availability, we seek servers that are almost always available, with due allowance for measurement bias due to packet loss. Based on Fig. 2 we believe a cutoff of 97% is safe. For Leap Performance, we insist that servers are in the Adequate class. Next, we use S1Downtime to order the servers that pass the above two criteria. Our Best-50 servers are then defined as the first 50 servers in this ordering (starting from the zero S1Downtime end) whose Clock Error class is either **G** or **R**.

Server errors in a given server are further quantified through the metrics of **Size** (the median over all error zones of the error range over that zone), and **Errtime** (the proportion of the trace taken up by error zones).

The resulting Best-50 servers are given in Table 4. Within each continent group, servers are ordered according to country code first, and then lexicographically according to their URL. The mapping from URL to IP address is provided in the Appendix.

Beyond the identities of the servers themselves and their geographical breakdown, the most important observation from the table is the fact that even excellent performance under each of Availability, Stratum Constancy and Leap Performance does not mean that the server is error free. Indeed, out of 15 servers with detected server errors, 9 give no warning of this with a S1Downtime of zero, yet have Sizes ranging from 2.1 to 1000 ms, albeit with Errtime being generally low (0.9 s in the hour on average in the worst case of 0.025%). The worst

Table 4. Best-50 public timeservers organised by continent, country, and URL. Cyan URLs marks National Laboratory servers.

CONT	URL	CY	Strata		Server Error			Avail. (%)	Leap Perf
			List	S1Down time(%)	Class	Size [ms]	Errtime (%)		
AF	stratum1.neology.co.za	ZA	{1}	0	R	2.1	7.0e-5	99.87	Adeq.
AN	–	–	–	–	–	–	–	–	–
OC	ntp1.net.monash.edu.au	AU	{1}	0	R	180	1.4e-4	99.86	Adeq.
EU	ntp1.oma.be	BE	{0,1}	2.9e-4	R	28	0.032	99.04	Adeq.
	ntp.freestone.net	CH	{1}	0	G	–	–	99.80	Ideal
	netopyr.hanacke.net	CZ	{1}	0	G	–	–	99.25	Ideal
	ntp.nic.cz	CZ	{1}	0	G	–	–	99.86	Adeq.
	ptbtime1.ptb.de	DE	{0,1}	2.9e-4	R	1.1	2.9e-4	99.78	Adeq.
	ptbtime3.ptb.de	DE	{1}	0	R	5.46	0.014	99.78	Ideal
	hora.roa.es	ES	{0,1,2}	2.9e-4	R	120	5.8e-3	99.40	Adeq.
	ntp.i2t.ehu.es	ES	{1}	0	G	–	–	98.94	Ideal
	unknown1	GB	{1}	0	G	–	–	99.71	Ideal
	unknown2	GB	{1}	0	G	–	–	99.71	Ideal
	ntp2.litnet.lt	LT	{1}	0	G	–	–	99.87	Ideal
	metronoom.dmz.cs.uu.nl	NL	{1}	0	G	–	–	99.66	Ideal
	unknown3	NO	{1}	0	G	–	–	98.88	Ideal
	goblin.nask.net.pl	PL	{1}	0	G	–	–	99.79	Ideal
	ntp.certum.pl	PL	{1}	0	R	7.0	0.025	97.55	Adeq.
	ntp.fizyka.umk.pl	PL	{1}	0	G	–	–	99.45	Ideal
	time.assecobs.pl	PL	{1}	0	G	–	–	99.10	Ideal
	ntp1.niiftri.irkutsk.ru	RU	{1}	0	G	–	–	98.83	Ideal
	ntp2.niiftri.irkutsk.ru	RU	{1}	0	G	–	–	98.94	Ideal
	ntp1.gbg.netnod.se	SE	{1}	0	R	1000	1.8e-5	99.89	Adeq.
	ntp2.gbg.netnod.se	SE	{1}	0	R	1000	1.8e-5	99.89	Adeq.
	ntp1.mmo.netnod.se	SE	{1}	0	R	1000	3.6e-5	99.87	Adeq.
	ntp2.mmo.netnod.se	SE	{1}	0	G	–	–	99.88	Adeq.
	ntp1.sth.netnod.se	SE	{1}	0	G	–	–	99.82	Adeq.
	ntp2.sth.netnod.se	SE	{1}	0	R	1000	8.8e-4	99.81	Adeq.
NA	istntpprd–02.corenet.ualberta.ca	CA	{1}	0	G	–	–	99.89	Ideal
	tick.usask.ca	CA	{1}	0	G	–	–	99.86	Adeq.
	tock.usask.ca	CA	{1}	0	R	17	2.5e-4	99.58	Adeq.
	clepsydra.dec.com	US	{1}	0	G	–	–	97.82	Ideal
	m4c2236d0.tmodns.net	US	{1}	0	G	–	–	99.87	Ideal
	m4d2236d0.tmodns.net	US	{1}	0	G	–	–	99.88	Ideal
	montpelier.ilan.caltech.edu	US	{1}	0	G	–	–	99.76	Ideal
	navobs1.gatech.edu	US	{1}	0	G	–	–	99.70	Adeq.
	ntp.colby.edu	US	{1}	0	G	–	–	99.71	Adeq.
	ntp1.digitalwest.net	US	{1}	0	G	–	–	99.82	Ideal
	tick.ucla.edu	US	{1,2}	2.6e-4	G	–	–	99.50	Adeq.
	time–a.netgear.com	US	{1}	0	G	–	–	99.78	Ideal
	time–a.stanford.edu	US	{1}	0	G	–	–	99.92	Adeq.
	tock.phyber.com	US	{1}	0	G	–	–	99.87	Adeq.
	usatl4-ntp-002.aaplimg.com	US	{0,1,2}	5.7e-5	R	1.5	0.063	99.83	Adeq.
	usno.hpl.hp.com	US	{1}	0	G	–	–	97.82	Ideal
	usnyc3-ntp-003.aaplimg.com	US	{0,1}	1.8e-3	R	6.4	0.052	99.85	Adeq.
AS	f2.kns1.eonet.ne.jp	JP	{0,1}	2.8e-4	G	–	–	99.83	Adeq.
	jptyo5-ntp-001.aaplimg.com	JP	{1,2}	2.3e-4	R	39	0.029	99.11	Adeq.
	ntp1.noc.titech.ac.jp	JP	{1}	0	G	–	–	99.82	Adeq.
	ntp-b2.nict.go.jp	JP	{1}	0	G	–	–	99.90	Ideal
	unknown4	SG	{1}	0	G	–	–	99.91	Ideal
SA	ntp.shoa.cl	CL	{1}	0	G	–	–	99.70	Ideal

Table 5. Five categories of examples of servers outside the Best-50 in one or more criteria. Bold column entries mark failed criteria.

CONT	URL	CY	Strata		Server Error			Avail. (%)	Leap Perf
			List	S1Down time(%)	Class	Size [ms]	Errtime (%)		
OC	ntp10.net.monash.edu.au	AU	{1}	0	**C**	18.46	0.002	99.86	Adeq.
NA	time-a.timefreq.bldrdoc.gov	US	{1}	0	**H**	23.16	100	99.47	Adeq.
NA	time-c.timefreq.bldrdoc.gov	US	{1}	0	**H**	8.98	100	99.69	Adeq.
OC	ntp.waia.asn.au	AU	{0,1,3}	**0.040**	R	700	0.128	99.44	Adeq.
EU	ntp1.fau.de	DE	{1,2}	**0.381**	R	1.76	0.628	99.70	Adeq.
NA	srcf-ntp.stanford.edu	US	{1}	0	G	–	–	99.93	**CGO**
SA	a.st1.ntp.br	BR	{0,1}	1.1e-4	G	–	–	99.72	**CGO**
EU	ntp1.vniiftri.ru	RU	{0-3,12}	**0.029**	R	2.30	1.852	98.05	**CNG**
EU	ntp3.fau.de	DE	{1,2}	**0.401**	**H**	6.3	100	99.69	Adeq.
NA	ntp.myfloridacity.us	US	{0,1}	3.9e-4	**H**	14.61	100	98.73	**CNG**
NA	time-b.nist.gov	US	{1}	0	**C**	2.10	0.254	**63.73**	Adeq.
NA	t2.timegps.net	US	{0,1,2}	**0.011**	R	333.50	0.043	99.59	**CGO**
EU	rustime01.rus.uni-stuttgart.de	DE	{1,2}	**0.380**	R	4.50	3.485	**95.05**	**CGO**
EU	ntp2.usv.ro	RO	{0,1}	**0.003**	G	–	–	**96.70**	**CNG**

S1Downtime in the table, NA server *usnyc3-ntp-003.aaplimg.com*, which is also an **R** server, only drops from Stratum-1 (to Stratum-0 in this case) 0.0018% of the time. This is 29 times less often than its Errtime at 0.052%. Thus for this server, error is a more serious concern than stratum stability.

The Best-50 are marked via symbols within Fig. 3, where certain observations are more immediate. For example we clearly see that 9 of the Constant S1 servers in the Best-50 have clock errors, and that only 2 in the Best-50 take 3 or more stratum values.

Another observation of note is that, with the exception of *ptbtime3.ptb.de*, servers with Ideal Leap Performance and zero S1Downtime enjoy Server Error ratings of **G**, suggesting that this pair could serve as a useful indicator of an exceptionally well managed server, and hence be predictive of exemplary Error behaviour. Useful does not mean foolproof however: in addition to the exception above the two NIST servers in Table 5 provide sobering counter-examples.

The server list contains 35 servers from Apple's *17.253* domain. Three of these make it into the Best-50, though all exhibit server errors with relatively large Errtime values. Finally, it is worth noting that despite having 66 servers from National Laboratories in the list, only 12, those colored cyan, make it into the Best-50 (an additional 5 from the NMI in Australia are excluded as they are not publicly accessible).

Because the criteria of entry into the Best-50 are so strict, there is a limit to what one can say about these servers: they are indeed very well behaved. However, if one relaxes the criteria in different dimensions, a much wider variety of behaviour is quickly revealed. To make this concrete, and to indicate what could have been included in the Best-50 had things been a little different, a number of contrasting examples are provided in Table 5, separated into five categories. For each server bolded column entries mark the criteria which did not meet the Best-50 standard.

In the first category we give 3 of the 5 servers (of which {2,3} were rated {C,H} respectively) that failed to make the Best-50 because of excessive server errors. By definition, and as noted earlier, such servers illustrate the fact that the (Availability, Stratum, Leap) three-tuple is not sufficient to predict the absence or otherwise of clock errors, nor their severity in terms of Size or Errtime. Particularly noteworthy is the fact that **H** servers, which by definition have an Errtime over 25%, and typically have Errtime of a dramatic 100%! can and do appear. The second category exhibits two examples of servers that failed only due to being too low in the S1Downtime ranking, one of which has Size of 700 ms and Errtime three times higher than its S1Downtime. The third category gives examples failing only the Leap criterion, that are exemplary in other respects. There were no examples of servers which failed in Availability only. The fourth category includes five diverse examples where two criteria were not met. Finally, the fifth category includes servers that are still generally respectable despite failing in three criteria.

5 Discussion

We discuss the limitations, implications and future of our work.

Source Coverage. Because of the widespread usage of the Pool service, and the high profile of the Org list, we expect the server list to contain most of the widely used public S-1 servers, but how representative are they of the (unknown) complete set? There is in fact a high degree of overlap, 50% or more, between each of the three main sources: Org, Pool and LBL, leading to speculation in [5] that the server list contains a significant percentage of the global public facing Stratum-1 server population. We now consider how to evaluate this claim.

Population estimation based on re-sampling a marked sub-population is known as the *capture-recapture* problem in statistics. To fit within this framework, it is natural to group the Org and Pool sources together as they are both community based, and have a strong, non-random relationship. Thus we have $n = |\mathbf{Org} \cup \mathbf{Pool}| = 356$ servers which represent a 'marked' sample of the total unknown population N. The LBL source now represents a random sample of $K = 257$ servers, of which $k = 175$ lie in $\mathbf{Org} \cup \mathbf{Pool}$, that is they are marked servers that are 'recaptured'. The population can now be estimated from n, K and k. For example the Chapman estimator [3,15], yields $\hat{N} = \lfloor (K+1)(n+1)/(k+1) \rfloor - 1 = 522$. A corresponding (non-symmetric) 95% coverage interval for N is [497, 562]. This suggests that our Best-50 is well founded as it is based on a number, 453, being between 80% and 91% of all public servers.

The random sampling assumptions underlying the Chapman estimator do not hold strictly here, so the above estimate can only be viewed as a rough indication. To determine the true value of N a better approach, for IPv4 servers, is simply to exhaustively probe the IPv4 address space. We did not do so here, as that would not have given us the leap second performance information we require.

List Shelf Life. As it derives from a static data set, the utility of our Best-50 will decrease over time. Some indication of its expected lifetime can be gained from the longitudinal results in [18], which report on a subset of Org servers using data collected over 151 days in 2011–12 (Exp1), and 124 days in 2014–15 (Exp2). Although Availability, Leap performance, and Errtime are not given, we can compare with respect to Stratum Constancy, and Error Classification.

Of the Best-50 servers, there are 13 which also appear in that study. All 13 (100%) were found to be error-free in each of Exp1 and Exp2, as well as having zero S1Downtime for Exp2 (stratum data was unavailable for Exp1). For the metrics available, this represents perfect agreement.

Of the 14 servers which feature in Table 5, 13 also appear in the study, of which 3 are suitable for direct comparison as they pass our criteria for S1Downtime and have Error class in {G,R,C}. Of these, all 3 exhibit close agreement, with no detected errors in each of Exp1 and Exp2, and again with zero S1Downtime. Finally, at the other end of the spectrum, of the 4 servers in the continuously errored H class in Table 5, 3 were also classed as H in [18].

Based on the above, we expect that the level of churn in the Best-50 list provided here will be low on useful timescales, for example 5 years. Knowledge of server configuration would be of interest here also to attempt root cause analysis, as would correlating against network failures. We have attempted to contact administrators, however the response rate was minimal.

Measurement Cost. The analysis used here requires specialist hardware, techniques, unusual data (leap events), and significant effort. A priori, this does not scale. A goal of future work must be to develop lighter weight approximate techniques and more automated server error detection using standard hardware. The work here can serve to evaluate the effectiveness of such techniques.

Scalability cost divides substantially along criteria lines. Stratum Constancy measurement scales trivially, as it depends neither on special hardware nor the network path. Availability also scales readily, though to remove packet loss bias requires measurement close to the server and/or path diversity, and hence client placement diversity ideally. Leap Performance is inherently difficult as opportunities to measure it occur only every ≈ 2.5 years. On the other hand this also limits the workload, and the protocol aspects are as scalable as Stratum Constancy. Rankings could be defined which exclude leap second criteria for applications where this is not needed, for example Internet measurement campaigns not covering leap events, which are announced months in advance.

The Clock Error criteria is the expensive one, and the most critical. The hardware cost could be avoided by using a robust clock synchronization and timestamping approach such as RADclock [16] as a Stratum-2, with its Stratum-1 server selected from the Best-50 provided here. Although timestamping errors would of course be higher, they would still be well below server error sizes in most cases. In terms of the error analysis itself, it is feasible, albeit non-trivial, to automate this to a good level of accuracy, and this is a direction for our future work. Such a capability would enable, for example, ongoing monitoring and error querying for important servers. However, this is not essential for the purpose of maintaining the Best-50 as we have defined it here, as the construction of the list, combined with its expected low churn, implies that only a small number of high quality servers (which are faster to process) would have to be evaluated from scratch each year to keep it current. Those remaining would also have to be re-evaluated, but this is less onerous when they have been seen before.

Server Ranking. From the quality dimensions we have considered various rankings could be defined. An obvious way to rank the Best-50 is the S1Downtime ordering employed in the list construction, however this cannot be extended over all servers, as many will not satisfy the minimum requirements in other criteria. A candidate which avoids this problem is *Badtime*, defined to be the sum of Errtime and 1−Availability, being the proportion of time a server should be avoided. This should suit contexts where leap second performance is not critical.

Great care must be taken in how any ranking is used, to prevent high ranking servers from receiving high loads. It would be a mistake (and is not the intent of this paper!) to recommend that clients make use of the Best-50 en masse. Instead, server rank should be used within broader systems designed to tradeoff load balancing and server quality appropriately. Indeed, NTP Pool's *score* is an attempt to do this (Sect. 2), however it is not grounded in knowledge of actual server error. The larger problem is that NTP Pool breaks NTP's inherent load balancing mechanism, namely the server hierarchy, while simultaneously preferencing its own load balancing over server quality. Thus pools contain servers of mixed strata, and clients are given different servers over time with quality which may vary enormously. Instead, we argue that the hierarchy needs to be enforced, and within that, well defined notions of rank given higher prominence.

Client Impacts. Finally, a separate, but natural question to ask is, how important is it for a client to select a server of Best-50 calibre? The client impact will depend strongly on many factors including the robustness of the clock synchronization algorithm in use, the policy regarding back-up servers and if they are available, the size of server errors, their duration, the length of non-availability periods, the stratum of the client, the characteristics of the path to the server, and whether a leap second is involved. Potential errors can range from negligible ($< 10\mu$s) and short-term (few seconds) at one extreme, to permanent (until server change) and extreme (10's of ms to seconds or well beyond plus high variability) at the other. The onus on the Stratum-1 server is to show near perfect behaviour to anchor and lift performance across the timing system. This is possible, as many in the Best-50 demonstrate.

6   Conclusion

Our Best-50 list is not definitive. It is however the first serious attempt to quantify timeserver best practice that we are aware of. We believe that it will be of use for a number of years at least, by which time the methodology could be improved to make such a list more comprehensive, dynamic and less expensive to generate. It is in any event, feasible to maintain it even with current technology.

Acknowledgment. Partially supported by Australian Research Council's Discovery Projects funding scheme #DP170100451.

Appendix

(see Tables 6 and 7).

Table 6. URL to IP mapping of the servers in Table 4.

CONT	URL	IP	CY
AF	stratum1.neology.co.za	41.73.40.11	ZA
AN		–	–
OC	ntp1.net.monash.edu.au	130.194.1.96	AU
EU	ntp1.oma.be	193.190.230.65	BE
	ntp.freestone.net	193.5.68.2	CH
	netopyr.hanacke.net	94.124.107.190	CZ
	ntp.nic.cz	217.31.202.100	CZ
	ptbtime1.ptb.de	192.53.103.108	DE
	ptbtime3.ptb.de	192.53.103.103	DE
	hora.roa.es	150.214.94.5	ES
	ntp.i2t.ehu.es	158.227.98.15	ES
	unknown1	188.39.213.7	GB
	unknown2	81.187.202.142	GB
	ntp2.litnet.lt	193.219.61.120	LT
	metronoom.dmz.cs.uu.nl	131.211.8.244	NL
	unknown3	148.252.105.132	NO
	goblin.nask.net.pl	195.187.245.55	PL
	ntp.certum.pl	213.222.200.99	PL
	ntp.fizyka.umk.pl	158.75.5.245	PL
	time.assecobs.pl	195.189.85.132	PL
	ntp1.niiftri.irkutsk.ru	46.254.241.74	RU
	ntp2.niiftri.irkutsk.ru	46.254.241.75	RU
	ntp1.gbg.netnod.se	192.36.133.17	SE
	ntp2.gbg.netnod.se	192.36.133.25	SE
	ntp1.mmo.netnod.se	192.36.134.17	SE
	ntp2.mmo.netnod.se	192.36.134.25	SE
	ntp1.sth.netnod.se	192.36.144.22	SE
	ntp2.sth.netnod.se	192.36.144.23	SE
NA	istntpprd–02.corenet.ualberta.ca	129.128.5.211	CA
	tick.usask.ca	128.233.154.245	CA
	tock.usask.ca	128.233.150.93	CA
	clepsydra.dec.com	204.123.2.5	US
	m4c2236d0.tmodns.net	208.54.34.76	US
	m4d2236d0.tmodns.net	208.54.34.77	US
	montpelier.ilan.caltech.edu	192.12.19.20	US
	navobs1.gatech.edu	130.207.244.240	US
	ntp.colby.edu	137.146.28.85	US
	ntp1.digitalwest.net	72.29.161.5	US
	tick.ucla.edu	164.67.62.194	US
	time–a.netgear.com	209.249.181.52	US
	time–a.stanford.edu	171.64.7.105	US
	tock.phyber.com	207.171.30.106	US
	usatl4-ntp-002.aaplimg.com	17.253.6.253	US
	usno.hpl.hp.com	204.123.2.72	US
	usnyc3-ntp-003.aaplimg.com	17.253.14.123	US
AS	f2.kns1.eonet.ne.jp	60.56.214.78	JP
	jptyo5-ntp-001.aaplimg.com	17.253.68.125	JP
	ntp1.noc.titech.ac.jp	131.112.125.48	JP
	ntp-b2.nict.go.jp	133.243.238.163	JP
	unknown4	210.23.25.77	SG
SA	ntp.shoa.cl	200.54.149.24	CL

Table 7. URL to IP mapping of the servers in Table 5.

CONT	URL	IP	CY
OC	ntp10.net.monash.edu.au	130.194.10.150	AU
NA	time-a.timefreq.bldrdoc.gov	132.163.4.101	US
NA	time-c.timefreq.bldrdoc.gov	132.163.4.103	US
OC	ntp.waia.asn.au	218.100.43.70	AU
EU	ntp1.fau.de	131.188.3.221	DE
NA	srcf-ntp.stanford.edu	171.66.97.126	US
SA	a.st1.ntp.br	200.160.7.186	BR
EU	ntp1.vniiftri.ru	89.109.251.21	RU
EU	ntp3.fau.de	131.188.3.223	DE
NA	ntp.myfloridacity.us	71.40.128.146	US
NA	time-b.nist.gov	129.6.15.29	US
NA	t2.timegps.net	69.75.229.43	US
EU	rustime01.rus.uni-stuttgart.de	129.69.1.153	DE
EU	ntp2.usv.ro	80.96.120.252	RO

References

1. Archipelago monitor locations. http://www.caida.org/projects/ark/locations/
2. Bajpai, V., Schönwälder, J.: A survey on internet performance measurement platforms and related standardization efforts. IEEE Commun. Surv. Tutorials **17**(3), 1313–1341 (2015)
3. Brittain, S., Böhning, D.: Estimators in capture-recapture studies with two sources. AStA Adv. Stat. Anal. **93**(1), 23–47 (2009)
4. Cao, Y., Veitch, D.: TimeServer Dataset 2016–2017. https://data.research.uts.edu.au/public/DVTSD/. Per-server results also available
5. Cao, Y., Veitch, D.: Network timing, weathering the 2016 leap second. In: Proceedings of IEEE INFOCOM 2018, Honolulu, USA, 15–19 April 2018
6. Guyton, J.D., Schwartz, M.F.: Experiences with a Survey Tool for Discovering Network Time Protocol Servers (1994). Accessed 31 July 2015
7. Hong, C.-Y., Lin, C.-C., Caesar, M.: Clockscalpel: understanding root causes of internet clock synchronization inaccuracy. In: Spring, N., Riley, G.F. (eds.) PAM 2011. LNCS, vol. 6579, pp. 204–213. Springer, Heidelberg (2011). https://doi.org/10.1007/978-3-642-19260-9_21
8. Malone, D.: The leap second behaviour of NTP servers. In: Proceedings of the Traffic Monitoring and Analysis workshop, 7–8 April 2016. IFIP Digital Library (2016). http://tma.ifip.org/2016/#program
9. Minar, N.: A Survey of the NTP Network (1999). http://xenia.media.mit.edu/nelson/research/ntp-survey99/ntp-survey99-minar.ps
10. Murta, C., Torres, P., Mohapatra, P.: Characterizing quality of time and topology in a time synchronization network. In: Global Telecommunications Conference, GLOBECOM 2006, pp. 1–5 (2006). IEEE, November 2006
11. ntp.org. NTP Pool Project (2018). Accessed 2 May 2018
12. pool.ntp.org. How do I use pool.net.org? http://www.pool.ntp.org/en/use.html
13. pool.ntp.org. NTP Pool server selection. http://support.ntp.org/bin/view/Servers/NTPPoolServers
14. Staff, R.N.: Ripe atlas: a global internet measurement network. Internet Protoc. J. **18**(3) (2015)

15. Sutherland, W.J.: Ecological Census Techniques: A Handbook. Cambridge University Press, Cambridge (2006)
16. Veitch, D., Ridoux, J., Korada, S.B.: Robust synchronization of absolute and difference clocks over networks. IEEE/ACM Trans. Netw. **17**(2), 417–430 (2009)
17. Veitch, D., Vijayalayan, K.: Network timing and the 2015 leap second. In: Proceedings of PAM 2016, Heraklion, Crete, Greece, 31 March - 1 April 2016
18. Vijayalayan, K., Veitch, D.: Rot at the roots? Examining public timing infrastructure. In: Proceedings of IEEE INFOCOM 2016, San Francisco, CA, USA, 10–15 April 2016

Service Traceroute: Tracing Paths
of Application Flows

Ivan Morandi[1], Francesco Bronzino[1(✉)], Renata Teixeira[1],
and Srikanth Sundaresan[2]

[1] Inria, Paris, France
{ivan.morandi,francesco.bronzino,renata.teixeira}@inria.fr
[2] Princeton University, Princeton, USA
srikanth@icsi.berkeley.edu

Abstract. Traceroute is often used to help diagnose when users experience issues with Internet applications or services. Unfortunately, probes
issued by classic traceroute tools differ from application traffic and hence
can be treated differently by routers that perform load balancing and
middleboxes within the network. This paper proposes a new traceroute
tool, called *Service traceroute*. Service traceroute leverages the idea from
paratrace, which passively listens to application traffic to then issue
traceroute probes that pretend to be part of the application flow. We
extend this idea to work for modern Internet services with support for
identifying the flows to probe automatically, for tracing of multiple concurrent flows, and for UDP flows. We implement command-line and
library versions of Service traceroute, which we release as open source.
This paper also presents an evaluation of Service traceroute when tracing
paths traversed by Web downloads from the top-1000 Alexa websites and
by video sessions from Twitch and Youtube. Our evaluation shows that
Service traceroute has no negative effect on application flows. Our comparison with Paris traceroute shows that a typical traceroute tool that
launches a new flow to the same destination discovers different paths than
when embedding probes in the application flow in a significant fraction of
experiments (from 40% to 50% of our experiments in PlanetLab Europe).

1 Introduction

Internet services and applications rely on highly distributed infrastructures to
deliver content. When applications stop working or when their performance
degrades, service providers and more sophisticated users often resort to traceroute to narrow down the likely location of the problem. Traceroute issues probes
with increasing TTL to force routers along the path towards a destination to
issue an ICMP TTL exceeded message back to the source, which iteratively
reveals the IP addresses of routers in the path [4].

Traceroute, however, may fail to reveal the exact path that a given application flow traverses. For example, Luckie et al. [8] have shown that depending
on the traceroute probing method (ICMP, UDP, and TCP) the set of reached

© Springer Nature Switzerland AG 2019
D. Choffnes and M. Barcellos (Eds.): PAM 2019, LNCS 11419, pp. 116–128, 2019.
https://doi.org/10.1007/978-3-030-15986-3_8

destinations and discovered links differ. The authors explain these differences by the presence of middleboxes in the path such as load balancers and firewalls that make forwarding decisions based on flow characteristics. These results imply that diagnosing issues on application flows must ensure that traceroute probes have the same characteristics as the application's packets.

This paper develops a traceroute tool, called *Service traceroute*, to allow discovering the paths of individual application flows. Service traceroute passively listens to application traffic to then issue probes that pretend to be part of the application flow. Some traceroute tools (for instance, paratrace [6], TCP sidecar [13], and 0trace [5]) already enable probes to piggyback on TCP connections. These tools observe an active TCP connection to then insert traceroute probes that resemble retransmitted packets. TCP sidecar was developed for topology mapping, whereas paratrace and 0trace for tracing past a firewall. As such, they lack the support for tracing paths of modern application sessions, which fetch content over multiple flows that change dynamically over time. First, these tools provide no means to identify the set of application flows to trace. They require as input the destination IP address and the destination port to detect the target application flow. Second, they trace one target application flow at a time. Finally, these tools lack the support for tracing application flows using UDP as transport protocol, which are increasing thanks to the adoption of QUIC protocol [7].

Our work makes the following contributions. First, we develop and implement Service traceroute (Sect. 2), which we release as open source software. Service traceroute is capable of identifying application flows to probe and of tracing the paths of multiple concurrent flows of both TCP and UDP flows. For example, a user may simply specify trace 'Youtube' and Service traceroute will identify Youtube flows and then trace all of their paths. Service traceroute is configurable to cover a large variety of Internet services.

Our second contribution is to conduct the first thorough evaluation of the effect of embedding tracetoute probes within application flows. One issue with this approach is that we may hurt application performance. Our evaluation shows that in the vast majority of cases, Service traceroute has no side-effect on the target application (Sect. 4). Finally, we compare Service traceroute with 0Trace, which also embeds probes within a target application flow, and with Paris Traceroute, which launches a new flow for probing (Sect. 5). Our comparison with Paris traceroute shows that when we launch a new flow with traceroute probes we observe a different path in around 40% to 50% of paths depending on the application. This difference reduces considerably for the majority of applications when we run Paris traceroute with the same flow ID as the target application flow, which shows that differences are mostly due to middleboxes that make forwarding decisions per flow. These results highlight the need for Service traceroute, which automatically identifies the flow IDs of the target application to create probes.

2   Tool Design and Implementation

Service traceroute follows the same high-level logic as paratrace or 0trace. Given a *target application flow*, which we define as the application flow whose path we aim to trace, Service traceroute proceeds with two main phases. The first phase is the passive observation of a target application flow to define the content of the probes. Then, the second phase involves active injection of TTL-limited probes within the application flow. The main difference is that Service traceroute identifies the flows to trace automatically and supports tracing paths traversed by multiple application flows concurrently. The user can either directly specify the set of target application flows or simply describe a high-level service (e.g., Youtube). Service traceroute will then trace paths traversed by all the flows related to the target service. This section first describes the two phases focusing on the new aspects of Service traceroute to allow per service tracing and then presents our implementation. Library and command-line versions of Service traceroute, together with the scripts to perform data analysis are available as open source projects [1].

2.1   Observation of Target Application Flow

Service traceroute passively observes traffic traversing a network interface to search for packets with the flow-id of the target application flows.[1] Service traceroute takes a set of target application flows as input, in contrast with previous tools which can only trace the path traversed by one single application flow. Users can either explicitly specify one or more target application flows or they can simply specify a service. Service traceroute uses a database of signatures of known services to inspect DNS packets in real-time and identify flows that match the target service. We release the DB as open source, so users can contribute to add or update the signatures in the database [1]. We define as signature the set of domains and IP addresses corresponding to a specific service. For instance, 'google.com' or the corresponding IP addresses can be used in the signature to detect Google services. Our current database has signatures for popular video streaming services such as Netflix, Youtube, and Twitch. We identify web flows simply from the domain or the host name given as input. For additional flexibility, it is possible to add domains and IP addresses via command line parameters or through the library API.

2.2   Path Tracing

Only once it identifies a packet belonging to the target application flow, Service traceroute will start the tracing phase. This phase works as classic traceroute implementations sending probes with increasing TTL, but Service traceroute creates a probe that takes the form of an empty TCP acknowledgement that

---

[1] We use the traditional 5-tuple definition of a flow (protocol, source and destination IP, as well as source and destination port).

copies the 5-tuple of the flow as well as its sequence number and acknowledgement number (similar to paratrace and 0trace). We rely on the flow-id plus the IPID field to match issued probes with the corresponding ICMP responses. We note that this is sufficient to correctly identify probes even when tracing multiple concurrent target application flows. The maximum number of concurrent target application flows varies based on the used configuration as the IPID field is dynamically sliced based on the number of probes that have to be generated. For example, with traceroute standard parameters, i.e. maximum distance of 32 and 3 packets per hop, Service traceroute can trace paths of more than 600 target application flows in parallel.

Service traceroute stops tracing when the target application flow closes to avoid any issues with middleboxes (which may interpret probes after the end of the connection as an attack) and also to reduce any network and server overhead. In contrast to prior tools that only support TCP, we add support for UDP. In this case, we create probes with empty UDP payload, but with the same 5-tuple flow-id as the target application flow. Given UDP has no explicit signal of the end of the flow (like the FIN in TCP), we stop tracing if the flow produces no further packets (either received or sent) after a configurable time interval.

2.3   Implementation

We implement Service traceroute in *Go* and release command-line and library versions. The command-line version is useful for ad-hoc diagnosis, whereas the library allows easy integration within monitoring systems. The library version of Service traceroute outputs a json data structure that contains the discovered interfaces with the observed round-trip-time values. For the command line version, Service traceroute shows the results of each trace in the traceroute format, i.e., the list of hops with the corresponding round-trip times.

Service traceroute is configurable to adapt to different applications. It includes three types of probing algorithms that capture the tradeoff between tracing speed and network overhead. *PacketByPacket* sends only one probe at a time. *HopByHop* sends a configurable number of probes with the same TTL at a time (3 by default). *Concurrent* sends all probes to all hops at once. Given that Service traceroute requires the target application flow to be active during tracing, some applications with short flows (e.g., Web) require the higher overhead of Concurrent to complete all the probes within the flow duration. Service traceroute also allows configuring the number of probes for each TTL, the inter-probe time, and inter-iteration time (i.e., the time between packets with different TTL) to further control the tradeoff between tracing speed and overhead. Finally, Service traceroute allows to specify three types of stop conditions: the maximum distance from the source, the maximum number of non-replying hops, like Paris Traceroute, or explicit stop points in the form of IP addresses. The stop condition is particularly important for Service traceroute because the destination host will never respond with an ICMP error message as probes are part of the target application flow.

Following extensive calibration tests (reported in Sect. 3), we set Service traceroute to use as default the *Concurrent* mode, together with a maximum distance of 32 and 3 probes per hop.

3 Evaluation Method

We design our evaluation around two questions. First, *does Service traceroute affect the target application flows?* Service traceroute injects new packets within the application flow. Although the majority of these packets will be discarded before they reach the servers, a few probe packets will reach the end-host and can potentially affect the target application flows. Second, *do paths discovered with Service traceroute differ from those discovered by other traceroute methods?* One assumption of our work is that paths taken by classic traceroute probes may not follow the same paths as the packets of the target application flows. We present a preliminary evaluation to help answer these questions, where we use Service traceroute to trace paths of target application flows corresponding to the two most popular Internet services: Web and video. We compare our results with that of Paris traceroute [2] and 0Trace [5].

Web. We select the top-1000 Alexa webpages on April 14 2018 as target web flows.

Video. We focus on two popular video streaming services: Twitch and YouTube. We select Twitch videos on their homepage where Twitch shows dynamically a popular live streaming video. While for YouTube, we select 20 random videos from the catalogue obtained after arbitrarily searching with the keyword "4K UHD". With YouTube, we evaluate both TCP and QUIC.

Calibration. We run extensive experiments to calibrate Service traceroute for these two applications varying the probing algorithm and the number of probes per hops [9]. Our results (not shown for conciseness) indicate that the best settings to maximize the fraction of completed traceroutes while minimizing the probing overhead is different for video and Web. For video, we use the HopByHop probing algorithm with a timeout of 2 seconds to wait for ICMP replies, whereas for web we use the Concurrent probing algorithm. For both, we set the maximum distance to 32 and the number of probes per hop to 3.

Comparison with Paris Traceroute. We select Paris traceroute because its Multipath Detection Algorithm (MDA) [16] can discover with high probability all paths between the source and the destination in case there is a load balancer in the path. This allows us to disambiguate whether the differences we may encounter between Paris traceroute and Service traceroute are because of load balancing or some other type of differential treatment. We evaluate four versions of Paris traceroute with MDA enabled using the three protocols ICMP, UDP, and TCP as well as Paris traceroute to trace a single path with the same 5-tuple as the target application flow.

Comparison with 0Trace. We select 0Trace as it implements the idea of embedding probes in a target application flow and it has a working implementation.[2] 0Trace, however, requires as input the flow to probe, which is hard to know in advance. We used Service traceroute's DNS resolution to detect the flow to probe and then launch 0Trace. Unfortunately, the download time for web pages is extremely short and our script was too slow to detect the target application flows and then run 0Trace. Hence, for this comparison we focus only on Twitch and Youtube. This experience illustrates the challenge of running 0Trace in practice and highlights the importance of integrating flow identification in Service traceroute.

Experiment Setup. We run our tests during 30 days in July 2018 from 27 PlanetLab nodes in Europe.[3] Experiments for video and Web are similar. We first launch Service traceroute, then we start streaming a video or downloading a webpage, once that is done we run the four versions of Paris traceroute and 0Trace back-to-back. Then, we stream again the same video or download the same webpage without Service traceroute. We have run a total of 459 videos, 153 for Twitch and 306 equally split between YouTube with TCP and with QUIC, and 1000 Web experiments. All datasets collected in our experiments are available [1].

Data Representativeness. Webpages in the Alexa top-1000 list are often hosted on CDNs [12]. This choice guarantees that we cover the large majority of locations hosting web content (i.e., all major CDN providers), but we may fail to capture the behavior of smaller webpages. Another bias comes from our choice of PlanetLab nodes as it is well known that they are mostly connected via academic networks [3,14] and hence may fail to capture the behavior of commercial ISPs. Even with these limitations, our European-scale evaluation is useful to determine whether or not Service traceroute affects the application flows of popular services (top-1000 Alexa as well as Twitch/Youtube). It is also useful to shed some light on whether there are differences between paths discovered with Service traceroute and more traditional traceroute paths. The generalization of these results to vantage points located in other areas of the Internet and to other services would require larger scale experiments.

4   Side Effects of Service Traceroute

This section evaluates whether Service traceroute affects target application flows. Firewalls or servers may mistakenly interpret too many duplicated packets within a flow as an attack or losses, which in turn may cause application flows to be

---

[2] To make 0Trace work on PlanetLab nodes, we had to replace the library to issue probes from dnet to scapy.

[3] Service traceroute failed to run on PlanetLab US nodes due to compatibility issues. PlanetLab US nodes use an old Linux distribution (Fedora 2), which lacks many required tools and libraries necessary to run our program.

blocked or achieve lower throughput. Although the idea of piggybacking tracer-oute probes within application flows has been around for approximately a decade, there has been no prior evaluation of whether it can hurt target application flows. TCP sidecar evaluates the intrusiveness of their method, but only by measuring the number of abuse reports [13].

4.1 Metrics

We select different metrics to measure properties of target application flows. *Flow duration* refers to the time between the first and the last packet of a flow. For TCP, we measure the time from the server SYN to the first FIN or RST. For UDP, we measure the time from the first and the last packet coming from the server. We compute the *average throughput* of a target application flow as the total application bytes divided by the flow duration. In addition to these metrics, which we can compute for both TCP and UDP flows, we have three other TCP specific metrics: the *number of resets*, which capture the number of target application flows closed by resets; *window size* is the difference between the minimum and the maximum TCP window size of the server for an application flow; and the *number of retransmissions* is the number of retransmission from the server per application flow.

4.2 Aborted Flows

We first study whether Service traceroute causes flows to be aborted. We have seen no video sessions that ended with resets in our experiments. Even though our analysis is only from PlanetLab vantage points in Europe, we believe that this result will hold more generally for both Twitch and Youtube as these type of large video providers deploy multiple versions of the same software across servers/caches [10, 17]. Any differences will depend on middleboxes placed either close to the clients or in the path towards the service. Our results for webpage downloads are also encouraging, we see no aborted flows. In some preliminary experiments we observe resets for three of the top-1000 websites only with Service traceroute. Our manual analysis suggests that either some firewall close to the website or the web server itself is resetting the flows due to the duplicate packets.

4.3 Flow Performance

We next evaluate whether Service traceroute affects flow performance. Figure 1 presents the cumulative distribution function of the flow duration in seconds with and without Service traceroute. We present eight curves: two for video sessions over TCP both for Twitch and Youtube, two for Youtube sessions over UDP, and two for all web page downloads. We see that the distributions with and without Service traceroute are mostly the same. Similarly, our analysis (omitted due to space constraints) shows that the distributions of average throughput, TCP window size, and retransmissions are similar with and without Service traceroute. We conclude that Service traceroute has no effect on the performance of target application flows.

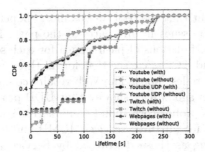

Fig. 1. Flow duration of target application flows with and without Service traceroute

5   Comparison with Traceroute Tools

The key motivation for building Service traceroute is that we must send probes within the target application flow to discover its path. Although Luckie et al. [8] have observed different paths depending on the traceroute method (UDP, ICMP, or TCP), no prior work has studied how often piggybacking traceroute probes within application flows will discover different paths. This section compares Service traceroute with different traceroute probing methods using Paris traceroute, which discover all paths between a source and destination in the presence of load balancing, and 0Trace, which also piggybacks probes inside an application flow.

5.1   Metrics

We select two metrics to compare the discovered paths. The *path length* captures the distance from the source to the last hop that replies to probes. For Paris traceroute, we take the length of the longest path in case of multiple paths. The *path edit distance* captures the edit distance between the path discovered with Service traceroute and that discovered with another traceroute (0Trace or Paris traceroute). The edit distance is the minimum number of operations (insertion, deletion, and substitution) needed to transform one string (in our case, one path) into the other. In case Paris traceroute returns multiple paths, we select the one with the smallest edit distance. This allows us to focus on the best case. We treat empty hops (marked with a ∗) as any other character. When we observe differences between paths, we analyze where the differences are in the path: origin AS, middle of the path, or destination AS. We map IPs to ASes using the RIPEstat Data API [11]. The location where the two paths diverge help us understand the placement of middleboxes.

5.2   Path Lengths

We study the length of paths discovered with Service traceroute, Paris traceroute MDA (TCP, ICMP, and UDP), and 0Trace. The comparison of path lengths helps capture which versions of traceroute discover more hops. For application diagnosis it is important that the tool reveals most (hopefully all) of the path, so that we can identify issues in any parts of the path. Figure 2 presents the cumulative distribution functions of path length for each service: Web, Twitch, and Youtube (UDP and TCP). We see that for all three services, probing with TCP and UDP discovers less hops. The Web results confirm Luckie et al. [8]'s analysis from ten years ago, which showed that UDP probes cannot reach the top Alexa web sites as probes correspond to no active flow. Service traceroute discovers longer paths for all three services. ICMP and 0Trace discover paths that are almost as long as those discovered by Service traceroute. The next sections characterize the path edit distance and the location of path differences to shed light on the causes of the differences we observe in path length.

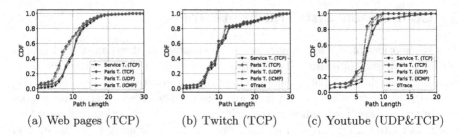

(a) Web pages (TCP)   (b) Twitch (TCP)   (c) Youtube (UDP&TCP)

Fig. 2. Length of paths discovered with different versions of traceroute.

5.3   Path Differences When Tracing with Different Flow IDs

This section studies the differences in paths discovered by Service traceroute versus by other traceroutes in the most typical case, i.e., when traceroute starts a new flow and picks the port numbers with no knowledge of the target application flow ID. We compare with Paris traceroute MDA using TCP, UDP, and ICMP.

Figure 3 presents the cumulative distribution functions of path edit distance between Service traceroute and Paris traceroute for Web, Twitch, and Youtube (UDP and TCP). A path edit distance of zero corresponds to the case when the Paris traceroute output contains the path discovered by Service traceroute. We see that even though we select the closest path in Paris traceroute's output to compute the edit distance, the path discovered with Service traceroute only matches that discovered by Paris traceroute MDA in about 55% of the web-page downloads, 50% of the Twitch sessions, and almost 75% of the Youtube streaming sessions. When paths discovered by Service traceroute differ from paths discovered by Paris traceroute, the edit distance is relatively high as the vast majority of paths towards these services is less than 15 hops long. In general, Twitch has longer paths (up to 30 hops) and Youtube shorter (up to 20 hops), which explains the differences in the values of edit distance we observe. For Twitch, UDP discovers paths that are the most similar to Service traceroute's paths, whereas for both Web and Youtube, ICMP leads to the most similar paths.

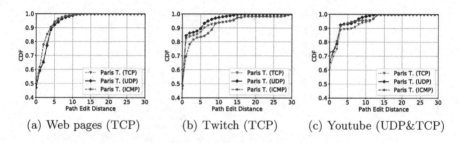

(a) Web pages (TCP)   (b) Twitch (TCP)   (c) Youtube (UDP&TCP)

Fig. 3. Path edit distance between Service traceroute and Paris traceroute.

5.4 Path Differences When Tracing with Same Flow ID as Application

One possible explanation for the differences we observe in the previous section is the fact that the flow ID of Paris traceroute probes is different than the ID of the target application flow, which can trigger different forwarding decisions in middleboxes that act per flow. In this section, we compare Service traceroute's output with Paris traceroute when it uses the same flow ID as the target application flow. Note that in this case Paris traceroute still runs after the target application flow finishes, we get the correct flow ID based on the Service traceroute's run just before in order to guarantee a complete match.

Figure 4 compares the path discovered by Service traceroute with that discovered by Paris traceroute when using the exact same flow ID as the target application flow. In this case, Paris traceroute discovers the same path as Service traceroute more often than when probing with MDA: about 65% of Twitch sessions, 91% of Youtube sessions, and 93% of web downloads. This result shows that issuing probes with a different flow ID than that of the target application flow causes most of the differences we observe in the previous section. The remaining differences are due to three possible causes: (i) path changes that might occur between the runs of Service traceroute and Paris traceroute; (ii) per-packet load balancing; or (iii) middleboxes (such as application-layer proxies or firewalls) that track the state of TCP connections and may hence drop packets after connections are terminated. In fact, in our initial testing we noticed cases of probes not generating any ICMP response if issued after the target application flow finishes. We further examine the paths for Twitch to shed light on the reasons for the large fraction of paths that are different between Paris traceroute and Service traceroute. It is unlikely to have routing changes for about 45% of paths and we verified that there are no middleboxes dropping our probes (which would appear as stars). Thus, we conjecture that the differences are likely due to per-packet load balancing, but we must run further experiments to verify this conjecture.

We also compare Service traceroute with 0Trace. Unfortunately, due to how web browsers loop across a large number of different ports, both Twitch and Youtube often change port numbers between consecutive runs. Given that we launch a new video session to probe with 0Trace, the result is that Service

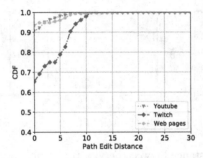

Fig. 4. Path edit distance between Service traceroute and Paris traceroute using the same flow ID.

traceroute and 0Trace often issue probes with different flow IDs. This issue biases our experiments, and hence we omit these results (available at [9]).

5.5 Location of Path Divergence Points

To help explain our results we study the location of the points where Service traceroute's and Paris traceroute's paths diverge, which we call the *divergence point*. Table 1 shows the fraction of experiments with divergence points at the origin AS, the middle of the path, and the destination AS. We conduct this analysis to help explain the results in the previous sections, but we note that the findings are heavily biased by our vantage points and destinations.

Table 1. Location of divergence points [% of all flows]

Configuration	Web pages (TCP)			Twitch (TCP)			Youtube (TCP and UDP)		
	Origin	Middle	Dest.	Origin	Middle	Dest.	Origin	Middle	Dest.
MDA UDP	7.33	39.82	4.92	0.41	50.56	0.64	12.49	19.52	3.15
MDA TCP	15.13	34.37	2.86	4.28	49.17	0.51	15.67	19.13	3.92
MDA ICMP	9.11	19.04	17.44	7.35	44.50	1.99	6.81	19.95	1.55
PT same flow ID	4.06	1.81	1.03	8.43	24.72	2.18	4.08	0.87	4.61

For the three applications, when comparing with MDA most of the divergence points are in the middle (from 19% for Youtube to above 40% for Twitch). Given the middle contains more hops it is not too surprising that it also contains more divergence points. When using Paris traceroute with the same flow ID, however, the percentage of divergence points in the middle decreases substantially to less than 2% for Web and Youtube and to 24% for Twitch. This result indicates that divergence points in the middle mostly correspond to middleboxes that perform per-flow forwarding. Paris traceroute's MDA discovers all possible interfaces for every hop of the path and we compare the closest path MDA finds to Service traceroute's output, but MDA often uses different flow IDs than the target application flow and hence it may not get the exact same sequence of hops end-to-end. For Paris traceroute with the same flow ID, we observe more divergence points at the origin, which may indicate path changes. The only exception is Twitch, which still has around 24% of divergence points in the middle. Our analysis of these divergence points shows that half of them are within a single ISP: GTT Communications (AS 3257).

6   Related Work

Since Jacobson's original traceroute tool [4], a number of new versions have emerged with different features and with new methods for constructing probes (e.g., Paris traceroute [2,16] and tcptraceroute [15]). All these traceroute versions have a drawback for the goal of diagnosing a target application flow because they start a new flow to send probes. As such, middleboxes may treat them differently than the target application flow. Service traceroute avoids this issue by piggybacking traceroute probes within active application flows. This idea was first introduced in paratrace [6], which is no longer available, and then re-implemented in 0trace [5] with the goal of tracing through firewalls and in TCP sidecar [13] for reducing complaints of large-scale traceroute probing for topology mapping. Unfortunately, none of these tools is actively maintained. Service traceroute adds the capability of automatically identifying application flows to trace by a domain name, of tracing UDP flows as well as of tracing multiple concurrent flows that compose a service. We release both a command-line and a library version as open source. Furthermore, we present an evaluation of the side-effects of piggybacking traceroute probes within application traffic as well as of its benefit by comparing the differences with Paris traceroute and with 0Trace. Our characterization reappraises some of the findings from Luckie et al. [8], which show that the discovered paths depend on the protocol used in the probes. Their study, however, includes no traceroute tools that piggyback on application flows.

7   Conclusion

In this paper we present Service traceroute, a tool to trace paths of flows of modern Internet services by piggybacking TTL-limited probes within target application flows. Our evaluation of paths to popular websites and video services from PlanetLab Europe shows that Service traceroute's probing has no effect on target application flows. Moreover, a typical traceroute tool that launches a new flow to the same destination discovers different paths than when embedding probes in the application flow in a significant fraction of experiments (from 40% to 50% of our experiments) as our comparison with Paris traceroute shows. When we set Paris traceroute's flow ID to that of the target application flow, the resulting paths are more similar to Service traceroute's. Identifying the flow ID to probe, however, is not trivial. Modern applications rely on a large pool of servers/ports.

Even to run 0Trace, which implements the same idea of piggybacking probes in the application flow, we had to rely on Service traceroute's functionality to identify target application flow IDs to probe. In future work, we plan to add the support of IPv6 to Service traceroute. We further plan to perform a larger scale characterization of results of Service traceroute across a wide variety of services and a larger set of globally distributed vantage points.

Acknowledgements. This work was supported by the ANR Project N^o ANR-15-CE25-0013-01 (BottleNet), a Google Faculty Research Award, and Inria through the IPL BetterNet and the associate team HOMENET.

References

1. Service Traceroute. https://github.com/inria-muse/service-traceroute
2. Augustin, B., et al.: Avoiding traceroute anomalies with Paris traceroute. In: Proceedings of IMC (2006)
3. Banerjee, S., Griffin, T.G., Pias, M.: The interdomain connectivity of PlanetLab nodes. In: Barakat, C., Pratt, I. (eds.) PAM 2004. LNCS, vol. 3015, pp. 73–82. Springer, Heidelberg (2004). https://doi.org/10.1007/978-3-540-24668-8_8
4. Jacobson, V.: Traceroute, February 1989
5. Edge, J.: Tracing behind the firewall (2007). https://lwn.net/Articles/217076/
6. Kaminsky, D.: Parasitic Traceroute via Established TCP Flows & IPID Hopcount. https://man.cx/paratrace
7. Langley, A., et al.: The QUIC transport protocol: design and internet-scale deployment. In: Proceedings of the Conference of the ACM Special Interest Group on Data Communication, pp. 183–196. ACM (2017)
8. Luckie, M., Hyun, Y., Huffaker, B.: Traceroute probe method and forward IP path inference. In: Proceedings of IMC, Vouliagmeni, Greece (2008)
9. Morandi, I.: Service traceroute: tracing paths of application flows. Master thesis, UPMC-Paris 6 Sorbonne Universités (2018). https://hal.inria.fr/hal-01888618
10. Netflix Open Connect Overview. https://openconnect.netflix.com/Open-Connect-Overview.pdf
11. RIPEstat Data API. https://stat.ripe.net/docs/data_api
12. Scheitle, Q., et al.: A long way to the top: significance, structure, and stability of internet top lists. arXiv preprint arXiv:1805.11506 (2018)
13. Sherwood, R., Spring, N.: Touring the internet in a TCP sidecar. In: Proceedings of the 6th ACM SIGCOMM Conference on Internet Measurement, pp. 339–344. ACM (2006)
14. Spring, N., Peterson, L., Bavier, A., Pai, V.: Using Planetlab for network research: myths, realities, and best practices. ACM SIGOPS Oper. Syst. Rev. **40**(1), 17–24 (2006)
15. Torren, M.: Tcptraceroute-a traceroute implementation using TCP packets. Man page, UNIX (2001). http://michael.toren.net/code/tcptraceroute
16. Veitch, D., Augustin, B., Friedman, T., Teixeira, R.: Failure control in multipath route tracing. In: Proceedings of IEEE INFOCOM (2009)
17. Google Cloud Overview. https://cloud.google.com/cdn/docs/overview

Mapping an Enterprise Network
by Analyzing DNS Traffic

Minzhao Lyu[1,2(✉)], Hassan Habibi Gharakheili[1], Craig Russell[2],
and Vijay Sivaraman[1]

[1] University of New South Wales, Sydney, Australia
{minzhao.lyu,h.habibi,vijay}@unsw.edu.au
[2] Data61, CSIRO, Sydney, Australia
craig.russell@data61.csiro.au

Abstract. Enterprise networks are becoming more complex and dynamic, making it a challenge for network administrators to fully track what is potentially exposed to cyber attack. We develop an automated method to identify and classify organizational assets via analysis of just 0.1% of the enterprise traffic volume, specifically corresponding to DNS packets. We analyze live, real-time streams of DNS traffic from two organizations (a large University and a mid-sized Government Research Institute) to: (a) highlight how DNS query and response patterns differ between recursive resolvers, authoritative name servers, web-servers, and regular clients; (b) identify key attributes that can be extracted efficiently in real-time; and (c) develop an unsupervised machine learning model that can classify enterprise assets. Application of our method to the 10 Gbps live traffic streams from the two organizations yielded results that were verified by the respective IT departments, while also revealing new knowledge, attesting to the value provided by our automated system for mapping and tracking enterprise assets.

Keywords: Enterprise network · DNS analysis · Machine learning

1 Introduction

Enterprise networks are not only large in size with many thousands of connected devices, but also dynamic in nature as hosts come and go, web-servers get commissioned and decommissioned, and DNS resolvers and name servers get added and removed, to adapt to the organization's changing needs. Enterprise IT departments track such assets manually today, with records maintained in spreadsheets and configuration files (DHCP, DNS, Firewalls, etc.) – this is not only cumbersome, but also error prone and almost impossible to keep up-to-date. It is therefore not surprising that many enterprise network administrators are not fully aware of their internal assets [12], and consequently do not know the attack surface they expose to the outside world.

The problem is even more acute in university and research institute campus networks for several reasons [6]: (a) they host a wide variety of sensitive and lucrative data including intellectual property, cutting-edge research datasets, social

© Springer Nature Switzerland AG 2019
D. Choffnes and M. Barcellos (Eds.): PAM 2019, LNCS 11419, pp. 129–144, 2019.
https://doi.org/10.1007/978-3-030-15986-3_9

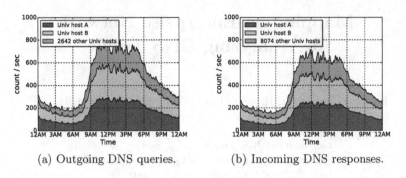

(a) Outgoing DNS queries.   (b) Incoming DNS responses.

Fig. 1. University campus: outgoing queries and incoming responses, measured on 3 May 2018. (Color figure online)

security numbers, and financial information; (b) their open-access culture, decentralized departmental-level control, as well as federated access to data makes them particularly vulnerable targets for unauthorized access, unsafe Internet usage, and malware; and (c) they typically have high-speed network infrastructure that makes them an attractive target for volumetric reflection attacks.

Our aim in this paper is to develop an automated method to map internal hosts of an enterprise network by focusing only on DNS traffic which: (a) is a key signaling protocol that carries a wealth of information yet bypasses firewalls easily; (b) constitutes a tiny faction of total network traffic by volume (less than 0.1% from our measurements in two networks); and (c) is easy to capture with only a couple of flow entries (i.e mirroring UDP packets to/from port 53) in an Openflow-based SDN switch. By capturing and analyzing DNS traffic in/out of the organization, we dynamically and continually identify the DNS resolvers, DNS name-servers, (non-DNS) public-facing servers, and regular client hosts behind or not behind the NAT in the enterprise. This can let network administrators corroborate changes in host roles in their network, and also equip them with information to configure appropriate security postures for their assets, such as to protect DNS resolvers from unsolicited responses, authoritative name servers from amplification requests, and web-servers from volumetric DNS reflection attacks.

Our specific contributions are as follows. We analyze real-time live streams of DNS traffic from two organizations (a large University and a mid-sized Government Research Institute) to: (a) highlight how DNS query and response patterns differ amongst recursive resolvers, authoritative name servers, and regular hosts; (b) identify key DNS traffic attributes that can be extracted efficiently in real-time; and (c) develop an unsupervised machine learning model that can classify enterprise assets. Application of our method to the traffic streams from the two organizations yielded results that were verified by the respective IT departments while revealing new information, such as unsecured name servers that were being used by external entities to amplify DoS attacks.

2   Profiling Enterprise Hosts

In this section, we analyze the characteristics of DNS traffic collected from the border of two enterprise networks, a large University campus (*i.e.,* UNSW) and a medium-size research institute (*i.e.,* CSIRO). In both instances, the IT department of the enterprise provisioned a full mirror (both inbound and outbound) of their Internet traffic (each on a 10 Gbps interface) to our data collection system from their border routers (**outside** of the firewall), and we obtained appropriate ethics clearances for this study[1]. We extracted DNS packets from each of enterprise Internet traffic streams in real-time by configuring rules for incoming/outgoing IPv4 UDP packets for port 53 on an SDN switch (extension to IPv6 DNS packets is left for future work). The study in this paper considers the data collected over a one week period of 3–9 May 2018.

2.1   DNS Behavior of Enterprise Hosts

Enterprises typically operate two types of DNS servers: (a) **recursive resolvers** are those that act on behalf of end-hosts to resolve the network address of a URL and return the answer to the requesting end-host (recursive resolvers commonly keep a copy of positive responses in a local cache for time-to-live of the record to reduce frequent recursion), and (b) **authoritative servers** of a domain/zone are those that receive queries from anywhere on the Internet for the network address of a sub-domain within the zone for which they are authoritative (*e.g.,* organizationXYZ.net).

In order to better understand the DNS behavior of various hosts (and their role) inside an enterprise network, we divide the DNS dataset into two categories: (a) DNS queries from enterprise hosts that leave the network towards a server on the Internet along with DNS responses that enter the network, (b) DNS queries from external hosts that enter the network towards an enterprise host along with DNS responses that leave the network.

This analysis helps us identify important attributes related to host DNS behavior, characterizing its type/function including authoritative name server, recursive resolver, generic public-facing server (e.g web/VPN servers), or end-host inside the enterprise that may not always be fully visible to the network operators. This also enables us to capture the normal pattern of DNS activity for various hosts.

Outgoing Queries and Incoming Responses. Figure 1 shows a time trace of DNS outgoing queries and incoming responses for the university campus[2], with a moving average over 1-minute intervals on a typical weekday. The university network handles on average 353 outgoing queries and 308 incoming responses per

---

[1] UNSW Human Research Ethics Advisory Panel approval number HC17499, and CSIRO Data61 Ethics approval number 115/17.

[2] We omit plots for *the research institute* in this section due to space constraint, they are shown in Appendix 1.

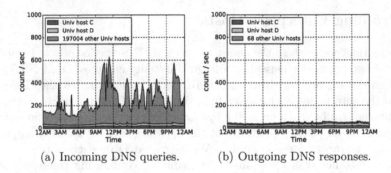

(a) Incoming DNS queries.   (b) Outgoing DNS responses.

Fig. 2. University campus: incoming queries and outgoing responses, measured on 3 May 2018. (Color figure online)

second. By checking the transaction ID of queries and responses, we found that 17.28% of outgoing queries are "unanswered" (*i.e.*, 5.26M out of 30.46M) on 3 May 2018. It is also important to note that 5.24% of incoming responses to the university campus network (*i.e.*, 1.39M out of 26.59M) are "unsolicited" on the same day[3]. A similar pattern with lower number of outgoing queries and incoming responses (*i.e.*, average of 107 and 80 per second respectively) is observed in the research institute network. This network experiences approximately double the amount of unanswered queries (*i.e.*, 34.14%) and unsolicited responses (*i.e.*, 12.15%) compared to the university network.

Query per Host: We now consider individual hosts in each enterprise. Unsurprisingly, the majority of outgoing DNS queries are generated by only two hosts A and B in both networks, *i.e.*, 68% of the total in the university campus (shown by blue and yellow shades in Fig. 1(a)) and 82% of the total in the research institute – these hosts are also the major recipients of incoming DNS responses from the Internet. We have verified with the respective IT departments of the two enterprises that both hosts are the primary recursive resolvers of their organizations.

In addition to these recursive resolvers, we observe a number of hosts in both organizations, shown by red shades in Fig. 1(a), that generate DNS queries to outside of the enterprise network. The 2,642 other Univ hosts in Fig. 1(a) are either: end-hosts configured to use public DNS resolvers that make direct queries out of the enterprise network, or secondary recursive servers operating in smaller sub-networks at department-level. We found that 286 of these 2,642 University hosts actively send queries (at least once every hour) over the day and contact more than 10 Internet-based DNS servers (resolvers or name-servers). These 286 hosts display the behavior of recursive resolvers but with fairly low throughput, thus we deem them secondary resolvers. The remaining 2,356 hosts are only active for a limited interval (*i.e.*, between 5 min to 10 h) and contact a small

---

[3] We acknowledge that some DNS packets could have been dropped by the switches on which the span-port was configured, especially during periods of overload.

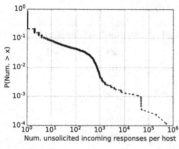
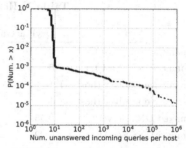

(a) Unsolicited incoming responses.   (b) Unanswered incoming queries.

Fig. 3. University campus: CCDF of (a) unsolicited incoming responses and (b) unanswered incoming queries per host, measured on 3 May 2018.

number of public resolvers (*e.g.*, 8.8.8.8 or 8.8.4.4 of Google) over the day. We found that 15 of 340 hosts in the research institute display behavior of secondary resolvers.

Response per Host: Considering incoming responses (Fig. 1(b) for the university network), a larger number of "other" hosts in both organizations are observed – approximately 8 K hosts in the University and 5.8 K hosts in the research institute. Most of these "other" hosts (*i.e.*, 67%) are the destinations of unsolicited responses. To better understand the focus target of these potentially malicious responses, we analyze unsolicited incoming responses for the two enterprises. Figure 3(a) shows the CCDF of total unsolicited incoming responses per each host over a day for the university campus. Interestingly, the primary recursive resolvers in both organizations are top targets: (a) in the University campus, hosts A and B respectively are the destinations of 522 K and 201 K unsolicited incoming responses (*i.e.*, together receive 52% of total unsolicited DNS responses), and (b) in the research institute, hosts A and B respectively are the destination of 435 K and 135 K unsolicited incoming responses (*i.e.*, together receive 69% of total unsolicited DNS responses).

Incoming DNS Queries. Enterprises commonly receive DNS queries from the Internet that are addressed to their authoritative name servers.

It can be seen that two hosts of the University campus (*i.e.*, hosts C and D in Fig. 2) and one host (we name it Host C) of the research institute are the dominant contributors to outgoing DNS responses – we have verified (by reverse lookup) that these hosts are indeed the name servers of their respective organizations. Interestingly, for both organizations we observe that a large number of hosts (*i.e.*, 197K hosts of the University campus and 244K hosts of the research institute (shown by red shades in Fig. 2(a) for the university network) receive queries from the Internet, but a significant majority of them are unanswered (*i.e.*, 82.18% and 62.09% respectively) – these hosts are supposed to neither receive

Table 1. Host attributes.

	QryFracOut	numExtSrv	numExtClient	actvTimeFrac
Univ name server (host C)	0	0	0.29	0
Rsch name server (host C)	0	0	0.61	0
Univ recursive resolver (host A)	1	0.26	0	1
Rsch recursive resolver (host A)	1	0.49	0	1
Univ mixed DNS Server	0.55	0.03	0.06	1
Rsch mixed DNS Server	0.29	0.0008	0.0018	1
Univ end-host	1	0.00002	0	0.375
Rsch end-host	1	0.00003	0	0.25

nor respond to incoming DNS queries, highlighting the amount of unwanted DNS traffic that targets enterprise hosts for scanning or DoS purposes.

To better understand the target of these potentially malicious queries, we analyze unanswered incoming queries over a day for the two enterprises. Figure 3(b) is the CCDF of total incoming unanswered queries per each host for the university campus. It is seen that two hosts of the university campus receive more than a million DNS queries over a day from the Internet with no response sent back, whereas one host in the research institute has the similar behaviour. By reverse lookup, we found that the University hosts are a DHCP server and a web server that respectively received 9.4M and 4.4M unanswered queries (together contributing to 72% of red shaded area in Fig. 2(a)).

Furthermore, we analyzed the question section of unanswered incoming queries that originated from a distributed set of IP addresses. Surprisingly, in the University dataset we found that 72% of domains queried were irrelevant to its zone (e.g., 47% for "nist.gov", 5% for "svist21.cz", and even 2% for "google.com"), and in the research institute dataset we found 84% of domains queried were irrelevant to its zone (e.g., 8% for "qq.com", 7% for "google.com", and 5% for "com").

Considering outgoing responses (shown in Fig. 2(b) for the university network), there are 68 hosts in the campus network (shown by the red shade) and 21 hosts in the research network that respond to incoming DNS queries in addition to name servers (i.e., hosts C and D). We have verified (by reverse lookup) that all hosts that generate "no Error" responses are authoritative for sub-domains of their organization zone. We also note that some hosts that reply with "Refused", "Name Error" and "Server Failure" flags to some irrelevant queries (e.g., com) – these are secondary name servers.

2.2   Attributes

Following the insights obtained from DNS behavior of various hosts, we now identify attributes that help to automatically (a) map a given host to its function, including authoritative name server, recursive resolver, mixed DNS server (i.e.,

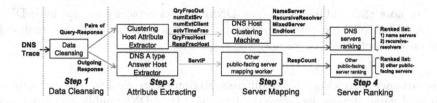

Fig. 4. Automatic classification and ranking of enterprise hosts.

both name server and recursive resolver), a (non-DNS) public-facing server, or a regular client; and (b) rank the importance of servers.

Dataset Cleansing. We first clean our dataset by removing unwanted (or malicious) records including unsolicited responses and unanswered queries. This is done by correlating the transaction ID of responses with the ID of their corresponding queries. In the cleaned dataset, incoming responses are equal in number to outgoing queries, and similarly for the number of incoming queries and outgoing responses.

Functionality Mapping. As discussed in Sect. 2.1, recursive resolvers are very active in terms of queries-out and responses-in, whereas name servers behave the opposite with high volume of queries-in and responses-out. Hence, a host attribute defined by the *query fraction of all outgoing DNS packets* (*QryFraqOut*) should distinguish recursive resolvers from name servers. As shown in Table 1, this attribute has a value close to 1 for recursive resolvers and a value close to 0 for name servers.

In addition to recursive resolvers, there are some end-hosts configured to use public resolvers (*e.g.*, 8.8.8.8 of Google) that have a non-zero fraction of DNS queries out of the enterprise network. We note that these end-hosts ask a limited number of Internet servers during their activity period whereas the recursive resolvers typically communicate with a larger number of external servers. Thus, we define a second attribute as the *fraction of total number of external servers queried (numExtSrv)* per individual enterprise host. As shown in Table 1, the value of this attribute for end-hosts is much smaller than for recursive resolvers. Similarly for incoming queries, we consider a third attribute as the *fraction of total number of external hosts that initiate query in (numExtClient)* per individual enterprise host. Indeed, this attribute has a larger value for name servers compared with other hosts, as shown in Table 1.

Lastly, to better distinguish between end-hosts and recursive resolvers (high and low profile servers), we define a fourth attribute as the *fraction of active hours for outgoing queries (actvTimeFrac)*. Regular clients have a smaller value of this attribute compared with recursive resolvers and mixed DNS servers, as shown in Table 1.

We note that public-facing (non-DNS) servers typically do not have DNS traffic in/out of the enterprise networks. To identify these hosts, we analyzed the answer section of *A-type* outgoing responses.

Importance Ranking. Three different attributes are used to rank the importance of name servers, recursive resolvers, and (non-DNS) public-facing servers respectively. Note that we rank mixed DNS servers within both name servers and recursive resolvers for their mixed DNS behaviour.

For recursive resolvers, we use **QryFracHost** defined as the *fraction of outgoing queries* sent by each host over the cleaned dataset. And for name servers, we use **RespFracHost** as the *fraction of outgoing responses* sent by each host. For other public-facing servers, we use **RespCount** as the *total number of outgoing responses that contain the IP address of a host* – external clients that access public-facing servers obtain the IP address of these hosts by querying the enterprise name servers.

3   Classifying Enterprise Hosts

In this section, we firstly develop a machine learning technique to determine if an enterprise host with a given DNS activity is a "name server", "recursive resolver", "mixed DNS server", or a "regular end-host". We then detect other public-facing (non-DNS) servers by analyzing the answer section of A-type outgoing responses. Finally, we rank the enterprise server assets by their importance.

Our proposed system (shown in Fig. 4) automatically generates lists of active servers into three categories located inside enterprise networks, with the real-time DNS data mirrored from the border switch of enterprise networks. The system first performs *"Data cleansing"* that aggregates DNS data into one-day granularity and removes unsolicited responses and unanswered queries (*i.e.,* step 1); then *"Attribute extraction"* in step 2 computes attributes required by the following algorithms; *"Server mapping"* in step 3 detects DNS servers and other public-facing servers; and finally *"server ranking"* in step 4 ranks their criticality. The output is a classification and a ranked order of criticality, which an IT manager can then use to accordingly adjust security policies.

3.1   Host Clustering Using DNS Attributes

We choose unsupervised clustering algorithms to perform the grouping and classification process because they are a better fit for datasets without ground truth labels but nevertheless exhibit a clear pattern for different groups/clusters.

Selecting Algorithm. We considered 3 common clustering algorithms, namely Hierarchical Clustering (HC), K-means and Expectation-maximization (EM). HC is more suitable for datasets with a large set of attributes and instances that

Table 2. University campus: host clusters (3 May 2018).

	Count	QryFracOut	numExtSrv	numExtClient	actvTimeFrac
Name server	42	0.0057	1e-5	0.02	0.03
Recursive resolver	14	0.99	0.06	0	0.94
Mixed DNS server	14	0.57	0.01	0.02	0.66
End-host	2195	1	2e-5	0	0.31

Table 3. Research institute: host clusters (3 May 2018).

	Count	QryFracOut	numExtSrv	numExtClient	actvTimeFrac
Name server	12	7e-7	5e-6	0.07	0.01
Recursive resolver	4	0.99	0.20	9e-5	1
Mixed DNS server	6	0.21	0.001	0.019	0.625
End-host	249	1	7e-4	0	0.25

have logical hierarchy (*e.g.,* genomic data). In our case however, hosts of enterprise networks do not have a logical hierarchy and the number of attributes are relatively small, therefore HC is not appropriate. K-means clustering algorithms are distance-based unsupervised machine learning techniques. By measuring the distance of attributes from each instance and their centroids, it groups datapoints into a given number of clusters by iterations of moving centroids. In our case there is a significant distance variation of attributes for hosts within each cluster (*e.g.,* highly active name servers or recursive resolvers versus low active ones) which may lead to mis-clustering.

The EM algorithm is a suitable fit in our case since it uses the probability of an instance belonging to a cluster regardless of its absolute distance. It establishes initial centroids using a K-means algorithm, starts with an initial probability distribution following a Gaussian model and iterates to achieve convergence. This mechanism, without using absolute distance during iteration, decreases the chance of biased results due to extreme outliers. Hence, we choose an EM clustering algorithm for *"DNS Host Clustering Machine"*.

Number of Clusters. Choosing the appropriate number of clusters is the key step in clustering algorithms. As discussed earlier, we have chosen four clusters based on our observation of various types of servers. One way to validate the number of clusters is with the "elbow" method. The idea of the elbow method is to run k-means clustering on the dataset for a range of k values (say, k from 1 to 9) that calculates the sum of squared errors (SSE) for each value of k. The error decreases as k increases; this is because as the number of clusters increases, the SSE becomes smaller so the distortion also gets smaller. The goal of the elbow method is to choose an optimal k around which the SSE decreases abruptly (*i.e.,*

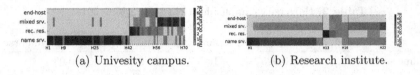

(a) Univesity campus. (b) Research institute.

Fig. 5. Hosts clustering results across one week.

ranging from 3 to 5 in our results, hence, k = 4 clusters seems a reasonable value for both the university and the research institute).

Clustering Results. We tuned the number of iterations and type of covariance for our clustering machine to maximize the performance in both enterprises. Tables 2 and 3 show the number of hosts identified in each cluster based on data from 3 May 2018. We also see the average value of various attributes within each cluster. For the cluster of name servers, *QryFracOut* approaches 0 in both organizations, highlighting the fact that almost all outgoing DNS packets from these hosts are responses rather than queries, which matches with the expected behavior. Having a high number of external clients served also indicates the activity of these hosts – in the University campus and research institute respectively 42 and 12 name servers collectively serve 84% (*i.e.*, 42 × 2% and 12 × 7%) of external hosts.

Considering recursive resolvers in Tables 2 and 3, the average *QryFracOut* is close to 1 for both organizations as expected. It is seen that some of these hosts also answer incoming queries (from external hosts) possibly due to their misconfiguration. However, the number of external clients served by these hosts is very small (*i.e.*, less than 10 per recursive resolver) leading to an average fraction near 0. Also, looking at the number of external servers queried (*i.e.*, *numExtSrv*), the average value of this attribute for recursive resolvers is reasonably high, *i.e.*, 14 and 4 hosts in the University and the research network respectively contribute to 84% and 80% of total *numExtSrv* – this is also expected since they commonly communicate with public resolvers or authoritative name servers on the Internet.

Hosts clustered as mixed DNS servers in both organizations have a moderate value of the *QryFracOut* attribute (*i.e.*, 0.57 and 0.21 for the University and the research network respectively) depending on their varying level of inbound/outbound DNS activity. Also, in terms of external clients and servers communicated with, the mixed servers lie between name servers and recursive resolvers. Lastly, regular end-hosts generate only outbound DNS queries (*i.e.*, *QryFracOut* equals to 1), contact a small number of external resolvers, and are active for shorter duration of time over a day (*i.e.*, *actvTimeFrac* less than 0.5).

Interpreting the Output of Clustering. Our clustering algorithm also generates a confidence level as an output. This can be used as a measure of reliability for our classifier. If adequate information is not provided by attributes of an instance then the algorithm will decide its cluster with a low confidence level.

The average confidence level of the result clustering is 97.61% for both organizations, with more than 99% of instances classified with a confidence-level of more than 85%. This indicates the strength of our host-level attributes, enabling the algorithm to cluster them with a very high confidence-level.

Server Clusters Across a Week. We now check the performance of our clustering algorithm over a week. Figure 5 shows a heat map for clusters of servers. Columns list server hosts that were identified in Tables 2 and 3 (*i.e.,* 70 hosts in the University network and 22 hosts in the research network). Rows display the cluster into which each server is classified. The color of each cell depicts the number of days (over a week) that each host is identified as the corresponding cluster – dark cells depict a high number of occurrences (approaching 7), while bright cells represent a low occurrence closer to 0.

In the University network we identified 42 name servers, shown by H1 to H42 in Fig. 5(a); the majority of which are repeatedly classified as a name server over a week, thus represented by dark cells at their intersections with the bottom row, highlighting the strong signature of their profile as a name server.

Among 14 recursive resolvers of the university campus, shown by H43 to H56 in Fig. 5(a); two of them (*i.e.,* hosts A and B in Fig. 1) are consistently classified as recursive resolver, and the rest are classified as either mixed DNS server or even end hosts (due to their varying activity). Lastly, 14 mixed servers, shown by H57 to H70 in Fig. 5(a), are classified consistently though their behavior sometimes is closer to a resolver or a name server.

Our results from the Research Institute network are fairly similar – Fig. 5(b) shows that hosts H1-H12 are consistently classified as name servers, while hosts H13-H16 are recursive resolvers and H17-H22 are mixes servers.

3.2 Server Ranking

Our system discovered 5097 public-facing (non-DNS) servers in the University, and 6102 at the Research Institute. However, only top 368 and 271 of these servers respectively appeared in the answer section of more than 100 outgoing DNS responses over a day. Additionally, 6 top ranked DNS servers, in each organization, contribute to more than 90% of outgoing queries and responses. Servers ranking provides network operators with the visibility into the criticality of their internal assets.

3.3 IT Verification

IT departments of both organizations were able to verify the top ranked DNS resolvers, name-servers, and non-DNS public-facing servers found, as they are directly configured and controlled by IT departments of the two organizations,(*e.g.,* major name-servers and web-servers). Additionally, we revealed unknown servers configured by departments of the two enterprises (we verified their functionality by reverse DNS lookup and their IP range allocated by IT departments). Interestingly, 3 of the name-servers our method identified were implicated in a DNS amplification attack soon after, and IT was able to confirm that these were managed by affiliated entities (such as retail stores that lease space and Internet connectivity from the University) - this clearly points to the use of our system in identifying and classifying assets whose security posture the network operators themselves may not have direct control over.

3.4   Clustering of End-Hosts: NATed or Not?

Lastly, to draw more insights we further applied our clustering algorithm (using the same attributes introduced in Sect. 2.2) to IP address of end-hosts, determining whether they are behind a NAT gateway or not (*i.e.,* two clusters: NATed and not-NATed). In both networks, all WiFi clients are behind NAT gateways. Additionally, some specific departments of the two enterprises use NAT for their wired clients too. We verified our end-host clustering by reverse lookup for each enterprise network. Each NATed IP address has a corresponding domain name in specific forms configured by IT departments. For example the University campus wireless NAT gateways are associated with domain-names as "SSID-pat-pool-a-b-c-d.gw.univ-primay-domain", where "a.b.c.d" is the public IP address of the NAT gateway, and SSID is the WiFi SSID for the University campus network (we will disclose SSID and univ-primay-domain when this paper is de-anonymized). Similarly, in the Research institute NAT gateways use names in form of "c-d.pool.rsch-primary-domain" where "c.d" is the last two octets of the public IP address of the NAT gateway in the Research institute. On 3rd May, our end-host clustering shows that 292 and 19 of end-hosts IP addresses are indeed NATed in the University campus and the Research institute respectively – we verified their corresponding domain names configured by their IT departments.

We note that the two clusters of end-hosts are distinguished primarily by one attribute *actvTimeFrac* – a NATed IP address (representing a group of end-hosts) is expected to have a longer duration of DNS activity compared to a not-NATed IP address (representing a single end-host)[4]. We observe that some IPs with domain-names of NAT gateways are incorrectly classified as not-NATed end-hosts. This is because their daily DNS activity was fairly low, *i.e.,* less than an hour. On the other hand, not-NATed end-hosts with long duration of DNS activity (*i.e.,* almost the whole day) were misclassified. Verifying end-hosts classified as NATed, 84.3% of them in the University campus and 86% in the Research institute have corresponding domain-names as for NAT gateways allocated by IT departments. For end-hosts classified as not-NATed, 80.7% and 90.0% in the respective two organizations do not map to any organizational domain-names.

---

[4] We omit CCDF plots due to space constraint, they are shown in Appendix 2.

Looking into the performance of end-hosts clustering across a week, we note that 78.3% end-hosts in the University campus are consistently labeled as NATed over 7 days[5]. However, for the research institute, only 32.0% of NATed IPs are consistent across the entire week – 34.5% of IPs were absent on some days and the remaining 33.4% were misclassified as not-NATed for their low activity (*e.g.*, only active 2 h during a day).

4   Related Work

DNS traffic has been analyzed for various purposes, ranging from measuring performance (effect of Time-to-Live of DNS records) [3,7,13] to identifying malicious domains [2,8,9] and the security of DNS [5,10,11,14]. In this paper we have profiled the pattern of DNS traffic for individual hosts of two enterprise networks to map network assets to their function and thereby identify their relative importance for efficient monitoring and security.

Considering studies related to malicious domains, [8] inspects DNS traffic close to top-level domain servers to detect abnormal activity and PREDATOR [9] derives domain reputation using registration features to enable early detection of potentially malicious DNS domains without capturing traffic. From a security viewpoint, the authors of [5] study the adoption of DNSSEC [1], highlighting that only 1% of domains have implemented this secure protocol due to difficulties in the registration process and operational challenges; [10,11] focus on authoritative name servers used as reflectors in DNS amplification attacks; some researchers [14] have reported that the amplification factor of DNSSEC is quite high (*i.e.*, up to 44 to 55) whereas this measure is 6 to 12 for regular DNS servers.

DNS data can be collected from different locations (such as from log files of recursive resolvers [4,7] or authoritative name servers) or with different granularity (such as query/response logs or aggregated records). Datasets used in [5,10,11] contain DNS traffic for top level domains such as .com, and .net. We collect our data at the edge of an enterprise network, specifically outside the firewall at the point of interconnect with the external Internet. We note that while using data from resolver logs can provide detailed information about end hosts and their query types/patterns, this approach limits visibility and may not be comprehensive enough to accurately establish patterns related to the assets of the entire network.

5   Conclusion

Enterprise network administrators find it challenging to track their assets and their network behavior. We have developed an automated method to map internal hosts of an enterprise network by focusing only on DNS traffic which carries a wealth of information, constitutes a tiny faction of total network traffic and is

---

[5] We omit consistency plots due to space constraint, they are shown in Appendix 2.

easy to capture. By analyzing real-time live streams of DNS traffic from two organizations we highlighted how DNS query and response patterns differ amongst recursive resolvers, authoritative name servers, and regular hosts. We then identified key DNS traffic attributes that can be extracted efficiently in real-time. Lastly, we developed an unsupervised machine learning model that can classify enterprise assets, and we further applied our technique to infer the type of an enterprise end-host (NATed or not-NATed). Our results have been verified with IT departments of the two organizations while revealing unknown knowledges.

Acknowledgements. This work was completed in collaboration with the Australian Defence Science and Technology Group.

Appendix 1. DNS Behavior of Hosts (Research Institute)

(see Figs. 6 and 7).

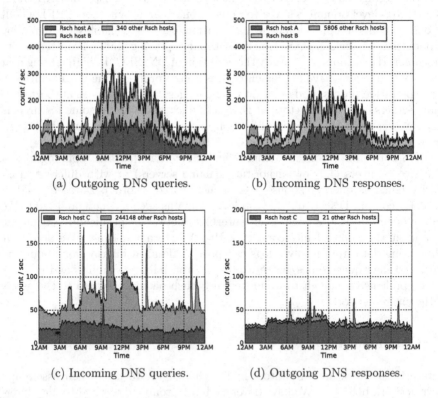

(a) Outgoing DNS queries.   (b) Incoming DNS responses.

(c) Incoming DNS queries.   (d) Outgoing DNS responses.

Fig. 6. Research institute: outgoing queries, incoming responses, incoming queries and outgoing responses, measured on 3 May 2018.

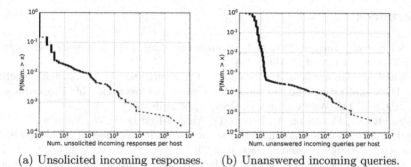

(a) Unsolicited incoming responses.   (b) Unanswered incoming queries.

Fig. 7. Research institute: CCDF of (a) unsolicited incoming responses and (b) unanswered incoming queries per host, measured on 3 May 2018.

Appendix 2. NATed vs. not-NATed End-Hosts

(see Figs. 8 and 9).

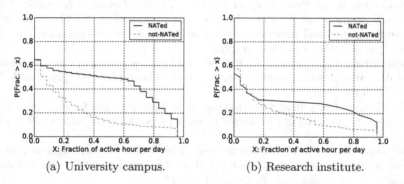

(a) University campus.   (b) Research institute.

Fig. 8. CCDF: fraction of active hour per day for end-host IP addresses with/without domain names.

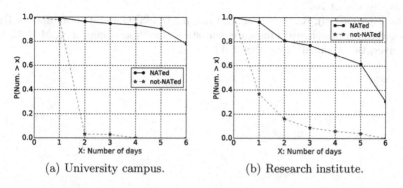

(a) University campus.   (b) Research institute.

Fig. 9. CCDF: Consistency of end-hosts clustering across a week.

References

1. DNS Security Introduction and Requirements (2018). https://www.ietf.org/rfc/rfc4033.txt. Accessed 28 May 2018
2. Ahmed, J., Gharakheili, H.H., Russell, C., Sivaraman, V.: Real-time detection of DNS exfiltration and tunneling from enterprise networks. In: Proceedings of IFIP/IEEE IM, Washington DC, USA, April 2019
3. Almeida, M., Finamore, A., Perino, D., Vallina-Rodriguez, N., Varvello, M.: Dissecting DNS stakeholders in mobile networks. In: Proceedings of ACM CoNEXT, Incheon, Republic of Korea, December 2017
4. Choi, H., Lee, H.: Identifying botnets by capturing group activities in DNS traffic. Comput. Netw. **56**(1), 20–33 (2012)
5. Chung, T., et al.: Understanding the role of registrars in DNSSEC deployment. In: Proceedings of ACM IMC, London, UK, November 2017
6. Deloitte: Elevating cybersecurity on the higher education leadership agenda (2018). https://www2.deloitte.com/insights/us/en/industry/public-sector/cybersecurity-on-higher-education-leadership-agenda.html
7. Gao, H., et al.: Reexamining DNS From a global recursive resolver perspective. IEEE/ACM Trans. Netw. **24**(1), 43–57 (2016)
8. Hao, S., Feamster, N., Pandrangi, R.: Monitoring the initial DNS behavior of malicious domains. In: Proceedings of ACM IMC, Berlin, Germany, November 2011
9. Hao, S., Kantchelian, A., Miller, B., Paxson, V., Feamster, N.: PREDATOR: proactive recognition and elimination of domain abuse at time-of-registration. In: Proceedings of ACM CCS, October 2016
10. MacFarland, D.C., Shue, C.A., Kalafut, A.J.: Characterizing optimal DNS amplification attacks and effective mitigation. In: Proceedings of PAM, New York, NY, USA, March 2015
11. MacFarland, D.C., Shue, C.A., Kalafut, A.J.: The best bang for the byte: characterizing the potential of DNS amplification attacks. Comput. Netw. **116**(C), 12–21 (2017)
12. Marshall, S.: CANDID: classifying assets in networks by determining importance and dependencies. Technical report, Electrical Engineering and Computer Sciences, University of California at Berkeley, May 2013
13. Müller, M., Moura, G.C.M., de O. Schmidt, R., Heidemann, J.: Recursives in the wild: engineering authoritative DNS servers. In: Proceedings of ACM IMC, London, UK, November 2017
14. van Rijswijk-Deij, R., Sperotto, A., Pras, A.: DNSSEC and its potential for DDoS attacks: a comprehensive measurement study. In: Proceedings of ACM IMC, Vancouver, BC, Canada, November 2014

Domain Names

A First Look at QNAME Minimization in the Domain Name System

Wouter B. de Vries[1]([✉]), Quirin Scheitle[2], Moritz Müller[1,3], Willem Toorop[4], Ralph Dolmans[4], and Roland van Rijswijk-Deij[1,4]

[1] University of Twente, Enschede, The Netherlands
w.b.devries@utwente.nl
[2] TUM, Munich, Germany
[3] SIDN Labs, Arnhem, The Netherlands
[4] NLnet Labs, Amsterdam, The Netherlands

Abstract. The Domain Name System (DNS) is a critical part of network and Internet infrastructure; DNS lookups precede almost any user request. DNS lookups may contain private information about the sites and services a user contacts, which has spawned efforts to protect privacy of users, such as transport encryption through DNS-over-TLS or DNS-over-HTTPS.

In this work, we provide a first look on the resolver-side technique of query name minimization (*qmin*), which was standardized in March 2016 as RFC 7816. *qmin* aims to only send minimal information to authoritative name servers, reducing the number of servers that full DNS query names are exposed to. Using passive and active measurements, we show a slow but steady adoption of *qmin* on the Internet, with a surprising variety in implementations of the standard. Using controlled experiments in a test-bed, we validate lookup behavior of various resolvers, and quantify that *qmin* both increases the number of DNS lookups by up to 26%, and also leads to up to 5% more failed lookups. We conclude our work with a discussion of *qmin*'s risks and benefits, and give advice for future use.

Keywords: DNS · Privacy · QNAME minimization · Measurements

1 Introduction

The Domain Name System (DNS) plays a crucial role on the Internet. It is responsible for *resolving* domain names to IP addresses. The DNS is a hierarchical system where each so-called authoritative name server in the hierarchy is responsible for a part of a domain name. Recursive caching name servers – or 'resolvers' for short – query each level of authoritative name servers in turn to obtain the final answer. Resolvers usually cache responses to improve lookup speed.

On the Internet every domain resolution, given an empty cache, starts at the root of the DNS, which has knowledge of the name servers that are responsible

© Springer Nature Switzerland AG 2019
D. Choffnes and M. Barcellos (Eds.): PAM 2019, LNCS 11419, pp. 147–160, 2019.
https://doi.org/10.1007/978-3-030-15986-3_10

for all the Top-Level Domains (TLDs). Those name servers typically then refer the recursive resolver on towards yet another name server. This can keep going indefinitely, only limited by the maximum query name (*qname*) length, until finally the authoritative name server for the requested *qname* is reached (in practice the recursive resolver can give up earlier).

In the standard DNS resolution process, outlined in RFC 1034 [24], the recursive resolver, unaware of zone cuts in which different parts of the domain are under control of different authorities, sends the full *qname* to each of the authoritative name servers in this chain. Since the first two (root and TLD) name servers in the recursion are very unlikely to be authoritative for the requested *qname*, this particular aspect causes unnecessary exposure of potentially private information [6]. E.g., exposing the *qname* of a website that is illegal in some countries to more parties than necessary might put the querying end-user at serious risk. A solution for this issue is proposed in RFC 7816 [7], which introduces query name minimization (*qmin*), preventing recursive resolvers from sending the full *qname* until the authoritative name server for that *qname* is reached [7].

End-users typically do not run a recursive resolver, but instead depend on others, such as their ISP, to enable this privacy-preserving feature. From a user's perspective, *qmin* is difficult to detect, making it hard to judge adoption.

In this paper we study the adoption, performance, and security implications of RFC 7816. Specifically, we: **(1)** develop novel methodology to detect whether a resolver has *qmin* enabled, and quantify the adoption of *qmin* over time, both with active measurements from the end-user perspective, and passive measurements from the authoritative name server perspective, at a root and TLD server, **(2)** develop an algorithm to fingerprint *qmin* implementations, and classify the use of *qmin* algorithms in the Internet and, **(3)** provide insight into the impact of *qmin* on performance and result quality for three resolver implementations.

In order to facilitate reproducibility we make our scripts and datasets available publicly [33].

2   Background and Related Work

When DNS was first introduced in the 1980s, there was no consideration for security and privacy. These topics have now gained considerable importance, leading to a plethora of RFCs that add security and privacy to the DNS. For example, DNSSEC [28–30] introduces end-to-end authenticity and integrity, but no privacy. More recently, DNS-over-TLS [21] and DNS-over-HTTPS [20] added transport security. "Aggressive Use of DNSSEC-Validated Cache" [18], reduces unnecessary leaks of non-existing domain names. Furthermore, running a local copy of the root zone at a resolver avoids sending queries to root servers completely [19].

Typically, resolvers send the full *qname* to each authoritative name server involved in a lookup. Consequently, root servers receive the same query as the final authoritative name server. Since the IETF states that Internet protocols should minimize the data used to what is necessary to perform a task [12], *qmin* was introduced to bring an end to this. Resolvers that implement *qmin* only query name servers with a name stripped to one label more than what that name server is known to be authoritative for. E.g., when querying for *a.b.domain.example*, the resolver will first query the root for *.example*, instead of *a.b.domain.example*. The reference algorithm for *qmin* also hides the original query type by using the NS type instead of the original until the last query. In Table 1 we show what queries are performed for both standard DNS and the *qmin* reference implementation.

This reference algorithm, however, faces two challenges on the real Internet: First, it does not handle configuration errors in the DNS well [26]. E.g., in case *b.domain.example* does not have any RRs but *a.b.domain.example* does, a name server should respond with NOERROR for a query to *b.domain.example* [8], but in fact often responds with NXDOMAIN, or another invalid RCODE. This would force resolvers that conform to the standard to stop querying and thereby not successfully resolve the query. Also, operators report other issues, such as name servers that do not respond to NS queries, which would break *qmin* as well [25].

Table 1. DNS queries and responses without (left) and with (right) *qmin*.

Standard DNS resolution			*qmin* Reference (RFC 7816)		
a.b.example.com.	A	→ .	com.	NS	→ .
com.	*NS*	*← .*	*com.*	*NS*	*← .*
a.b.example.com	A	→ com.	example.com	NS	→ com.
example.com	*NS*	*← com.*	*example.com*	*NS*	*← com.*
a.b.example.com	A	→ example.com.	b.example.com	NS	→ example.com.
a.b.example.com	*A*	*← example.com.*	*b.example.com*	*NS*	*← example.com*
			a.b.example.com	NS	→ example.com.
			a.b.example.com	*NS*	*← example.com*
			a.b.example.com	A	→ example.com.
			a.b.example.com	*A*	*← example.com*

Second, *qmin* can lead to a large number of queries. For example, a name with 20 labels would make the resolver issue 21 queries to authoritative name servers, causing excessive load at the resolver and authoritative. Attackers can abuse this for DoS attacks by querying excessively long names for victim domains. Both of these issues led resolver implementors to modify their *qmin* implementations, as well as adding so called "strict" and "relaxed" modes, which we investigate in Subsect. 3.2 and Sect. 5.

As of October 2018, three major DNS resolvers support *qmin*. Unbound supports *qmin* since late 2015 and turned relaxed *qmin* on by default in May 2018 [25]. Knot resolver uses relaxed *qmin* since its initial release in May 2016 [13], and the recursive resolver of BIND supports *qmin* and turned the relaxed mode on by default in July 2018 [23]. Another frequently used resolver, PowerDNS Recursor, does not support *qmin* yet [9].

Related Work: Hardaker et al. [19] showed that root servers receive a considerable amount of privacy-sensitive query names, and propose using local instances of root servers to alleviate this issue. Imana et al. [22] study this aspect from a broader perspective, covering all name servers above the recursive resolver, and report similar privacy issues.

Schmitt et al. [32] propose Oblivious DNS, an obfuscation method introducing an additional intermediate resolver between recursive resolver and authoritative name servers. Oblivious DNS prevents the additional resolver from learning the user's IP address and the recursive resolver from learning the query name.

Recent work [34] has also shown that *qmin* increases the number of queries per lookup, increasing the load on authoritative name servers. They provide a technique called NXDOMAIN optimization that reduces the number of queries in case the resolver encounters an NXDOMAIN. We extend this by providing longitudinal measurements, showing various implementations of *qmin* algorithms and quantifying the increase in queries per resolver implementation.

3   Active Internet-Wide Measurements

We conduct active Internet-wide measurements using two methods. First, we use RIPE Atlas probes to query a domain under our control. Second, we query open resolvers for the same domain. RIPE Atlas is a global measurement network with over 10,000 small devices called probes, and 370 larger probes, called anchors. In this section, we measure *qmin* adoption over time, classify the various *qmin* implementations in use, and shed light on *qmin* use by open resolvers.

3.1   Resolver Adoption over Time

We detect *qmin* support by relying on the fact that a non-*qmin* resolver will miss any delegation that happens in one of the labels before the terminal label. So, if we delegate to a different name server, with a different record for the terminal label in one of the labels *before* the terminal label, *qmin* resolvers will find a different answer than non-*qmin* resolvers.

We scheduled a RIPE Atlas measurement for all probes to perform a lookup with all the probe's resolvers for *"a.b.qnamemin-test.domain.example"* with type TXT [1], repeating every hour. Each probe uses its own list of resolvers, typically obtained via DHCP, and assumed typical for the network that hosts the probe.

A non-*qmin* resolver will send a query for the full qname to the authoritative name server for "qnamemin-test.domain.example", and will end up with a TXT reply containing the text: "qmin NOT enabled." A *qmin* resolver will send a query for just the second-to-last label, "b.qnamemin-test.domain.example", to the authoritative name server for "qnamemin-test.domain.example". For this minimized query, it will receive a delegation to a different name server, which will return a TXT record containing the text: "qmin enabled."

This measurement runs since April 2017, and allows us to see the long term adoption of *qmin*. Figure 1b shows the overall adoption of *qmin* as seen from all

RIPE Atlas probes. We count both probes and probe/resolver combinations, as a significant number of probes uses multiple resolvers. Adoption grew from 0.7% (116 of 17,663) of probe/resolver pairs in April 2017 to 8.8% (1,662 of 18,885) in October 2018. Also in April 2017, 0.9% (82 of 9,611) of RIPE Atlas probes had at least one *qmin* resolver, growing to 11.7% (1,175 of 10,020) in October 2018.

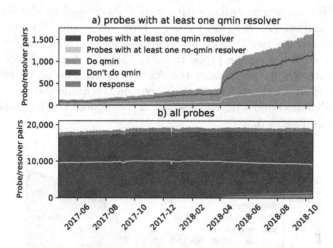

Fig. 1. Adoption over time

In Fig. 1a only probe/resolver pairs supporting *qmin* are shown. We see a steep rise of *qmin* resolvers in April 2018. Figure 1a also shows probes that have at least one *qmin* resolver as well as at least one resolver that does not do *qmin*. It is noteworthy that at the last measurement (October 15, 2018) at least 31% of probes that have a *qmin* resolver, also have at least one non-*qmin* resolver.

Alongside the *qmin* measurement, we run measurements that return the IP address of the resolver as seen from an authoritative name server [2,3,5]. By identifying the Autonomous System Numbers (ASNs) associated with the IP addresses seen at the authoritative name server we gain insight in the organizations providing the *qmin* resolvers. From this we learn that the adoption of Cloudflare (1.1.1.1) is responsible for the fast rise of *qmin* resolvers in April 2018.

We also found some public resolvers, such as Google Public DNS, that in some cases appear to support *qmin* according to our test, but in fact do not. This is likely caused by a *qmin*-enabled *forwarding* resolver, which forwards to, in Google's case, 8.8.8.8. Additionally, the non-*qmin* resolver successively caches the authoritative for the second-last label and will appear to support *qmin* for the TTL of the delegation (10 s in our test). We have developed an improved test without these issues in the course of this research, but this corrected test did not yet exist during scheduling of the RIPE Atlas measurement in April 2017.

The improved test, "a.b.*random-element*.domain.example. TXT", uses a random pattern as the third-last label which is uniquely chosen for each query, preventing other measurement queries to find a cached delegation for the second-last label. This improved test is used in measuring the adoption by open resolvers in Subsect. 3.3, removing false positives from that measurement.

We argue that this flaw had little impact on our results, as *(i)*, RIPE Atlas measurements are spread out over an hour, whereas our test record has a small TTL, reducing this risk and *(ii)* the overall trend over time is still indicative.

The ASNs seen at the authoritative were further used to classify resolvers in three categories: **(1)** *Internal* resolvers have the same ASN for the probe and the observed resolver IP, **(2)** *External* resolvers for which the ASN of the resolver IP configured on the probe matches the ASN for the IP observed on the authoritative, but differs from the ASN in which the probe resides, **(3)** *Forwarding* resolvers, for which the ASN seen on the authoritative differs from both the ASN associated with the resolver IP configured on the probe and the ASN the probe resides in.

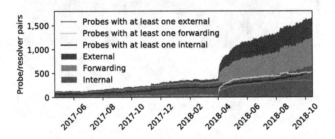

Fig. 2. Internal, Forwarding and External resolvers supporting *qmin*

Figure 2 shows that both *External* and *Forwarding* probe/resolver pairs supporting *qmin* are on the rise, which is mainly due to adoption of the Cloudflare resolver in April 2018. We can also see that *qmin* support is steadily growing with *Internal* resolvers, which do not include the larger public resolvers.

Looking more closely at the *Internal* resolvers we have identified, we see that several ISPs started supporting *qmin* over the past 1.5 years. Most notably "Versatel Deutschland GmbH" started supporting *qmin* on November 9th, 2017; "Init Seven AG" on August 2nd, 2017; "OVH Systems" on February 1st, 2018; and "M-Net Telekommunikations GmbH, Germany" on May 1st, 2018. Note that these do not necessarily cause a visible change in Fig. 2.

3.2 Fingerprinting Resolver Algorithms

As described in Sect. 2, the RFC [7] provides a reference algorithm for *qmin*. This is an aggressive algorithm in the sense that it maximizes potential privacy gains at the cost of performance. It iteratively increases the name length by one label, querying for the NS type, until it reaches the full name. Then, it switches to the original query type, thus also this type from all but the final name server.

While this algorithm is good for privacy, it can significantly impact performance, security, and result quality (see Sect. 5). Since the reference algorithm is merely a suggestion, resolver implementors are free to write their own algorithm.

Using RIPE Atlas measurements, we explore *qmin* algorithms implemented in practice. To measure this, we performed a one-off DNS measurement [4] from all RIPE Atlas probes able to resolve A records correctly (9,410 probes). We control the authoritative name server for the queried name, permitting us to identify query behavior. The queried name consists of 24 labels, including random values and the probe ID to permit mapping inbound DNS queries to originating probes. We see inbound queries from 8,894 unique probes (out of 9,410) from 8,179 unique resolvers. Most probes have at least two resolvers configured, many overlapping with those of other probes, resulting in 20,716 total inbound queries.

Assigning Signatures: To group resolver behavior, we map the incoming query behavior observed at our authoritative name server to signatures, containing length, order, and type of inbound queries. Our test domain is at the second label depth, so we observe queries starting from the third label depth. For example, an algorithm asking for NS at the 3rd label, then for NS at the 4th label, and then for A at the final, 24th, label, will be mapped to the signature 3NS-4NS-24A.

Signatures of BIND, Knot and Unbound: To have a basis for comparison, we run our domain through each of these three resolvers, which are known to implement *qmin*, and determine each of their *qmin* signatures. BIND and Unbound also support an additional *strict mode*, however, this has no effect on the signature and is related to how NXDOMAIN responses are handled. The resulting signatures, and the reference algorithm signature, are shown in Table 2.

Table 2. Top 6 signatures seen at Authoritative Resolvers, mapped to resolver implementations. Reference implementation not observed.

Type	Signature	Implementation	Count
1	24A		13,892
2	3NS-24A	Knot 3.0.0	784
3	3A-4A-5A-8A-11A-14A-17A-21A-24A		239
3	3A-4A-5A-6A-9A-12A-15A-18A-22A-24A		193
3	3A-4A-7A-10A-13A-16A-20A-24A	Unbound 1.8.0	16
4	3NS-4NS-5NS-24A	BIND 9.13.3	11
	3NS-4NS-5NS-6NS-7NS-...-24NS-24A	Reference	0

Signatures in the Wild: We identify four types of signatures, with some types having multiple variations, see Table 2. The first, most common type (*#1*) applies no *qmin*. These resolvers directly query the full length DNS name. The second type (*#2*) is a minimalistic *qmin* approach. After a no-delegation check below the base domain, the full query name is sent. This is used by the Knot resolver, and, for example, by Cloudflare's public DNS resolver. The third type, with variations (*#3*), is closer to the reference algorithm, but displays various ways of skipping labels, as well as always using the A query type instead of the NS type as suggested by the reference algorithm. Unbound is known to have a similar implementation [16], confirmed in our experiments. The final signature, (*#4*) uses the NS query type, and jumps to querying for the full name after not finding a zone cut for three labels. This is consistent with the BIND implementation.

Besides the specific signatures seen in Table 2, there are many variations of type #3. This indicates that not only do different resolvers implement different algorithms, but they also appear to be configurable or change over time (e.g. a new version changes the behavior). In total we see 20 different signatures, many of which only from one specific resolver. Interestingly, we did not observe the reference algorithm from any resolver.

3.3   Adoption by Open Resolvers

Aside from resolvers that can be reached from inside networks, such as those offered by ISPs, there are also a large number of open resolvers on the Internet. These can range from unsecured corporate DNS resolvers, to large scale public DNS services, such as those run by Google, OpenDNS, Quad9 and Cloudflare.

Rapid7 provides a list of servers that are responsive on UDP port 53, which are typically DNS servers. We query each such server using the method outlined in Subsect. 3.1. The list contains a total of 8M IPv4 addresses, we receive a response from 64% of these. Of those responding, 32% respond with a NOERROR reply, of which only 72% ($\approx$1.2M) provide a correct reply.

Of those 1.2M, only 19,717 (1.6%) resolvers support *qmin*. On the authoritative side, we only observe 110k unique source IPs, which suggests that many of the queried resolvers are in fact forwarders. Of the resolvers that implement *qmin*, 10,338 send queries from a Cloudflare IP, 2,147 from an OVH IP, and 1,616 from a TV Cabo Angola IP address. This shows that most *qmin*-supporting open resolvers simply forward to larger public DNS resolvers that implement *qmin*.

For *qmin*-enabled resolvers, we compare the ASN of the IP we send our query to with the ASN of the IP seen at the authoritative for that same query. We find 11.5k resolvers to resolve externally, and 8.2k resolvers to resolve internally.

The takeaway is that many open resolvers on the Internet use centralized public DNS services. Thus, efforts to drive adoption of *qmin* should focus on large public DNS providers (e.g. Google, which does not support *qmin* yet).

4   Passive Measurements at Authoritative Name Servers

As *qmin* limits the visible information of a query at authoritative name servers, adoption of *qmin* likely changes the query profile of resolvers as observed on the authoritative side. We measure the impact and adoption of *qmin* with query data collected at the authoritative name servers of the ccTLD *.nl* and of K-Root.

Name servers of *.nl* are authoritative for the delegation of 5.8 million domain names. If they receive queries for a *.nl* domain name with 2 or more labels then they almost always (except for DS records) respond with a set of name servers that are actually responsible for the queried domain name. Thus, a query for the NS record of a second level domain name is sufficient for the *.nl* name servers to answer the query. Similarly, the root servers are authoritative for the 1.5k TLDs as of October 9, 2018, and a query for just the TLD is sufficient in most cases.

We cannot be certain whether resolvers send minimized queries to the authoritative name servers, but we can count the queries that follow the expected patterns if resolvers were to send minimized queries. For the rest of this section, and following the observations made in Sect. 3, we count queries as minimized if the query contains only 2 labels (at *.nl*) or 1 label (at K-Root). With increasing *qmin* adoption, we expect to see an increase in queries that follow these criteria.

Identifying qmin. First, we measure how query patterns seen at the authoritative name servers differ when resolvers implement *qmin*. We use the list of open resolvers from Subsect. 3.3 of which we know whether they have *qmin* enabled. Then, we count how many queries these resolvers send to the authoritative name servers of *.nl* for names with just two labels on 2018-10-11. In total, we observe 1,918 resolvers that *do* and 27,251 resolvers that *do not* support *qmin*.

In Fig. 3 we see that *qmin*-enabled resolvers send a median of 97% of queries classified as minimized, whereas resolvers that have not enabled this feature send only 12% of their queries classified as minimized. This confirms that *qmin* has an observable impact at authoritative name servers.

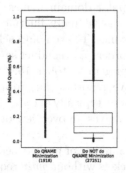
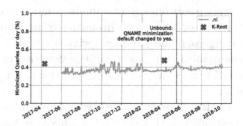

Fig. 3. Minimized queries to *.nl.* Whiskers at 0.05 and 0.95.

Fig. 4. Share of minimized queries sent to *.nl* and K-Root

Resolver Adoption Over Time. Based on the results of the previous section we expect a visible impact from increasing adoption of *qmin* at authoritative name servers. To verify this expectation we count how many queries overall are sent for 2nd level domain names and TLDs respectively. We analyze *.nl* data collected from 2017-06-01 to 2018-09-30 at 2 of the 4 authoritative name servers [35] and rely on the "Day In The Life of the Internet" (DITL) data sets of K-Root on 2017-04-11 and 2018-04-10 collected by DNS-OARC [15]. We observe more than 400B queries from 2017-06-01 to 2018-09-30 at .nl and 12B queries on the two days of the DITL data sets. Figure 4 shows the fraction of minimized queries.

In the beginning of our measurement, roughly 33% of the queries to .nl where minimized. A year later, at least 40% of queries were minimized. A peak around May 2018 correlates with the date on which Unbound enabled *qmin* by default. This peak, however, is followed by a steep decline shortly after, which means we cannot confirm if Unbound enabling *qmin* by default caused this peak.

At K-Root we also observe an increase from 44% to 48% in queries for domain names with only one label. Note that query patterns at the root may strongly vary from one day to another and that many queries are sent to non existing domain names which can influence our results [10].

5   Controlled Experiments: Impact on Resolver Performance and Result Quality

As *qmin* is deployed at the recursive resolver, we explore how *qmin* impacts the *performance* and the *result quality* of such a recursive resolver. We compare three popular *qmin*-enabled resolvers in their most recent version: Unbound 1.8.0, Knot 3.0.0, and BIND 9.13.3. We use all three resolvers with their default options, only adjusting to an equal cache size of 4GB and turning DNSSEC validation off[1]. We cycle through all configurable *qmin* behaviors for Unbound and BIND; Knot has *relaxed qmin* hardcoded. As target domains, we use the Cisco Umbrella Top 1M [11] list as a sample of popular domain names, and aggregate all domains names for a 2-week period to avoid daily fluctuations and weekly patterns [31], resulting in 1.56M domain names. To even out caching effects, we sort our target domain names in 4 different orders. We conduct several iterations of these measurements from October 1 through October 15, 2018, starting each measurement with an empty cache. We report means from all measurement runs, and find little variation in all numbers, typically one standard deviation σ is smaller than 2% of the mean μ. Table 3 gives an overview of our results.

Performance: *qmin* shows a clear impact on the number of packets sent to resolve our 1.56M domains. For Unbound, the 5.7M packets without *qmin* require 6.82M (relaxed) and 6.71M (strict) packets with *qmin*, a 17–19% increase. For BIND, the increase is 15–26%. It is to be expected that the strict mode requires fewer packets, as it will give up on receiving an error, whereas relaxed modes continue through SERVFAIL or NXDOMAIN error codes. This increase in packet count is not offset by smaller packets, across resolvers we see average packet sizes only decrease by 5% or less with *qmin* enabled.

---

[1] We turn DNSSEC validation off to achieve comparable behavior (validating DNSSEC requires more queries to be sent); we also note that the combination of *qmin* and DNSSEC may induce further complexities beyond the scope of this work.

Table 3. Performance and result quality across *qmin* modes and resolvers. Results are mean (μ) across all runs, with all standard deviations $\sigma < 2\%\mu$. We also show the *qmin* algorithm signature per resolver for the *qmin*-enabled case (signature without *qmin* is always 24A).

	Unbound 1.8.0			Knot 3.0.0	Bind 13.3.2		
qmin Signature	3A-4A-7A-...-24A			3NS-24A	3NS-4NS-5NS-24A		
qmin mode	Off	Relaxed	Strict	Relaxed	Off	Relaxed	Strict
# packets	5.70M	6.82M	6.71M	5.94M	5.07M	6.39M	5.84M
Errors	12.6%	12.6%	15.9%	13.5%	16.6%	17.1%	21.6%

This confirms that *qmin* in its current form does come with a performance penalty of up to 26%. We argue that the full cache in a production resolver will soften that overhead. Please note that a comparison of packet counts between different resolvers implicitly compares many other details such as caching strategies, which is why comparison between resolvers should be conducted very carefully. While it may seem intuitive that Unbound's 3A-4A-7A-10A-13A-16A-20A-24A *qmin* approach requires more packets than Knot's 3NS-24A and BIND's 3NS-4NS-5NS-24A approaches (cf. Subsect. 3.2), a comparison of the number of packets between resolvers would require a much deeper exploration of root causes of packets sent, such as caching and time-out strategies.

Result Quality: Another critical aspect of resolver performance is the result quality: Will a resolver be able to work through numerous edge cases and misconfigurations to deliver a response, or will it hang up on certain errors? To answer this question, we compare the amount of errors (NXDOMAIN or SERVFAIL) in our resolution results between different resolver and *qmin* approaches. Across resolvers, we see a significantly higher share of errors with strict *qmin* enabled. For example, the 3.3% increase for Unbound translates to ≈50k domains, a significant share of these popular DNS domain names. The difference in resolvers corresponds to our observations on resolver behavior: As reported in Sect. 2, a portion of authoritative name servers fails to respond to NS queries. As Unbound uses type A queries to discover zone boundaries, and Knot and BIND use NS queries (as suggested by RFC 7816), higher error rates are expected for Knot and BIND. The surprisingly high baseline of non-resolving domains of 12–16% is a characteristic of the Umbrella Top 1M list recently discussed in [31].

These findings show that *qmin* comes with two drawbacks: Packets and bytes transferred increase, and, depending on the detailed algorithm, also a significant share of popular DNS names fails to resolve.

6   Discussion and Conclusions

Our study covered *qmin* from various angles: we performed (**1**) controlled experiments that confirm that *qmin* can have negative performance and result quality implications, and **(2)** active and passive measurements in the Internet that confirm from both the client and authoritative server side that *qmin* adoption is rising. We also explored the various problems and workarounds that have been deployed, and want to conclude and discuss further aspects:

qmin **Is Complex:** Like many DNS mechanisms, *qmin* sounds simple, but broken deployments make it difficult to implement without collateral damage. Resolvers' iterations towards a relaxed *qmin* algorithm reflect this, and important take-aways are: *(i)* Using NS queries to detect zone cuts results in a considerable number of failures; using A queries instead seems reasonable. *(ii)* responding to SERVFAIL/NXDOMAIN by sending the full name (*i.e.,* disabling *qmin* for this query) is currently a necessity to avoid significant error rates.

qmin **Can Be a Security Risk:** Having a resolver step through many iterations for a name with an excessive number of labels is a DoS attack vector. All implementations we encountered mitigate this. Unbound jumps over labels to decrease the number of queries to some maximum, considerably saving on query count. Knot's (3NS-24A) and BIND's (3NS-4NS-5NS-24A) approaches go further: Knot stops *qmin* if it encounters a label that has not been delegated (except for some exceptions, such as *.co.uk*). BIND has both a limit on the maximum number of labels (default 9), in addition to having a maximum number of undelegated labels (default 3). We consider these approaches good, as they mitigate security risks while still providing *qmin* privacy against the top levels in the DNS hierarchy.

qmin **Can Impact Resolver Performance and Result Quality:** Currently, *qmin* comes with a 15%+ performance penalty, and unless implemented very carefully, will also impair result quality. Please note that, as *qmin* queries are sent sequentially, the measured increase in query volume will correlate to latency.

Recommendations: Based on the insights collected in this paper, we conclude with the following recommendations: *(i)*, despite its performance and quality caveats, *qmin* improves privacy and should be universally deployed. *(ii)* *qmin* deployment must be conducted carefully: We recommend an algorithm that combines Unbound's and BIND's algorithms, *i.e.,* conducts fallback upon error, replaces NS (and other) query types by A queries, and stops *qmin* after a configurable number of labels. *(iii)* over time, heuristics may be added to alleviate certain cases where *qmin* will unlikely add privacy. For example, DANE-TLSA labels such as _443._tcp could be exempt from *qmin*.

Conclusion: The currently still rather low *qmin* adoption already causes a significant positive effect for query privacy at both Root and TLD authoritative name servers. While there are legitimate performance, result quality, and security concerns, we already see resolver implementers tackle these, and are confident that these negative implications will be further reduced, assisted by the quantitative evidence and tangible recommendations in this study. We fully expect more and more DNS operators to enable *qmin* to further improve privacy of end-users on the Internet.

Ethical Considerations and Reproducibility: We carefully considered ethical implications of our work. We followed scanning best practices [17], and received no complaints. Our passive data collection has been cleared by the respective IRBs, and we follow the recommendations by Dittrich *et al.* [14] and Partridge *et al.* [27]. To encourage other researchers to validate and/or build upon our results we publish our scripts, code and data publicly [33].

Acknowledgements. This work was partially funded by the German Federal Ministry of Education and Research under project X-Check (grant 16KIS0530). Partial funding was also supplied by SURFnet Research on Networks.

References

1. RIPE Atlas measurement for `a.b.qnamemin-test.internet.nlTXT` (2017). https://atlas.ripe.net/measurements/8310250/
2. RIPE Atlas measurement for `o-o.myaddr.l.google.comTXT` (2017). https://atlas.ripe.net/measurements/8310237/
3. RIPE Atlas measurement for `ripe-hackathon6.nlnetlabs.nlAAAA` (2017). https://atlas.ripe.net/measurements/8310366/
4. RIPE Atlas measurement for `ripe-hackathon6.nlnetlabs.nlAAAA`. Ripe MSM IDs: 16428213, 16428214, 16428215, 16428216, 16428217, 16428218, 16428219, 16428220, 16428221, 16428222 (2017)
5. RIPE Atlas measurement for `whoami.akamai.netA` (2017). https://atlas.ripe.net/measurements/8310245/
6. Bortzmeyer, S.: DNS privacy considerations. RFC 7626 (Informational), August 2015. https://www.rfc-editor.org/rfc/rfc7626.txt
7. Bortzmeyer, S.: DNS query name minimisation to improve privacy. RFC 7816 (Experimental), March 2016. https://www.rfc-editor.org/rfc/rfc7816.txt
8. Bortzmeyer, S., Huque, S.: NXDOMAIN: there really is nothing underneath. RFC 8020 (Proposed Standard), November 2016. https://www.rfc-editor.org/rfc/rfc8020.txt
9. Bortzmeyer, S.: PowerDNS - add qname minimisation (2015). https://github.com/PowerDNS/pdns/issues/2311
10. Castro, S., Wessels, D., Fomenkov, M., Claffy, K.: A day at the root of the internet. ACM SIGCOMM Comput. Commun. Rev. **38**(5), 41–46 (2008)
11. Cisco: Cisco Umbrella Top 1M List, September 14–30 2018. https://s3-us-west-1.amazonaws.com/umbrella-static/index.html
12. Cooper, A., et al.: Privacy Considerations for Internet Protocols. RFC 6973, July 2013. https://rfc-editor.org/rfc/rfc6973.txt
13. CZ.NIC: Knot resolver 1.0.0 released (2016). https://www.knot-resolver.cz/2016-05-30-knot-resolver-1.0.0.html
14. Dittrich, D., Kenneally, E., et al.: The Menlo Report: Ethical Principles Guiding Information and Communication Technology Research. US Department of Homeland Security (2012)
15. DNS OARC: Day In The Life of the Internet (2017 and 2018). https://www.dns-oarc.net/oarc/data/ditl
16. Dolmans, R.: QNAME Minimization in Unbound, RIPE 72 (2016). https://ripe72.ripe.net/wp-content/uploads/presentations/120-unbound_qnamemin_ripe72.pdf

17. Durumeric, Z., Wustrow, E., Halderman, J.A.: ZMap: fast internet-wide scanning and its security applications. In: USENIX Security (2013)
18. Fujiwara, K., Kato, A., Kumari, W.: Aggressive Use of DNSSEC-Validated Cache. RFC 8198 (Proposed Standard), July 2017. https://www.rfc-editor.org/rfc/rfc8198.txt
19. Hardaker, W.: Analyzing and mitigating privacy with the DNS root service. In: NDSS: DNS Privacy Workshop, 2018 (2018)
20. Hoffman, P.E., McManus, P.: DNS queries over HTTPS (DoH). RFC 8484, October 2018. https://rfc-editor.org/rfc/rfc8484.txt
21. Hu, Z., Zhu, L., Heidemann, J., Mankin, A., Wessels, D., Hoffman, P.E.: Specification for DNS over transport layer security (TLS). RFC 7858, May 2016. https://rfc-editor.org/rfc/rfc7858.txt
22. Imana, B., Korolova, A., Heidemann, J.: Enumerating privacy leaks in DNS data collected above the recursive. In: NDSS: DNS Privacy Workshop, 2018. San Diego, California, USA, Feburary 2018. https://www.isi.edu/%7ejohnh/PAPERS/Imana18a.html
23. ISC: Release notes for bind version 9.13.2 (2018). https://ftp.isc.org/isc/bind9/9.13.2/RELEASE-NOTES-bind-9.13.2.txt
24. Mockapetris, P.: Domain names - concepts and facilities. RFC 1034, November 1987. https://rfc-editor.org/rfc/rfc1034.txt
25. NLnet Labs: Nlnet labs: Unbound chanelog (2018). https://nlnetlabs.nl/svn/unbound/tags/release-1.8.0/doc/Changelog
26. Pappas, V., Wessels, D., Massey, D., Lu, S., Terzis, A., Zhang, L.: Impact of configuration errors on DNS robustness. IEEE J. Sel. Areas Commun. **27**(3), 275–290 (2009)
27. Partridge, C., Allman, M.: Ethical considerations in network measurement papers. Commun. ACM **59**, 58–64 (2016)
28. Rose, S., Larson, M., Massey, D., Austein, R., Arends, R.: DNS security introduction and requirements. RFC 4033, March 2005. https://rfc-editor.org/rfc/rfc4033.txt
29. Rose, S., Larson, M., Massey, D., Austein, R., Arends, R.: Protocol modifications for the DNS security extensions. RFC 4035, March 2005. https://rfc-editor.org/rfc/rfc4035.txt
30. Rose, S., Larson, M., Massey, D., Austein, R., Arends, R.: Resource records for the DNS security extensions. RFC 4034, March 2005. https://rfc-editor.org/rfc/rfc4034.txt
31. Scheitle, Q., et al.: A long way to the top: significance, structure, and stability of internet top lists. In: IMC 2018, Boston, USA. arXiv:1805.11506 November 2018
32. Schmitt, P., Edmundson, A., Feamster, N.: Oblivious DNS: practical privacy for DNS queries. arXiv:1806.00276 (2018)
33. de Vries, W.B., Scheitle, Q., Müller, M., Toorop, W., Dolmans, R., van Rijswijk-Deij, R.: Datasets and Scripts (2019). https://www.simpleweb.org/wiki/index.php/Traces#A_First_Look_at_QNAME_Minimization_in_the_Domain_Name_System
34. Wang, Z.: Understanding the performance and challenges of DNS query name minimization. In: 17th IEEE International Conference On Trust, Security And Privacy In Computing And Communications/12th IEEE International Conference On Big Data Science And Engineering (TrustCom/BigDataSE), pp. 1115–1120. IEEE (2018)
35. Wullink, M., Moura, G.C., Müller, M., Hesselman, C.: ENTRADA: a high-performance network traffic data streaming warehouse. In: 2016 IEEE/IFIP Network Operations and Management Symposium (NOMS), pp. 913–918. IEEE (2016)

Clustering and the Weekend Effect: Recommendations for the Use of Top Domain Lists in Security Research

Walter Rweyemamu[✉], Tobias Lauinger, Christo Wilson, William Robertson, and Engin Kirda

Northeastern University, Boston, MA, USA
walter@iseclab.org

Abstract. Top domain rankings (e.g., Alexa) are commonly used in security research, such as to survey security features or vulnerabilities of "relevant" websites. Due to their central role in selecting a sample of sites to study, an inappropriate choice or use of such domain rankings can introduce unwanted biases into research results. We quantify various characteristics of three top domain lists that have not been reported before. For example, the weekend effect in Alexa and Umbrella causes these rankings to change their geographical diversity between the workweek and the weekend. Furthermore, up to 91% of ranked domains appear in alphabetically sorted clusters containing up to 87k domains of presumably equivalent popularity. We discuss the practical implications of these findings, and propose novel best practices regarding the use of top domain lists in the security community.

1 Introduction

In recent years, security research has seen the emergence of Internet measurements as a subdiscipline aiming to quantify the prevalence of security risks or vulnerabilities in practice. Since many types of security assessments do not easily scale to the entire Internet, researchers typically consider only a subset of registered domains. Often, they decide to cover the most popular domains, that is, those receiving the most visitors [14,18,27,32]. In doing so, they rely on "top site" rankings such as the lists compiled by Alexa [2], Majestic [6], Quantcast [7] and Umbrella [4]. Consequently, these top site lists play a central role in many studies; they decide which domain will or will not be included in the measured sample. Alexa's list in particular has become nearly ubiquitous, with multiple papers using it at any major security and Internet measurement conference [20,30].

Many authors have commented individually on shortcomings of Alexa's ranking (e.g., lack of reliability in the bottom ranks [29], presence of malicious domains [23,24,28]) and devised their own ad-hoc mitigations to make their research results more robust against these issues (e.g., using only a list prefix [9,22], using multiple domain lists [13,19], and using only domains that have been present on the list for a longer time period [9,22]). Yet, researchers are

D. Choffnes and M. Barcellos (Eds.): PAM 2019, LNCS 11419, pp. 161–177, 2019.
https://doi.org/10.1007/978-3-030-15986-3_11

just beginning to investigate these issues in a more systematic way. In 2018, Scheitle et al. [30] and Le Pochat et al. [20] performed rigourous analyses on the nature of top lists. These works aim to understand the construction of these lists, including: how they model popularity, what their data sources are, how fast they change, and how resilient they are to manipulation attempts. While these papers have shed light on many important characteristics of top domain lists, several aspects have gone unnoticed, or have received less attention than they deserve.

Specifically, Scheitle et al. mention a periodic *weekend effect* in Alexa's and Umbrella's lists [30], becoming manifest in a higher degree of change each weekend. We conduct a more in-depth analysis of the weekend effect by studying the content categories of the respective websites, confirming the authors' cursory finding that the weekend effect is likely due to a dominance of leisure traffic during the weekend, and office traffic during the workweek. In addition, we show that the weekend effect causes changes even among the highest ranked domains in Umbrella, whereas these domains tend to be more stable in Alexa. The weekend effect also affects country representation in the lists. These phenomena highlight the need for a more robust and stable domain selection process.

Beyond the brief reference by Le Pochat et al. [20], we are the first to quantify in detail how Alexa and Umbrella cluster domain names of equivalent popularity, while assigning them individual ranks. In fact, more than 54% of domains in Alexa, and 91% in Umbrella, appear in such alphabetically ordered clusters that can reach a size of up to 87k domains. If not accounted for, the alphabetic ordering caused by clustering can cause anomalies when correlating a domain's rank with a measured property.

By characterising clustering and the weekend effect, we contribute to a better understanding of the limitations of top domain lists. We distill our findings into concrete recommendations by proposing novel best practices for the use of domain lists.

Overall, this paper makes the following contributions:

- We provide a detailed look at weekend changes in Alexa and Umbrella, the extent of these changes in different parts of the list, and the implications on the content categories and geographical diversity of listed domains.
- We are the first to quantify and explain the presence of alphabetically sorted clusters of domains in Alexa's and Umbrella's rankings.
- We discuss the implications of these phenomena for researchers using the lists in their measurements, and propose novel best practices to minimise unwanted biases.

2   Background and Related Work

In this paper, we often refer to entries of rankings or lists, but language can be confusingly ambiguous as to a "high" rank being good or bad. As a convention, when we write that a rank is *higher*, we mean that it is a *better* rank, *numerically lower*, towards the top of the list with the most popular entries.

Table 1. Data sources of common top site lists.

Ranking	Data source	List contents
Alexa	Browser toolbar	Typed-in website domains
Majestic	Web crawl	Linked website domains
Quantcast	Website instrumentation	Measured website domains
Umbrella	DNS resolver	Resolved (sub)domains

Alexa and Umbrella data from 2018-02-01 to 2018-05-31

Majestic data from 2018-02-28 to 2018-05-31

Table 2. Hidden entries in quantcast (2018-06-17).

List prefix	Hidden #	%
$1 - 10$	0	0.0
$1 - 100$	15	15.0
$1 - 1,000$	136	13.6
$1 - 10,000$	594	5.9
$1 - 100,000$	1,892	1.9
$1 - 511,804$	5,045	1.0

2.1 Use of Top Lists in Security Research

Top domain lists such as the Alexa Top Sites are frequently used in security research. Le Pochat et al. [20] found 102 papers using the Alexa ranking at the four main security conferences from 2015 to 2017/2018, and Scheitle et al. [30] found 68 studies using Alexa published at the top measurement, security, and systems conferences in 2017.

Researchers can use top domain lists in different ways. In this paper, we focus on measurement studies that use these lists to select a "representative" sample of domains to analyse, in the sense that these lists designate the "largest" or "most popular" domains (e.g., [14,18,27,32]). When measurement studies compute aggregates over the domains on these lists, their results depend on how the lists select and rank domains [20,30].

A less frequent, but common use of domain lists in security research is to obtain samples of "benign" domains. In this context, domain lists are sometimes used to train models or evaluate proposed security systems (e.g., [9,10,15,22]). In a few cases, any ranked domain is whitelisted to improve classifier performance [21,26]. This use is most sensitive to malicious domains not appearing in the ranking, and other list properties such as stability or ordering are less critical. Maliciousness of ranked domains has been studied before [23,24,28], and this scenario is beyond the scope of this paper.

2.2 List Compilation Methodology

We are aware of four major measurement-based top site lists: Amazon Alexa Top Sites [2], The Majestic Million [6], Quantcast Top Websites [7], and Cisco Umbrella Top 1 Million [4]. Table 1 summarises the data source and popularity model of each ranking.

Alexa. The data for the ranking originates primarily from "millions of users" [3] who have installed the Alexa toolbar and share their browsing history with Alexa. Its website documents Alexa's methodology as follows: The toolbar only collects URLs that appear in the address bar of the browser window or tab. Sudomains are not ranked separately from the main domain, unless they can be determined to be blogs or personal homepages. Domains are ranked according to a combination of the number of users visiting the site, and the unique URLs on that site visited by each user. Ranks below 100k are not statistically meaningful because the data collected about those domains is too scarce [3,5]. The ranking is updated daily. Our work uses the ranking from the file download [1]. In contrast to the API and website, ranks in the file do not appear to be smoothed.

Majestic. Majestic's ranking is based on the link graph built from a continuously updated, proprietary web crawl comprising over 528 B URLs as of June 2018 [6]. Domains are ranked by the number of unique /24 IP networks hosting inbound links [17].

Quantcast. Ranks are based on direct traffic measurements through client-side tracking code embedded by Quantcast's customers into their websites and mobile applications, as well as estimated traffic (from unspecified sources) for non-customer websites [7]. Quantcast customers can choose to hide their identity in the ranking. Table 2 shows that around 1% of all list entries are hidden, but for some list prefixes the percentage can be much higher, such as 15% in the top 100. These censored entries make it challenging to compare this ranking to others. Therefore, we do not consider it further in this paper.

Umbrella. The ranking is computed from incoming DNS lookups observed in Cisco's Umbrella Global Network and the OpenDNS service, which amount to over 100 B daily requests from 65 M users in 165 countries [4]. Consequently, the list reflects the popularity of domains used in any Internet protocol, not only web traffic. According to Umbrella, ranks are based on the unique client IPs looking up a domain [16].

2.3   Related Work

In 2006, Lo and Sharma Sedhain compared the lists available at that time to determine how similar and reliable they were [25]. Out of the lists we initially considered relevant for this study, they included only Alexa. Given the long time that has passed since then, it is likely that the ranking methodology and list composition have changed.

Scheitle et al. [30,31] study the domains on the lists compiled by Alexa, Umbrella and Majestic, how these lists differ, how they evolve over time, how they are being used in research studies, how list parameters influence the outcome of research studies, and how the rankings could be manipulated. The authors describe a weekend effect in Alexa and Umbrella, a periodic change in list composition between weekday and weekend rankings. While the authors convey an intuition as to why this effect exists, we provide a more detailed analysis of the reasons and implications of this phenomenon. We describe an additional phenomenon, clustering of equivalent domains in Alexa and Umbrella, which is not mentioned by Scheitle et al. and discuss potential implications.

Le Pochat et al. [20] also quantify several properties of domain lists and reproduce prior studies using different lists, but the focus of their work is on attacks to influence the rankings. While the weekend effect is visible in one of the figures, it is not further mentioned or analysed. The authors do mention clustering, but only in an attack context, and without discussing the implications for research studies relying on these lists.

When discussing their results, both papers make high-level recommendations how other researchers should use domain lists in their studies. We believe that this topic warrants more discussion and conclude our paper with several additional recommendations.

3   List Analysis

In the following, we study weekend effects and clustering in the top 1 M rankings of Alexa, Majestic, and Umbrella. We downloaded the respective ranking file every day. We label the data with the date one day prior to downloading, as a list updated and downloaded on Monday, for instance, appears to contain the ranks computed from Sunday data.

3.1   List Stability

We begin our analysis with a look at *how much* and *how fast* the rankings change. In contrast to prior work [20,30], we divide each ranking into non-overlapping intervals of exponentially increasing length 1–10, 11–100, 101–1,000, etc. This provides a better view on *which parts* of the ranking change. The exact order of domains within each interval does not matter for many uses in security research, thus we allow for reordering or minor rank changes by calculating set intersections. We pick a single reference day, 2018-02-07 for Alexa and Umbrella, 2018-03-28 for Majestic, and compare all subsequent days upto 2018-05-31 to this day. This allows us to visually distinguish long-term drift from transient changes. Figure 1 uses a Wednesday as a representative of the workweek; similar heatmaps using a Sunday for the weekend can be seen in Fig. 6 in the appendix.

At a high level, the heatmaps show that the top ranked domains exhibit less change than the lower intervals of the ranking. This is in line with Scheitle et al. [30], who showed that longer list prefixes tend to exhibit lower stability. In contrast to prior work, our representation reveals that the higher ranks in Alexa are more stable than in Umbrella, where changes occur within the top 10 domains on a regular basis. The bottom 900k domains, however, are considerably less stable in Alexa than they are in Umbrella. In the bottom of the plot, most intervals get lighter in color, corresponding to long-term drift.

Scheitle et al. [30] describe a *weekend effect* in Alexa and Umbrella, a weekly pattern where change is highest on the weekend. This pattern appears in the heatmaps as regular horizontal bands. While only implied by Scheitle et al. the heatmaps in Fig. 1 confirm that the change is indeed transient, that is, the ranking tends to revert back to the original domains after the weekend. Furthermore,

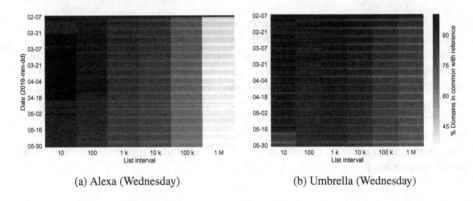

(a) Alexa (Wednesday)   (b) Umbrella (Wednesday)

Fig. 1. Heatmaps showing the set intersection of ranked domains with the reference day, Wed. 7 February, in exponentially increasing list intervals 1–10, 11–100, 101–1,000, etc. Horizontal lines correspond to the weekend effect, which is stronger in Umbrella, whereas Alexa has stronger long-term drift. For Majestic, see Fig. 7 in the appendix.

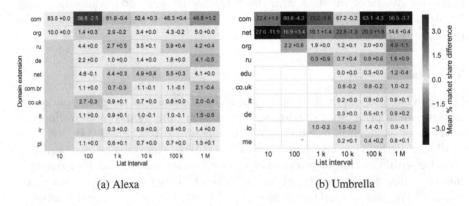

(a) Alexa   (b) Umbrella

Fig. 2. Heatmaps showing domain extensions' mean Wednesday market share ± the difference to the mean Sunday market share (also used to colour each cell) in exponentially increasing list intervals 1–10, 11–100, 101–1,000, etc., from February to May 2018. Extensions ordered by Wednesday top 1 M mean market share. Weekends cause a change in geographic representation. For Majestic, see Fig. 9 in the appendix. (Color figure online)

close inspection of the heatmaps shows that the weekend differences are strongest on Sundays. Figure 6 in the appendix contains similar heatmaps using a Sunday as the reference day, and shows the expected inverted pattern of a greater difference during the workweek, and less during the weekend, relative to the Sunday list. Umbrella has the strongest weekend effect, with changes occurring even in the top 10. For example, Table 4 in the appendix shows that Netflix moves from ranks two and three to one and two, and Hola appears with two new entries. Majestic, shown in Fig. 7 in the appendix, has no discernible weekend effect, as its ranks appear stable.

Table 3. Top 5 unresolvable public suffixes in Umbrella, Feb. to May 2018.

Suffix	Wednesday (mean freq./best rank)	Sunday (mean freq./best rank)
localhost	18/18,583	7,852/11,829
local	835/2,211	1,080/1,530
home	705/2,629	1,266/1,331
lan	566/6,246	948/3,687
localdomain	208/13,852	315/8,723

3.2 The Weekend Effect

Alexa and Umbrella exhibit strong, temporary changes each weekend. Using domain extensions and website categories, we quantify how this affects the type of listed domains.

Domain Extensions. To judge how the lists represent different geographical regions, we look at country-code domain extensions, or more precisely, public suffixes. The public suffix of a domain is the domain extension under which domains can be registered, such as .cl or .co.uk. Country-code domain extensions are only a coarse-grained approximation of country-level popularity, as many regions use generic top-level domains such as .com in addition to their country-code domain, and the U.S. in particular makes comparatively little use of their .us extension. However, the way how each region splits its traffic across generic and country-code domains should be stable, which means that we can use domain extensions to uncover weekday to weekend changes.

Figure 2 shows the most common public suffixes used in Alexa and Umbrella on Wednesdays from February to May 2018, ordered by their mean market share. Different list intervals often exhibit variation in the relative popularity of domain extensions. For example, .jp is the sixth most frequent extension in Alexa's top 100k, whereas it is ranked twenty-fourth in the full list. Extension diversity differs between the lists, with Alexa containing 33 extensions in the top 100, Majestic 13, and Umbrella only 4.

The weekend effect affects the geographical diversity of Alexa and Umbrella. On weekends, Alexa loses domains from European countries and gains in Russia, India, and for .com (from mean of 47.0 to 48.1%); Umbrella also includes more Russian domains, and more domains with invalid extensions, but has fewer .com domains (from 57.1 to 53.4% in the full list). Only Majestic remains relatively stable, most likely due to its ranking reflecting structural properties of a website link graph and not visitor popularity.

Invalid Domains. All of the domains in Alexa use a well-known public suffix, but a mean of 0.5% (Wednesday) and 1.6% (Sunday) of Umbrella domains and 0.004% of Majestic domains have a non-delegated domain extension. Such domains cannot currently be registered or resolved on the public Internet. In fact, Umbrella appears to contain domains used internally in corporate networks. These domains can appear quite high in the ranking, such as the domain tcs at rank 820. Table 3 shows the five most frequently used invalid domain extensions in Umbrella. Each Wednesday, Umbrella contains a mean of 18 domains with the localhost extension, the highest of which was observed at rank 18,583, while each Sunday, localhost contains a mean of 7,852 domain with a best rank of 11,829. This trend is consistent with other invalid domains, showing that invalid domains peak on the weekend. The list also contains a mean of 198 corp domains, and entries corresponding to the names of networking equipment manufacturers such as belkin and dlink. Chen et al. [11,12] describe how internal domain name lookups can leak into the public Internet, where they are susceptible to attacks.

Website Categories. Similar to country-level representations, the lists may exhibit differences in the content-level types of domains they contain. We utilise Symantec/BlueCoat WebPulse [8] to categorise the top 10k domains of each list, assuming that they are websites. For subdomains, the category usually refers to the registered parent domain.

We successfully retrieve categories for 97.8–98.3% of domains in the top 10k from March and April 2018. Domains listed in Alexa and Majestic are classified into 63 and 62 categories, respectively, whereas Umbrella covers only 53 distinct categories. This effect is even more pronounced in the top 1k, where Alexa contains 48 categories, Majestic 39, and Umbrella only 23. Umbrella contains many subdomains [20,30], which results in a significantly less diverse set of websites. Figure 3 shows the most frequent categories ordered by their Wednesday market share. The category market share distribution in Alexa is much more balanced than in Umbrella, resulting in a better representation of websites of different categories.

The types of categories also differ between the lists. The Wednesday Alexa in the interval 100–1k contains 7.5% websites that could be considered "unsafe for work" environments, whereas in Umbrella, the percentage is only 0.2%. This suggests that the Umbrella ranking may be based on a larger share of corporate traffic. Similarly, while the News/Media category is ranked first in Sunday Alexa, it appears at rank 12 in Umbrella. In contrast, Umbrella highly ranks several categories that appear to apply to internal subdomains and subresources such as Web Ads/Analytics, the highest ranked category at (38.4% Wed.), as well as Content Servers (7.7% Wed.) and Non-Viewable/Infrastructure (4.0% Wed.). For comparison, in the Alexa top 1k, the former categories account for only 2.8% and 0.5%, respectively, and the latter category does not appear. This further illustrates the effects of Umbrella's subdomain inclusion.

From the weekdays to the weekend, Alexa and Umbrella both lose in business-related categories and gain in various forms of entertainment. In the Umbrella interval 100–1 k, the Business/Economy category loses 1.1 percentage points, whereas the Chat category gains 0.9 percentage points; Games increase their mar-

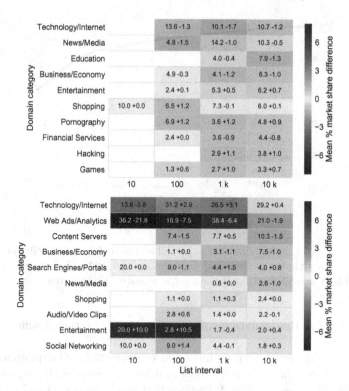

Fig. 3. Alexa (top) and Umbrella (bottom) heatmaps showing website categories' mean Wednesday market share ± the difference to the mean Sunday market share (also used to colour each cell) in exponentially increasing list intervals 1–10, 11–100, 101–1,000, etc., from March to April 2018. Categories ordered by Wednesday top 1 M mean market share. Sundays see fewer office-related domains, and more entertainment. For Majestic, see Fig. 10 in the appendix. (Color figure online)

ket share threefold. Furthermore, categories appear to be slightly more evenly distributed during the weekend. The categories of the top 10 domains (Table 4) in Alexa, and to some extent also the top 100, remain stable between the workweek and the weekend. In Umbrella, however, there is significant change in the categories in the top 10 because of the addition of two new domains. Taken together, these results confirm the preliminary finding by Scheitle et al. [30] (based on popularity changes of a handful of domains listed with many subdomains) that Alexa and Umbrella are dominated by office traffic during the workweek, and leisure traffic during the weekend.

3.3   Clusters

The rankings of Alexa and Umbrella contain large alphabetically sorted clusters of domain names. (Umbrella appears to apply an atypical sorting order when dashes and prefixes are involved: ab-c before ab.) We assume that these clusters

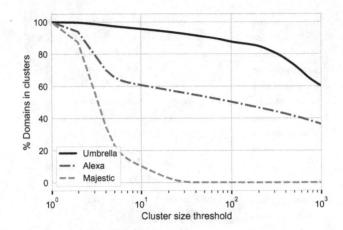

Fig. 4. Percentage of the ranking that is part of a cluster, for varying minimum length thresholds for an alphabetically sorted sequence to be considered a cluster. Alexa and Umbrella cluster a large fraction of their respective list, Majestic does not.

represent domains that cannot be distinguished based on their traffic characteristics.

Alphabetically sorted sublists may occur coincidentally. To explore minimum size thresholds for when a sorted sublist may be considered a cluster, we plot in Fig. 4 the resulting percentage of domains that would be considered part of any cluster. Majestic has only very small clusters; fewer than 0.05% of the list would be part of clusters if they were required to be larger than 42 domains. Applying the same threshold to the other lists, more than 54% of Alexa, and more than 91% of Umbrella appear in a cluster.

To understand the sizes and rank locations of clusters, Fig. 5 plots the length of each alphabetically ordered sublist against its first rank. In Alexa, larger clusters start appearing at ranks around 49k. Clusters can grow very large, with outliers of 40k and 87k domains, and their size does not increase monotonically. Majestic, shown in Fig. 8 in the appendix, has no significant clusters except for a few outliers in the last third of the list. In Umbrella, clusters larger than 42 domains start at rank 83k (rank 126k with a threshold of 100). The size of clusters appears to grow exponentially towards the end of the list, but the last cluster of the list is likely truncated as it does not follow the increasing trend. Furthermore, clusters on the two Wednesdays are one third to a half smaller than the clusters observed on Sundays. This suggests that Umbrella's ranking is based on less traffic on Sundays, as larger clusters imply more domains that cannot be distinguished.

These clusters have a number of important implications for users of the lists. First, while one may expect that domains equivalent in terms of traffic would receive the same rank, Alexa and Umbrella do in fact assign individual ranks to each domain in alphabetical order. Inside a large cluster, the first few characters of a domain can cause a large rank difference, such as 87k in Alexa. The last

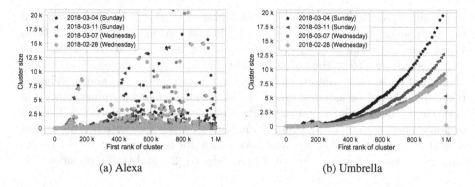

(a) Alexa   (b) Umbrella

Fig. 5. Scatterplots of each alphabetically sorted cluster's size by its highest rank. No size threshold, but clusters with 42 or fewer domains are downsampled to 1% for printability (difference invisible). In Alexa, ten very large outlier clusters of up to 87k domains not shown. Umbrella clusters have a trend of increasing size towards the end of the list, except for the last (truncated) cluster; weekends tend to increase cluster sizes.

cluster of the ranking is cut off, as including it entirely would extend the length of the list beyond 1 M entries. Similar effects can occur when researchers use a list prefix without accounting for clusters. In both cases, domains are excluded from consideration not because of their popularity, but because of their relative lexicographical order. Furthermore, clustering effects have implications on the stability of the list. A domain with stable traffic may receive a worse rank when domains with equivalent traffic but a lower lexicographical ordering are added to the list. Similarly, when a domain switches to an adjacent cluster, the rank difference can be consequential, even though the actual change in traffic may be minor.

4   Discussion: Best Practices for Using Top Domain Lists

Our analysis has revealed various characteristics of the lists compiled by Alexa, Majestic, and Umbrella. To minimise any negative impact that these character-istics can have on measurement results, we propose the following best practices.

Avoid Direct Correlation with a Domain's Rank. Alexa and Umbrella contain large clusters of domains with the same popularity, yet each domain is assigned an individual rank in alphabetical order. For example, 56% of Alexa, and 99.9% of Umbrella entries in the bottom 900k are part of clusters. This can cause anomalies, e.g. when looking for a linear correlation between the rank and a security property ("do more popular websites have a higher security score?"). Furthermore, especially the lower domain ranks can fluctuate considerably on a daily basis. Instead of using the rank directly, we suggest looking at aggregates based on exponentially increasing rank intervals, such as 1–10, 11–100, 101–1000 etc., which perhaps results in less precision, but more robustness.

Use Contemporaneous Rankings to Label Historical Datasets. A domain that was popular in the past is not necessarily highly ranked today, and vice versa. When labelling a dataset with domain ranks, it is important to use the rank that was current at the time of the recorded event. For example, a Web vulnerability database may contain entries spanning multiple years, and a website's popularity should be assessed based on the ranking when the vulnerability was discovered ("do popular websites receive more vulnerability reports?"). The fast responsiveness of Alexa and Umbrella implies that this precaution is also necessary at shorter time scales. A malicious domain, for instance, may be active and popular for just a few days before it is blacklisted [28] and traffic subsides.

Measure a Static Set of Domains, if Possible. We have shown that the weekend effect in Alexa and Umbrella causes different types of domains to be included (e.g., changing country and content category distributions). This pattern is also visible in multiple network, transport and application layer measurements reproduced daily with the newest domain lists by Scheitle et al. [30]. However, such a measurement setup does not allow to distinguish changes due to list composition from changes that occur on a measured domain. For example, a domain that is present in the ranking during all days may cease to use a certain form of tracking, or a domain that always uses this form of tracking may drop out of the ranking, to the same overall effect. We argue that *short-term* noise from list composition, such as the weekend effect, is usually undesirable in measurements. It makes it challenging to interpret observed changes, and it is typically of little interest to break down the prevalence of tracking, for instance, based on sites' weekend or workweek popularity. We believe that measurements can often be carried out with a static list of domains, such as to study the evolution of tracking on a fixed set of sites. *Medium* and *long-term* list changes may be more relevant to account for permanent popularity changes.

To create a set of domains to be measured, we suggest collecting list data over the course of one or more weeks, and using the union or intersection of all days, depending on the scenario. To improve comparability and reproducibility of measurements, researchers could agree on a common list of domains that is updated on a quarterly or yearly basis.

Account for Subdomains. Umbrella contains so many subdomains that the set of unique registered domains is only around 28% [30], three times smaller than in Alexa or Majestic. In some contexts, measuring all subdomains may be desirable. For example, subdomains may serve different web content, and subdomains include mail servers that may use a different TLS configuration than web servers. In other contexts, subdomains may be aliases, or may be configured and managed identically since they are part of the same infrastructure. For example, if they share the same authoritative name server, they likely have identical DNSSEC capabilities. This can result in duplicates, and bias aggregates towards services that are listed with more subdomains. In such cases, it may be preferable to use only one (sub)domain per unique registered domain. Similar issues exist due to Content Distribution Networks [30]. The large difference in unique registered domains also makes it challenging to compare results derived from Umbrella to Alexa or Majestic.

For completeness, we discuss recommendations from prior work in the paragraphs below.

Use Lists According to What They Represent. Each list uses different data, which implies a different definition of popularity. Alexa contains (desktop) type-in website domains, Majestic models website popularity by inbound links instead of visitors, Umbrella ranks domains that may not host web content, and Quantcast allows customers to hide their identity. These missing ranks are not uniformly random (Table 2), and we recommend against the use of Quantcast when representativity or comparability are desired.

Use Only the Highest-Ranked 100k Domains, or Fewer. The publishers of the Alexa list caution that only the top 100k domains are statistically significant [3,5]. The reverse conclusion is a degree of imprecision, or randomness, in the remaining 900k list entries; this could refer both to their relative ranking, and to their presence or absence. Research results aggregated over the full 1 M list are based on 90% "unreliable" data points.

Use Multiple Sources, Including Unranked Sets of Domains. The limitations of individual lists could be mitigated by measuring domains selected from multiple lists in parallel and contrasting the results, as suggested [30] and done [19] in prior work. Researchers could base their analysis on one ranked domain list and a random sample of the .com zone (or IPv4 address space). The first set of domains would be "representative" in terms of visits and mirror the security aspects that users face, while the second set would be "representative" in terms of sites and reflect security from the point of view of developers.

Do Not Assume that Ranked Domains are Benign. This paper and the previous recommendations focus on measurement studies, where domains do not need to be benign. In fact, several prior studies have reported evidence that malicious domains exist in the Alexa ranking [23,24,28]. This can be an issue for security systems using domain lists as sources of "benign" examples for model training, validation or whitelisting [9,10,15,21,22,26].

5 Conclusion

Many security research papers utilise top domain rankings such as the ones published by Alexa, Majestic, or Umbrella to select domains or websites to consider in their study. Each list models popularity in a different way. Alexa contains only type-in website domains based on their popularity with toolbar users, Majestic ranks websites based on structural properties rather than popularity with actual visitors, and Umbrella includes any type of domain observed at a large public DNS resolver, including many internal, non-web domains. Consequently, the lists differ in the country and category distribution of their domains, and some exhibit immediate reactivity to momentary changes in traffic volume and distribution, making weekday and weekend rankings look quite distinct. If not properly accounted for, these characteristics can hamper reproducibility, and introduce unwanted bias into research results derived from the domains in the rankings. To that end, we have proposed best practices for the use of top domain lists in security measurements.

Acknowledgements. This work was supported by Secure Business Austria and the National Science Foundation under grants CNS-1563320, CNS-1703454, and IIS-1553088.

Appendix

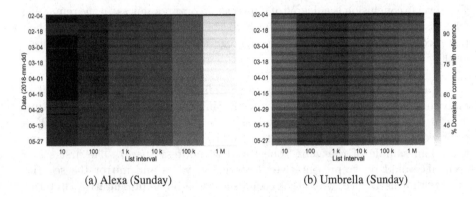

(a) Alexa (Sunday)   (b) Umbrella (Sunday)

Fig. 6. Alexa and Umbrella changes over time in exponentially increasing list intervals, using Sunday 4 February as the reference day. See Fig. 1 for full legend.

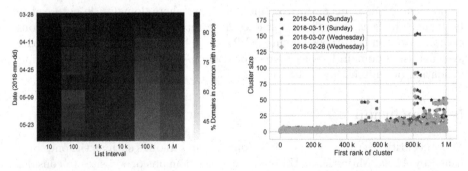

Fig. 7. Changes in Majestic over time in exponentially increasing list intervals, using Wednesday 24 March as the reference day. See Fig. 1 for full legend. Majestic is remarkably stable.

Fig. 8. Scatterplot of each alphabetically sorted cluster's size by its highest rank in Majestic. Partially visible downsampling of small clusters. See Fig. 5 for full legend. Majestic has only small clusters.

Table 4. Top 10 domains on Wed. 4 and Sun. 8 April 2018 in Alexa and Umbrella.

Alexa	Umbrella	
Wednesday & Sunday	Wednesday	Sunday
1 `google.com`	`google.com`	`netflix.com`
2 `youtube.com`	`netflix.com`	`api-global.netflix.com`
3 `facebook.com`	`api-global.netflix.com`	`google.com`
4 `baidu.com`	`www.google.com`	`microsoft.com`
5 `wikipedia.org`	`microsoft.com`	`ichnaea.netflix.com`
6 `yahoo.com`	`facebook.com`	`www.google.com`
7 `reddit.com`	`doubleclick.net`	`facebook.com`
8 `google.co.in`	`g.doubleclick.net`	`hola.org`
9 `qq.com`	`googleads.g.doubleclick.net`	`dns-test1.hola.org`
10 `taobao.com`	`google-analytics.com`	`doubleclick.net`

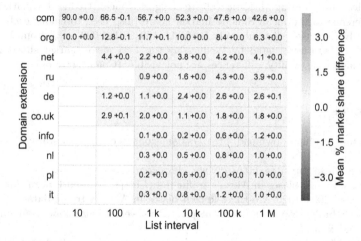

Fig. 9. Heatmap showing Majestic domain extensions' mean Wednesday market share ± the difference to the mean Sunday market share (also used to colour each cell) in exponentially increasing list intervals 1–10, 11–100, 101–1,000, etc., from March to May 2018. Extensions ordered by Wednesday top 1 M mean market share. Due to Majestic's high list stability, differences are not visible. (Color figure online)

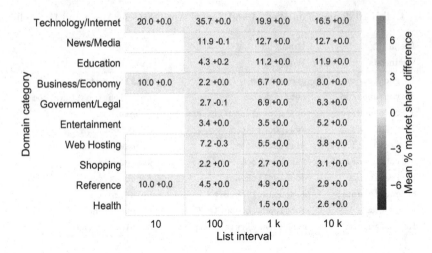

Fig. 10. Heatmap showing Majestic website categories' mean Wednesday market share ± the difference to the mean Sunday market share (also used to colour each cell) in exponentially increasing list intervals 1–10, 11–100, 101–1,000, etc., from March to April 2018. Categories ordered by Wednesday top 1 M mean market share. Due to Majestic's high list stability, differences are not visible. (Color figure online)

References

1. Alexa top 1 million download. http://s3.amazonaws.com/alexa-static/top-1m.csv.zip
2. Amazon Alexa top sites. https://www.alexa.com/topsites
3. Are there known biases in Alexa's traffic data? https://support.alexa.com/hc/en-us/articles/200461920-Are-there-known-biases-in-Alexa-s-traffic-data-
4. Cisco Umbrella top 1 million. https://s3-us-west-1.amazonaws.com/umbrella-static/index.html
5. How are Alexa's traffic rankings determined? https://support.alexa.com/hc/en-us/articles/200449744-How-are-Alexa-s-traffic-rankings-determined-
6. Majestic million. https://majestic.com/reports/majestic-million
7. Quantcast top websites. https://www.quantcast.com/top-sites/
8. Symantec BlueCoat WebPulse site review. https://sitereview.bluecoat.com/
9. Alrwais, S., et al.: Under the shadow of sunshine: understanding and detecting bulletproof hosting on legitimate service provider networks. In: Security and Privacy Symposium (2017)
10. Bilge, L., Kirda, E., Kruegel, C., Balduzzi, M.: EXPOSURE: finding malicious domains using passive DNS analysis. In: NDSS (2011)
11. Chen, Q.A., Osterweil, E., Thomas, M., Mao, Z.M.: MitM attack by name collision: cause analysis and vulnerability assessment in the new gTLD era. In: Security and Privacy Symposium (2016)
12. Chen, Q.A., et al.: Client-side name collision vulnerability in the new gTLD era: a systematic study. In: CCS (2017)
13. Durumeric, Z., Kasten, J., Bailey, M., Halderman, J.A.: Analysis of the HTTPS certificate ecosystem. In: IMC (2013)

14. Englehardt, S., Narayanan, A.: Online tracking: a 1-million-site measurement and analysis. In: CCS (2016)
15. Heiderich, M., Frosch, T., Holz, T.: ICESHIELD: detection and mitigation of malicious websites with a frozen DOM. In: Sommer, R., Balzarotti, D., Maier, G. (eds.) RAID 2011. LNCS, vol. 6961, pp. 281–300. Springer, Heidelberg (2011). https://doi.org/10.1007/978-3-642-23644-0_15
16. Hubbard, D.: Cisco Umbrella 1 million (2016). https://umbrella.cisco.com/blog/2016/12/14/cisco-umbrella-1-million/
17. Jones, D.: Majestic million CSV now free for all, daily (2012). https://blog.majestic.com/development/majestic-million-csv-daily/
18. Larisch, J., Choffnes, D., Levin, D., Maggs, B.M., Mislove, A., Wilson, C.: CRLite: a scalable system for pushing all TLS revocations to all browsers. In: Security and Privacy Symposium (2017)
19. Lauinger, T., Chaabane, A., Arshad, S., Robertson, W., Wilson, C., Kirda, E.: Thou Shalt not depend on me: analysing the use of outdated JavaScript libraries on the Web. In: NDSS (2017)
20. Le Pochat, V., van Goethem, T., Tajalizadehkhoob, S., Korczynski, M., Joosen, W.: Rigging research results by manipulating top websites rankings. In: NDSS (2019)
21. Lee, S., Kim, J.: WarningBird: detecting suspicious URLs in Twitter stream. In: NDSS (2011)
22. Lever, C., Kotzias, P., Balzarotti, D., Caballero, J., Antonakakis, M.: A lustrum of malware network communication: evolution and insights. In: Security and Privacy Symposium (2017)
23. Lever, C., Walls, R.J., Nadji, Y., Dagon, D., McDaniel, P., Antonakakis, M.: Domain-Z: 28 registrations later. In: Security and Privacy Symposium (2016)
24. Li, Z., Zhang, K., Xie, Y., Yu, F., Wang, X.: Knowing your enemy: understanding and detecting malicious web advertising. In: CCS (2012)
25. Lo, B.W.N., Sedhain, R.S.: How reliable are website rankings? Implications for e-business advertising and internet search. Issues Inf. Syst. 7(2), 233–238 (2006)
26. Nadji, Y., Antonakakis, M., Perdisci, R., Lee, W.: Connected colors: unveiling the structure of criminal networks. In: Stolfo, S.J., Stavrou, A., Wright, C.V. (eds.) RAID 2013. LNCS, vol. 8145, pp. 390–410. Springer, Heidelberg (2013). https://doi.org/10.1007/978-3-642-41284-4_20
27. Pearce, P., Ensafi, R., Li, F., Feamster, N., Paxson, V.: Augur: internet-wide detection of connectivity disruptions. In: Security and Privacy Symposium (2017)
28. Pitsillidis, A., Kanich, C., Voelker, G.M., Levchenko, K., Savage, S.: Taster's choice: a comparative analysis of spam feeds. In: IMC (2012)
29. Felt, A.P., Barnes, R., King, A., Palmer, C., Bentzel, C., Tabriz, P.: Measuring HTTPS adoption on the Web. In: USENIX Security (2017)
30. Scheitle, Q., t al.: A long way to the top: significance, structure, and stability of internet top lists. In: IMC (2018)
31. Scheitle, Q., Jelten, J., Hohlfeld, O., Ciprian, L., Carle, G.: Structure and stability of internet top lists. In: eprint arXiv:1802.02651 [cs.NI] (2018)
32. Starov, O., Nikiforakis, N.: XHOUND: quantifying the fingerprintability of browser extensions. In: Security and Privacy Symposium (2017)

Funny Accents: Exploring Genuine Interest in Internationalized Domain Names

Victor Le Pochat$^{(\boxtimes)}$ [iD], Tom Van Goethem, and Wouter Joosen

imec-DistriNet, KU Leuven, 3001 Leuven, Belgium
{victor.lepochat,tom.vangoethem,wouter.joosen}@cs.kuleuven.be

Abstract. International Domain Names (IDNs) were introduced to support non-ASCII characters in domain names. In this paper, we explore IDNs that hold *genuine interest*, i.e. that owners of brands with diacritical marks may want to register and use. We generate 15 276 candidate IDNs from the page titles of popular domains, and see that 43% are readily available for registration, allowing for spoofing or phishing attacks. Meanwhile, 9% are not allowed by the respective registry to be registered, preventing brand owners from owning the IDN. Based on WHOIS records, DNS records and a web crawl, we estimate that at least 50% of the 3 189 registered IDNs have the same owner as the original domain, but that 35% are owned by a different entity, mainly domain squatters; malicious activity was not observed. Finally, we see that application behavior toward these IDNs remains inconsistent, hindering user experience and therefore widespread uptake of IDNs, and even uncover a phishing vulnerability in iOS Mail.

Keywords: Internationalized Domain Names · Phishing ·
Domain squatting · Homograph attack

1 Introduction

The Internet has become a global phenomenon, with more than half of the world's households being estimated to have Internet access [2]. The English language and Latin alphabet remain dominant, but multilingual content is enjoying increased popularity [19,59]. However, one crucial part of the Internet, the Domain Name System (DNS), has historically been limited to ASCII characters [5,27,46].

Internationalized Domain Names (IDNs) [20,35] have been introduced to address this problem, and domain names can now contain (Unicode) characters from various languages and scripts. IDNs allow end users to refer to websites in their native language, and have helped to increase linguistic diversity, with a strong correlation between a website's language and the script of its IDN [19].

Acceptance of IDNs relies on support by web applications, and while this has been improving, significant gaps that present a barrier to user recognition and

© Springer Nature Switzerland AG 2019
D. Choffnes and M. Barcellos (Eds.): PAM 2019, LNCS 11419, pp. 178–194, 2019.
https://doi.org/10.1007/978-3-030-15986-3_12

adoption remain [19]. Moreover, IDNs have seen abuse, with malicious actors registering domains that use visually similar characters to impersonate popular domains for phishing attacks [21,28,41]. This further complicates how browsers choose between displaying IDNs and protecting end users [1,44].

In this paper, we explore (ab)use of IDNs for over 15 000 popular brands and phrases that contain non-ASCII characters (e.g. "Nestlé"), obtained through the presence of their ASCII equivalent in a set of popular domains (nestle.com). For these, we define IDNs that hold *genuine interest* (nestlé.com): these IDNs can enhance user experience as they are easier and more natural to read and correctly understand, and both end users and brand owners may therefore prefer to use them. Moreover, country-specific keyboard layouts often feature dedicated keys for characters with accents, making typing them no more difficult than non-accented letters. We study whether owners of popular domains where an IDN with genuine interest exists have made the effort to register and use it.

However, these IDNs can also attract malicious activity. While previous work studied abuse of IDNs resembling very popular brands [41], these brands generally do not feature accents, meaning that users are less prone to use or trust the IDNs, and brand owners are not inclined to own them except for defensive purposes. In contrast, as our IDNs with genuine interest appear 'valid' to end users, it becomes even more difficult to distinguish a legitimate website from an attempt at phishing, and the domains are therefore more valuable to malicious actors. This also enables attacks akin to typosquatting [16], as users may type the (non-)accented version of a domain, even though this may host a different website. We determine whether these IDNs are still open for or already see abuse.

In summary, we make the following contributions: (1) we generate 15 276 candidate IDNs with genuine interest as derived from the page titles of popular domains; (2) we see that 43% can still easily be registered, e.g. for domain squatting or abuse by malicious parties; (3) we estimate at least 50% of the IDNs to share ownership with the original domain, but 35% to have different owners, mostly domain squatters; (4) we see that browsers and email clients display IDNs inconsistently: our survey even leads us to discover a vulnerability in iOS Mail that enables phishing for domains with ß.

2   Background and Related Work

Internationalized Domain Names. Through the Domain Name System (DNS), user-friendly domain names are translated into IP addresses. Domain names represent a hierarchy, with the registries managing the top-level domains (e.g. .com) usually delegating the public offering of second-level domains (e.g. example.com) to registrars. Originally, the *LDH* convention restricted domain names to ASCII *l*etters, *d*igits and *h*yphens [5,27,46]. However, languages like French and German use Latin characters with diacritics, and e.g. Arabic and Chinese use different character sets altogether. To provide a universal character encoding of these writing systems, the Unicode Standard [65] was developed.

To support domain names with Unicode labels, IETF developed the Internationalized Domain Names in Applications (IDNA2003) protocol in 2003 [20]. To maintain compatibility with existing protocols and systems, this protocol uses the Punycode algorithm [10] to convert Unicode labels ("U-label") to an ASCII Compatible Encoding (ACE) label starting with xn-- and containing only ASCII characters ("A-label"). In 2010, the standard was revised (IDNA2008) [35], mainly to add support for newer versions of the Unicode Standard.

Homograph Attacks. Homographs are strings that contain homoglyphs or visually resembling characters, and can be used to trick users into thinking that they are visiting one domain while actually browsing another, opening up opportunities for web spoofing or phishing [14,28]. While certain ASCII characters (e.g. lower case l and upper case I) already allowed for confusion, the introduction of IDNs gave rise to a whole new set of potential homographs, using either diacritics or resembling characters from other scripts. Evaluations over time of browser and email client behavior regarding IDNs have found that browsers have implemented countermeasures in response to vulnerabilities to homograph attacks, but that they are not (yet) fully effective [24–26,41,45,71].

Previous studies have shown IDNs confusable with popular domains to exist on a modest scale and for relatively benign purposes such as parking [21,28]. In 2018, Liu et al. [41] detected 1 516 out of 1.4 million registered IDNs to exploit homographs for targeting domains in Alexa's top 1 000. Only 4.82% belonged to the same owner as the original domain. Moreover, they generated 42 434 additional IDNs with sufficient visual similarity that are still unregistered. Tian et al. [66] searched for phishing sites that impersonate a set of 702 popular brands both in content and in domain, a.o. through homograph domains. Several industry reports have addressed homograph attacks in the wild, seeing circumvention of spam filters [70], phishing, malware and botnet abuse [38] and popular as well as financial websites being main targets [56].

Domain Squatting. Domain names can be exploited for deceiving end users: involuntary errors redirect traffic to unintended destinations [3,15,16,50,63,67, 69], while credible domain names may create the perception of dealing with a legitimate party [34,43,48]. Spaulding et al. [61] reviewed techniques to generate, abuse and counteract deceptive domains. Liu et al. [41] found 1 497 IDNs that combine domains from Alexa's top 1 000 with keywords containing non-ASCII characters. They also mention a type of abuse where the IDN is the translation of a brand name to another language, but do not conduct any experiments.

3 Methods

3.1 Generating Candidate Domains

In order to obtain IDNs with genuine interest, we start from a list of popular domains. While the Alexa top million ranking is commonly used, Scheitle et al. [55] and Le Pochat et al. [39] have shown that it has become very volatile and disagrees with other rankings, while the latter proved that manipulation by malicious actors requires very low effort. Therefore, we use the Tranco list[1]

---

[1] https://tranco-list.eu/list/RQ4M/1000000.

Table 1. Candidate IDNs are generated by searching relevant substitutions within a domain name using its root page title.

Original domain	Root page title	Converted to lowercase, punctuation removed	Diacritics removed/ substitutions applied	Derived IDN
example.com	Example domain	example domain	example domain	*No IDN*
nestle.com	Home | Nestlé Global	home nestlé global	home nestle global	nestlé.com
uni-koeln.de	Universität zu Köln	universität zu köln	universitat zu koln universitaet zu koeln	– uni-köln.de

proposed by Le Pochat et al. [39], a list of one million domains generated by combining four rankings over 30 days (here 30 July to 28 August 2018), in order to require prolonged popularity from multiple vantage points.

We check for each domain whether it corresponds to a string that contains diacritical marks, i.e. where there could be genuine interest in adopting a variant IDN. For this purpose, we look for plausible substitutions with accented words in the title of its root page. To collect these title strings, we use a distributed crawler setup of 4 machines with 4 CPU cores and 8 GB RAM, using Ubuntu 16.04 with Chromium version 66.0.3359.181 in headless mode.

We then convert this title to lowercase and remove punctuation, after which two strings are generated: either diacritical marks are simply removed, or language-specific substitutions are applied (as listed in Appendix A). The latter covers the common practice in for example German to use replacements such as ae for ä. We then compare these converted (ASCII) strings with the domain name: we favor the case where the full domain is found, but also consider cases where single words are shared. Finally, if such cases are found, we retrieve the corresponding accented form from the original title and apply this substitution to the original domain name, resulting in the candidate IDN. Table 1 illustrates our approach.

3.2 Retrieving Domain-Related Data

To understand if and how these IDNs are used, we collect the following data:

DNS Records. To check whether candidate IDNs exist in the DNS (i.e. are registered) and how they are configured, we request A, MX, NS and SOA records for both the original and candidate domain. If all records return an NXDOMAIN response, we assume the domain to be unregistered. Otherwise, we verify whether the nameserver is properly set up (no SERVFAIL) and if there are A records (suggesting a reachable website) or only other records (suggesting another purpose).

Domain Eligibility. A TLD registry is free to support IDNs or not, and if they do, they may only allow a specific set of characters. For country code TLDs this set usually consists of the characters in languages spoken in that TLD's country, which can help in avoiding homograph attacks by prohibiting confusable characters that would normally not be used in those languages.

ICANN's IDN guidelines [29] require registries to publish "Label Generation Rulesets" (LGR), i.e. lists with permitted Unicode code points, in IANA's Repository for IDN Practices [30]. However, as of this publication, only six TLDs had published these machine readable LGRs. For 626 other TLDs, the repository contains simple text files that list the code points. Where possible, we parse these files and generate the corresponding LGRs with ICANN's LGR Toolset [31]. For the remaining TLDs, no information is available from the repository. We manually search the IDN policy and generate an LGR for 30 additional TLDs. Finally, we validate our candidate domains against these LGRs with the LGR Toolset to determine whether they are allowed by their respective registries.

Domain Availability. To determine whether unregistered domains can be readily bought through a popular registrar, we query GoDaddy's API [22] for their availability. This data complements the eligibility data, as further restrictions may apply for certain TLDs (e.g. being based in that TLD's country): in this case the API returns an error indicating that the TLD is unsupported, otherwise the API returns whether the domain is (un)available.

WHOIS Records. To obtain ownership information for the domains in our data set, we retrieve and parse their WHOIS records with the Ruby Whois library [7]. However, WHOIS data has several limitations, especially for bulk and automated processing. The format of WHOIS data varies widely between providers (which can be registries or registrars); it may be human-readable, but both parser-based and statistical methods cannot retrieve all information flawlessly [42]. Moreover, rate limits prevent bulk data collection.

Even if data can be adequately obtained, it may not be of high quality. Registrant details can contain private contact information, so privacy concerns and malicious intent have spurred a number of privacy and proxy services, whose details replace those of the real owner [9]. The European General Data Protection Regulation (GDPR) has also cast doubt on whether such data can still be released [32], with e.g. the .de registry already withholding any personal details [13]. Finally, WHOIS data may be outdated, e.g. not reflecting company name changes, or the same registrant may use different data across domains.

Web Pages. To determine what content the accented and non-accented domains serve, we visit the root page for each domain pair where the IDN has a valid A record. By limiting our crawl to one page, we minimize the impact on the servers hosting the websites. As with our title crawl, we use a real browser to capture the request and response headers, the redirection path and final URL of the response, TLS certificate data, the HTML source and a screenshot.

To classify domains, we first compute a perceptual hash of the screenshot based on the discrete cosine transform [37]. As visually similar images have similar hash values, we cluster their pairwise Hamming distances using DBSCAN [18] to find groups of websites with (nearly) the same content, which we then manually label. We also compare the hashes of the original domain and its IDN to detect equal but non-redirecting domains. Finally, for domains that were not

Table 2. Summary of the registration properties of our candidate IDNs.

Candidates	15 276	(100.0%)			
Unregistered	12 087	(79.1%)	Readily available	6 608	(54.7%)
			Unavailable/Additional restrictions	4 116	(34.1%)
			Non-compliant with TLD policy	1 363	(11.3%)
Registered	3 189	(20.9%)			

classified using their hash, we check for the presence of certain keywords (e.g. 'parking') in the HTML source, or else decide that we cannot classify the domain.

Blacklists. To detect whether our candidate IDNs exhibit malicious behavior, we match them and the domains they redirect to against the current blacklists provided by Google Safe Browsing [23] (malware and phishing), PhishTank [53] (phishing), Spamhaus DBL [60] (spam), SURBL [62] (spam, phishing, malware and cracking) and VirusTotal [8] (malware).

3.3 Limitations

We restrict our search to IDNs with variations on characters of the Latin alphabet. Our exploration could be broadened to popular domains that are a romanized (converted to Latin alphabet) version of brands or phrases in another character set. However, a script often has multiple romanization standards that may be language-dependent [64]: for example, Яндекс (Yandex) can be romanized to Iandeks, Jandeks or Yandeks. We therefore ignore other character sets to avoid false positives and negatives caused by these differing systems.

Our approach to select candidate IDNs is conservative: our requirement that whole words from the title and domain match, may mean that we miss some candidate IDNs, e.g. if the domain is an abbreviation of words in the title. However, through this approach we limit erroneous candidate IDNs, which we estimate would more likely be either unregistered or maliciously used, as no one would have a genuine interest in owning the domain.

4   Results

In this section, we determine whether IDNs with genuine interest share ownership with the popular domain they are based on, and for what purpose they are used. Through a crawl conducted between 30 August and 28 September 2018, we were able to retrieve a non-empty title from the root page of 849 341 out of 1 million domains (website rankings are known to contain unreachable domains [39]). Using the process described in Sect. 3.1, we generated 15 276 candidate IDNs.

Table 3. Summary of the classification of the registered IDNs with genuine interest.

(a) Domain ownership.

Same owner	1 595 (50.0%)
Same configuration	289 (9.1%)
Different owner	1 102 (34.6%)
Insufficient data	203 (6.4%)

(b) DNS records.

A same	704 (22.1%)
NS or SOA same	736 (23.1%)
NS and SOA different	624 (19.6%)
All records different	838 (26.3%)
Other/no data	287 (9.0%)

(c) WHOIS records.

Same contact	319 (10.0%)
Same nameserver	378 (11.9%)
Other	923 (28.9%)
No data	1 569 (49.2%)

(d) Website availability.

No A record	455 (14.3%)
HTTP status 200	2 466 (77.3%)
Other HTTP status	160 (5.0%)
Not reachable	108 (3.4%)

(e) Website content.

Redirect to original	1 215 (49.3%)
Identical content	112 (4.5%)
Parked/for sale	751 (30.5%)
Empty/default	132 5.4%
Unknown	256 (10.4%)

(f) TLS setup.

Same certificate	479 (22.1%)
Different certificate	1 687 (77.9%)
Secure	171 (7.9%)
Insecure	964 (44.5%)
No connection	1 031 (47.6%)

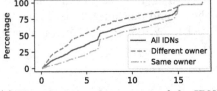
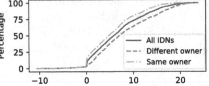

(a) Years between the creation of the IDN and October 15, 2018, for 3 IDN types.

(b) Difference in years between the creation of the original domain and the IDN.

Fig. 1. Cumulative distribution functions for the creation dates of registered IDNs.

4.1 Registration and Ownership

Table 2 lists whether our candidate IDNs with genuine interest are still available for registration. Of the 79.1% unregistered IDNs, 11.3% do not comply with their respective TLD's LGR policy, meaning that an owner of a popular domain cannot register the corresponding IDN and loses out on the user experience benefits. Through the GoDaddy API, we find that 43.3% of all candidate IDNs are readily available; 26.9% are unavailable for registration, because the registry either blocks visually similar registrations or applies further restrictions to registrants, which could also increase the burden for a malicious registration.

For the 20.9% registered domains, we compare the DNS (Table 3b) and WHOIS (Table 3c) records and web crawl data (Tables 3e and f) to estimate whether the original domain and its IDN have the same owner (summarized in Table 3a). For 50.0%, we believe both domains to have the same owner: they have overlapping WHOIS contact data, have the same A record, serve the same web content and/or present a TLS certificate for the same domains. For an additional 9.1%, shared nameservers or SOA records also allow us to reasonably assume shared ownership. For 34.6%, we believe both domains to have a different owner: either their NS and SOA records are both different, or the domain is parked or for sale. Brand owners would be unlikely to use the latter for monetizing their IDN, as they could better serve the actual website the visitor is looking for, and the domain would not be displaying content from a third party.

Figure 1 shows the distribution of creation dates of the IDNs. Brand owners tend to have registered their IDNs earlier than average, while domain squatters registered them later (Fig. 1a). The majority of IDNs was registered after the original domain, although 3.7% of IDNs were registered earlier (Fig. 1b).

In our data set, we can see examples of companies that do or do not cover IDNs when protecting their brand on the Internet. Nestlé, L'Oréal, Mömax and Citroën own several candidate IDNs, usually redirecting to the original domain, but still see some owned by third parties for parking. We also see 40 IDNs bought by brand protectors such as CSC, Nameshield and SafeBrands for their clients. However, the lack of support for certain characters hinders some companies in owning IDNs with genuine interest: e.g. the Š character in Škoda sees little support by TLD registries, causing relatively low IDN ownership.

4.2   Usage

Table 3d lists whether the IDNs host a website: 14.3% of registered IDNs have no configured A record, suggesting proactive registration without the intention to use the IDN. Table 3e lists what content the domains that returned HTTP status code 200 serve, with 53.8% displaying the same content as the original domain, meaning that they are very likely owned and operated by the same entity. 112 IDNs are even treated equally by not redirecting to the original; however, none of the original domains redirect to the IDN. 30.5% are parked/for sale, while 5.4% show an empty/default page (e.g. unconfigured server).

Manual inspection of the domains that could not be classified shows that these largely fall into two categories. The first consists of websites that are completely different to the original domain, owned by another entity. This can leverage the popularity of the original domain, and is an opportunity to own domains with desirable phrases, but also exposes end users to confusion and potential misdirection. The second has the IDN showing slightly different or older versions of the original domain. This indicates that they both belong to the same owner and that there was an intention to use the IDN, but that it was forgotten when the original domain was reconfigured and now points to an outdated website.

4.3   Security

Incidence on blacklists is very low: none of our candidate IDNs, nor the domains they redirect to appear on the Google Safe Browsing, PhishTank, Spamhaus or SURBL blacklists. VirusTotal reports malware detections on 5 domains, but only by at most 3 out of 67 engines; these detections appear to be based on outdated information. However, Tian et al. [66] have found that over 90% of phishing sites served through squatting domains could evade blacklisting, meaning that phishing may already be much more prevalent on our candidate IDNs. Finally, parked domains are known to only sometimes redirect to malicious content [68]: we manually saw instances of such intermittent redirects to blacklisted sites for several IDNs.

Through inspection of the redirection paths, we found no proof of affiliate abuse on IDNs (sending users to the intended domain, but adding an affiliate ID to earn a sales commission), as has been seen for several domain squatting techniques [47]. We manually found examples of other, questionable behavior: pokémongo.com offers a "cheat code" in an online survey scam [33], and has a cryptocurrency miner [17,54]; jmonáe.com redirects to the original domain through an ad-based URL shortener [49]; and www.preußische-allgemeine.de includes the site of a competing newspaper in a frame (Fig. 2).

From the WHOIS records, we find 81 domains to use a privacy/proxy service; while abusive domains tend to use such services [9], using them does not reliably demonstrate malicious intent [36]. Moreover, privacy concerns as well as the GDPR make that some registries and registrars hide private information by default, reducing the need to procure a privacy/proxy service.

As the web is rapidly adopting HTTPS, IDNs will also need a correct TLS setup for users to reach them without trouble. However, for the 2 166 reachable IDNs in our TLS crawl, Table 3f shows that only 7.9% are securely configured and would not cause a browser warning. The other domains either have an insecure setup (mostly because the presented certificate does not cover the IDN) or do not allow a TLS connection to be established.

For the domains with shared ownership, 60.2% are insecure or don't allow a TLS connection even though the original domain is securely configured. For 360 (26.9%) IDNs, the presented certificate is valid only for the original domain, suggesting that the domain owner has set up the original domain and the IDN identically, but has forgotten to obtain a certificate that is also valid for the IDN.

5   User Agent Behavior

Throughout the DNS protocol, the A-label (Punycode) of an IDN is used to maintain backward compatibility. However, developers of user interfaces may elect to display the U-label (Unicode) to provide the best user experience, as the A-label is less readable (e.g. köln.de becomes xn--kln-sna.de). In this section, we discuss the behavior of user agents regarding IDNs with diacritical marks from the Latin script, where the lack of homoglyphs makes abuse more difficult to prevent. We also uncover two edge cases that have an impact both on the value of IDNs to brand owners and on the vulnerability to IDN abuse.

Table 4 shows that popular web browsers and email clients vary widely in whether they show the A- or U-label when visiting a website or receiving email. The Gmail app on Android is a particular case, as it shows either the U-label or the A-label when email is received on a Gmail or IMAP account respectively.

Browsers based on Chromium, such as Chrome and several Android browsers, implement a special policy toward IDNs resembling very popular domains: the A-label is shown when the domain with diacritics removed appears on a hardcoded list based on Alexa's top 10 000 [1]. This policy affects 125 candidate IDNs, of which 74 are registered with 21 having the same owner: these cannot choose to prefer the IDN without affecting user experience. 2 domains already do not redirect, causing the display of the A-label. The seemingly arbitrary cut-off [58],

Table 4. Browser and email client behavior regarding IDNs with diacritical marks. For the top 10 000 pokémon.com was tested, for the other sites böll.de, and for "deviation" characters straße.de. 'A' denotes the display of the A-label, 'U' of the U-label. Appendix B lists the browser and email client versions used in our survey.

(a) Web browsers

		10K	other	ß/ss
Desktop	Chrome	A	U	ss
	Firefox	U	U	ß
	Safari	U	U	ß
	Opera	A	U	ss
	Internet Explorer	A	A	ss
	Edge	A	A	ss
Mobile	Chrome	A	U	ss
	Safari	U	U	ß
	Firefox	U	U	ß
	UC Browser	A	A	ß
	Samsung Internet	A	U	ss
	Opera	A	U	ss
	Microsoft Edge	A	U	ss

(b) Email clients

		10K	other	ß/ss receive	send
Desktop	Outlook	U	U	empty	ss
	macOS Mail	A	A	A (ß)	ss
	Thunderbird	A	A	A (ß)	ß
Mobile	Gmail	U	U	U (ß)	ss
	Gmail (IMAP)	A	A	A (ß)	fails
	Outlook	A	A	A (ß)	fails
	iOS Mail <12.1.1	U	U	ss	ß
	iOS Mail ≥12.1.1			U (ß)	
Webmail	Gmail	U	U	A (ß)	ss
	Yahoo	A	A	A (ß)	fails
	Yandex	U	U	A (ß)	ss
	Outlook	A	A	A (ß)	ss
	RoundCube	U	U	A (ß)	ß

manual addition of domains and lack of updates [57] suggest that this heuristic solution using a hardcoded list still leaves room for successful spoofing attacks.

Another edge case was introduced during the revision of the IDNA standard. Four characters (so-called "deviations") are valid in both versions, but are interpreted differently [12]: for example, the German ß is supported as-is in IDNA2008 but converted to ss in IDNA2003[2]. This results in two different domains, but the visited domain depends on which version of the standard a browser implements.

This does not only affect user experience, i.e. when links on web pages or outside the browser (e.g. in emails) point to different resources, but also has security implications. The ß domain may host a spoofing or phishing site replicating that of the ss domain [12]. Moreover, resources included from an ß domain could originate from another domain in different browsers, allowing to insert malicious content. Requiring the same owner for both domains will prevent such attacks, although errors due to misconfigured websites may persist. However, for example even the German .de registry does not currently enforce this for ß and ss.

Unfortunately, Table 4a shows that major browsers do not agree on which IDNA standard to implement, causing them to direct users to different websites as shown in Fig. 2. An ß character occurs in 55 candidate IDNs, of which 26 are registered, including several bank websites. 9 domains do not belong to the

---

[2] The other deviations are the Greek ς, converted to σ in IDNA2003, and the zero width non-joiner and joiner, both deleted by the IDNA2003 Punycode algorithm.

Fig. 2. Visiting preußische-allgemeine.de in Chrome and Firefox leads to different sites: preussische-allgemeine.de and xn--preuische-allgemeine-ewb.de.

same owner: the ß domain is then almost unreachable from Chromium-based and Microsoft browsers (users would have to type or follow a link to the already converted A-label), and there is potential for phishing or spoofing attacks.

Email clients also handle domains with ß differently, even between receiving and sending (Table 4b). On Outlook, the sender field remains empty. More worringly, we found that iOS Mail displayed an email received from an ß domain (e.g. user@straße.de) as coming from the domain with ss (user@strasse.de). This vulnerability enables phishing attacks by the owner of the ß domain; moreover, checks such as SPF will succeed as they are carried out by the mail exchangers and not the client. A reply will also be sent to the ß domain, potentially leaking sensitive information to a third party. We disclosed this vulnerability to Apple, and it was fixed in iOS 12.1.1 [4], which now displays the correct U-label.

6 Discussion

As registries are ultimately responsible for managing which domains can be registered and who can own them, they are in a prime position to combat IDN-related abuse. The most recent version of ICANN's IDN implementation guidelines [29] calls for registries to prohibit registrations of domain name variants with accented or homoglyph characters, or limit them to the same owner [40]. While certain registries implement these measures [6,11,51,52], other registries that support IDNs usually either only apply such policies to homograph domains but not domains with diacritics, or do not impose any restriction at all, allowing malicious actors or domain squatters to register the IDNs with genuine interest.

On the client side, browsers and email clients represent the most visible and widespread use of IDNs. However, we have shown that they do not yet universally support the display of IDNs in Unicode, degrading the user experience. Moreover, measures put in place by browser vendors to prevent homograph attacks have been shown to be insufficient on multiple occasions [21,41,71]; we have done the same for a popular email client. Mozilla has expressed the opinion that registries are responsible for preventing IDN abuse, and that browser restrictions risk degrading the usefulness of IDNs [44]. Indeed, the manually developed and heuristic-based defenses cannot be expected to comprehensively solve this issue. Other protection mechanisms such as TLS and SPF also cannot prevent these attacks, as e.g. certificates can legitimately be acquired for the malicious IDN.

Owners of popular brands and domains can register the IDN with genuine interest, either as a real replacement or supplementary domain, or to proactively stop others from abusing it. However, while this may be enough to combat (more dangerous) abuse of the 'valid' IDN with genuine interest, registering all other variant domains with homoglyphs, diacritics, and potential typos quickly becomes infeasible in terms of cost and coverage. Shared ownership of IDNs with genuine interest is already much more common than of other homograph IDNs (over 50% vs. almost 5% [41]). However, it is still concerning that at least 35% allow third parties to take hold of the valuable IDNs with genuine interest.

An unfortunate outcome of the issues surrounding IDNs would be to discourage the adoption of IDNs and to recommend that users distrust them. IDNs enable anyone to use the Internet in their native language, providing them a great benefit in user experience. IDNs also allow companies to create a better integration of brands with their Internet presence, e.g. combining a logo with a TLD in marketing material, providing additional economic value.

7   Conclusion

We have introduced the concept of Internationalized Domain Names for which there is *genuine interest*: domains that represent popular brands or phrases with diacritical marks. By comparing the page titles and domain names for 849 341 websites, we generated 15 276 such IDNs. We find 43% of them to be available for registration without restrictions, leaving the opportunity for a third party to exploit the IDN. For the 3 189 registered domains, we see that ownership is split: at least half have the same owner and content as the original domain, but at least a third belongs to another entity, usually domain squatters who have put the domain up for sale. The IDNs are not known to exhibit malicious activity, although cases of questionable behavior can be found. From insecure TLS setups and IDNs showing old versions of the original domain, we can see that brand owners who registered IDNs tend to 'forget' configuring them properly. Finally, we find applications to treat IDNs with diacritical marks inconsistently, displaying Unicode or a less readable alternative depending on resemblance to a popular domain or on the implemented version of the IDNA standard. We even found a phishing vulnerability on iOS Mail, where the actual sender domain differs from the one displayed. While brand owners have already somewhat found their way to IDNs with genuine interest, and while registries and browser vendors start to deploy tools to prevent IDN abuse, support for IDNs remains challenging, which unfortunately does not encourage their uptake in the near future.

Acknowlegdments. We would like to thank our shepherd Ignacio Castro for his valuable feedback, and Gertjan Franken and Katrien Janssens for their help in the user agent survey. This research is partially funded by the Research Fund KU Leuven. Victor Le Pochat holds a PhD Fellowship of the Research Foundation - Flanders (FWO).

A   Common Character Substitutions

Original	ä	ö	ü	ß	æ	ø	å	œ	þ
Substitution	ae	oe	ue	ss	ae	oe	aa	oe	th

B   Tested User Agent Versions

	Client	Version	Operating system
Browser desktop	Google Chrome	69.0.3497.100	Ubuntu Linux 18.04.1
	Firefox	62.0	Ubuntu Linux 18.04.1
	Safari	12.0.1 (13606.2.100)	macOS 10.13.6 (17G65)
	Opera	55.0.2994.61	Ubuntu Linux 18.04.1
	Internet Explorer	11.0.9600.18894	Windows 8.1
	Microsoft Edge	42.17134.1.0	Windows 10 17.17134
Browser mobile	Google Chrome	69.0.3497.100	Android 7.0.0
	Safari	–	iOS 12.0 (16A366)
	Firefox	62.0.2	Android 7.0.0
	UC Browser	12.9.3.1144	Android 7.0.0
	Samsung Internet	7.4.00.70	Android 7.0.0
	Opera	47.3.2249.130976	Android 7.0.0
	Microsoft Edge	42.0.0.2529	Android 7.0.0
Email desktop	Outlook 2016	16.0.4738.1000	Windows 10 17.17134
	macOS Mail	11.5 (3445.9.1)	macOS 10.13.6 (17G65)
	Thunderbird	52.9.1	Ubuntu Linux 18.04.1
Email mobile	Gmail	8.9.9.213351932	Android 7.0.0
	Outlook	2.2.219	Android 7.0.0
	iOS Mail	–	iOS 12.0 (16A366)
			iOS 12.1.2 (16C104)
Webmail	Gmail	–	–
	Yahoo	–	–
	Yandex	–	–
	Outlook	–	–
	RoundCube	1.2.9	–

References

1. IDN in Google Chrome. https://dev.chromium.org/developers/design-documents/idn-in-google-chrome
2. Measuring the information society report 2017, vol. 1. Technical report, International Telecommunication Union (2017). https://www.itu.int/en/ITU-D/Statistics/Documents/publications/misr2017/MISR2017_Volume1.pdf
3. Agten, P., Joosen, W., Piessens, F., Nikiforakis, N.: Seven months' worth of mistakes: a longitudinal study of typosquatting abuse. In: 22nd Annual Network and Distributed System Security Symposium. Internet Society (2015). https://doi.org/10.14722/ndss.2015.23058
4. Apple Inc.: About the security content of iOS 12.1.1, December 2018. https://support.apple.com/en-us/HT209340
5. Braden, R.: Requirements for internet hosts - application and support. RFC 1123, October 1989
6. Canadian Internet Registration Authority: Domains with French accented characters, January 2018. https://cira.ca/register-your-ca/domains-french-accented-characters
7. Carletti, S.: Ruby Whois. https://whoisrb.org/
8. Chronicle: VirusTotal. https://www.virustotal.com
9. Clayton, R., Mansfield, T.: A study of Whois privacy and proxy service abuse. In: 13th Annual Workshop on the Economics of Information Security (2014)
10. Costello, A.: Punycode: a bootstring encoding of Unicode for internationalized domain names in applications (IDNA). RFC 3492, March 2003
11. CZ.NIC: Czechs refused diacritics in domain names again, February 2017. https://www.nic.cz/page/3499/czechs-refused-diacritics-in-domain-names-again/
12. Davis, M., Suignard, M.: Unicode IDNA compatibility processing. Technical Standard 46, The Unicode Consortium, May 2018. https://www.unicode.org/reports/tr46/
13. DENIC: DENIC putting extensive changes into force for .DE Whois Lookup Service by 25 May 2018, May 2018. https://www.denic.de/en/whats-new/press-releases/article/denic-putting-extensive-changes-into-force-for-de-whois-lookup-service-as-of-25-may-2018/
14. Dhamija, R., Tygar, J.D., Hearst, M.: Why phishing works. In: SIGCHI Conference on Human Factors in Computing Systems, pp. 581–590. ACM (2006). https://doi.org/10.1145/1124772.1124861
15. Dinaburg, A.: Bitsquatting: DNS hijacking without exploitation. White Paper #2011-307, Raytheon Company (2011)
16. Edelman, B.: Large-scale registration of domains with typographical errors. Technical report, Berkman Center for Internet & Society - Harvard Law School, September 2003. http://cyber.law.harvard.edu/people/edelman/typo-domains
17. Eskandari, S., Leoutsarakos, A., Mursch, T., Clark, J.: A first look at browser-based cryptojacking. In: 3rd IEEE European Symposium on Security and Privacy Workshops - Security on Blockchains, pp. 58–66 (2018). https://doi.org/10.1109/EuroSPW.2018.00014
18. Ester, M., Kriegel, H.P., Sander, J., Xu, X.: A density-based algorithm for discovering clusters in large spatial databases with noise. In: 2nd International Conference on Knowledge Discovery and Data Mining, pp. 226–231. AAAI Press (1996)
19. EURid, UNESCO: World report on internationalised domain names 2018, August 2018. https://idnworldreport.eu/2018-2

20. Faltstrom, P., Hoffman, P., Costello, A.: Internationalizing domain names in applications (IDNA). RFC 3490, March 2003
21. Gabrilovich, E., Gontmakher, A.: The homograph attack. Commun. ACM **45**(2), 128 (2002). https://doi.org/10.1145/503124.503156
22. GoDaddy: The GoDaddy API. https://developer.godaddy.com/
23. Google: Safe Browsing. https://safebrowsing.google.com/
24. Hannay, P., Baatard, G.: The 2011 IDN homograph attack mitigation survey. In: International Conference on Security and Management, pp. 653–657 (2012)
25. Hannay, P., Bolan, C.: An assessment of internationalised domain name homograph attack mitigation implementations. In: 7th Australian Information Security Management Conference (2009). https://doi.org/10.4225/75/57b405aa30dee
26. Hannay, P., Bolan, C.: The 2010 IDN homograph attack mitigation survey. In: International Conference on Security and Management, pp. 611–614 (2010)
27. Harrenstien, K., Stahl, M., Feinler, E.: DoD internet host table specification. RFC 952, October 1985
28. Holgers, T., Watson, D.E., Gribble, S.D.: Cutting through the confusion: a measurement study of homograph attacks. In: USENIX Annual Technical Conference, pp. 261–266. USENIX Association (2006)
29. IDN Guidelines Working Group: Guidelines for the implementation of internationalized domain names, version 4.0, May 2018. https://www.icann.org/en/system/files/files/idn-guidelines-10may18-en.pdf
30. Internet Assigned Numbers Authority: Repository of IDN Practices. https://www.iana.org/domains/idn-tables
31. Internet Corporation for Assigned Names and Numbers: Label Generation Rules Tool. https://www.icann.org/resources/pages/lgr-toolset-2015-06-21-en
32. Internet Corporation for Assigned Names and Numbers: Data Protection/privacy Issues, July 2017. https://www.icann.org/dataprotectionprivacy
33. Kharraz, A., Robertson, W., Kirda, E.: Surveylance: automatically detecting online survey scams. In: 39th IEEE Symposium on Security and Privacy, pp. 70–86 (2018). https://doi.org/10.1109/SP.2018.00044
34. Kintis, P., et al.: Hiding in plain sight: a longitudinal study of combosquatting abuse. In: 24th ACM SIGSAC Conference on Computer and Communications Security, pp. 569–586. ACM (2017). https://doi.org/10.1145/3133956.3134002
35. Klensin, J.: Internationalized domain names for applications (IDNA): definitions and document framework. RFC 5890, August 2010
36. Korczyński, M., et al.: Cybercrime after the sunrise: a statistical analysis of DNS abuse in new gTLDs. In: 13th Asia Conference on Computer and Communications Security, pp. 609–623. ACM (2018). https://doi.org/10.1145/3196494.3196548
37. Krawetz, N.: Looks like it, May 2011. https://www.hackerfactor.com/blog/index.php?/archives/432-Looks-Like-It.html
38. Larsen, C., van der Horst, T.: Bad guys using internationalized domain names (IDNs), May 2014. https://www.symantec.com/connect/blogs/bad-guys-using-internationalized-domain-names-idns
39. Le Pochat, V., Van Goethem, T., Tajalizadehkhoob, S., Korczyński, M., Joosen, W.: Tranco: a research-oriented top sites ranking hardened against manipulation. In: 26th Annual Network and Distributed System Security Symposium, February 2019. https://doi.org/10.14722/ndss.2019.23386
40. Levine, J., Hoffman, P.: Variants in second-level names registered in top-level domains. RFC 6927, May 2013

41. Liu, B., et al.: A reexamination of internationalized domain names: the good, the bad and the ugly. In: 48th Annual IEEE/IFIP International Conference on Dependable Systems and Networks, pp. 654–665 (2018). https://doi.org/10.1109/DSN.2018.00072
42. Liu, S., Foster, I., Savage, S., Voelker, G.M., Saul, L.K.: Who is .com?: learning to parse WHOIS records. In: Internet Measurement Conference, pp. 369–380. ACM (2015). https://doi.org/10.1145/2815675.2815693
43. Lv, P., Ya, J., Liu, T., Shi, J., Fang, B., Gu, Z.: You have more abbreviations than you know: a study of AbbrevSquatting abuse. In: Shi, Y., et al. (eds.) ICCS 2018. LNCS, vol. 10860, pp. 221–233. Springer, Cham (2018). https://doi.org/10.1007/978-3-319-93698-7_17
44. Markham, G.: IDN display algorithm, April 2017. https://wiki.mozilla.org/IDN_Display_Algorithm
45. McElroy, T., Hannay, P., Baatard, G.: The 2017 homograph browser attack mitigation survey. In: 15th Australian Information Security Management Conference, pp. 88–96 (2017). https://doi.org/10.4225/75/5a84f5a495b4d
46. Mockapetris, P.: Domain names - concepts and facilities. RFC 1034, November 1987
47. Moore, T., Edelman, B.: Measuring the perpetrators and funders of typosquatting. In: Sion, R. (ed.) FC 2010. LNCS, vol. 6052, pp. 175–191. Springer, Heidelberg (2010). https://doi.org/10.1007/978-3-642-14577-3_15
48. Nikiforakis, N., Balduzzi, M., Desmet, L., Piessens, F., Joosen, W.: Soundsquatting: uncovering the use of homophones in domain squatting. In: Chow, S.S.M., Camenisch, J., Hui, L.C.K., Yiu, S.M. (eds.) ISC 2014. LNCS, vol. 8783, pp. 291–308. Springer, Cham (2014). https://doi.org/10.1007/978-3-319-13257-0_17
49. Nikiforakis, N., et al.: Stranger danger: exploring the ecosystem of ad-based URL shortening services. In: 23rd International Conference on World Wide Web, pp. 51–62. ACM (2014). https://doi.org/10.1145/2566486.2567983
50. Nikiforakis, N., Van Acker, S., Meert, W., Desmet, L., Piessens, F., Joosen, W.: Bitsquatting: exploiting bit-flips for fun, or profit? In: 22nd International Conference on World Wide Web, pp. 989–998. ACM (2013). https://doi.org/10.1145/2488388.2488474
51. Nominet: .wales and .cymru domains - IDN policy, August 2015. https://nominet-prod.s3.amazonaws.com/wp-content/uploads/2015/08/CymruWalesIDNPolicy_0.pdf
52. Núcleo de Informação e Coordenação do Ponto BR: Regras do domínio. https://registro.br/dominio/regras.html
53. OpenDNS: PhishTank. https://www.phishtank.com
54. Rüth, J., Zimmermann, T., Wolsing, K., Hohlfeld, O.: Digging into browser-based crypto mining. In: Internet Measurement Conference, pp. 70–76. ACM (2018). https://doi.org/10.1145/3278532.3278539
55. Scheitle, Q., et al.: A long way to the top: significance, structure, and stability of Internet top lists. In: Internet Measurement Conference, pp. 478–493. ACM (2018). https://doi.org/10.1145/3278532.3278574
56. Schiffman, M.: Global internationalized domain name homograph report, Q2/2018. Technical report, Farsight Security, June 2018
57. Shin, J.: Establish a process to update "top domain" skeleton list for confusability check, May 2017. https://bugs.chromium.org/p/chromium/issues/detail?id=722022
58. Shin, J.: Mitigate spoofing attempt using Latin letters, April 2017. https://codereview.chromium.org/2784933002

59. Sommers, J.: On the characteristics of language tags on the web. In: Beverly, R., Smaragdakis, G., Feldmann, A. (eds.) PAM 2018. LNCS, vol. 10771, pp. 18–30. Springer, Cham (2018). https://doi.org/10.1007/978-3-319-76481-8_2

60. Spamhaus Project: The domain block list. https://www.spamhaus.org/dbl/

61. Spaulding, J., Upadhyaya, S., Mohaisen, A.: The landscape of domain name typosquatting: techniques and countermeasures. In: 11th International Conference on Availability, Reliability and Security, pp. 284–289 (2016). https://doi.org/10.1109/ARES.2016.84

62. SURBL: SURBL URI reputation data. http://www.surbl.org/

63. Szurdi, J., Kocso, B., Cseh, G., Spring, J., Felegyhazi, M., Kanich, C.: The long "taile;; of typosquatting domain names. In: 23rd USENIX Security Symposium, pp. 191–206. USENIX Association (2014)

64. The Unicode Consortium: Unicode transliteration guidelines. http://cldr.unicode.org/index/cldr-spec/transliteration-guidelines

65. The Unicode Consortium: The Unicode Standard, Version 11.0.0 (2018). http://www.unicode.org/versions/Unicode11.0.0/

66. Tian, K., Jan, S.T.K., Hu, H., Yao, D., Wang, G.: Needle in a haystack: tracking down elite phishing domains in the wild. In: Internet Measurement Conference, pp. 429–442. ACM (2018). https://doi.org/10.1145/3278532.3278569

67. Vissers, T., Barron, T., Van Goethem, T., Joosen, W., Nikiforakis, N.: The wolf of name street: hijacking domains through their nameservers. In: 24th ACM SIGSAC Conference on Computer and Communications Security, pp. 957–970. ACM (2017). https://doi.org/10.1145/3133956.3133988

68. Vissers, T., Joosen, W., Nikiforakis, N.: Parking sensors: analyzing and detecting parked domains. In: 22nd Annual Network and Distributed System Security Symposium. Internet Society (2015)

69. Wang, Y.M., Beck, D., Wang, J., Verbowski, C., Daniels, B.: Strider typo-patrol: discovery and analysis of systematic typo-squatting. In: 2nd Workshop on Steps to Reducing Unwanted Traffic on the Internet, pp. 31–36. USENIX Association (2006)

70. Wood, P., Johnston, N.: Spammers taking advantage of IDN with URL shortening services, February 2011. https://www.symantec.com/connect/blogs/spammers-taking-advantage-idn-url-shortening-services

71. Zheng, X.: Phishing with Unicode domains, April 2017. https://www.xudongz.com/blog/2017/idn-phishing/

Failures

BGP Zombies: An Analysis of Beacons Stuck Routes

Romain Fontugne[1]([⊠]), Esteban Bautista[2], Colin Petrie[3], Yutaro Nomura[4], Patrice Abry[5,6], Paulo Goncalves[2], Kensuke Fukuda[6], and Emile Aben[3]

[1] IIJ Research Lab, Tokyo, Japan
romain@iij.ad.jp
[2] Univ Lyon, Ens de Lyon, Inria, CNRS, UCB Lyon 1, 69342 Lyon, France
[3] RIPE NCC, Amsterdam, Netherlands
[4] The University of Tokyo, Tokyo, Japan
[5] Univ Lyon, Ens de Lyon, Univ Claude Bernard, CNRS, Laboratoire de Physique, Lyon, France
[6] NII/Sokendai, Tokyo, Japan

Abstract. Network operators use the Border Gateway Protocol (BGP) to control the global visibility of their networks. When withdrawing an IP prefix from the Internet, an origin network sends BGP withdraw messages, which are expected to propagate to all BGP routers that hold an entry for that IP prefix in their routing table. Yet network operators occasionally report issues where routers maintain routes to IP prefixes withdrawn by their origin network. We refer to this problem as BGP zombies and characterize their appearance using RIS BGP beacons, a set of prefixes withdrawn every four hours. Across the 27 monitored beacon prefixes, we observe usually more than one zombie outbreak per day. But their presence is highly volatile, on average a monitored peer misses 1.8% withdraws for an IPv4 beacon (2.7% for IPv6). We also discovered that BGP zombies can propagate to other ASes, for example, zombies in a transit network are inevitably affecting its customer networks. We employ a graph-based semi-supervised machine learning technique to estimate the scope of zombies propagation, and found that most of the observed zombie outbreaks are small (i.e. on average 10% of monitored ASes for IPv4 and 17% for IPv6). We also report some large zombie outbreaks with almost all monitored ASes affected.

1 Introduction

BGP is the protocol that governs inter-domain routing on the Internet. As such understanding the boundaries of its behaviour is of prime importance. The tens of thousands of Autonomous Systems (ASes) that constitute the Internet expect to rapidly be able to change the routing and reachability of the address space they are originating towards all other ASes. The process of announcing and withdrawing address space is of utmost importance.

When an origin AS withdraws a prefix, it sends a withdrawal message to its BGP neighbours, who will in turn propagate it to their neighbours. Sometimes a

© Springer Nature Switzerland AG 2019
D. Choffnes and M. Barcellos (Eds.): PAM 2019, LNCS 11419, pp. 197–209, 2019.
https://doi.org/10.1007/978-3-030-15986-3_13

network sees the best path that it propagated to neighbours disappears, but in a rich topology the network still has alternative paths yet to be withdrawn. In that case the neighbours will not receive a withdrawal, but the best alternative path. This process, called *path hunting*, typically causes several BGP path changes in the matter of minutes, before a BGP prefix is fully withdrawn [9]. The richer the topology between the origin AS and a BGP speaker, the larger the number of path changes.

Theoretically this withdrawal process ends with the prefix completely withdrawn from all BGP speakers, as announcements and withdrawals propagate through the entire Internet similarly. In practice, this sometimes fails, a phenomenon known by network operators as *stuck routes* or *zombie routes*. In this case, path hunting gets stuck in a state where BGP routes are still visible at some BGP routers, something we can easily observe with route collector systems like RIS, Routeviews, and Isolario [2,6,7].

This work is motivated by the operational confusion that missing withdrawal causes. We have witnessed several cases where zombie routes caused confusion about the state of the withdrawn address space. In addition, troubleshooting and cleaning zombie routes is a burden for network operators. This phenomenon is relatively unknown outside network operator circles, and generally not well understood. We intend to shed light on BGP zombies in order to make the research community aware of this problem and to assist operators.

In this study we characterize zombie routes in a controlled setting using the RIS routing beacons. In this controlled environment, we can measure the frequency of failed withdrawals, and alternative paths that are seen in the withdrawal phase. The key contributions of this paper are to provide the first characterization of BGP zombies and a method to infer the scope of zombie outbreaks with the help of a graph-based semi-supervised machine learning algorithm. Our experiments reveal a surprisingly high number of zombies. Zombies are seen daily in our dataset, but we found that the number of affected ASes is usually limited (on average 10% of monitored ASes in IPv4 and 17% for IPv6). The appearance of zombie routes is very erratic. Zombie routes rarely emerge for numerous prefixes at the same time and for the same RIS peers. The average likelihood of observing a zombie for a given RIS peer and beacon prefix is 1.8% for IPv4 and 2.7% for IPv6. Finally, we show that numerous zombie paths are revealed during path hunting and the scope of an outbreak is usually related to the affected transit networks.

2   BGP Zombies

Before diving into the detailed analysis of BGP zombies, we define all the related terminology and explain our experimental setup. A **BGP zombie** refers to an active Routing Information Base (RIB) entry for a prefix that has been withdrawn by its origin network, and is hence not reachable anymore. In this paper we also refer to **zombie ASes** and **zombie peers** for ASes and BGP peers whose routers have BGP zombies. We refer to all zombies that correspond to the same prefix and appear during the same two-hour time slot as a **zombie outbreak**, the outbreak size is the number of zombie ASes.

2.1 Experimental Setup

In order to observe BGP zombies one needs to withdraw an IP prefix from its origin AS and inspect RIB changes, or lack thereof, in other ASes. We conduct such controlled experiments with the help of RIPE's Routing Information Service (RIS) BGP beacons [4,14] and RIS BGP data repository [6].

The RIS BGP beacons are a set of IPv4 and IPv6 prefixes that are used solely for studying Internet inter-domain routing. These IP prefixes are announced and withdrawn at predetermined time intervals. Namely, RIS BGP beacons are announced every day at 00:00, 04:00, 08:00, 12:00, 16:00, and 20:00 UTC, and they are withdrawn two hours after the announcements (i.e. at 02:00, 06:00, 10:00, 14:00, 18:00, and 22:00 UTC). We are monitoring 27 beacon prefixes (13 IPv4 and 14 IPv6) announced from Europe, U.S.A., Russia, Japan, and Brazil.

RIS also archives RIB and BGP update messages collected at diverse places on the Internet. RIS collectors (named rrc00, rrc01, etc.) are mainly located at Internet eXchange Points (IXP) and peer with hundreds of different ASes. Using this archive we can monitor how these ASes respond to the BGP beacons stimuli and characterize the emergence of BGP zombies.

For beacon prefixes, the detection of zombies in RIS peers is straightforward. We keep track of the visibility of beacons for all RIS peers and report a zombie for each RIB entry that is still active 1.5 h after the prefix was withdrawn. The 1.5 h delay is set empirically to avoid late withdrawals due to BGP convergence [14], route flap damping [20], or stale routes [17]. Each beacon's visibility is monitored in near-real time using the RIPEstat looking glass [5] so we can trigger active measurements (e.g. traceroutes) during detected zombie outbreaks.

We conducted experiments during the three periods of time listed in Table 1 and detected for the 27 monitored prefixes a total of 5115 zombie outbreaks, each composed of one or more zombie routes for the same prefix.

Table 1. Measurement periods and number of detected zombie outbreaks for the 27 monitored beacons.

Start	End	#IPv4 outbreaks	#IPv6 outbreaks
2017-03-01	2017-04-28	1732	591
2017-10-01	2018-12-28	384	1202
2018-07-19	2018-08-31	520	686

2.2 Example

Figure 1 illustrates the visibility for beacon 84.205.71.0/24 from all RIS peers on September 9th and 10th, 2017. Peers are sorted on the y axis and time is represented by the x axis. From 12:00 to 18:00 UTC, all peers behave as expected. At

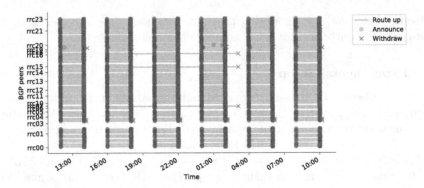

Fig. 1. Visibility for 84.205.71.0/24 from all RIS collectors on September 9th and 10th, 2017. A zombie outbreak happened from 18:00 to 20:00 UTC and another one from 22:00 to 00:00 UTC. Both outbreaks are visible from three RIS peers.

12:00, RIS peers announce the availability of the beacon prefix and maintain an active route to the prefix until 14:00. One peer from rrc19 withdraws the prefix a bit late (14:19), but this is not considered as a zombie because the prefix is withdrawn reasonably quickly. However, at 18:00 three peers do not withdraw the beacon although this prefix is not reachable at that time. This zombie outbreak ends at 20:00 when the beacon is re-announced. A similar zombie outbreak appears at 22:00 for the same three peers.

During the first zombie outbreak (18:00–20:00), we found other zombies for the same three peers but another beacon (84.205.67.0/24). The 25 other beacons are withdrawn as expected at that time. For the second outbreak (22:00–00:00), we found no other zombie. These observations give an early glimpse of the relationship between outbreaks for different prefixes. Zombie outbreaks for different beacons can be related but are usually independent. We formally investigate the co-occurrence of outbreaks from different beacons in Sect. 4.1.

2.3   Are Zombies Real?

To ensure that no artificial zombies are caused by measurement artifacts, we also looked for zombie evidences in other datasets.

First, for each zombie detected with the RIPEstat looking glass, we also accessed the raw data from the RIS archive using BGPstream [16] and checked that the withdraw messages are indeed missing in the raw traces. We found 794 outbreaks that are reported by the looking glass but not present in the raw data. We ignored these events in our analysis; these are not listed in Table 1.

Then, we also looked at the presence of zombies in Routeviews data and NLNOG looking glass during large zombie outbreak and confirmed that zombies are also present there. As Routeviews and RIS are now using completely different software for data collection (ExaBGP vs. Quagga/Zebra) we assume that observed zombies are not caused by malfunctioning collectors.

Finally, during zombie outbreaks we performed traceroute measurements towards beacon prefixes from Atlas probes located in zombie ASes. The traceroutes reveal that border routers in zombie ASes are indeed forwarding packets whereas other routers usually drop these packets. We also use these traceroute results to evaluate our method to infer zombie ASes on AS paths (Sect. 3.2).

3   Hunting Zombies

With the simple zombie detection technique described above, we observe zombies only in ASes that are peering with RIS collectors. In this section, we show that the withdrawn and zombie AS paths collected by RIS also enable us to infer zombie ASes beyond RIS peers and estimate the scope of outbreaks.

For each outbreak we retrieve the AS path of zombie entries and the last valid path for peers that have correctly withdrawn the beacon. A path alone provides little information, but put together they reveal topological similarities that we consider evidence for the locations of zombies.

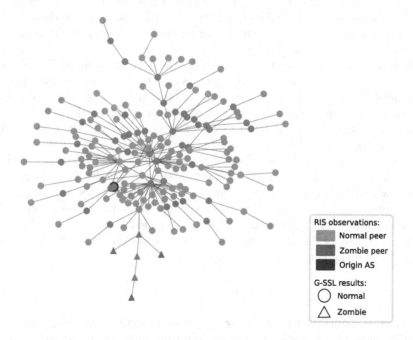

Fig. 2. AS paths for the second outbreak in Fig. 1. Each node is an AS, red and green nodes are RIS peers. Gray nodes are ASes seen on the paths but not peering with RIS. (Color figure online)

Figure 2 depicts AS paths for the second outbreak in Fig. 1. Each node represents an AS and consecutive ASes in the AS paths are connected by an edge. The green nodes represent RIS peers that have correctly withdrawn the prefix at 22:00. The red nodes represent zombie peers observed from 22:00 to 00:00. The gray nodes represent ASes that are not peering with RIS collectors, hence we have no direct observations for these ASes though they appear in collected AS paths. Here, the three observed zombies share the same upstream provider which is strong evidence that this provider and all its downstream ASes (depicted by triangles in Fig. 2) are also zombies.

To systematically identify these clusters of zombies, we build such graphs for each outbreak then we classify unknown ASes using the graph-based machine learning technique described in the next section. The results of the classification are illustrated in Fig. 2 with the shape of the nodes: triangles represent detected zombies; circles represent other ASes.

3.1 Graph-Based Semi-supervised Learning

Graph-based Semi-Supervised Learning (G-SSL) is a generic framework permitting efficient classification of graph nodes by jointly exploiting the graph topology and prior information consisting of a small fraction of nodes being a priori classified by *experts* [19] (i.e. RIS peers). There already exist several documented examples where G-SSL has outperformed other state-of-the-art classification strategies (e.g., BitTorrent content and user classification [10], text recognition [18], bio-medical diagnoses [21]).

Amongst the several versions of G-SSL, the PageRank-based G-SSL is a popular and commonly used one [11]. It relies on a coding of the graph topology via a specific operator, the (combinatorial) Laplacian L. Namely, let us consider an N node undirected graph encoded by the adjacency matrix W, with $W_{i,j} = 1$ when nodes i and j are connected and 0 otherwise. Further, let $d_i = \sum_j W_{ij}$ denote the degree of node i, $D = diag(d_1, \ldots, d_N)$ the diagonal matrix of vertex degrees, and form $L = D - W$. The PageRank K-class classification procedure can be sketched as follows. The labeled information is encoded in a matrix $Y \in \mathbb{R}^{N \times K}$, where $Y_{ik} = 1$ if node i is declared by expert to belong to class k and 0 elsewhere. In the present work, Y conveys the information provided by RIS; normal and zombie peers are respectively coded as $Y_{i1} = 1$ and $Y_{i2} = 1$. The classification of the unlabeled nodes amounts to estimate a vectorial signal $X \in \mathbb{R}^{N \times K}$ on the graph as:

$$\min_x \left\{ x^T D^{-1} L D^{-1} x + \mu (y - x)^T D^{-1} (y - x) \right\}. \tag{1}$$

This functional minimization is known to have an analytical closed-form solution, providing access to X, without recourse to a time/memory consuming iterative minimization procedure:

$$X^T = \frac{\mu}{\mu + 2} \mathbf{y}^T \left(\mathbb{I} - \alpha \mathbf{D}^{-1} \mathbf{W} \right)^{-1}. \tag{2}$$

Once X is computed, node i is assigned to the class k selected by $\mathrm{argmax}_k X_{ik}$.

The hyper-parameter μ balances the confidence granted to the *expert knowledge* versus the information conveyed by the graph (and the graph Laplacian L). It is tuned by means of a standard leave-one-out cross validation procedure, tailored to the context of semi-supervised learning: From the set of documented vertices, one element, per class, is selected as a labeled example, while the rest is added to the group of not documented and used for validation. The procedure is repeated and μ is selected as maximizing average detection performance.

3.2 Validation

G-SSL produces a list of zombie ASes that are not necessarily peering with RIS collectors. To evaluate the classification accuracy of G-SSL we performed timely traceroute measurements from ASes found on the zombie paths and compared the traceroute results with G-SSL results.

Our traceroute measurements are done with the RIPE Atlas measurement platform [3]. We select five Atlas probes for each AS found in zombie paths, and perform traceroutes towards the corresponding beacon prefix every 5 min until the prefix is announced again.

Comparing traceroute results to G-SSL results requires certain precautions. We intuitively expect routers from zombie ASes to forward traceroute packets and other routers to either drop these packets or return an ICMP network unreachable error. However, the presence of default routes in intra-AS routing is inevitably exhibiting router IP addresses although the AS border routers have withdrawn the prefix. Another difficulty is to identify borders between two ASes and avoid making wrong inferences when mapping IP addresses to AS numbers [13,15].

To address both issues we employ the following heuristics. First, we discard the first public IP found in traceroutes as it usually stands for a gateway with a default route. We group all traceroutes initiated from the same AS, if these traceroutes consist only of ICMP network unreachable errors and unresponsive routers then we consider that AS as normal, that is the AS has correctly withdrawn the route and is not forwarding packets. For traceroutes with responsive routers we retrieve the routers' ASN using longest prefix match and compute F_A, the number of IP addresses from ASN A that forwarded packets, and, E_A the number of IP addresses from ASN A that sent an ICMP error. We consider an AS A as zombie if the majority of its routers are forwarding packets, $F_A > E_A$.

The AS classification using traceroutes and the observations from RIS peers constitute the ground truth data we use to evaluate G-SSL results. For the three measurement periods G-SSL retrieved 97% of the zombies identified in the ground truth and 99% of the normal AS, which is more than acceptable for the following characterization of zombies. Since G-SSL classifies all nodes in the graph, we also obtain 35% more classified ASes than using traceroutes and RIS peers.

4   Zombie Characteristics

We now investigate temporal and topological characteristics of zombies directly observed at RIS peers and those inferred using the G-SSL method. Our aim here is to quantify the frequency of zombies, uncover their locality, and estimate the scale of zombie outbreaks.

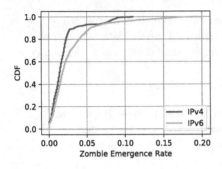 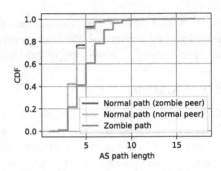

(a) Frequency of zombie appearance for   (b) AS path length for IPv4 beacons.
each RIS peer and beacon prefix.

Fig. 3. Zombies observed by RIS peers.

4.1   Zombies Observed at RIS Peers

Starting with zombies observed at RIS peers, we compute the zombie emergence rate, that is the number of times zombies are reported for each peer and each beacon normalized by the number of times beacons have been withdrawn during our measurement study. This metric corresponds to the likelihood of pair ⟨*peer, beacon*⟩ to cause a zombie. Figure 3a depicts the distribution of the values obtained with our dataset. We observe only 6.5% ⟨*peer, beacon*⟩ pairs with no zombie during our entire measurement periods. However, zombies are uncommon for RIS peers, 50% of the ⟨*peer, beacon*⟩ pairs have zombie entries for less than 1.3% of the beacon withdraws (average value is 1.8% for IPv4 and 2.7% for IPv6). We found some outlier values, meaning that a few RIS peers are more prone to zombies, which is better understood with G-SSL results (Sect. 4.2).

We also compared the zombie AS paths to the paths that are advertised before the beacon withdraw. For IPv4, 50% of the zombie paths are different than the paths that are used before the withdraw (69% for IPv6). Figure 3b illustrates the distribution of path length for zombie paths, paths that were previously advertised by zombie ASes (Normal path (zombie peer)), and paths that were advertised by peers that correctly withdrawn the beacon (Normal path (normal peer)). The distribution of zombie paths is clearly shifted to the right hence zombie paths are usually longer. These observations imply that zombie paths are mostly different from the paths that are selected during BGP path convergence, and numerous zombies appear during path hunting.

Then we examine if certain beacons are more prone to zombies. Figure 4a shows the number of zombie outbreaks observed per beacon. On average we detect about 200 outbreaks per beacon in our dataset. For IPv6 beacons announced from DE-CIX in Frankfurt and VIX in Vienna are responsible for the largest number of outbreaks. For IPv4 the beacon with the most outbreaks is the one announced from both AMS-IX and NL-IX in Amsterdam. To understand the relationship between zombies detected across the various beacons, we

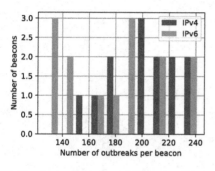 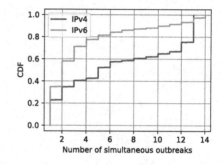

(a) Total number of zombie outbreaks per beacon.

(b) Number of simultaneous zombie outbreaks.

Fig. 4. Dependency of outbreaks across BGP beacons.

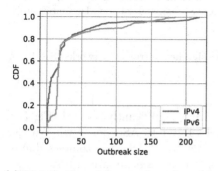 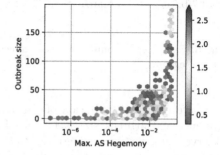

(a) Distribution of the number of zombie ASes per outbreak.

(b) Relation between main zombie transit and outbreak size.

Fig. 5. All detected Zombies (i.e. observed by RIS and inferred by G-SSL).

compute the number of outbreaks that happened simultaneously but for different beacons. For 23% of instances where we detect IPv4 zombies (35% for IPv6) we found zombies only for a single beacon. For IPv4 we also found multiple instances (25%) where we detect simultaneous zombies outbreaks for all monitored beacons. The rest of the distribution is uniform, meaning that we observe little correlation between outbreaks on different beacons. These observations reveal that usually outbreaks emerge independently across different prefixes, yet in certain cases some peers altogether miss withdraws for all monitored beacons.

4.2 Zombies Beyond RIS Peers

Using G-SSL results we can explore the scale of zombie outbreaks beyond the monitored RIS peers. For each zombie outbreak we count the total number of ASes with detected zombies (i.e. zombies observed at RIS peers and zombies inferred by G-SSL). On average, a zombie outbreak affects 24 ASes for IPv4 and 30 ASes for IPv6, that is 10% of the IPv4 monitored ASes and 17% for IPv6.

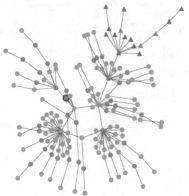
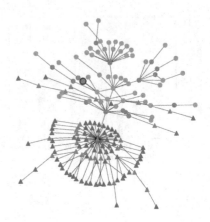

(a) Zombie detected in Init7 for beacon 2001:7fb:fe06::/48 on March 1st, 2017.

(b) Zombie detected in Level(3) for beacon 84.205.70.0/24 on December 6th, 2017.

Fig. 6. Examples of zombie outbreak affecting significant transit networks. See Fig. 2 for the legend.

However, the distribution of outbreak size is significantly skewed (Fig. 5a). The median outbreak size is 11 ASes for IPv4 and 16 ASes for IPv6. We also observe a few instances where most of the monitored ASes are zombies due to zombies that appeared close to the beacons' origin AS or in large ISPs.

For IPv6 we found that a remarkably high number of outbreaks (63%) contain between 12 and 19 ASes. For IPv4, the number of outbreaks with that particular size is also significant (18%), but we also observe a large proportion of smaller outbreaks, 45% of the IPv4 outbreaks have between 1 and 6 ASes.

By manually looking at the results we noticed certain patterns among outbreaks. We hypothesize that the number of zombie ASes is usually related to the importance of the transit networks affected by zombies. To illustrate this we select for each outbreak the most prominent transit network affected by the outbreak using global AS hegemony [8,12]. AS hegemony measures the centrality of an AS in the Internet, higher values standing for Tier-1 ISPs. Comparing the size of outbreaks to the largest AS hegemony score of affected ASes (Fig. 5b) shows that small outbreaks consist only of edge networks (i.e. low AS hegemony) and large transit networks belong only to the largest outbreaks.

Figure 6 illustrates two outbreaks where we detected zombies in large transit networks. The left hand side graph (Fig. 6a) represents an outbreak where the zombie AS with the highest hegemony score is Init7 and all ASes downstream are also affected by the outbreak. The right hand side graph (Fig. 6b) depicts another outbreak where we inferred a zombie in a Tier-1 network, Level(3). As Level(3)'s customer cone is larger the scope of the outbreak is also more important. This results in about half of the RIS peers having zombie routes through Level(3).

Table 2. Top 5 affected transit ASes for IPv4, IPv6, and each measurement period. Each percentage is the number of outbreaks that include the AS divided by the total number of outbreaks for the corresponding measurement period.

(a) IPv4

Mar./Apr. 2017		Oct./Dec. 2017		Jul./Aug. 2018	
AS3303 Swisscom	46.13%	AS6939 HE	14.84%	AS6667 Elisa	19.81%
AS12874 Fastweb	46.07%	AS1103 SURFnet	9.90%	AS680 DFN	17.69%
AS8359 MTS	9.93%	AS7575 AARNet	9.38%	AS7018 AT&T	16.73%
AS680 DFN	9.18%	AS286 KPN	9.38%	AS3549 Level3 GBLX	15.96%
AS7018 AT&T	8.60%	AS6453 TATA	9.11%	AS7575 AARNet	15.19%

(b) IPv6

Mar./Apr. 2017		Oct./Dec. 2017		Jul./Aug. 2018	
AS8455 Atom86	39%	AS13030 Init7	57%	AS13030 Init7	74%
AS13030 Init7	39%	AS8455 Atom86	55%	AS8455 Atom86	73%
AS5580 Hibernia	36%	AS8928 Interoute	36%	AS7018 AT&T	15%
AS7018 AT&T	8%	AS9002 RETN	35%	AS23106 CEMIG	13%
AS28917 Fiord	6%	AS33891 Core-Backbone	22%	AS1916 RNP	13%

In the absence of zombies we observe much less AS paths that contain Init7 or Level(3). This demonstrates again the role of path hunting in zombie propagation. When a beacon is withdrawn and a zombie appears on a transit network, downstream ASes are selecting that zombie path as other paths get discarded.

The frequency of zombies at transit networks is hence directly related to the topological spread of zombie outbreaks reported earlier (Fig. 5a). In Table 2 we list transit networks that appeared the most in zombie outbreaks. We again employ AS hegemony to focus only on large transit ASes, we arbitrarily picked ASes with an hegemony higher than 0.001. For IPv4 the top-5 ASes vary significantly across the three measurement periods. For IPv6 we found that Init7 and Atom86 are always the top two affected networks. Our manual inspection of the data reveals that Atom86 is downstream of Init7, so is affected every time Init7 has zombies. Init7's zombies usually propagate to 14 downstream ASes (example shown in Fig. 6a), which explains the large number of outbreaks composed of about 15 ASes in IPv6 in our results (Fig. 5a).

Network operators at Init7 acknowledged these issues with IPv6 routes, likely due to misbehaving vendor software, and expressed the need for zombie reporting systems, as it creates customer complaints every few months. Mitigation of the BGP zombies usually required the clearing of some Route Reflector iBGP sessions within Init7's network. Init7 operates its backbone using Extreme Networks MLXe (formerly known as Brocade MLXe) platform, which seems to be uncommon. Upgrading to later firmware version did not resolve the problem. Notice that we do not imply that detected outbreaks are caused by the transit networks listed in Table 2. Finding the root cause of zombie outbreaks requires additional measurements within these networks and their peers.

5   Discussion

While detecting BGP zombies with RIS beacons is straightforward, we faced significant challenges in pinpointing the root cause of observed zombies. Given the erratic patterns observed in our study and the investigations conducted with network operators, we believe zombies are mainly the results of software bugs in routers, BGP optimizers, and route reflectors. The systematic identification of zombie root causes on the Internet has proven to be very challenging, even for operators, as it requires timely and detailed information from a complex and occasionally misbehaving infrastructure. It is however a crucial challenge to ensure that this issue will not cause an increasing amount of difficult to debug issues for network operators.

If the fraction of zombie routes in the wild is in the same order of magnitude as what we see for RIS beacons, this can have interesting consequences that would merit further research. For instance, in the case of large route leaks, zombie routes could add significantly to the complexity of mitigating these incidents.

Our study focuses only on RIS beacons as we know their withdraw times a priori. However, these results cannot be easily extrapolated for any routed prefix. We could infer zombies for cases where a prefix is withdrawn in a short period of time for most, but not all route collector peers, and it remains difficult to distinguish this from a routing configuration change intended to limit the visibility of a prefix. Furthermore, in the case of large zombie outbreaks, which are of prime interest, one may confuse the few observed withdraws with a local routing issue. We plan to address these challenges in future works. A rigorous method for detecting zombies in the wild would allow us to estimate the overall impact of zombies on routing tables and to provide network operators with tools to effectively identify zombies.

6   Conclusions

In this paper, we investigated the emergence of BGP zombies with the help of RIS beacons. Our study spans across a year and half of data and revealed that BGP zombies are seen daily, although the scope of outbreaks is usually limited to a small fraction of monitored ASes (on average 10% for IPv4 and 17% for IPv6). We found almost no regularity in the appearance of zombies. They rarely emerge synchronously on all monitored prefixes. Numerous zombie paths are revealed during path hunting and the scope of an outbreak is usually related to the affected transit networks. Our future plans are to identify zombies for any prefix announced on the Internet (i.e. not only beacon prefixes) and quantify the impact of zombies in the wild. Finally, we make our tools and traceroute results publicly available [1] in order to share our findings and assist researchers in their zombie hunt.

References

1. BGP Zombie: Tools and Data. https://github.com/romain-fontugne/BGPzombies SSL
2. Isolario Project. https://www.isolario.it/
3. RIPE NCC, Atlas. https://atlas.ripe.net
4. RIPE NCC, Current RIS Routing Beacons. https://www.ripe.net/analyse/internet-measurements/routing-information-service-ris/current-ris-routing-beacons
5. RIPE NCC, RIPEstat: BGP Looking Glass. https://stat.ripe.net/widget/looking-glass
6. RIPE NCC, RIS Raw Data. https://www.ripe.net/analyse/internet-measurements/routing-information-service-ris/ris-raw-data
7. The RouteViews Project. http://www.routeviews.org/
8. AS Hegemony Results (2017). http://ihr.iijlab.net/ihr/hegemony/
9. Asturiano, V.: The Shape of a BGP Update. https://labs.ripe.net/Members/vastur/the-shape-of-a-bgp-update
10. Avrachenkov, K., Gonçalves, P., Legout, A., Sokol, M.: Classification of content and users in BitTorrent by semi-supervised learning methods. In: 8th International Wireless Communications and Mobile Computing Conference (IWCMC), pp. 625–630, August 2012
11. Avrachenkov, K., Mishenin, A., Gonçalves, P., Sokol, M.: Generalized optimization framework for graph-based semi-supervised learning. In: Proceedings of the 2012 SIAM International Conference on Data Mining, pp. 966–974 (2012)
12. Fontugne, R., Shah, A., Aben, E.: The (thin) bridges of AS connectivity: measuring dependency using AS hegemony. In: Beverly, R., Smaragdakis, G., Feldmann, A. (eds.) PAM 2018. LNCS, vol. 10771, pp. 216–227. Springer, Cham (2018). https://doi.org/10.1007/978-3-319-76481-8_16
13. Luckie, M., Dhamdhere, A., Huffaker, B., Clark, D., Claffy, K.: bdrmap: Inference of borders between IP networks. In: Proceedings of the 2016 Internet Measurement Conference, IMC 2016, pp. 381–396. ACM, New York (2016)
14. Mao, Z.M., Bush, R., Griffin, T.G., Roughan, M.: BGP beacons. In: Proceedings of the 3rd ACM SIGCOMM Conference on Internet Measurement, pp. 1–14. ACM (2003)
15. Marder, A., Smith, J.M.: MAP-IT: multipass accurate passive inferences from traceroute. In: Proceedings of the 2016 Internet Measurement Conference, IMC 2016, pp.397–411. ACM, New York (2016)
16. Orsini, C., King, A., Giordano, D., Giotsas, V., Dainotti, A.: BGPStream: a software framework for live and historical BGP data analysis. In: IMC, pp. 429–444. ACM (2016)
17. Sangli, S., Chen, E., Systems, C., Fernando, R., Scudder, J., Rekhter, Y.: Graceful restart mechanism for BGP (No. RFC 4724). Technical report (2007)
18. Subramanya, A., Bilmes, J.: Soft-supervised learning for text classification. In: Proceedings of the Conference on Empirical Methods in Natural Language Processing, pp. 1090–1099 (2008)
19. Subramanya, A., Talukdar, P.P.: Graph-Based Semi-supervised Learning. Morgan & Claypool Publishers, San Rafael (2014)
20. Villamizar, C., Chandra, R., Govindan, R.: BGP route flap damping (No. RFC 2439). Technical report (1998)
21. Zhao, M., Chan, R.H.M., Chow, T.W.S., Tang, P.: Compact graph based semi-supervised learning for medical diagnosis in Alzheimer's disease. IEEE Sig. Process. Lett. **21**(10), 1192–1196 (2014)

How to Find Correlated Internet Failures

Ramakrishna Padmanabhan[1,2(✉)], Aaron Schulman[3], Alberto Dainotti[2],
Dave Levin[1], and Neil Spring[1]

[1] University of Maryland, College Park, USA
{dml,nspring}@cs.umd.edu
[2] CAID/UCSD, La Jolla, USA
{ramapad,alberto}@caida.org
[3] UCSD, San Diego, USA
schulman@cs.ucsd.edu

Abstract. Even as residential users increasingly rely upon the Internet, connectivity sometimes fails. Characterizing small-scale failures of last mile networks is essential to improving Internet reliability.

In this paper, we develop and evaluate an approach to detect Internet failure events that affect multiple users simultaneously using measurements from the Thunderping project. Thunderping probes addresses across the U.S. When the areas in which they are geo-located are affected by severe weather alerts. It detects a disruption event when an IP address ceases to respond to pings. In this paper, we focus on simultaneous disruptions of multiple addresses that are related to each other by geography and ISP, and thus are indicative of a shared cause. Using binomial testing, we detect groups of per-IP disruptions that are unlikely to have happened independently. We characterize these dependent disruption events and present results that challenge conventional wisdom on how such outages affect Internet address blocks.

1 Introduction

Even as residential users rely increasingly upon the Internet, last-mile infrastructure continues to be vulnerable to connectivity outages [1–3,5,18,20–24]. Measurement-driven approaches to study residential Internet failures will help improve reliability by identifying vulnerable networks and their challenges.

Techniques that detect outages at the Internet's edge often seek, using terminology from Richter et al. [19], *disruption events*: the abrupt loss of Internet connectivity of a substantial set of addresses. The set of addresses may comprise those belonging to the same /24 address block [18,19], BGP prefix [9], or country [4]. Techniques seek such disruption events because individually, each large disruption has impact and their size makes them easier to confirm, e.g., with operators. In contrast, disruptions affecting only a few users are harder to detect with confidence. For example, the lack of response from a single address might best be explained by a user switching off their home router—hardly an outage. However, residential Internet outages may be limited to a small neighborhood or apartment block; prior techniques are likely to miss such events.

D. Choffnes and M. Barcellos (Eds.): PAM 2019, LNCS 11419, pp. 210–227, 2019.
https://doi.org/10.1007/978-3-030-15986-3_14

In this work, we demonstrate a technique that detects disruption events with quantifiable confidence, by investigating the potential dependence between disruptions of multiple IP addresses in a principled way. We apply a simple statistical method to a large dataset of active probing measurements towards residential Internet users in the US. We find times when multiple addresses experience a disruption simultaneously such that they are unlikely to have occurred independently; we call the occurrence of such events *dependent disruptions*. Our preliminary results shed light on when, how large, and with which structure in the address space dependent disruptions happen. We show that even some large outages do not disrupt entire /24 address blocks.

Our contributions are:

- We demonstrate a technique to detect dependent disruption events using the binomial test.
- We show that dependent disruption events occur more frequently at night for some ISPs.
- The majority of dependent disruption events last less than an hour.
- We show that dependent disruption events do not always affect entire /24 address blocks and can therefore be missed by prior techniques that detect disruptions at this granularity [18,19].

2   Background and Related Work

In this section, we begin with a presentation of edge Internet disruption detection techniques. These techniques typically detect disruptions affecting a large group of addresses. Next, we provide a description of the Thunderping dataset [21] that yields per-IP address disruptions required for our detection technique.

2.1   Prior Work

Prior techniques that detect edge Internet disruptions typically detect disruptions that affect a group of addresses *collectively*. Like us, they also leverage the *dependence* among the per-IP address "disruptions" that these disruptions cause. However, they differ from our technique in that they look for dependence in large aggregates (that is, so many addresses are affected at the same time that there must be an evident anomaly) or limit their resolution to small address blocks, looking only for outages that cause dependent disruptions for most addresses in a monitored block.

Several systems investigate disruptions affecting a substantial set of addresses. The IODA system looks for the most impactful outages, those causing an extensive loss of connectivity for a geographical area or Autonomous System [4,7]. Hubble detects prefix-level unreachability problems [9] using a hybrid monitoring scheme that combines passive BGP monitoring and active probing.

Other systems detect disruptions affecting many addresses within /24 address blocks. For example, Trinocular uses historical data from the ISI census [6] to model the responsiveness of blocks and finds addresses within each block that are likely to respond to pings. The system pings a few of these addresses from each block at random in 11-minute rounds. It then employs Bayesian inference to reason about responses from blocks. When a block's responsiveness is lower than expected, Trinocular probes the block at a faster rate and eventually detects an outage when the follow-up probes also suggest the block's lack of Internet connectivity. Since Trinocular may not identify an outage even if a single address in a block responds to probing, it potentially neglects outages affecting /24 blocks only partially, including larger outages affecting multiple /24 blocks. Recently, Richter et al. used proprietary CDN logs to detect disruptions affecting multiple addresses within /24 address blocks [19]. They showed that many disruptions do not affect all addresses in a /24; we revisit this result in Sect. 4.4.

Disco [22] shares some features with our work: they also detect simultaneous disconnects of multiple RIPE Atlas probes within an ISP or geographic region to infer outages. However, there are two major differences between the Thunderping and RIPE Atlas datasets. At any given point in time, the Thunderping dataset typically consists of pings sent to thousands of addresses in relatively small geographical areas in the U.S. with active severe weather alerts. The Disco dataset consists of 10,000 RIPE Atlas probes distributed around the world; this sparse distribution may prevent the detection of smaller outages localized to one area (like a U.S. state). The second difference is that unlike Thunderping ping data whose timestamps are only accurate to minutes, the timestamps available in the RIPE Atlas datasets are accurate to seconds, permitting the use of Kleinberg's burst detection to detect bursts in probe disconnects.

2.2   The Thunderping Dataset Yields Per-Address Disruptions

The key insight behind our technique is that simultaneous disruptions of multiple individual IPv4 addresses could occur due to a common underlying cause. We therefore require per-IP address disruptions.

Such data is present in the Thunderping dataset [21]. Thunderping pings sampled IPv4 addresses from multiple ISPs in geographic areas in the United States. Originally designed to evaluate how weather affects Internet outages, the system uses Planetlab vantage points to ping 100 randomly sampled IPv4 addresses per ISP, from multiple ISPs, in each U.S. county with active weather alerts. Each address is pinged from multiple Planetlab vantage points (at least 3) every 11 min, and addresses in a county are pinged six hours before, during, and after a weather alert.

Here, we analyze a dataset of Thunderping's ping responses to detect disruptions for each probed address using Schulman and Spring's technique [21]. When an address that is responsive stops responding to pings from all vantage points that are currently probing it, we detect a disruption for that address. Since a disruption is detected only when all vantage points declare unreachability, the minimum duration of a disruption is 11 min (at the end of 11 min each vantage point has pinged the address at least once).Thunderping continues to probe an address after it has become unresponsive, allowing us to estimate how long the unresponsive period lasted.

While per-IP address disruptions allow the detection of small disruption events, all per-address disruptions are not necessarily the result of Internet connectivity outages (e.g., a user might turn off their home router). This paper shows how to detect dependent disruption events using per-address disruptions.

3   Detecting Dependent Disruptions

In this section, we apply binomial testing to identify dependent disruptions in the outage dataset. First, we show how the binomial test works to rule out independent events and show how to apply the test to outages in reasonably sized aggregates of addresses. Second, we apply this method to the outage dataset, omitting addresses with excessive baseline loss rates and evaluating our chosen aggregation method. Finally we summarize the dependent disruptions we found in this dataset. This sets up analysis of these events (time of day, geography, and scope) which we defer to the following section.

3.1   Finding Dependent Events in an Address Aggregate

When many addresses experience a disruption simultaneously, there could be a common underlying cause. Such disruptions are statistically *dependent*. To identify these dependent events, our insight is to model address disruptions as *independent* events; when disruptions co-occur in greater numbers than the independent model can explain, the disruptions must be *dependent*. Binomial testing provides precisely this ability to find events that are highly unlikely to have occurred independently.

Given N addresses, the binomial distribution gives the probability that D of them were disrupted *independently* as:

$$\Pr[D \text{ independent failures}] \quad = \quad \binom{N}{D} \cdot P_d^D (1 - P_d)^{N-D} \tag{1}$$

where P_d represents the probability of disruption for the aggregate N. To apply this formula, we must first set a threshold probability below which we consider the simultaneous disruption to be too unlikely to be independent. We set this threshold to 0.01%. We then solve for D_{min}, the smallest (whole) number of simultaneous disruptions with a smaller than 0.01% chance of occurring independently. Table 1 in the appendix presents computed values of D_{min} for various values of N and P_d. This table shows that, even for large aggregates of IP addresses, often few simultaneous disruptions are necessary to be able to confidently conclude that a dependent disruption has occurred. As we will see, when applied to our dataset, D_{min} values are typically below 8.

There are two practical challenges in applying this test. First, we must choose aggregates of N IP addresses that define the scope of a dependent disruption:

too large an aggregate will have too large a chance of simultaneous independent failures and drive up D, while too small an aggregate may fail to include all the addresses in an event. Second, we must estimate P_d for each aggregate. We address each in turn.

3.1.1 Choosing Aggregate Sets of IP Addresses

Our technique assumes some *aggregate* set of IP addresses among which to detect a dependent disruption. We note that the *correctness* of our approach does not depend on how this set is chosen—the binomial test will apply so long as independent failures can be modeled by P_d. When applying our technique, IP addresses must be aggregated into sets that are large enough to span interesting disruption events, but not so large as to become insensitive to them.

In this paper, we aggregate IP addresses based on the U.S. state and the ASN they are in.*State-ASN* aggregates have the benefit of spanning multiple prefixes (so we can observe whether more than one /24 is affected by a given disruption event), but also being constrained to a common geographic region (so hosts in an aggregate are likely to share similar infrastructure). There are two limitations with this approach: states are not of uniform size, though the test elegantly handles varying N, and a few ISPs use multiple ASNs, which may hide some dependent failures. Alternate aggregations are possible (Appendix A.4).

3.1.2 Calculating the Probability of Disruption (P_d)

As a final consideration, we discuss how to estimate the probability of disruption, P_d, from an empirical dataset of disruptions. We assume that the dataset can be separated into a set of discrete "time bins"; this is common with ping-based outage detection, such as Thunderping and Trinocular, which both consider 11-minute bins of time. P_d can be estimated using the following equation:

$$P_d = \frac{\#\text{disruptions}}{\#\text{timebins}} \qquad (2)$$

Here, #timebins represents the total number of observation intervals used: if a single host was measured across 10 time intervals and five other hosts were all measured across 3, then #timebins $= 10 + 3 \cdot 5 = 25$.

We only consider state-ASN aggregates where we were able to obtain a statistically significant value for P_d. For statistical significance, we adhere to the following rule of thumb [25, Chap. 6]: we accept a state-ASN aggregate with t timebins and estimated probability of disruption P_d only if:

$$tP_d(1 - P_d) \geq 10 \qquad (3)$$

3.2 Applying Our Method to the Thunderping Dataset

We investigate all ping responses in the Thunderping dataset from January 1, 2017 to December 31, 2017 and detect disruptions according to the methodology described above. During this time, Thunderping had sent at least 100 pings to 3,577,895 addresses and detected a total of 1,694,125 individual address disruptions affecting 1,193,812 unique addresses. The top ISPs whose addresses

Thunderping sampled most frequently include large cable providers (Comcast, Charter, Suddenlink), DSL providers (Windstream, Qwest, Centurytel), WISP providers (RISE Broadband), and satellite providers (Viasat). While most addresses have low loss rates, 2% of addresses had loss rates exceeding 10%; we remove these addresses to avoid biasing the analysis. We report additional details about these addresses in [15,17].

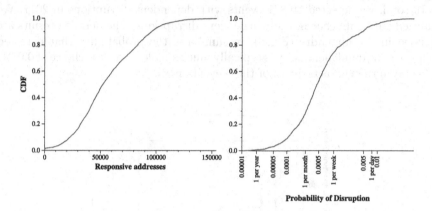

Fig. 1. Potential N and P_d values in the Thunderping dataset: on the left, we show the distribution of all addresses (across all state-ASN aggregates) pinged by Thunderping that can potentially fail in each 11 min time bin. On the right, we show the distribution of the probability of disruption (P_d) for the 1559 state-ASN address aggregates we studied.

Detecting Dependent Disruptions in the Thunderping Dataset
We use Fig. 1 to describe potential N and P_d values in the Thunderping dataset. On the left, we show the distribution of addresses pinged by Thunderping in each 11 min timebin in 2017. The median number is roughly 50,000 addresses across all U.S. states and ISPs. Since many weather alerts tend to be active at any given point of time, these addresses are likely to be distributed among tens of state-ASN aggregates. In 2017, the maximum addresses that could potentially fail in any state-ASN aggregate was 15,863. On the right, we show the distribution of P_d values for all state-ASN aggregates that we considered. There is extensive variation: addresses in some of these aggregates experience disruptions only once every year, whereas in other aggregates they experience disruptions more often than once per day.[1]

---

[1] Since disruptions are a superset of outages and dynamic reassignment [16], frequent disruptions are not necessarily indicative of poor Internet connectivity. Also, the existence of many aggregates with few disruptions indicates that Thunderping often pinged addresses during weather conditions that were not conducive to disruptions.

For each state-ASN aggregate, for each 11-min window during which Thunderping had pinged addresses, we identify the maximum number of addresses that can potentially fail, N, *i.e.*, all the addresses that are responsive to pings at the beginning of the window. Next, we apply the binomial test for each of these windows since we know N and P_d. When the number of disruptions in a window is at least D_{min}, we determine that a dependent disruption event occurred in that window with a probability greater than 0.9999.

In total, we detected 20,831 events with dependent disruptions in 2017. We analyzed our confidence in these dependent disruptions. The detailed results are included in the appendix (Fig. 8); in summary, the probabillity that detected events occurred independently is typically much smaller than our choice of 0.01%. We analyze the characteristics of these events next.

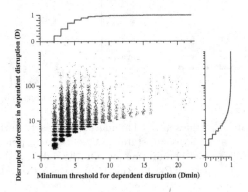

Fig. 2. For each detected dependent disruption event, Fig. 2 shows the D_{min} value on the x-axis and the corresponding number of observed disruptions on the y-axis. 62% of the 20,831 detected events had more than D_{min} observed disruptions. The scatterplot adds a random gaussian offset to both x and y with mean of 0.1, clamped at 0.45, to show density.

How Many Addresses Are Disrupted Dependently?

The binomial test does not say that *all* of the addresses that were observed to be disrupted during a dependent event were disrupted in a dependent manner. Consider if D_{min} is 4 and we detect an event where 7 addresses were disrupted. The binomial test shows us that the event took place with very low probability. However, that does not necessarily mean all 7 addresses were disrupted in a dependent manner; up to 3 of them $(D_{min} - 1)$ could have been disrupted independently with up to 99.99% probability.

We call the set of addresses in a state-ASN aggregate that were disrupted in the time-bin of a dependent event the observed group of addresses that were disrupted, or the *observed disrupted group* for short. In the example above, the observed disrupted group contains 7 addresses. Of the observed disrupted group, our assumption is that some were disrupted together in a dependent manner:

we call this subset the actual group of addresses that were disrupted, or *actual disrupted group*. We obtain a minimum bound on the actual disrupted group by subtracting $D_{min} - 1$ from the observed disrupted group; thus in the example above, the minimum number of addresses in the actual disrupted group is 4. For the 20,831 dependent disruption events, the total addresses in all the observed disrupted groups is 229,413 and the minimum total addresses in all the actual disrupted groups is 165,328.

We study the relationship between D_{min} for a state-ASN aggregate on the x-axis and the corresponding number of addresses in the observed group of disrupted addresses (on the y-axis) in Fig. 2. Each point corresponds to one of the 20,831 detected events. Sometimes, a state-ASN aggregate had such low P_d that even a single disruption in a 11-min bin occurred with less than 0.01% probably and therefore had a D_{min} value of 1. However, since we are looking for unlikely disruptions of multiple addresses, at least two addresses were disrupted in the same time-bin for all our detected events. For 12,911 (62%) detected events, *more* than D_{min} addresses experienced disruptions in the same time-bin, corroborating the result from Fig. 8 (in the appendix) that most detected events would have been detected even with a stricter threshold.

We detected dependent disruption events with various sizes as shown in Fig. 2. There are 693 (3%) events with more than 50 observed disrupted addresses. The largest detected event had 913 addresses experience disruptions in the same time-bin in AS33489 (Comcast) in Florida at 2017-09-13T20:33 UTC time. This detected event correlates to the minute with a known failure event for Comcast that was discussed in the Outages mailing list [14]. However, for most of the events, the size of the observed group of disrupted addresses is small: there were 2,593 (12%) with two, 2,969 (14%) with three, 2,776 (13%) with four, and 2,175 (10%) with five observed disrupted addresses. These results highlight the ability of our technique to detect even small sized disruptions with confidence.

4   Properties of Dependent Disruptions

In this section, we study various properties of dependent disruptions. For some properties, we conduct additional analyses on specific ISPs in the Thunderping dataset: Comcast (cable), Qwest (DSL) and Viasat (Satellite). These are three ISPs whose addresses are pinged frequently by Thunderping and where we were able to detect in excess of a thousand dependent disruption events (3109 events for Comcast, 1855 for Viasat, 1734 for Qwest). The appendix contains additional detail on per-ISP dependent disruption events.

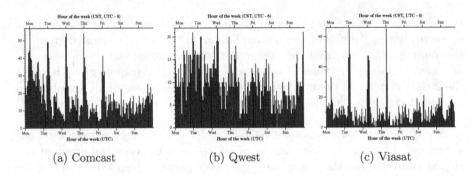

(a) Comcast   (b) Qwest   (c) Viasat

Fig. 3. The y-axis shows dependent disruption events that began in each hour of the week. 'Mon' on the bottom x-axis refers to midnight on Monday in UTC time. On the top x-axis, 'Mon' refers to midnight at UTC-6 (CST).

4.1 Dependent Disruptions Are More Frequent at Night for Some ISPs

Richter et al. have recently shown that disruptions tend to happen more frequently during maintenance intervals close to midnight local time [19]. They did so using proprietary data from a CDN, collected at the granularity of every hour. Here, we investigate if our technique can identify similar patterns.

Figure 3 shows that individual ISPs can have different behavior. Comcast and Viasat have more dependent disruption events occurring close to midnight, CST, on weekday nights. Qwest, on the other hand, does not appear to have a clearly discernible pattern. Our results confirm those from prior work [19], lending credence to our technique.Moreover, we are able to do so using public (Thunderping) data and a granularity of every 11 min.

4.2 Dependent Disruptions Can Recover Together

Here, we investigate whether dependent disruption events are accompanied by *dependent recovery*. Since Thunderping continues to probe an IP address even after it becomes unresponsive (until six hours after the end of the weather alert [21]), it can observe when the address becomes responsive again. This responsiveness may signal that the disruption for the address has ended. Multiple addresses that are disrupted together and also recover together offer evidence that: (a) the event was indeed dependent and (b) the event has ended, allowing estimation of the disruption's duration.

Most dependent disruptions also have correlated recoveries. Of 20,831 dependent disruption events, 6,869 (33%) had *all* disrupted addresses recover during the same 11-min time-bin. Further, 14,789 (71%) disruption events had at least half of the disrupted addresses recover together. Across all of the 20,831 dependent disruption events, there were 229,413 observed disrupted addresses in total. Of these, 121,648 (53%) disrupted addresses—from 15,117 (73%) disruption events—exhibited a dependent recovery with other addresses from that same group. This indicates that dependent recovery is quite common.

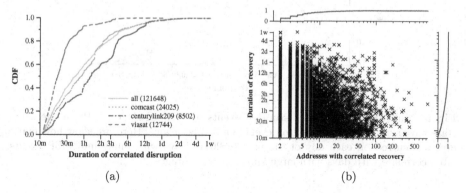

(a)   (b)

Fig. 4. (a) The distribution of durations of dependent disruptions for all addresses that recovered in a correlated manner. 60% of addresses recovered in less than an hour. (b) For dependent disruption events where at least two addresses recovered, this shows the number of addresses that recovered on the x-axis and the corresponding recovery duration for the event on the y-axis. Dependent disruption events vary in their duration irrespective of the number of affected addresses.

Recovery Times are Often Shorter than an Hour

Next, we turn our attention to the time it takes dependent disruptions to recover. Figure 4(a) shows that 60% of recovered addresses recovered in less than an hour. Our technique is able to identify this, because we operate at the precision of the 11-min time-bins from standard outage detection datasets. Conversely, recent work that finds disruptions spanning an entire calendar hour [19] would miss these disruptions.

Next, we examine whether short recovery durations can be attributable to small disruption events: that is, do the recoveries appear quick because only a couple hosts were disrupted? Figure 4(b) shows that the answer is no: Even dependent disruptions with hundreds of addresses that recovered together often last less than an hour.

4.3   Dependent Disruptions Can Be Multi-ISP

Dependent disruption events can also span multiple ISPs within a single state: these events indicate a fault of infrastructure shared by the ISP or their customers. Here, we broaden our analysis to examine whether dependent disruption events are correlated across multiple ISPs within the same state.

We observe 333 instances where multiple ISPs in the same state had simultaneous dependent disruption events, and we are able to confirm that many occurred on days when the media reported large power outages in those

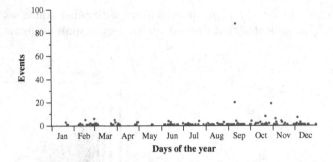

Fig. 5. Multi-ISP dependent disruption events over time: several ISPs in the same state have simultaneous disruption events on 333 occasions. Here, we show how many events occurred on each day of the year in 2017. Days with many multi-ISP events often correlate with days with large known power outages.

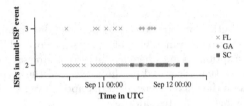

Fig. 6. Multi-ISP dependent disruption events during Hurricane Irma in Florida (FL), Georgia (GA), and South Carolina (SC). Of 111 events during this time, 15 affected 3 ISPs simultaneously and 96 affected 2.

areas. Figure 5 shows days in 2017 when multi-ISP dependent disruption events occurred. Of the 333 instances, 88 (26%) occurred on a single day during Hurricane Irma (Sep 11). Figure 6 shows multi-ISP events during Hurricane Irma by state and by the number of individual ISPs affected during each multi-ISP event. We observed 20 multi-ISP events in Florida on Sep 10, when Irma made landfall [8]. As Irma moved northwards, we saw multi-ISP events in Georgia and South Carolina as well. Other days with many such events include Oct 30 with 19 events across six states in the Northeastern U.S. (Maine, New Hampshire, Vermont, Connecticut, Massachusetts, Rhode Island); there were recorded power outages during this time as a result of a severe storm [11–13]. On Oct 22, there were 4 multi-ISP events in Oklahoma and 2 in Arkansas; there are corresponding reports of power outages during these times as well [10].

4.4 Dependent Disruptions May Not Disrupt Entire /24s

Here, we examine if dependent disruption events disrupt entire /24 address blocks. If so, they would likely be detected by prior work that looks for outages at these granularities [18,19]. If there continue to be responding addresses within a /24 with a disrupted address, however, prior work may miss the disruption.

To analyze how dependent disruptions affect /24 address blocks, we find all addresses in the observed disrupted group for a dependent disruption event and group them by /24s. As a running example in this section, consider a dependent disruption event comprising 3 addresses in 1.2.3.0/24, 5 addresses in 2.3.4.0/24, and 2 addresses in 4.5.6.0/24. We call these the *observed disrupted* /24s for this event. For each of these /24s, we also find how many addresses were pinged by Thunderping that were responding to pings *before* the dependent disruption and that continued to respond for at least 30 min *after* the time-bin where the dependent disruption occurred. We term these addresses the responsive addresses in a /24 since these addresses were not affected by the disruption.

Our goal is to find how many /24 address blocks exist where at least one address within the /24 was an actual address in a dependent disruption but there were other addresses within the same /24 that continued to be responsive. Such /24s only experience a *partial* disruption (as defined in [19]). First, we checked how many of the 20,831 dependent disruption events had at least one responsive address in *all* of the observed disrupted /24s; there were 12,825 (61%) such events. For each of these events, even if some of the observed disrupted /24s for the event have addresses that failed independently, since all disrupted /24s continue to have at least one responsive address, all affected /24s only experienced partial disruptions (that could be missed by prior work).

Next, we investigate the subset of observed disrupted /24s where there were at least D_{min} failures within the /24 itself. Since the entire state-ASN aggregate only required D_{min} failures, when D_{min} or more addresses are disrupted within a single /24, the /24 has at least one actual disrupted address. We obtain the minimum bound on the number of actual disrupted addresses in a /24 by subtracting $D_{min} - 1$ from the observed disrupted addresses in that /24. Suppose the D_{min} for the example dependent disruption event above was 3. We would obtain a minimum bound of at least 1 actual disrupted address in 1.2.3.0/24. In 2.3.4.0/24, the minimum bound is 3. In 4.5.6.0/24, the minimum bound is 0 and we are unable to determine if the addresses in this /24 had a dependent disruption. Of 92,777 observed disrupted /24s (across all dependent disruption events), we find that 14,702 (16%) have at least D_{min} disrupted addresses. Each of these is a point in Fig. 7.

We find that many disrupted /24s with actual disrupted addresses have other addresses that continued to be responsive. 10,164 (69%) /24s had at least one responsive address, 9327 (63%) had at least two responsive addresses, and 6,096 (41%) had at least 10 responsive addresses. 1,691 /24s had at least 10 actual disrupted addresses; of those, 550 (33%) had at least 10 responsive addresses. In the appendix, we show that such behavior occurs across ISPs and we also discuss the implications of these results for prior work.

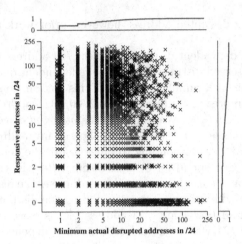

Fig. 7. Minimum actual disrupted addresses in a /24 vs. responsive addresses in a /24, for all /24s with at least D_{min} address that were disrupted during a detected dependent disruption event.

5   Discussion and Conclusion

We developed a technique to detect dependent disruption events with high confidence using the binomial test. The technique is general enough to apply to any dataset of disruptions; we applied it to the Thunderping dataset [21]. This dataset has the benefit of containing per-address disruption data from thousands of addresses in relatively small geographic regions (like a U.S. state) that may experience failures due to common underlying causes. We inherit the limitations of the Thunderping probing scheme—the system only measures residential addresses in one country (the U.S.), it probes mostly during times of predicted severe weather, and the minimum duration of disruptions is 11 min—so our conclusions may be limited in that they apply to this data.

Our application of the binomial test upon this dataset allowed us to show the feasibility of detecting large disruption events (such as power outages during times of severe thunderstorms) and also much smaller events. The majority of dependent disruptions last less than an hour although a small fraction continued for days. Corroborating prior work, we observe that disruption events occur more frequently at night for some ISPs. However, many disruptions do not affect entire /24 address blocks, suggesting that prior work may miss detecting them.

Simultaneous renumbering of entire prefixes by an ISP would manifest as a dependent disruption event. However, Richter et al. show that such events occur rarely in the U.S.; even elsewhere, they occur only in a few ASes [19]. Since Thunderping pings only U.S. addresses, the dependent disruption events we detected are unlikely to be caused by simultaneous renumbering. We believe that most of these events are caused by outages and are pursuing efforts to corroborate our inferences against ground truth.

Acknowledgments. We thank Arthur Berger, Philipp Richter, our shepherd Georgios Smaragdakis, and the anonymous reviewers for their thoughtful feedback. This research is supported by the U.S. Department of Homeland Security (DHS) Science and Technology Directorate, Cyber Security Division (DHS S&T/CSD) via contract number 70RSAT18CB0000015 and by NSF grants CNS-1619048 and CNS-1526635.

A   Appendix

A.1   Determining D_{min}

Section 3.1 described our technique for detecting dependent disruptions through the calculation of D_{min}. Table 1 presents D_{min}, computed for various values of N and P_d. This table shows that, even for large aggregates of IP addresses, often few simultaneous disruptions are necessary to be able to confidently conclude that a dependent disruption has occurred.

Table 1. D_{min} values for varying values of N and P_d. There is less than 0.01% probability according to the binomial test that D_{min} or more addresses fail for each N and P_d.

N	D_{min}			
	$P_d = 1$/hour	1/day	1/week	1/month
10	8	3	2	2
50	21	5	3	2
100	35	7	4	3
500	126	14	6	4
1000	231	21	8	5
5000	1021	64	17	8
10000	1980	112	26	11
50000	9491	457	85	29

A.2   Analyzing the Confidence of Detected Disruption Events

Here, we examine our confidence in the 20,831 detected dependent disruption events from Sect. 3.2. The occurrence of D_{min} disruptions has less than 0.01% probability according to the binomial test. We test if most detected dependent disruption events have exactly 0.01% probability of occurring or if they are well clear of this threshold.

Figure 8 shows the distribution of the probability that we incorrectly classify an independent event as dependent. The probability of occurring independently is less than 0.005% for 90% of the events and less than 0.001% for 75%. Thus, the probabillity that detected events occurred independently is typically much smaller than our choice of 0.01%.

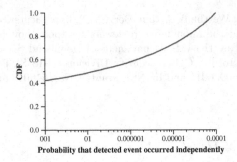

Fig. 8. Figure 8 shows the distribution of the probability that the 20,831 detected dependent disruption events could have occurred independently. For 90% of events, the probability of occurring independently is less than 0.00005.

A.3   Dependent Disruption Events Across ISPs

We grouped dependent disruption events by ISP to check if any ISPs contribute an unusual number of events. Figure 9 shows the top 15 ISPs with dependent disruption events. These top 15 ISPs together account for 13,643 (65%) of all detected events.

We emphasize that these results are not meant to reflect any underlying problems with these ISPs; Thunderping samples and pings large ISPs more frequently and consequently, finds more disrupted addresses in them. The purpose of this analysis is to ensure that no ISP contributes unduly many events.

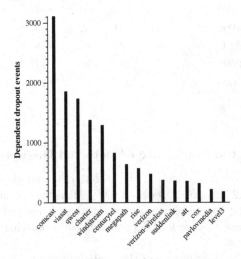

Fig. 9. Figure 9 shows the number of dependent disruption events detected per ISP. Note that these numbers are more a reflection of addresses sampled and pinged in the Thunderping dataset than any major underlying problem in their infrastructure. We leave per-ISP comparisons of dependent disruptions to future work.

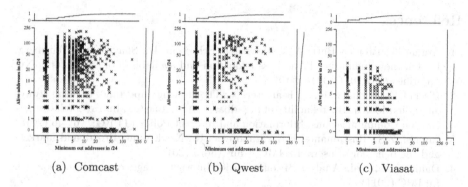

(a) Comcast   (b) Qwest   (c) Viasat

Fig. 10. For Comcast, Qwest, and Viasat: Minimum actual disrupted addresses in a /24 vs. responsive addresses in a /24, for all /24s with at least D_{min} address that were disrupted during a detected dependent disruption event. All ISPs have /24s with actual disrupted addresses where there continued to be responsive addresses throughout the disruption.

A.4   Dependent Disruptions May Not Disrupt Entire /24s: Implications

Continuing our analysis from Sect. 4.4, we investigated if the responsiveness of other addresses in /24s with actual disrupted addresses would vary across ISPs. Figure 10 shows per-ISP behavior. We see that all these ISPs have /24s with actual disrupted addresses where there continued to be responsive addresses throughout the disruption.

Prior work detecting outages within /24 aggregates may miss these events. Since a single positive response from an address within a /24 could lead Trinocular to conclude that the block is alive [18], it can miss dependent disruption events affecting only a subset of addresses within a /24 address block. Richter et al.'s technique is capable of detecting partial /24 disruptions [19]; indeed, many of their disruptions did not affect all addresses in the /24. However, their choice of the *alpha* parameter in their technique ($alpha = 0.5$) meant that they would only detect disruptions where at least half of the active addresses were disrupted. In this paper, we showed that many /24s with actual disrupted addresses continued to have more than half of their (sampled) addresses responsive.

We believe that prior work may be able to detect these events by analyzing broader address aggregates (such as the state-ASN aggregates we use), in addition to /24 aggregates. In preliminary investigations, we found that many of our dependent disruption events consisted of multiple observed disrupted /24s that were each only partially disrupted; that is, a few addresses from many /24s were disrupted simultaneously but there continued to be other responsive addresses in these /24s. One of the largest events had 811 addresses from 42 /24 blocks in the observed disrupted group and 40 of these blocks had responsive addresses. We leave additional analyses for future work but we believe that we detected such events due to the broader aggregate of addresses we considered.

References

1. Argon, O., Bremler-Barr, A., Mokryn, O., Schirman, D., Shavitt, Y., Weinsberg, U.: On the dynamics of IP address allocation and availability of end-hosts. arXiv preprint arXiv:1011.2324 (2010)
2. Bischof, Z., Bustamante, F., Feamster, N.: The growing importance of being always on - a first look at the reliability of broadband internet access. In: Research Conference on Communications, Information and Internet Policy (TPRC), vol. 46 (2018)
3. Bischof, Z.S., Bustamante, F.E., Stanojevic, R.: Need, want. Broadband markets and the behavior of users. In: IMC, Can Afford (2014)
4. Dainotti, A., et al.: Analysis of country-wide Internet outages caused by censorship. In: IMC (2011)
5. Grover, S., et al.: Peeking behind the NAT: an empirical study of home networks. In: IMC (2013)
6. Heidemann, J., Pradkin, Y., Govindan, R., Papadopoulos, C., Bartlett, G., Bannister, J.: Census and survey of the visible Internet. In: IMC (2008)
7. Internet Outage Detection and Analysis (IODA). https://www.caida.org/projects/ioda/
8. National Hurricane Center Tropical Cyclone Report: Hurricane Irma. https://www.nhc.noaa.gov/data/tcr/AL112017_Irma.pdf
9. Katz-Basset, E., Madhyastha, H.V., John, J.P., Krishnamurthy, A., Wetherall, D., Anderson, T.: Studying black holes in the internet with Hubble. In: NSDI (2008)
10. Line Of Storms Moves Through Oklahoma. http://www.newson6.com/story/36651816/tornado-watch-in-effect-for-ne-oklahoma
11. Northeast Storm Undergoes Bombogenesis, Bringing 70 MPH Gusts, Almost 350 Reports of Wind Damage, Flooding—The Weather Channel. https://weather.com/forecast/regional/news/2017-10-30-northeast-storm-damaging-winds-flooding
12. 29–30 October 2017 damaging winds, heavy rainfall & flooding. https://www.weather.gov/aly/October29-302017
13. More than 1 million power outages in the Northeast after blockbuster fall storm - The Washington Post. https://www.washingtonpost.com/news/capital-weather-gang/wp/2017/10/30/over-one-million-power-outages-in-the-northeast-after-blockbuster-fall-storm/
14. Comcast outage on Sep 13 2017 in the Outages Mailing List. https://puck.nether.net/pipermail/outages/2017-September/010754.html
15. Padmanabhan, R.: Analyzing internet reliability remotely with probing-based techniques. Ph.D. thesis, University of Maryland (2018)
16. Padmanabhan, R., Dhamdhere, A., Aben, E., Claffy, K., Spring, N.: Reasons dynamic addresses change. In: IMC (2016)
17. Padmanabhan, R., Owen, P., Schulman, A., Spring, N.: Timeouts: beware surprisingly high delay. In: IMC (2015)
18. Quan, L., Heidemann, J., Pradkin, Y.: Trinocular: understanding internet reliability through adaptive probing. In: SIGCOMM (2013)
19. Richter, P., Padmanabhan, R., Plonka, D., Berger, A., Clark, D.: Advancing the art of internet edge outage detection. In: IMC (2018)
20. Sánchez, M.A., et al.: Dasu: pushing experiments to the internet's edge. In: NSDI (2013)
21. Schulman, A., Spring, N.: Pingin' in the rain. In: IMC (2011)
22. Shah, A., Fontugne, R., Aben, E., Pelsser, C., Bush, R.: Disco: fast, good, and cheap outage detection. In: TMA (2017)

23. Shavitt, Y., Shir, E.: DIMES: let the internet measure itself. SIGCOMM Comput. Commun. Rev. **35**, 71–74 (2005)
24. Sundaresan, S., Burnett, S., Feamster, N., de Donato, W.: BISmark: a testbed for deploying measurements and applications in broadband access networks. In: USENIX ATC, June 2014
25. van Belle, G., Heagerty, P.J., Fischer, L.D., Lumley, T.S.: Biostatistics: A Methodology for the Health Sciences, 2nd edn. Wiley, Hoboken (2004)

Security and Privacy

On DNSSEC Negative Responses, Lies, and Zone Size Detection

Jonathan Demke and Casey Deccio[✉]

Brigham Young University, Provo, UT 84602, USA
{jpd0057,casey}@byu.edu
https://cs.byu.edu/

Abstract. The Domain Name System (DNS) Security Extensions (DNSSEC) introduced additional DNS records (NSEC or NSEC3 records) into negative DNS responses, which records can prove there is no translation for a queried domain name. We introduce a novel technique to estimate the size of a DNS zone by analyzing the NSEC3 records returned by only a small number of DNS queries issued. We survey the prevalence of the deployment of different variants of DNSSEC negative responses across a large set of DNSSEC-signed zones in the wild, and identify over 50% as applicable to our measurement technique. Of the applicable zones, we show that 99% are composed of fewer than 40 names.

Keywords: DNS · DNSSEC · Privacy

1 Introduction

Since its inception over thirty years ago, the Domain Name System (DNS) [19,20] has included provisions for so-called negative responses, which indicate that there is no translation for a queried domain name. While the essential characteristic of a negative response has always been the lack of an *answer* (i.e., translation), the DNS Security Extensions (DNSSEC) [8,19,20,23] introduced the requirement that additional DNS records (NSEC or NSEC3 records) be included in a negative DNS response, which records can *prove* the non-translation of the domain name. A side effect of including these extra records is that additional information is revealed about a domain—such as names that *do* exist. While this side effect is innocuous to some, to others it can be undesirable. In an attempt to reduce or eliminate unwanted disclosure of information via DNSSEC negative responses, new approaches have been introduced into the DNSSEC ecosystem. However, each comes with its own caveats.

In this paper, we present a novel method for learning the *size* of a DNS zone—using DNSSEC negative responses—by issuing only a relatively small number of queries. From a standpoint of minimum information disclosure, even revealing the size of a zone might be a privacy concern to some entities. However, more generally it stands alone as a way to estimate zone size to learn more about how the DNS ecosystem is being utilized. We list the following as the major contributions of this paper:

© Springer Nature Switzerland AG 2019
D. Choffnes and M. Barcellos (Eds.): PAM 2019, LNCS 11419, pp. 231–243, 2019.
https://doi.org/10.1007/978-3-030-15986-3_15

- The presentation of a technique to estimate DNS zone size for NSEC3-signed zones;
- A measurement study on the use of different strategies of DNSSEC negative responses in the wild; and
- A survey of the sizes of various NSEC3-signed zones using the technique introduced in this paper.

As part of our study, we systematically issue queries to DNS servers authoritative for over two million DNSSEC-signed zones, eliciting negative DNS responses of various types. We find that over 50% of the zones we analyzed are signed with traditional NSEC3, and are thus candidates for zone size estimation using relatively few queries. We also observed that 99% of the NSEC3 zones we analyzed have an estimated size of less than 40 names.

2   Background

The Domain Name System (DNS) [19,20] protocol primarily consists of queries and responses. *Queries* are messages requesting the translation of a given *domain name* (i.e., example.com) and type (e.g., A, for IPv4 address). *Responses* are made of multiple DNS *records*, where a record is a mapping of domain name and type to some resource. The records in a DNS response collectively constitute either an *answer*, a *referral* to which server(s) might have the answer, or a definitive indication that there is no resource to which the name and type maps, i.e., there is no answer. A DNS *zone* is a group of DNS records with names under a common domain (i.e., suffix) and served from the same set of servers.

When there is no translation for a given name and type, the response includes no answer records, yielding an empty answer section. The NSEC record was introduced, with DNSSEC, to *prove* that for a given query (a) the queried domain name doesn't exist or (b) no record of the queried type exists at that name [8,9]. An NSEC (next secure) record consists largely of two parts: (1) a pair of domain names that, using a defined canonical ordering, are in sequence; and (2) the list of types that exist for the first of the names in the NSEC record. If a queried name doesn't exist, the server returns the NSEC record that contains the names between which the queried name would fall, if it existed—the NSEC *covering*. If the queried name exists but the queried type does not, then the server returns the NSEC record corresponding to the name, and the list of types in the record prove that the queried type does not exist.

While NSEC records in a response provide a useful non-existence proof, their inclusion makes it possible for a server to divulge all existing domain names in a given zone through systematic querying. This exposure is a privacy concern for some organizations, but the introduction of NSEC3 addressed this concern, in part [23]. With NSEC3, names within a DNS zone are hashed, and the ordered sequence of *hashes* that cover the hash of the queried name, are returned by a server, instead of the names that cover the queried name. Thus, the client receiving the response can prove non-existence of a given name, but doesn't immediately learn about any other names that do exist.

3   Previous Work

While NSEC3 effectively obfuscates the names from simple disclosure, research has shown that with a relatively small number of queries, a significant portion of zone contents can be enumerated using an offline dictionary "attack" [12,24]. We complement this research to show that the *size* of a zone can also trivially be learned.

Further measures to protect DNS privacy by revealing less about a DNS zone involve servers sending minimal proofs—effectively "lying" about zone contents. Two major variants exist, one for NSEC3 records ("white lies") and one for NSEC records ("black lies"). The notion of NSEC3 white lies was introduced by Dan Kaminsky in his Phreebird DNSSEC software [18]. Upon receiving a query for a given domain name, d, rather than returning the NSEC3 record with the hashes corresponding to existing names that surround the hash of d, $h(d)$, the server dynamically creates an NSEC3 record with hashes $h(d) - 1$ and $h(d) + 1$. With the black lies approach—a term coined by Cloudflare—the server dynamically generates an NSEC record with (1) the name queried and (2) the next possible name in DNSSEC canonical ordering (i.e., foo.com and \000.foo.com) [16]. The result in both cases is an NSEC or NSEC3 proof that satisfies any validator without disclosing any existing names or hashes of existing names and does not disclose additional information. In the case of black lies, the response indicates that the name exists (even though it doesn't), but that the type does not.

Generating a dynamic response requires a server to have access to the private key(s) associated with the zone, so DNSSEC signatures (RRSIG records) can also be generated dynamically. This is in contrast to traditional static signing methods, in which RRSIG records can be created on a server, possibly even offline. This potentially creates concerns for zones served by third-party organizations [11,22]; providing private keys to a third party allows them access to create arbitrary zone content. The NSEC5 mechanism was proposed to address this concern by providing a separate key to third parties, which was only good for providing a dynamic signature for an intermediate record that played a role in the proof [15]. Because this key cannot sign the records found in the zone proper, they cannot be used to manipulate. Despite the privacy advantages, NSEC5 has faced challenges with its standardization and adoption.

4   NSEC3 Zone Size Discovery

In this section we discuss the foundations and methodology for estimating the size of an NSEC3-signed zone.

It is well known that contents of zones signed with traditional NSEC (i.e., without black lies) can be trivially enumerated with a number of queries equal to the number of unique owner names in the zone [21]. As a side effect, zone size—as measured by the number of unique owner names—is also discovered.

Zones signed with NSEC3 cannot be similarly enumerated. This is because the hashes returned in the NSEC3 records of one response cannot be used as query names in subsequent responses, as they can in NSEC [23]. However, with traditional NSEC3 (i.e., no white lies), an interested party can accumulate a large number of NSEC3 records with repeated queries. With sufficient queries, the collection of records retrieved might approach the entire set of NSEC3 records for the zone. In that case, the investigator can not only carry out an offline dictionary "attack" [12, 24], but also learn the size of the zone.

Throughout the remainder of this paper, we refer to three types of queries used to elicit negative response, which we describe here:

- *q-nxdomain*: a type A query for a domain name within the zone, formed by pre-pending an arbitrary label of our choosing to the subject domain, e.g., foobar123.example.com, which domain name (presumably) does not exist.
- *q-nodata*: a type CNAME query for the domain name at the zone apex (i.e., the domain name corresponding to the zone itself), which record should also not exist (because a record of type CNAME cannot co-exist with the NS records also at the zone apex) [13].
- *q-nodata-type*: a query for an undefined type at the zone apex, which record should also not exist because the type has not been defined.

4.1 NSEC3 Distance

Like all DNS records, NSEC3 records have an owner name and record data. The first (left-most) label in the owner name is the Base32-encoded (using the "Extended Hex" alphabet [17]) value of the SHA1 hash of a domain name [23]. This label is 32 characters long, with each character having 32 possible values. The record data for an NSEC3 record includes, among other fields, the next field, which is the hash of another owner name in the zone—the next hash in the zone, in canonical ordering. The hash value in the next field can also be represented as a 32-byte string of Base32 characters. The maximum value of the Base32 representation of either is $H = 2^{160} = 32^{32}$.

The *distance*, $d(n)$, of an NSEC3 record, n, is the result of subtracting the next field's value, n_{next}, from the value of the first label of the owner name, n_{owner}. If the next hash value is greater than the hash value in the owner name, then the absolute difference is subtracted from the maximum hash space:

$$d(n) = \begin{cases} n_{owner} - n_{next} & \text{if } n_{owner} \geq n_{next} \\ H - |n_{next} - n_{owner}| & \text{otherwise} \end{cases} \tag{1}$$

For a given zone, Z, the sum of the distances of all the NSEC3 records must equal the total hash space, H:

$$\sum_{n \in Z} d(n) = H \tag{2}$$

4.2 NSEC3 Distance Distribution

To understand the distribution of distances within a zone, Z, we generated random names using the Natural Language Toolkit (NLTK) [10] to create 100 DNS zones for each of the following zone sizes: 10^2, 10^3, 10^4, 10^5, and 10^6. Each of the resulting 500 zones was signed with NSEC3 using BIND's dnssec-signzone [1]. We then computed the distance for each NSEC3 record and plotted the Cumulative Distribution Function (CDF) of all the distances, categorized by zone size, in Fig. 1.

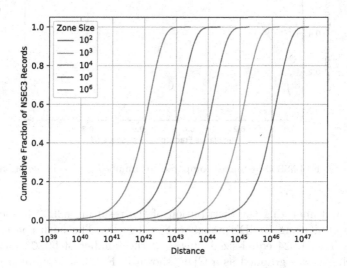

Fig. 1. The CDF of NSEC3 distances for zones of various sizes.

The plots exhibit several noteworthy features. First, the plots of distances for each zone size are nearly identical, with each distribution being shifted from any other distribution according to the inverse proportionality of their respective zone sizes. For example, the median distance for the zone of size 10^2, is 100 (i.e., $10^4/10^2$) times greater than the median distance for the zone of size 10^4. Second, the CDF for each zone size increases logarithmically, rather than exhibiting a normal distribution. Thus, there is a much larger proportion of small NSEC3 distances in each of the zones than large distances. It follows that for an NSEC3-signed zone, the majority of the hash space is covered by relatively few NSEC3 records. Specifically, 90% of the hash space, H, is covered by only about 60% of the NSEC3 records in a zone, and only 19% of the NSEC3 records cover half of the hash space. Relatedly, the lower 50% of NSEC3 distances for a given zone covers only 15% of the overall hash space, H.

The distribution of cumulative NSEC3 distances to cumulative hash space, for the 500 zones we created, is shown in Fig. 2. Notably, Fig. 2 plots the same NSEC3 distance data as Fig. 1, consolidating the distance data from all the zones. Because the distribution of NSEC3 across the hash space is the same for any zone size, the resulting plot is a single, unified line.

The hashes of query names, however, are distributed uniformly across the hash space. We confirmed this by generating 100,000 unique query names within

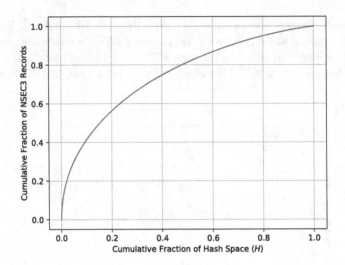

Fig. 2. The CDF of NSEC3 distances compared to cumulative percentage of hash space.

a domain and analyzing the distribution of the resulting NSEC3 hashes, which were computed using BIND's `nsec3hash` utility [1]. The hash space, H, was divided up into 1,024 equal-sized bins, and the number of NSEC3 hashes that fell in each bin was graphed as a CDF, shown in Fig. 3. The number of NSEC3 hashes per bin were normally distributed with a median value of 98, which is the expected value for 100,000 queries, i.e., $100000/1024 = 98$.

The apparent disparity between the uniform distribution of hashes and the exponential distribution of the distances between them is actually an example of a Poisson process. The NSEC3 hashes represent "arrival times" across the hash space, which are uniformly distributed according to constant *intensity* (or *arrival rate*) λ, which is a function of the size of the zone. The NSEC3 distances represent the inter-arrival times and are distributed according to $\mathbf{Exp}(\lambda)$ [14].

Let $z = |Z|$ denote the actual size of DNS zone Z, and let z' represent the estimate of z, derived from NSEC3 distances. If the distances of all NSEC3 records were somewhat uniform, then calculating z' would be as simple as calculating the average distance of the collection of NSEC3 records, N, returned in negative responses to *q-nxdomain* queries and dividing H by that average:

$$z' = \frac{H}{\left(\frac{\sum_{n \in N} d(n)}{|N|}\right)} \tag{3}$$

However, the fact that the distribution of NSEC3 distances—for a zone of any size—follows an exponential distribution across the hash space, while the distribution of NSEC3 hashes are uniformly distributed across the hash space, means that not all queries are equal. That is, the NSEC3 hash corresponding to an arbitrary *q-nxdomain* query is more likely to be covered by an NSEC3 record with a large distance, but that distance is less representative of the zone's NSEC3 records

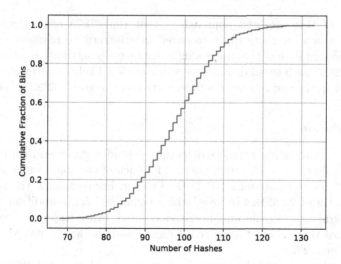

Fig. 3. The distribution of NSEC3 hashes resulting from random query names, graphed as a CDF representing the number of hashes per 1,024th part of the hash space, H.

because of the relatively large percentage of NSEC3 records having a smaller distance. Thus, if all NSEC3 distances in N were weighted equally (i.e., following Eq. 3), then the resulting average would be too high, resulting in a proportionally too-low value for z'.

A more accurate approach to estimating the size of a zone using the collection of NSEC3 records, N, returned in negative responses to q-*nxdomain* queries, is to weight each NSEC3 record according to its statistical representation of the hash space. If the NSEC3 records in N are divided into q quantiles, according to their distance, $N = N_1 + N_2 + \ldots + N_q$, then the distance for all records in N_i are weighted using the fraction of the hash space that that ith quantile represents. The weights for $q = 10$ (i.e., decile or 10th percentiles) were derived from the distance distribution of the NSEC3 records from the 100 zones of size 10^6 that we created and are shown in Table 1. These weights correspond to the difference in cumulative hash space, x, for consecutive quantile values of NSEC3 distances, i.e., $y_1 = \frac{i-1}{q}$ and $y_2 = \frac{i}{q}$. The resulting formula to approximate zone size, letting w_i correspond to the weight for quantile i, is the following:

$$z' = \frac{H}{\left(\sum_{1 \leq i \leq q} \frac{w_i \sum_{n \in N_i} d(n)}{|N_i|} \right)} \tag{4}$$

Table 1. Distance weights for zone size detection using decile divisions (i.e., $q = 10$).

Decile (i)	1	2	3	4	5	6	7	8	9	10
Weight (w_i)	0.41	0.15	0.10	0.08	0.07	.05	.05	0.04	0.03	0.02

The result of this weighted approach is that the NSEC3 records with larger distances—which are more likely to cover an arbitrary *q-nxdomain* query but are less representative of the zone's NSEC3 distances—contribute less to the average than NSEC3 with small distances—which are less likely to cover an arbitrary *q-nxdomain* query and are more representative of the zone's NSEC3 distances.

4.3 Validation

To test the validity of our zone size detection methodology, we issued 1,000 trials, each consisting of 18 *q-nxdomain* queries, for each of the zones we created. The zones were served locally on a BIND DNS server. For each trial, the 18 queries yielded a total of 20 NSEC3 records, which comprised N; in addition to the 18 NSEC3 records covering the unique names queried, every response included the NSEC3 record that covers the wildcard record and the NSEC3 record matching the zone name [23].

First, we investigated the accuracy of our methodology using different quantile (q) values. Specifically, we evaluated the 1,000 trials against the zone of size 10,000 using quantile values of 20, 10, and 5. We measured accuracy in terms of percentage of error based on the actual zone size, i.e.,

$$e = \frac{z' - z}{z} \tag{5}$$

Thus, values of e closer to 0 indicate higher accuracy of zone size prediction, $e < 0$ indicates a low guess ($z' < z$), and $e > 0$ indicates a high guess ($z' > z$). The results are shown in Fig. 4 as a CDF.

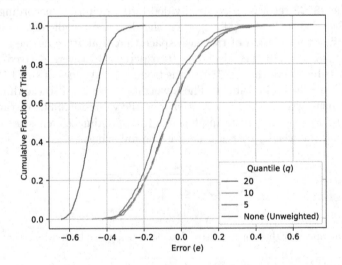

Fig. 4. Error (e) for size prediction of a DNS zone of size 10^6 for various values of q.

Weighting the NSEC3 distances, by any quartile value (Eq. 4) significantly improved the accuracy from the zone size estimates based on unweighted distance averages (Eq. 3). Even the highest zone size estimates calculated using unweighted averages were lower than the actual zone size, with the median error being about 48% low. In contrast, for about 60% of the trials (between the 30 and 90 percentiles) for $q = 10$ and $q = 20$, z' was within 15% of z. And for about 30% of the trials (between the 50 and 80 percentiles), the z' was within 7% of z. Because the error for $q = 10$ and $q = 20$ were comparable, and $q = 10$ requires fewer queries to have at least one NSEC3 record in every quantile, we use $q = 10$ for the remainder of our experiments.

We next tested the accuracy of zone size prediction against zones of different sizes, the results of which are shown in Table 2 and Fig. 5. Consistent among the zones of all sizes was that z' was low more often than not, with the median values of e ranging between -6% and -16%. For zones smaller than 100,000, 75% or more of the trials had error values that were within 20% of the size of the zone.

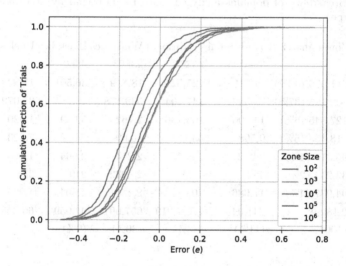

Fig. 5. Error (e) for zone size prediction of DNS zones of various sizes using $q = 10$.

Table 2. Statistics for zone size prediction of DNS zones of various sizes using $q = 10$.

Zone size	10^2	10^3	10^4	10^5	10^6
Median error	-0.06	-0.05	-0.07	-0.16	-0.11
Fraction of trials $-0.20 \leq e \leq 0.20$	0.77	0.78	0.76	0.61	0.70

5 DNS Zone Size Measurement Study

To perform our DNS zone size measurement on deployed DNS zones, we analyzed 2,182,987 DNSSEC-signed zones to determine the strategy they employ for negative responses. This would allow us to identify our candidate DNS zones. The list of zones consisted of DNSSEC-signed second-level domains extracted from the zone files for 821 top-level domains (TLDs). The TLD zone files themselves were obtained from the following sources: Verisign's Zone File Access [6]; the Centralized Zone Data Service (CZDS) [2]; the Public Interest Registry (PIR) [5]; the Internet Foundation in Sweden (IIS) [4]; and Domains Index [3], from which we acquired domains under gov. DNSSEC-signed domains were identified as those with at least one delegation signer (DS) record in the TLD zone file. The breakdown of the domains and their TLD are shown in Table 3. Nearly 80% of the zones analyzed were under the com and se TLDs. This was because of the significant presence of DS records in those domains.

Table 3. Breakdown of domains analyzed, both by TLD and by detected negative response type.

TLD	Zones analyzed	Traditional NSEC	Traditional NSEC3	White lies NSEC3	Black lies NSEC	Unclassified
com	911,576 (42%)	112,168	725,521	18,879	36,501	17,823
se	802,198 (37%)	77,549	147,294	539,178	408	37,072
net	127,545 (6%)	14,390	103,136	2,762	5,089	1,920
nu	118,158 (5%)	9,508	33,801	66,690	74	7,623
org	95,319 (4%)	9,252	79,557	2,214	2,964	1,076
app	33,254 (2%)	492	7,223	25,232	219	33
Other	94,937 (4%)	17,686	70,687	2,136	2,804	1,099
Total	2,182,987 (100%)	241,045 (11%)	1,167,219 (53%)	657,091 (30%)	48,059 (2%)	66,646 (3%)

5.1 Zone Analysis

For each zone in our data set, we identified the authoritative servers using DNS lookups for the NS (name server) records and the corresponding A and AAAA (IPv4 and IPv6 address) records. Having the set of IP addresses for servers authoritative for the domains, we issued three queries to every authoritative server: a *q-nxdomain* query, a *q-nodata* query, and a *q-nodata-type* query. The three queries were intended to elicit different types of negative response behavior, including any of the following:

- NXDOMAIN: a response indicating that the name queried name doesn't exist.
- wildcard: a response synthesized from a wildcard, with NSEC or NSEC3 records to indicate that the queried name didn't exist (as specified by DNSSEC [23]).

– NODATA: a response indicating that the name exists, but with no records corresponding to the type queried [7].

The expected response for *q-nxdomain* was either an NXDOMAIN or wildcard response, and the expected response for *q-nodata* and *q-nodata-type* was NODATA. Under DNSSEC requirements, all such responses would include NSEC or NSEC3 records. Table 3 shows the breakdown of response strategies observed by authoritative servers: traditional NSEC, traditional NSEC3, white lies with NSEC3, and black lies with NSEC. If at least one of the query responses matched a given negative response strategy, then the zone was included in the count for that strategy. We note that for a very small (less than 1%) percentage of the zones analyzed, we observed several different negative response behaviors, such that they are represented in multiple categories. For example, for some zones, white lies was used in response to our *q-nxdomain*, but NSEC records were returned in response to the *q-nodata-type*. Also, for 3% of the DNS zones we analyzed, none of our queries resulted in NSEC or NSEC3 records, so their negative response strategy remained unclassified.

The responses for the unclassified zones fell into several categories. Some of the *q-nxdomain* queries yielded non-wildcard positive responses (i.e., indicating that the record existed), the result of server-side record synthesis with online-signing. This method is employed by organizations in an effort to not even disclose the fact that the response is a wildcard—which would otherwise be apparent. Some responses lacked NSEC or NSEC3 records due to misconfiguration. For example, a DS record existed, but the zone was actually not DNSSEC-signed, or the response had response code SERVFAIL.

We observed nearly one-third of the zones employed white lies, while just over half used traditional NSEC3. About 11% of zones were signed with traditional NSEC, while about 2% of zones used black lies. The combined presence of white lies and black lies implied that a minimum of 32% of the zones we analyzed employed a online signing.

5.2   Detecting Zone Size in the Wild

We tested our zone detection methodology in the wild by issuing 20 queries to each of the zones in our dataset that were signed with plain NSEC3, i.e., without white lies. The results of this measurement are shown in Fig. 6. We found that 85% of the zones we probed were so small that even with only 20 queries, we received fewer than 10 unique NSEC3 records, which is the minimum size of N necessary to apply our methodology. The fact that NSEC3 records were being returned multiple times with these zones was evidence that the zone was small, and was—quite likely—being completely enumerated with our small number of queries. Thus, for $|N| < 10$, we simply use $z' = |N|$ as our zone size estimate. For the zones we measured, 99% were smaller than 40, but the top 1% reached up to nearly four million.

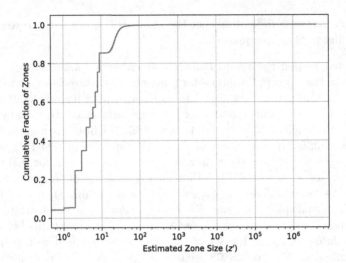

Fig. 6. Estimated zone sizes (z') for the NSEC3-signed zones in our data set (Table 3).

6   Conclusion

In this paper, we have presented methodology for learning the size of a DNS zone by issuing relatively few DNS queries. We demonstrated the accuracy of our technique in a lab environment and showed that in approximately 75% of cases, the methodology would yield a an estimate that is within 20% of the actual zone size, with only 18 queries. We deployed this methodology on over one million NSEC3 zones in our data set and learned that most of these zones are small, with 85% having fewer than 10 domain names.

As part of our study, we measured some of the DNSSEC negative response behaviors currently deployed. We learned that the most popular negative response strategy deployed in our data set is traditional NSEC3, which is used by 53% of zones, and makes them candidates for DNS zone size estimation, using our methodology. Privacy-preserving strategies such as NSEC3 with white lies and NSEC with black lies are also gaining some traction with 30% and 2% deployment, respectively.

The techniques presented in this paper serve as a general purpose tool to better understand the DNS ecosystem, in terms of the size of deployed DNS zones, specifically those signed with NSEC3. It also provides a new insight into information disclosure, regardless of how innocuous the revealing of the size of DNS zone might be to an organization. This knowledge can only benefit and empower the designers, maintainers, and users of the Internet.

References

1. BIND open source DNS server. https://www.isc.org/downloads/bind/
2. Centralized Zone Data Service. https://czds.icann.org/
3. Domains index. https://domains-index.com/
4. The Internet Foundation in Sweden. https://www.iis.se/
5. Public Interest Registry. https://pir.org/
6. Verisign. https://www.verisign.com/
7. Andrews, M.: RFC 2308: negative caching of DNS queries (DNS NCACHE), March 1998
8. Arends, R., Austein, R., Larson, M., Massey, D., Rose, S.: RFC 4033: DNS security introduction and requirements, March 2005
9. Arends, R., Austein, R., Larson, M., Massey, D., Rose, S.: RFC 4034: resource records for the DNS security extensions, March 2005
10. Bird, S., Loper, E., Klein, E.: Natural Language Processing with Python. O'Reilly Media Inc., Sebastopol (2009)
11. Deccio, C., Chen, C.C., Mohapatra, P., Sedayao, J., Kant, K.: Quality of name resolution in the domain name system. In: 2009 17th IEEE International Conference on Network Protocols, October 2009
12. DNSCurve: DNSCurve: Usable security for DNS. http://dnscurve.org/nsec3walker.html
13. Elz, R., Bush, R.: RFC 2181: clarifications to the DNS specification, July 1997
14. Gardiner, C.: Stochastic Methods: A Handbook for the Natural and Social Sciences. Springer, Heidelberg (2009)
15. Goldberg, S., Naor, M., Papadopoulos, D., Reyzin, L., Vasant, S., Ziv, A.: NSEC5: provably preventing DNSSEC zone enumeration. In: NDSS 2015, February 2015
16. Grant, D.: Economical with the truth: making DNSSEC answers cheap. https://blog.cloudflare.com/black-lies/
17. Josefsson, S.: RFC 4648: the base16, base32, and base64 data encodings, October 2006
18. Kaminsky, D.: Phreebird. https://dankaminsky.com/phreebird/
19. Mockapetris, P.: RFC 1034: domain names - concepts and facilities, November 1987
20. Mockapetris, P.: RFC 1035: domain names - implementation and specification, November 1987
21. Osterweil, E., Ryan, M., Massey, D., Zhang, L.: Quantifying the operational status of the DNSSEC deployment. In: Proceedings of the 6th ACM/USENIX Internet Measurement Conference (IMC 2008), October 2008
22. Ramasubramanian, V., Sirer, E.G.: Perils of transitive trust in the domain name system. In: IMC 2005 Proceedings of the 5th ACM SIGCOMM Conference on Internet Measurement, October 2015
23. Sisson, G., Arends, R., Blacka, D.: RFC 5155: DNS security (DNSSEC) hashed authenticated denial of existence, March 2008
24. Wander, M., Schwittmann, L., Boelmann, C., Weis, T.: GPU-based NSEC3 hash breaking. In: 2014 IEEE 13th International Symposium on Network Computing and Applications. IEEE, August 2014

Spectrum Protection
from Micro-transmissions Using
Distributed Spectrum Patrolling

Mallesham Dasari[✉], Muhammad Bershgal Atique, Arani Bhattacharya,
and Samir R. Das

Stony Brook University, Stony Brook, USA
mdasari@cs.stonybrook.edu

Abstract. RF spectrum is a limited natural resource under a significant demand and thus must be effectively monitored and protected. Recently, there has been a significant interest in the use of inexpensive commodity-grade spectrum sensors for large-scale RF spectrum monitoring. The spectrum sensors are attached to compute devices for signal processing computation and also network and storage support. However, these compute devices have limited computation power that impacts the sensing performance adversely. Thus, the parameter choices for the best performance must be done carefully taking the hardware limitations into account. In this paper, we demonstrate this using a benchmarking study, where we consider the detection an unauthorized transmitter that transmits intermittently only for very small durations (micro-transmissions). We characterize the impact of device hardware and critical sensing parameters such as sampling rate, integration size and frequency resolution in detecting such transmissions. We find that in our setup we cannot detect more than 45% of such micro-transmissions on these inexpensive spectrum sensors even with the best possible parameter setting. We explore use of multiple sensors and sensor fusion as an effective means to counter this problem.

Keywords: Distributed spectrum monitoring ·
Transmission detection

1 Introduction

RF spectrum is a natural resource that is in limited supply but is nevertheless in great demand due to the exponentiating increase of mobile network use. Naturally, just like any such resource the spectrum must be protected against unauthorized use. This issue has recently been exacerbated by the increasing affordability of software-defined radio technologies making RF transmissions of arbitrary waveforms in arbitrary spectrum bands practical.

One way to protect spectrum is via large-scale spectrum monitoring. Various spectrum monitoring efforts have been underway for many years (e.g., [13–15]). One issue in such efforts is that lab-grade spectrum sensors are large and

© Springer Nature Switzerland AG 2019
D. Choffnes and M. Barcellos (Eds.): PAM 2019, LNCS 11419, pp. 244–257, 2019.
https://doi.org/10.1007/978-3-030-15986-3_16

expensive both to procure and operate. This issue has recently been addressed by promoting the use of small and inexpensive spectrum sensors that can potentially be crowdsourced, e.g., SpecSense [8], Electrosense [30] and other projects [6,19,32]. This enables much wider deployment in practical settings. Some of these works [8,30] use inexpensive software-defined radios (such as RTL-SDR which costs ≈\$20 [27]) and inexpensive compute devices (such as the RaspberryPi which costs ≈\$40 [25]) attached to these spectrum sensors to enable compute, storage and network capability. ElectroSense has already deployed using these inexpensive spectrum sensors[1] to successfully monitor wide-area spectrum [26].

However, one major concern here is that these inexpensive spectrum sensors are too resource limited and may not be able to perform resource intensive spectrum sensing and detection tasks, e.g., Fast Fourier Transform (FFT) computation and signal detection algorithms [7]. Several sensor related parameters (such as sampling rate, FFT size) and device related parameters (CPU and memory) affect the signal detection performance. A natural question here is to ask how much of these parameters impact the transmitter detection performance given the fact that there are diverse heterogeneous sensors with diverse capabilities. Understanding the impact of these parameters is crucial to design and deploy this class of spectrum sensors.

To address this question, we consider *detecting an intermittent transmitter* as an example problem and characterize the impact of these parameters on detection performance. In our setup, the transmitter here generates a tone of certain duration (e.g., 1 μs) periodically. Detecting such 'micro-transmissions' on these inexpensive devices is hard because we cannot use the optimal parameters that are used in general, due to poor compute capabilities. To quantify this, we use detection ratio as a metric to evaluate the system. Detection ratio is the percentage of transmissions detected by the sensor. We characterize the detection ratio for four different parameters: (1) sampling rate, (2) integration size, (3) FFT size, and (4) device hardware. Our goal is to understand how each of these parameters on the inexpensive compute devices affect the detection of micro-transmissions.

Our key finding is that the inexpensive sensors perform very poorly (<45% accuracy) in detecting micro-transmissions on Odroid-C2 board [24] using USRP-B210 [1] and RTL-SDR [27] sensors. In particular, the detection ratio drops by almost 90% for an intermittent transmitter when the transmission duration drops from 1 s to 1 μs (Sect. 2.3). This is because the limited capabilities of the compute devices lead to dropping of samples while computing FFT and power spectral density (PSD). We also observe that increasing sampling rate from 1 Msps to 32 Msps leads to a drop in the detection ratio by 85% and decreasing it from 1 Msps to 512 Ksps drops by 30%. This performance impact is due to buffer overflow at the higher sampling rate or insufficient number of samples at lower sampling rate.

---

[1] We use the term spectrum sensor as sensor and compute device together.

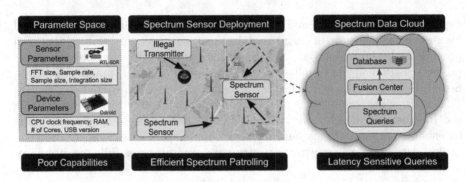

Fig. 1. Architecture of distributed spectrum patrolling. The sensors and attached compute devices are inexpensive and thus suitable for crowd sourcing, but are performance limited.

We also find that the detection ratio is greatly impacted by device hardware. For example, on Odroid-C2 the detection ratio is 70% and 30% less relative to a desktop PC during local and remote detection, respectively (Sect. 3.2). The detection performance can also be impacted by the received power which depends on sensor location, channel conditions as well as the Tx power. To model this behavior at different received power levels, we vary the Tx gain. As expected, the detection ratio reduces significantly on reducing the gain of transmitter (Sect. 3.3). Finally to tackle the above challenges in using low-cost spectrum sensors, we deploy multiple sensors in a given location. We show that using multiple sensors and sensor fusion the detection performance improves significantly (Sect. 4.2).

2 Distributed Spectrum Patrolling

2.1 Background

The increasing cost of spectrum has made it necessary to monitor its usage and detect illegal spectrum transmissions. Crowdsourcing approaches have been proposed in the past to deploy distributed spectrum sensors at a large-scale. However, that necessitates use of inexpensive sensors. To perform large-scale spectrum monitoring, the most commonly proposed technique is to deploy a distributed set of inexpensive sensors (see in Fig. 1). For example, SpecSense [8] and ElectroSense [30] are two successful, well-known examples of distributed spectrum monitoring. Each such spectrum sensor consists of a low-cost embedded compute platform device such as a RaspberryPi or Odroid-C2 connected to an RF front end such as RTL-SDR or USRP. Each sensor scans the different frequency bands and transfers the sampled IQ data to compute device over

Table 1. Spectrum sensor and compute configurations used in our experiments.

Parameters	RTL SDR	USRP B210	Parameters	Desktop	Odroid C2	RPi3	RPi1
Sampling rate (Msps)	2.5	62	Max clock (GHz)	3.35	1.5	1.2	0.7
Spectrum (MHz-GHz)	24-1.7	50-6	CPU cores	4	4	4	1
Bits/sample	8	12	Memory (GB)	8	2	1	0.5
Interface (USB version)	2	2/3	Interface	2/3	2	2	2
Cost ($\approx$\$)	20	1200	Cost ($\approx$\$)	1000	40	40	20

USB interface.[2] The compute device either runs signal detection algorithms on the data locally or sends the data to a remote server for processing. We refer to these two configurations as *local* and *remote* processing respectively. A number of such spectrum patrolling systems have been proposed and deployed [8,18,30].

A key design challenge for these distributed sensing systems is to decide the type of compute device, the sensor and the associated parameters to use. Devices with better compute power and spectrum sensors with higher sampling rates provide much higher accuracy, but also cost more. The higher sampling rate also increases the network bandwidth requirement which is challenging in a wireless environment. While various deployments use different compute devices and sensors, the performance impact of different device choices is not well understood. To address this question, we systematically benchmark the performance of multiple sensor and compute device parameters in the context of a specific spectrum patrolling problem where an intermittent transmitter needs to be detected.

2.2 Measurement Setup

Our measurement setup includes the type of spectrum sensors used, the compute devices attached with the sensors, and the data collection process. Each of these are explained below.

Spectrum Sensors: Commodity spectrum sensors vary widely in terms of cost, performance, and the maximum frequency that they can scan. We experiment with two types of sensors—a higher performing but relatively expensive sensor, USRP-B210 (\$1200) [1], and popular, inexpensive sensor, RTL-SDR (\$20) [27]. The RTL-SDR has a maximum sampling rate of 2.5 Msps while the maximum of the USRP-B210 is 62 Msps. The number of bits per sample is 8 for RTL and 12 for USRP. More bits means better accuracy because of lower quantization noise. The sensor capabilities are summarized in Table 1.

Compute Devices: This device is essentially a small form factor single board embedded computer that acts as a USB host to the sensor. There are many such

---

[2] I refers to the in phase component of the signal and Q refers to the quadrature component of the signal. I and Q representation of a signal contains information about the amplitude as well as the phase of the signal. The received IQ samples are used to reconstruct the received signal which is later demodulated to extract the message signal.

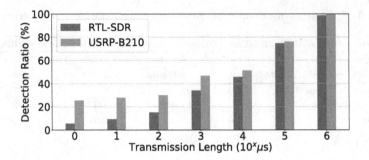

Fig. 2. Detecting intermittent transmissions using USRP-B210 and RTL-SDR sensors on Odroid-C2 board. The detection performance deteriorates significantly as we decrease the transmission length.

platforms. We experiment with three different types of devices—Odroid-C2 [24], RaspberryPi-3 (RPi-3) [25] and RaspberryPi-1 (RPi-1) [25], along with a desktop for a baseline comparison. Each of these devices vary significantly in terms of cost and performance. The CPU performance directly influences the transmitter detection performance because of the processing needed for the signal detection algorithms. Table 1 summarizes the capabilities of these devices.

Data Collection: For all the experiments, we place the transmitter and sensor at a distance of five meters. This transmitter is a USRP-B210 based software radio that transmits an intermittent tone in the 915 MHz band. The default transmitter gain for all the experiments is 100. We use an energy-based signal detection algorithm for detecting the transmitter [7]. The algorithm calculates total power within a frequency band by computing FFT on the IQ samples. The signal is detected if the total power in the channel is more than a predetermined threshold. The threshold can be determined by measuring noise in the channel when there is no transmission. For all the experiments, we use 1 ms transmission on Odroid-C2 board with either USRP or RTL sensors. We consider a single transmitter transmitting with a center frequency of 915 MHz. The default sampling rate is 1 Msps.

2.3 Motivation

As explained in Sect. 2.1, these systems employ expensive compute operations on the received signals at the deployed spectrum sensor. For example, most of this prior work performs FFT on the received IQ samples at the sensor itself, computes the PSD and sends the results to a remote server for further analysis. This computation however can slow down the sensor, leading to dropping of IQ samples and thereby making it hard to detect micro-transmissions. To quantify this, we conduct experiments to study the performance of detecting shorter intermittent transmissions by varying the Tx lengths from 1μs to 1 s (see Fig. 2).

Based on the length of transmitted signal, a significant difference exists in detection performance even if all other parameters and configurations are identi-

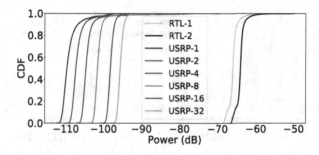

Fig. 3. Sampling rate versus Noise floor (the number in the label indicates sampling rate in Msps). Higher sampling rates bring challenges in detection in terms of noise floor and data rates.

cal. While the sensor is able to detect almost all the 1 s transmissions, the detection performance for 1 µs falls to less than 30% and 10% on USRP and RTL-SDR sensors respectively. This difference must stem from the sensing parameters used on both the sensor and compute device (see Sect. 3) as we observe significantly better performance on high-end desktops with the same sensors (not shown here). Note that the desktop machine has sufficient compute power, and we do not expect any drop of samples on it.

Based on this initial study, our goal is to (i) understand the factors that influence the performance of detecting micro-transmissions on the inexpensive spectrum sensors and (ii) explore an alternative to improve the signal detection performance.

3   Micro-benchmarking of Spectrum Sensors

Four different spectrum sensor parameters (Table 1) could influence the detection performance—sampling rate, integration size, FFT size, and compute device hardware. Sampling rate here is the number of IQ samples received per second. Integration size is the number of samples (i.e., the length of the signal in time) used in a single FFT computation. FFT size is the number of FFT bins. Apart from these parameters, placing the detection locally versus remote, and the transmitter behavior can also influence the detection performance. We study the impact of these properties.

3.1   Sensor Performance

Impact of Sampling Rate: In general, more the sampling rate, better the transmission detection performance. However, distributed spectrum patrolling with inexpensive sensors brings many challenges in using higher sampling rates: (1) Not all sensors support multiple sampling rates. For example, USRP B210 supports sampling rates from 64 Ksps to 62 Msps while RTL supports only from 1 Msps to 2.4 Msps. (2) Higher sampling rates also require proportionately higher backhaul network capacity. (3) Finally, there is a general concern where

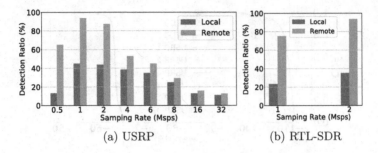

Fig. 4. Detection performance vs. Sampling rate for 1 ms transmission. Increase in sampling rate is decreasing the detection performance on USRP-B210.

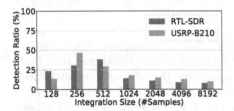

Fig. 5. Integration size vs. detection ratio. We use an FFT bin size of 1024 and run the experiment on Odroid-C2.

Fig. 6. FFT size vs. detection ratio. We use an integration size of 256 and run the experiment on Odroid-C2.

increasing the sampling rate increases the noise floor which makes it harder to detect micro-transmissions. We study this impact of sampling rate on the inexpensive spectrum sensors.

Figure 3 shows that the noise-floor increases from −110 dB to −90 dB when the sampling rate increases from 1 Msps to 32 Msps on USRP. This becomes much worse, greater than −70 dB, for RTL-SDR because of its inaccurate analog converter [5]. This increase in noise-floor makes it hard to choose a threshold for the transmission detection, especially given the fact that there can be many heterogeneous sensors deployed with different sampling rates.

Figure 4 shows the impact of sampling rate on detection performance. The detection performance using local and remote processing decreases by 30% and 80% respectively from 1 Msps to 32 Msps sampling rate. This is a counterintuitive result because we expect to see an increase in detection ratio with the increase in sampling rate. This is because the sensor is unable to cope with the speed at which the samples are received under higher sampling rates (remote), and FFT and PSD computation (local). Hence, the sensor is losing many of the important samples that could otherwise detect transmissions. The result is different with RTL-SDR against sampling rate. When sampling rate increases from 1 Msps to 2 Msps, the detection ratio increases by 15% and 20% for local and remote detection respectively. We explain this by noting that the bits per sample of RTL-SDR is less than USRP, and hence RTL-SDR data require less. Also, reducing the sampling rate below 1 Msps decreases detection ratio due to insufficient number of samples.

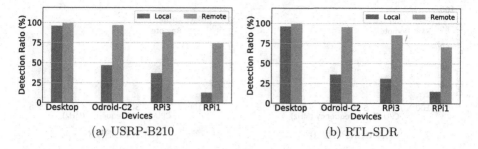

(a) USRP-B210   (b) RTL-SDR

Fig. 7. Impact of device performance on detection performance

Impact of Integration Size: Integration size is a critical parameter in detecting micro-transmissions in terms of both FFT accuracy and compute requirement. Increasing the integration size increases the accuracy of FFT computations, but also increases the amount of computation power needed to compute it. We study the impact of integration size while computing the PSD locally on both USRP and RTL-SDR sensors.

Figure 5 shows local detection performance against integration size on USRP and RTL-SDR on an Odroid-C2. We set the FFT size at 1024 for this experiment, as we find in the next experiment that it provides the best detection performance. The detection drops by more than 30% from an integration size of 256 to 8192 on USRP. The reason behind this impact is that more number of samples the FFT is computed on, harder it is to detect micro-transmissions as the power is averaged over many noise samples. Another interesting result is that if we decrease the integration time from 256 to 128, the detection rate also drops by over 20%. This discrepancy is because the increased number of FFTs become computationally intensive, and consequently, it is not able to handle all the incoming IQ samples. Similar trend exists with RTL-SDR. Therefore, we observe that the integration size should neither be too low nor be too high.

Impact of FFT Size: FFT size defines the number of bins while computing the FFT. Each bin represents the resolution of frequency. For example, if sampling rate is 1 Msps and FFT size is 1024, then the frequency resolution should be 1 MHz/1024 which is 1024 Hz. Smaller the frequency resolution (i.e., more bins), more accurately we can detect the power at a given frequency. Also, it increases the amount of computation needed. We evaluate detection ratio with different FFT sizes from 128 to 8192 with local processing on an Odroid-C2. We use an integration size of 256 samples, as we have observed in the previous experiment that it provides the best detection performance.

Figure 6 shows the impact of FFT size on detection performance. Both RTL and USRP sensors perform better at 1024 FFT size. Having more than 1024 FFT size causes compute and buffer overflow thereby missing IQ samples. Whereas having less than 1024 FFT size makes it hard to detect micro-transmissions. This is because the signal power gets averaged with noise floor due to larger bin size. On the other hand, we find that the optimal FFT size on desktop to detect micro-transmissions is 8192.

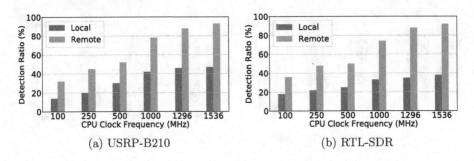

(a) USRP-B210   (b) RTL-SDR

Fig. 8. Impact of CPU clock frequency on detection performance

3.2   Device Performance

In the previous section, we studied impact of low-end hardware on the sensor parameters that affect detection performance. In this section, we study the direct influence of device hardware on detection. We keep the best performing sensor parameters such as sampling rate (1 Msps) and integration size (256) and evaluate the detection ratio across different devices – Odroid-C2, RPi-3, RPi-1, and a desktop (See Table 1).

Detection Performance Across Devices: Figure 7 shows the performance of detection for both local and remote processing. We observe that in each case, performance of detection reduces with a reduction in the computation power of the computing device. For both USRP and RTL sensors, as we go from more powerful to less powerful computing devices, the local detection ratio drops by over 50% and becomes the worst in case of RPi-1 (<20%). This must be due to the compute capacity of the device as the other parameters are unchanged.

We also find that remote processing has much higher detection ratio than local processing when other sensor and transmitter-related parameters are identical. The compute capacity is a bottleneck for local detection because of the FFT and PSD computation, as we observe that remote detection is as high as 97% on Odroid-C2. Even the remote detection performance degrades to only 60% of total transmissions on RPi-1 as its poor hardware is not able to cope with the sampling rate at which the sensors are sampling.

Critical Device Bottleneck: To further understand the impact of the device, we experiment with the most critical parameter of the device – CPU clock frequency (as we have seen relatively less impact with other device parameters such as memory and number of cores). A reduction in CPU clock frequency leads to slower computation on the board, and thus lower detection ratio. This is especially important because many such single board compute devices have varied clock frequencies. We conduct the same study for six different clock frequencies available on the Odroid-C2 board. Figure 8 shows the detection ratio against clock frequency. From 1536 MHz to 100 MHz clock frequency, the detection ratio for local and remote processing on USRP drops by almost 30% and

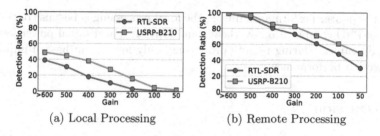

(a) Local Processing   (b) Remote Processing

Fig. 9. Detection performance vs. transmitter gain. The poor detection performance is because of a combination of factors – dropped IQ samples due to additional computation and poor received signal power level.

62% respectively. Similar trends can also be observed with RTL-SDR. An interesting observation is that the decrease in detection ratio in case of RTL-SDR is less than USRP despite being much cheaper. This is because RTL-SDR has smaller number of bits per sample compared to USRP and hence the compute requirement is less.[3]

3.3 Variation in Transmitter's Behavior

The detection performance depends on the received signal power relative to the noise floor. To model this we vary the transmitter's gain. Gain here is a scaling factor that decides the power of the transmitted signal. When the received signal power is low (due to the low gain in the Tx for example) there is a significant chance of false alarms. When the signal power is close to the noise floor, it becomes difficult for the sensors to differentiate between noise and the signal. As a result, signal detection becomes difficult because the sensors can falsely tag noise as signal. The false alarm rate increases in this scenario as it is very hard to detect the low power signals unless we keep the threshold close to noise. Keeping the threshold closer to noise increases the probability of false alarm (P_{FA}). We choose a threshold similar to [5] by assuming the P_{FA} as 10% and compute the detection performance based on this threshold.

We experiment with the transmitter changing its gain from 100 to 1000 in steps of 100. Figure 9 shows the detection performance during local and remote processing. The detection ratio drops to zero when the transmitter changes its gain to 50 during local processing on USRP-B210.[4] The performance is much worse on RTL-SDR, in that it becomes almost zero for gain around 200. This performance degradation also exists for remote processing. The detection ratio drops to 50% and 30% on USRP and RTL-SDR sensors respectively. The reason

---

[3] Note that RTL-SDR has detection ratio similar USRP when the received signal power is high. RTL-SDR performs poorly when the transmitter gain is very low and signal power is close to noise floor (See Sect. 3.3).

[4] Note that it is well known that signal power deteriorates as the transmitter decreases its gain. The goal of this experiment is to understand the significance of detecting micro-transmissions under poor capabilities.

behind the poorer performance during the local processing is because of the dual impact of PSD computation overheads and lower received signal power levels at lower gain values. During remote processing, only lower gain has an impact on the detection performance.

4   Discussion

In this section, we discuss the major findings of our study and provide a possible solution to improve the detection performance of the inexpensive sensors.

4.1   Summary of Main Observations

The key takeaways of our benchmark study are:

- The optimal parameters for spectrum sensing such as effective sampling rate, FFT size, integration size need to be rethought for low-end inexpensive sensors. For example, the optimal sampling rate of detecting 1 ms length micro-transmissions on a Desktop is 8 Msps while on Odroid-C2 it is 1 Msps.
- Even when all signal processing is done remotely, the performance impact of using low-end processors in the spectrum sensor could be significant ($<75\%$ on RPi-1 compared to Desktop, for 1 ms transmission). This is attributed to two factors – (1) inaccurate spectrum sensors, and (2) poor compute hardware that is not able to process high sampling rates.
- For local processing, availability of compute power is a much bigger factor affecting detection performance than the type of spectrum sensor. However, this is not true for remote processing as the amount of samples dropped in the network during shipping for remote processing is never high enough to reduce detection ratio significantly.

4.2   Data Fusion

In Sect. 3, we observed that inexpensive compute devices are limited in terms of computation power because of their hardware. Moreover, the spectrum sensors are also inaccurate in detecting the signal. We now overcome these limitations and improve the signal detection performance while retaining the cost-effective motivation behind distributed sensing. We follow a similar idea from the previous work [8] where the authors show that the inaccuracy of radios can be mitigated by having more radios that are sensing together. This is because the samples are dropped randomly by the devices due to computation bottleneck. The data is later fused from all the sensors. Taking this further, we deploy 10 sensors each with RTL-SDR and Odroid-C2 board at the same location in a campus area.

We use the same transmitter and the setup described in Sect. 2.1. The 10 sensors sense the single channel continuously, compute the PSD, and send the power data to our central server. We use Kaa framework [16] and MongoDB [21] to collect the data and store it in a central database. We use a fusing algorithm

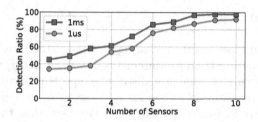

Fig. 10. Improvement in detection performance with number of sensors used.

similar to [5] to combine the data from all the sensors. The detection performance is shown in Fig. 10. We observe that using 8 sensors, a detection ratio of
almost 99% and 95% is reached in case of transmission lengths of 1 ms and 1 μs
respectively. This trade-off of cost versus performance benefits shows that detection performance of inexpensive spectrum sensors can be improved by deploying
more sensors. A more complicated scenario is to detect the transmissions where
the transmitter is changing its gain. This brings the challenges of dealing with
P_{FA} while fusing data and requires more sensors to detect all transmissions.

5   Related Work

The advent of inexpensive software radios has made the spectrum vulnerable to
unauthorized use [2,9,10,17,23,31]. We discuss two related lines of research: (1)
distributed spectrum patrolling, and (2) benchmarking of spectrum sensors.

Distributed Spectrum Patrolling: Multiple studies such as SpecSense [8],
ElectroSense [30] and RadioHound [18] have proposed deploying distributed
spectrum patrolling systems using commodity spectrum sensors. However, they
all deploy one or two different varieties of sensors and compute devices. For
example, RadioHound uses RPi's and laptops as the compute device whereas
ElectroSense and SpecSense use RPi's and Odroid-C2's respectively. Other studies such as [4] and [5] have focused on the heterogeneity of the sensors and their
impact on detection, or various performance issues related to distributed sensing,
such as inaccurate clocks [3] and noisy outputs [19,22]. However, these studies
do not investigate impact of sensing parameters or device hardware.

Benchmarking of Spectrum Sensors: A number of studies benchmark the
performance of individual spectrum sensors and the compute devices. For example, [7,28] benchmarks the energy and performance trade-off of RPi and compare
it with a smartphone and a laptop based sensor. Other studies investigate the
performance of multiple compute devices such as RPi-2, RPi-3 and Beaglebone-
Black in the context of audio processing [11,12,20]. Finally, [29] benchmark FFT
computations on multiple inexpensive compute devices to study their utility for
on-board processing for space missions.

6   Conclusion

The demand for wireless spectrum sharing and co-existence technologies makes large-scale, real-time spectrum measurements necessary. In this work, we explain the key issues that current wide-area distributed spectrum sensing systems face, by benchmarking the impact of sensor and device-related parameters when detecting unauthorized micro-transmissions. We show that the detection performance is no more than 45% even with optimal parameter settings for a 1 ms transmission. The poor performance is mainly attributed to limited computation capability of the device that results in lost samples. To improve this detection performance, we deploy multiple sensors and demonstrate a 98% of detection performance by fusing the data from all the sensors. We believe that this study also serves the validation and reappraisal of distributed sensing systems such as SpecSense [8] and ElectroSense [26].

Acknowledgments. This work is partially supported by NSF grant CNS-1642965 and a grant from MSIT, Korea under the ICTCCP Program (IITP-2017-R0346-16-1007).

References

1. USRP B210. https://www.ettus.com/product/details/ub210-kit
2. Bazerque, J.A., Giannakis, G.B.: Distributed spectrum sensing for cognitive radio networks by exploiting sparsity. IEEE Trans. Sig. Process. **58**(3), 1847–1862 (2010)
3. Calvo-Palomino, R., Giustiniano, D., Lenders, V., Fakhreddine, A.: Crowdsourcing spectrum data decoding. In: INFOCOM 2017-IEEE Conference on Computer Communications, pp. 1–9. IEEE (2017)
4. Calvo-Palomino, R., Pfammatter, D., Giustiniano, D., Lenders, V.: A low-cost sensor platform for large-scale wideband spectrum monitoring. In: Proceedings of the 14th International Conference on Information Processing in Sensor Networks, pp. 396–397. ACM (2015)
5. Chakraborty, A., Bhattacharya, A., Kamal, S., Das, S.R., Gupta, H., Djuric, P.M.: Spectrum patrolling with crowdsourced spectrum sensors. In: IEEE INFOCOM (2018)
6. Chakraborty, A., Das, S.R.: Measurement-augmented spectrum databases for white space spectrum. In: CoNEXT, pp. 67–74. ACM (2014)
7. Chakraborty, A., Gupta, U., Das, S.R.: Benchmarking resource usage for spectrum sensing on commodity mobile devices. In: Proceedings of the 3rd Workshop on Hot Topics in Wireless, HotWireless 2016, pp. 7–11. ACM, New York (2016)
8. Chakraborty, A., Rahman, Md.S., Gupta, H., Das, S.R.: SpecSense: crowdsensing for efficient querying of spectrum occupancy. In: INFOCOM, pp. 1–9. IEEE (2017)
9. Chen, R., Park, J.-M., Bian, K.: Robust distributed spectrum sensing in cognitive radio networks. In: INFOCOM, pp. 1876–1884. IEEE (2008)
10. Cordeiro, C., Challapali, K., et al.: Spectrum agile radios: utilization and sensing architectures. In: DySPAN, pp. 160–169. IEEE (2005)
11. Dasari, M., Kelton, C., Nejati, J., Balasubramanian, A., Das, S.R.: Demystifying hardware bottlenecks in mobile web quality of experience. In: Proceedings of the SIGCOMM Posters and Demos, pp. 43–45. ACM (2017)

12. Dasari, M., Vargas, S., Bhattacharya, A., Balasubramanian, A., Das, S.R., Ferdman, M.: Impact of device performance on mobile internet QOE. In: Proceedings of the Internet Measurement Conference 2018, pp. 1–7. ACM (2018)
13. NASA RF Propagation Database. https://propagation.grc.nasa.gov/
14. MTP Group et al.: Microsoft Spectrum Observatory, Seattle, November 2013
15. Iyer, A., Chintalapudi, K., Navda, V., Ramjee, R., Padmanabhan, V.N., Murthy, C.R.: SpecNet: spectrum sensing sans frontieres. In: NSDI, pp. 351–364. USENIX Association (2011)
16. KAA. https://www.kaaproject.org/
17. Khaledi, M., et al.: Simultaneous power-based localization of transmitters for crowdsourced spectrum monitoring. In: Proceedings of the 23rd Annual International Conference on Mobile Computing and Networking, pp. 235–247. ACM (2017)
18. Kleber, N., et al.: RadioHound: a pervasive sensing platform for sub-6 GHZ dynamic spectrum monitoring. In: 2017 IEEE International Symposium on Dynamic Spectrum Access Networks (DySPAN), pp. 1–2. IEEE (2017)
19. Li, Z., et al.: Identifying value in crowdsourced wireless signal measurements. In: WWW, pp. 607–616. International World Wide Web Conferences Steering Committee (2017)
20. McPherson, A.P., Jack, R.H., Moro, G., et al.: Action-sound latency: are our tools fast enough? (2016)
21. MongoDB. https://www.mongodb.com/
22. Nika, A., et al.: Empirical validation of commodity spectrum monitoring. In: SenSys, pp. 96–108. ACM (2016)
23. Nika, A., et al.: Towards commoditized real-time spectrum monitoring. In: Proceedings of the 1st ACM Workshop on Hot Topics in Wireless, pp. 25–30. ACM (2014)
24. ODROID-C2. https://wiki.odroid.com/odroid-c2/odroid-c2
25. Raspberry Pi. https://www.raspberrypi.org/
26. Rajendran, S., et al.: ElectroSense: open and big spectrum data. IEEE Commun. Mag. **56**(1), 210–217 (2018)
27. RTL-SDR. https://osmocom.org/projects/rtl-sdr/wiki/rtl-sdr
28. Saeed, A., Harras, K.A., Zegura, E., Ammar, M.: Local and low-cost white space detection. In: 2017 IEEE 37th International Conference on Distributed Computing Systems (ICDCS), pp. 503–516. IEEE (2017)
29. Schwaller, B.: Investigating, optimizing, and emulating candidate architectures for on-board space processing. Ph.D. thesis, University of Pittsburgh (2018)
30. Van den Bergh, B., et al.: ElectroSense: crowdsourcing spectrum monitoring. In: DySPAN, pp. 1–2. IEEE (2017)
31. Yucek, T., Arslan, H.: A survey of spectrum sensing algorithms for cognitive radio applications. IEEE Commun. Surv. Tutor. **11**(1), 116–130 (2009)
32. Zhang, T., Leng, N., Banerjee, S.: A vehicle based measurement framework for enhancing whitespace spectrum databases. In: MobiCom, pp. 17–28. ACM (2014)

Measuring Cookies and Web Privacy
in a Post-GDPR World

Adrian Dabrowski[1]([✉]) [iD], Georg Merzdovnik[1] [iD], Johanna Ullrich[2] [iD],
Gerald Sendera[1], and Edgar Weippl[2] [iD]

[1] SBA Research, Vienna, Austria
{adabrowski,gmerzdovnik,gsendra}@sba-research.org
[2] Christian Doppler Laboratory for Security and Quality Improvement
in the Production System Lifecycle, Institute of Information Systems Engineering,
TU Wien, Vienna, Austria
{johanna.ullrich,edgar.weippl}@tuwien.ac.at
http://www.sba-research.org

Abstract. In response, the European Union has adopted the General
Data Protection Regulation (GDPR), a legislative framework for data
protection empowering individuals to control their data. Since its adoption on May 25th, 2018, its real-world implications are still not fully
understood. An often mentioned aspect is Internet browser cookies, used
for authentication and session management but also for user tracking
and advertisement targeting.

In this paper, we assess the impact of the GDPR on browser cookies in the wild in a threefold way. First, we investigate whether there
are differences in cookie setting when accessing Internet services from
different jurisdictions. Therefore, we collected cookies from the Alexa
Top 100,000 websites and compared their cookie behavior from different
vantage points. Second, we assess whether cookie setting behavior has
changed over time by comparing today's results with a data set from
2016. Finally, we discuss challenges caused by these new cookie setting
policies for Internet measurement studies and propose ways to overcome
them.

Keywords: GDPR · Cookies · Privacy

1 Introduction

Privacy means freedom from (unauthorized) surveillance and is considered a
human right according to the United Nations. Nowadays, individual privacy
is increasingly eroding by our fully digitalized world: Enterprises of the digital
economy such as social networks or online advertisers but also nation-state actors
collect vast amounts of data via the Internet [8].

However, privacy legislation significantly differs among countries failing to
address the international aspects of the Internet. With the General Data Protection Regulation (GDPR), the European Union (EU) has taken the effort of

© Springer Nature Switzerland AG 2019
D. Choffnes and M. Barcellos (Eds.): PAM 2019, LNCS 11419, pp. 258–270, 2019.
https://doi.org/10.1007/978-3-030-15986-3_17

harmonization and adopted bold rules for personal data. Its overall goal is to empower individuals to control their personal data and is largely considered one of the strictest legislative framework for data protection worldwide [26]. As a novelty, the GDPR does not only apply to data collection and processing based in the EU, but also to data of European residents that is collected abroad. In theory, this implies changes to all Internet services offered to EU customers regardless of their origin.

As one of its aims, GDPR seeks to prevent the (unconsenting) creation of user profiles; in consequence, most common usages of browser cookies are affected.

As a reaction, Internet services appear to follow one of the strategies below for compliance with the GDPR: (1) A service refrains from using persistent cookies at all. (2) The service asks for explicit user consent and only then sets the cookies, leaving the site usable without consent. In practice, there is frequently a banner spanning over a service's pages asking for consent. (3) Alternatively, EU users are banned from using the service. For example, Los Angeles Times [16] remained inaccessible from Europe for some time, and even *GDPR shields as a service* preventing visits from Europe for a monthly fee are available [13].

In this paper, we assess the impact of the recent GDPR enactment on cookie setting behavior at large scale. In particular, our research is threefold:

- We investigate whether there are differences in cookie setting when accessing the Alexa Top 100,000 websites from different jurisdictions by collecting cookies in an Internet measurement study. We compare persistent cookie usage upon requests originating from the European Union with such from the United States.
- Further, we assess whether cookie setting behavior has changed with the implementation of the GDPR in May 2018. Therefore, we compare our 2018 results with a data set collected in 2016.
- Finally, we infer challenges for Internet measurement studies imposed by GDPR's implementation and discuss means to overcome them.

The remainder of the paper is organized as follows: Sect. 2 provides background on browser cookies and their subsumption under the GDPR framework. Section 3 describes our measurement methodology and data sets. Our results on differences in cookie setting behavior with respect to jurisdiction are presented in Sect. 4, on changes over time in Sect. 5. Section 6 discusses the impact of cookie setting policies on Internet-wide measurement studies, and Sect. 8 concludes.

2 Background and Related Work

This section provides background on HTTP cookies, the General Data Protection Regulation (GDPR) and finally presents related work.

2.1 HTTP Cookies

HTTP cookies are a state management mechanism [2], enabling stateful behavior for the per se stateless HTTP protocol [12]. Cookies are data pieces – to be precise: name-value pairs and metadata – and are set (1) in a server's HTTP response using a HTTP `Set-Cookie` header or alternatively (2) by Javascript running at the client. Either way, the cookie is stored in the client's browser and sent back to the server in subsequent requests; whether the cookie is included into a request is decided upon its metadata, e.g., its expiry date, domain and path. The server is able to adapt its behavior in dependence of the cookie information, or return a modified cookie to the client. Cookies have manifold usages, including user authentication, user tracking or targeted advertising. The latter two are typically permanent (or persistent) cookies; they are issued automatically at the first visit to a new site, stored non-volatile, remain valid for long periods of time – as a consequence of the chosen expiry date – and are used to link subsequent visits of the same user. In contrast, cookies for login purposes are only set during authentication. Working as a temporary session identifier, they are only kept in volatile memory, expire within hours and lost when the browser window is closed.

2.2   General Data Protection Regulation

The General Data Protection Regulation (GDPR) came into force on May 25th, 2018. Before that, cookies have been addressed in 2002 by the European Union's ePrivacy directive (Directive 2002/58/EC, Directive on privacy and electronic communications), also known as *Cookie directive*, and its adaption in 2009 (2009/136/EC). Publications of the European Commission address the correct use of cookies in regard of the European legal framework [10]. In case of cookies acting as a means to collect data for behavioral analytics or to facilitate user tracking, the legislation of the GDPR applies in addition.

According to the GDPR, a data controller will need a legal basis to process personal identifiable information (PII) at all. In general, this is either consent from the user or one of the exceptions in Article 6 of the GDPR.

1. *the data subject has given consent to the processing of his or her personal data for one or more specific purposes.* Almost any processing activity can be justified by informed consent, although the requirements for the underlying information are relatively high. For consent to be valid, it must be informed, specific, freely given and must constitute a real indication of the individual's wishes[1]. In any case, consent is only valid in the form of an active act of consent, or a so-called *opt-in*, the mere *opt-out* or tolerance would no longer be legal. An example in which consent would be required are behavioral analyses, e.g., by Google Analytics. Cookies are only exempted from this requirement, if they are used for the sole purpose of carrying out the transmission of a communication, and are strictly necessary in order for the provider of an information society service explicitly required by the user to provide that service.
2. *processing is necessary for the performance of a contract to which the data subject is party or in order to take steps at the request of the data subject*

---

[1] *Guidelines on Consent under Regulation 2016/679.* Adopted on 28 November 2017.

prior to entering into a contract. This applies to cases in which the cookie is necessary to provide the requested webpage or service, such as cookies for user authentication, or webshop carts.

3. *processing is necessary for the purposes of the legitimate interests pursued by the controller or by a third party, except where such interests are overridden by the interests or fundamental rights and freedoms of the data subject which require protection of personal data.* IT security, i.e. the protection from attacks or malware are considered a possible legitimate interest on the part of the person responsible.

Also in the case of transfer to a third country according to Article 44, which is often the case when using analysis, content delivery or social media (e.g. Google, USA), certain regulations must be observed in order to remain within a legal framework [11], e.g., in the case of the U.S. the Privacy Shield framework [9].

2.3 Related Work

Previous measurement studies collected cookies for various purposes; measurements are either active using crawling or probing a data set, e.g., [3,5,7,8] or passive relying on (already available or just captured) traffic logs, e.g., [14,25]: Hannak et al. [15] investigate price discrimination and personalization that is based on cookies. Englehardt et al. [8] studied the potential of passive mass surveillance, e.g., by intelligence services, exploiting third-party HTTP tracking cookies. Englehardt and Narayanan [7] developed a measurement platform for web privacy measurements. The platform allowed to assess cookie-based, stateful as well as fingerprinting-based, stateless tracking, and found previously unknown techniques for tracking. Merzdovnik et al. [21] provided a similar large scale study on tracking and tracker blocking, which was conducted on the Alexa Top 200,000 pages. Cahn et al. [3] crawled the Alexa Top 100,000 web sites for cookies; their assessment led to the development of a mathematical model to quantify user information leakage. Sivakorn et al. [25] assessed the extent of information that is revealed to adversaries hijacking HTTP cookies in cases of simultaneous deployment of HTTP and HTTPS. Based on a data set of cookies collected in the wild, Gonzalez et al. [14] developed a methodology extracting information from proprietary data formats that are frequently used in cookies. Lerner et al. [19] investigated the history of cookie-based web tracking from 1996 to 2016; their work is similar to ours insofar as historic changes in cookie utilization are observed. We progress this line of research by specifically assessing the practical impact of the GDPR adoption on cookie usage.

Degeling et al. [6] and Linden et al. [20] made studies on the related topic of how GDPR changes web sites' privacy policies. Kulyk et al. [18] observed user reaction to the former cookie information banners.

Beyond, there are works on effects of GDPR adoption on Internet measurement: Plonka and Berger [22] revised collection of IPv6 addresses – the latter considered as personal identifiable information (PII) under the GDPR – and proposed a method to anonymize data sets of IPv6 addresses. Trammell and

Kühlewind [27] showed that even simple round-trip measurements reveal sensitive information, i.e., geographical location, and might thus become subject to the GDPR. While these works consider the impact of GDPR on Internet measurement, they do not assess the impact of GDPR adaption in the wild.

3   Methodology and Data Sets

For our study we employed three measurements based on the Alexa Top 100,000 ranking (a subset of Alexa Top 1 Million [1]). While the ranking methodology is poorly documented [23,24], it remains a de-facto industry standard. In our opinion, it still depicts the World Wide Web better, than the protocol-agnostic Umbrella [4] list.

Two data sets were recorded in 2018 from different locations starting one week after GDPR's adoption. The third one had been recorded in 2016 but remapped to fit the 2018 ranking based on domain name. Thus, all data are shown and compared in 2018 ranking.

3.1   2018 Measurement

We crawled the Alexa Top 100,000 websites using the official Google Chrome v.66 browser in headless and network-deterministic mode. Every website was visited using HTTP and HTTPS, and each visit consisted of three retrievals. In the first retrieval, the main landing page is gained. For example, `microsoft.com` redirects to a specific regional page such as https://www.microsoft.com/nl-nl/ and de.wikipedia.org redirects to https://de.wikipedia.org/wiki/Wikipedia: Hauptseite. If the HTTP visit redirected to HTTPS or vice-versa, the other visit was skipped. The last two retrievals shared the user profile, but the browser process was closed in between. Thus removing all session cookies and leaving only persistent cookies. Finally, the internal *netlog* of the third retrieval was searched for transmitted cookies to the landing page. Unresponsive websites (e.g., due to down times or blocked IPs) and unresolvable websites were marked as erroneous.

This approach provides the following benefits: (1) The final netlog is not cluttered with redirect chains, e.g., HTTP redirects to HTTPS followed by further redirects to regional language pages. (2) In consequence, the first request in the netlog is the page actually shown to the user. (3) This way, subsequent requests to third party resources (e.g., advertisement banners) can be clearly separated. (4) Since persistent cookies can also be set dynamically among others by Javascript or in iframes, we have to observe the actual network traffic of an request to gain all cookies. It is not enough to look for `Set-Cookie` headers in server responses as the dynamic cookies are missed this way.

For the two measurements, we visited the Alexa Top 100,000 websites[2] from two locations. The first is based in a member state of the EU, the second in a

---

[2] We used Alexa Top 1 Million file [1] dating, May 24th, 2018, for all 2018 measurements after the introduction of GDPR.

US-based Amazon data center (east coast). Unreachable or unsuccessfully loaded websites were retried a few days later before being eventually marked as erroneous.

3.2 2016 Measurement

The 2016 measurement was conducted for a different study and thus used a slightly different approach. A scripted Firefox headless browser visited the Alexa Top 200,000 pages[3] from a US-based Amazon data center (west coast). These 200,000 measurements where later mapped to the 2018 ranking for comparison, matching 62,679 sites. A visit consisted of following initial redirects and then visiting three random sub pages of the site. Both, the HTTP and HTTPS traffic was recorded using a man-in-the-middle proxy with a custom-supplied certificate which was trusted by the browser.

This method is able to distinguish between session and persistent cookies that are set in HTTP headers using the expiry date from the `Set-Cookie` HTTP response header. However, it cannot make such a distinction on cookies that have been dynamically set (Javascript). The latter are only observed in subsequent requests but do not carry any indicator about their lifespan. In consequence, we can only provide an upper and lower bound for persistent cookies within this work representing the uncertainty span.

3.3 Unavailable Websites

In 2018, 2.5% of all websites were unavailable from the US but available from the EU; 0.7% were unavailable from the EU but available from the US and 1.9% were unavailable from both locations. Possible reasons include:

- Content delivery network (CDN) domains without an actual website. Examples include twimg.com (the Twitter CDN for images), cdninstagram.com, cloudfront.net (the CDN domain of cloudfront.com), ytimg.com, ebay-desc.com (used for user-supplied content to mitigate SOP-based problems such as XSS).
- Geographic blocking. For example, 92 Russian, 45 Iranian, and 58 Brasilian websites were exclusively blocked for US visitors, compared to 26, 5, and 13 respectively for EU visitors (based on ccTLD).
- Network and server failures during the measurement period.

3.4 Data Set Usage

For the 2018 measurements, we concluded that a website uses persistent cookies whenever at least one cookie was detected during the first HTTP(S) request in the third retrieval. We did not specifically look at third-party resources, such as advertisement networks. For the 2016 data set, we counted the `Set-Cookie`

---

[3] Alexa file from May 24th, 2016.

header in case it included an expiry date or if a new cookie not previously set by HTTP headers was observed in the traffic. For comparison of the 2018 data sets, we used websites reachable from both measurement locations only. For temporal analysis, we matched the 2018 and 2016 data sets by domain name and included only domains that have been prevalent in both data sets since the Alexa ranking changed considerably over time.

3.5 Ethical Considerations

In our measurements, no personal data of individuals was collected or processed, i.e., the GDPR does apply to our measurements. We pretended to be a regular user, and investigated how websites react in case of such legitimate use. However, personal data of real people was not involved at any stage of this study. Beyond, we did not inflict any negative impact on websites ranked in the Alexa ranking [1] as our line of action, i.e., accessing websites and storing the cookies in our browser, is considered regular behavior on the Internet.

4 Geographical Differences

In this section, we compare the results from our 2018 measurements from US and EU vantage points (Fig. 1). In total, 94,836 sites could be retrieved from both test locations. Thereof, 50,663 sites (53.4%) did not install a persistent cookie on first visit, neither when requested from the EU nor the US. 31,362 (33.0%)

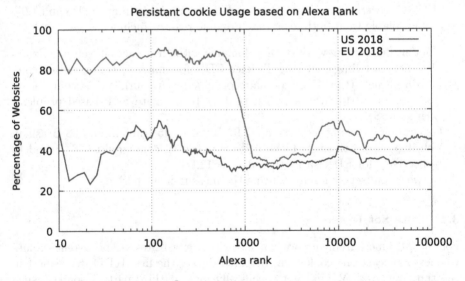

Fig. 1. Comparison of 2018 cookie usage. How to read: similar to a density plot. Example: around rank position 100, 87% of sites install a persistent cookie when visited from the US, but only 46% sites do the same for European visitors without prior consent.

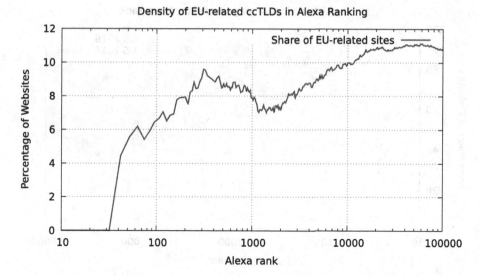

Fig. 2. Share EU-related top-level domains in the Alexa top 100,000 sites as of May 2018 based on ccTLD (Sect. 5.1)

installed a cookie in every case. However, 11,773 (12.4% of reachable and 26.6% of cookie-using) sites issued cookies for US-based visitors but not for EU-based ones. In comparison, only 1,038 (1% reachable, 2.3% cookie-using) of the sites set cookies for European, but not for US customers.

Interestingly, the discrepancy sharply increases for the top 1,000 websites: 49.3% of cookie-using websites choose to evade GDPR by using some form of geographic discrimination.

Figure 1 depicts the percentage of websites using persistent cookies, and shows the clear tendency of less persistent cookie usage for EU users. We have chosen a logarithmic scale for the Alexa rank as it better fits the long-tail characteristic of the rank.

We attribute the clear tendency to more geographically-based cookie differentiation on the higher ranks to the dominance of commercial and international websites. The Alexa list (and probably the WWW as a whole) is skewed towards non-EU sites on the top ranks (Fig. 2). As EU-based operators have to apply GDPR rules regardless of origin, those rules have larger effect on lower ranks. Additionally, lower ranked websites tend not to have made the same investment into a real-time geographical differentiation of their visitors, as higher ranked websites. The latter's business model might depend more on tracking, advertisement and user analytics.

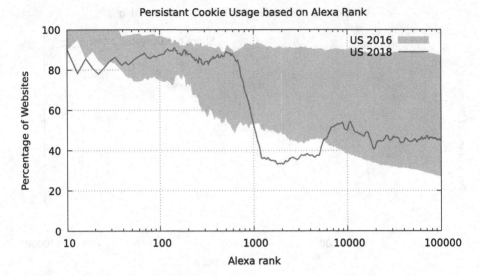

Fig. 3. Temporal comparison of cookie usage. Data for 2016 is given as an upper and lower limit (see Sect. 3.2) and mapped to Alexa ranking of May 2018

5   Temporal Changes

For temporal comparison, we normalized the 2016 ranking to fit the 2018 ranking. Thus, giving us a comparison about the development of cookie usage on a per-site basis. As for the above described uncertainty of the 2016 data, we can only provide ranges. The results are depicted in Fig. 3.

In the top 1,000 ranks, 84% of sites could be matched from the whole 2016 data set. Of those, between 10.3% and 24.3% dropped non-consensual persistent cookie usage between 2016 and 2018.

In comparison, for the top 100,000 sites, only 55% could be matched from 2016 to 2018. Between 30.88% and 46.7% decided to refrain from non-consensual persistent cookie use all together.

Overall, US customers seem to also have profited from EU restrictions on Cookie usage.

As mentioned in Sect. 4, the drop of cookie usage above rank 1,000 for non EU-consumers could be due to websites applying EU-sane settings without a geographical considerations.

5.1   EU Websites

Out of the Alexa Top 100,000 sites, we estimate are 10,584 are EU-related based on the country-code top-level domain (ccTLD)[4]. 7,668 have been valid and present in all three data sets (Fig. 4). Albeit some inaccuracies (e.g., vanity domains such as start.at, or multinationals such as siemens.com), the majority

---

[4] eu, at, be, bg, cz, cy, de, dk, ee, es, fi, fr, gg, uk, gb, gi, gr, hr, hu, ie, im, it, je, lt, lu, lv, mt, nl, pl, pt, ro, se, si, sk.

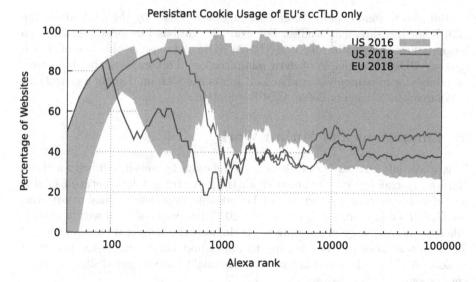

Fig. 4. Persistent cookie usage amount sites with EU-related domains, otherwise similar to Figs. 1 and 3.

of those websites target EU consumers of some sort. 36% use cookies regardless of the geographic location of an visitor. 11% set cookies for U.S.-based but not EU users and 2% vice-versa. Between 31% and 46% of websites with EU-related domain names chose to drop cookie usage in the last two years, whereas 3% introduced them.

6 Impact on Measurement Studies

The adoption of the GDPR in the European Union has apparently created a two-class Internet with regard to privacy. While Internet users benefit from this development, it poses several challenges for Internet measurement studies. Future measurements on website behavior, cookie usage, privacy options, and related matters will heavily depend on the location of the measurement and provide potentially vastly different results. This diversification will further proceed should more world-regions (state unions, political super-powers) put effective Internet-regulation for privacy protection in place.

This implies reduced significance and universality, especially for measurements on privacy. Researchers will either have to restrict their scope to certain geographical regions or have to invest in multiple measurement sites repeating tests from each site. Additionally, as many websites present geographically-selected GDPR-compliance banners, measurement studies comparing the visual representation of websites might lead to false results. Studies investigating cookies, e.g., the extent of tracking after providing consent, have to find a way to automatically overcome the banner to proceed to cookie setting.

But also beyond cookies, more challenges are caused by the adoption of the GDPR for measurement studies. For example, various European registrars no longer collect information for ICANN's WHOIS database as this line of action opposes GDPR's principle of data minimization. This impacts the database's usefulness for measurement studies as it limits the view on domain registrations in comparison to the era before GDPR adoption.

7   Limitations and Future Work

This study only compared snapshots of cookie usage by websites directly without third-party cookies (c.f. Iordanou et al. [17]). A stronger link between GDPR and changes in cookie usage would be possible by a longitudinal study during GDPR's adoption. Additionally, the 2016 data was collected with a slightly different methodology prohibiting to distinguish the temporal configuration of Javascript-set cookies, thus leading to upper and lower bounds for persistent cookies. Additionally, the different browsers might have triggered slightly different responses from websites.

Nevertheless, the current data suggests that EU's GDPR had a massive international impact on cookie usage in the web's ecosystem.

Some open topics remain for further investigation. First, we focused on persistent cookies in this study but neglected the use of sessions cookies which should become part of future inspections. Furthermore, as has been shown in the past, trackers can also rely on other information to identify users, like fingerprinting and local storage. Therefore the impact of GDPR on such types of user tracking needs to be analyzed as well. Additionally, since sites now need to ask the user's consensus before setting cookies, systems to detect and interact with such checks need to be devised to allow for a better analysis in future privacy measurements. Many cookies might still be set, after the user consent – however, if the user is willing to live with the banner, they might now enjoy many more websites cookie-free. We neglected, that some non-GDPR-compliant websites might offer the user to opt-out afterwards. Beyond, it should be investigated whether a website's real behavior is compliant with the declaration offered in the banners.

In our study we assumed geographical discrimination to be Source-IP or DNS-based. Other techniques exist, such as geographical routing announcements to different data centers.

8   Conclusion

General Data Protection Regulation (GDPR) has created a two-class Internet with regard to privacy. EU consumers encounter significantly less unconditional usage of persistent cookies when surfing the web than US visitors. 49.3% of cookie-using websites of the Alexa Top 1,000 choose to refrain from cookie setting without consent on the first visit when facing an EU visitor, when they would for other visitors. This figure drops to an overall of 26% when observing all Alexa

Top 100,000 websites. Further, the new regulations reduced cookie burdens for the rest of the Internet as well, i.e., even users from outside of the EU benefit from the GDPR's adoption and experience less cookies. When compared to data from 2016, the overall cookie load reduced by up to 46.7% for US consumers, albeit mostly for lower ranked websites.

For consumers, this is clearly great news for their privacy. However, researchers face an increasingly divided World Wide Web. Future Internet studies will have to account for different geographical regions or alternatively reduce their scope.

Acknowledgments. This research was funded by the *Christian Doppler Laboratory for Security and Quality Improvement in the Production System Lifecycle (CDL-SQI)*, *Institute of Information Systems Engineering*, TU Wien and the Josef Ressel Centers project TARGET. The competence center SBA Research (SBA-K1) is funded within the framework of COMET Competence Centers for Excellent Technologies by BMVIT, BMDW, and the federal state of Vienna.

References

1. Amazon: Alexa top sites (2018). https://aws.amazon.com/alexa/, direct download: http://s3.amazonaws.com/alexa-static/top-1m.csv.zip
2. Barth, A.: HTTP state management mechanism. RFC 6265 (Proposed Standard), April 2011. https://doi.org/10.17487/RFC6265. https://www.rfc-editor.org/rfc/rfc6265.txt
3. Cahn, A., Alfeld, S., Barford, P., Muthukrishnan, S.: An empirical study of web cookies. In: Proceedings of the 25th International Conference on World Wide Web, WWW 2016, pp. 891–901. International World Wide Web Conferences Steering Committee, Republic and Canton of Geneva, Switzerland (2016). https://doi.org/10.1145/2872427.2882991
4. Cisco: Cisco umbrella 1 million, December 2016. http://s3-us-west-1.amazonaws.com/umbrella-static/index.html
5. Dabrowski, A., Merzdovnik, G., Kommenda, N., Weippl, E.: Browser history stealing with captive Wi-Fi portals. In: 2016 IEEE Security and Privacy Workshops (SPW), pp. 234–240, May 2016. https://doi.org/10.1109/SPW.2016.42
6. Degeling, M., Utz, C., Lentzsch, C., Hosseini, H., Schaub, F., Holz, T.: We value your privacy... now take some cookies: measuring the GDPR's impact on web privacy. In: Network and Distributed System Security Symposium (NDSS) (2019)
7. Englehardt, S., Narayanan, A.: Online tracking: A 1-million-site measurement and analysis. In: Proceedings of the 2016 ACM SIGSAC Conference on Computer and Communications Security, CCS 2016, pp. 1388–1401. ACM, New York (2016). https://doi.org/10.1145/2976749.2978313
8. Englehardt, S., et al.: Cookies that give you away: the surveillance implications of web tracking. In: Proceedings of the 24th International Conference on World Wide Web, WWW 2015, pp. 289–299. International World Wide Web Conferences Steering Committee, Republic and Canton of Geneva, Switzerland (2015). https://doi.org/10.1145/2736277.2741679
9. European Commission: Adequacy of the protection of personal data in non-EU countries (2018). https://ec.europa.eu/info/law/law-topic/data-protection/data-transfers-outside-eu/adequacy-protection-personal-data-non-eu-countries_en

10. European Commission: Cookies (2018). http://ec.europa.eu/ipg/basics/legal/cookies/index_en.htm
11. European Commission: Data transfers outside the EU (2018). https://ec.europa.eu/info/law/law-topic/data-protection/data-transfers-outside-eu_en
12. Fielding, R., Reschke, J.: Hypertext transfer protocol (HTTP/1.1): message syntax and routing. RFC 7230 (Proposed Standard), June 2014. https://doi.org/10.17487/RFC7230. https://www.rfc-editor.org/rfc/rfc7230.txt
13. General Data Protection Regulation Shield: Gdpr shield (2018). https://gdprshield.co.uk
14. Gonzalez, R., et al.: The cookie recipe: untangling the use of cookies in the wild. In: 2017 Network Traffic Measurement and Analysis Conference (TMA), pp. 1–9, June 2017
15. Hannak, A., Soeller, G., Lazer, D., Mislove, A., Wilson, C.: Measuring price discrimination and steering on e-commerce web sites. In: Proceedings of the 2014 Conference on Internet Measurement Conference, IMC 2014, pp. 305–318. ACM, New York (2014). https://doi.org/10.1145/2663716.2663744
16. Hern, A., Belam, M.: LA times among US-based news sites blocking EU users due to GDPR (2018). https://www.theguardian.com/technology/2018/may/25/gdpr-us-based-news-websites-eu-internet-users-la-times
17. Iordanou, C., Smaragdakis, G., Poese, I., Laoutaris, N.: Tracing cross border web tracking. In: Proceedings of ACM IMC 2018, Boston, MA, October 2018
18. Kulyk, O., Hilt, A., Gerber, N., Volkamer, M.: "This website uses cookies": users' perceptions and reactions to the cookie disclaimer. In: European Workshop on Usable Security (EuroUSEC) (2018)
19. Lerner, A., Simpson, A.K., Kohno, T., Roesner, F.: Internet jones and the raiders of the lost trackers: an archaeological study of web tracking from 1996 to 2016. In: 25th USENIX Security Symposium (USENIX Security 16). USENIX Association, Austin, TX (2016). https://www.usenix.org/conference/usenixsecurity16/technical-sessions/presentation/lerner
20. Linden, T., Harkous, H., Fawaz, K.: The privacy policy landscape after the GDPR (2018). http://arxiv.org/abs/1809.08396
21. Merzdovnik, G., et al.: Block me if you can: a large-scale study of tracker-blocking tools. In: 2017 IEEE European Symposium on Security and Privacy (EuroS&P), pp. 319–333. IEEE (2017)
22. Plonka, D., Berger, A.W.: kIP: a measured approach to IPv6 address anonymization (2017). http://arxiv.org/abs/1707.03900
23. Pochat, V.L., van Goethem, T., Joosen, W.: Rigging research results by manipulating top websites rankings (2018). https://arxiv.org/abs/1806.01156v1
24. Scheitle, Q., et al.: A long way to the top: significance, structure, and stability of internet top lists. In: Proceedings of the Internet Measurement Conference 2018, IMC 2018, pp. 478–493. ACM, New York (2018). https://doi.org/10.1145/3278532.3278574
25. Sivakorn, S., Polakis, I., Keromytis, A.D.: The cracked cookie jar: HTTP cookie hijacking and the exposure of private information. In: 2016 IEEE Symposium on Security and Privacy (SP), pp. 724–742, May 2016
26. Tiku, N.: Europe's new privacy law will change the web, and more (2018). https://www.wired.com/story/europes-new-privacy-law-will-change-the-web-and-more/
27. Trammell, B., Kühlewind, M.: Revisiting the privacy implications of two-way internet latency data. In: Beverly, R., Smaragdakis, G., Feldmann, A. (eds.) PAM 2018. LNCS, vol. 10771, pp. 73–84. Springer, Cham (2018). https://doi.org/10.1007/978-3-319-76481-8_6

Web

The Value of First Impressions

The Impact of Ad-Blocking on Web QoE

James Newman[✉] and Fabián E. Bustamante

Northwestern University, Evanston, USA
jamesnewman2015@u.northwestern.edu

Abstract. We present the first detailed analysis of ad-blocking's impact on user Web quality of experience (QoE). We use the most popular web-based ad-blocker to capture the impact of ad-blocking on QoE for the top Alexa 5,000 websites. We find that ad-blocking reduces the number of objects loaded by 15% in the median case, and that this reduction translates into a 12.5% improvement on page load time (PLT) and a slight worsening of time to first paint (TTFP) of 6.54%. We show the complex relationship between ad-blocking and quality of experience - despite the clear improvements to PLT in the average case, for the bottom 10 percentile, this improvement comes at the cost of a slowdown on the initial responsiveness of websites, with a 19% increase to TTFP. To understand the relative importance of this trade-off on user experience, we run a large, crowd-sourced experiment with 1,000 users in Amazon Turk. For this experiment, users were presented with websites for which ad-blocking results in both, a reduction of PLT and a significant increase in TTFP. We find, surprisingly, 71.5% of the time users show a clear preference for faster first paint over faster page load times, hinting at the importance of first impressions on web QoE.

1 Introduction

The web advertisement industry has grown exponentially over the past decade and is now the primary source of income for most content providers [19]. A number of research efforts in the last few years have focused on understanding their scale, mechanisms, and economics [10,26,34].

While keeping most online content and services "free", web advertisements have raised serious security problems and privacy concerns, and attracted some negative press due to questionable practices [21,29,40]. In response, millions of users have adopted some form of ad-blocker. By February 2017, at least 615 million devices have an ad-blocker installed, and the total ad-block usage increased 30% between December 2015 and 2016, according to the latest PageFair Adblock Report from 2017 [8].

Besides increased security and fewer interruptions, a key motivation for the wide adoption of ad-blockers is speed [8]. While it seems intuitive that loading fewer objects would lead to an improved quality of experience (QoE), the exact

© Springer Nature Switzerland AG 2019
D. Choffnes and M. Barcelos (Eds.): PAM 2019, LNCS 11419, pp. 273–285, 2019.
https://doi.org/10.1007/978-3-030-15986-3_18

impact of ad-blocking on perceived website performance is still unclear, despite the importance of QoE on user engagement and profit [24,39].

This paper presents the first detailed analysis of ad-blocking's impact on user QoE. We use the most popular web-based ad-blocker to analyze the impact of ad-blocking on users' web experience when visiting the top-5,000 most popular websites according to Alexa. We rely on three commonly used metrics as proxies of users' QoE – Page Load Time, First Paint Time, and Speed Index.

Our results reveal a complex relationship between ad-blocking and web QoE. We find, as expected, that ad-blocking reduces the number of objects loaded by 15% in the median case. This reduction in loaded objects translates into a 12.5% improvement on PLT and a slight worsening of TTFP of 6.54%, on average. When focusing on the bottom 10 percentile, however, we find that while ad-blocking yields a 14% improvement on PLT, the worsening of TTFP is about 3x higher than in the average case.

To understand the relative importance of this trade-off for user experience, we conducted a large crowd-sourced experiment of ad-blocking and Web QoE with 1,000 users in Amazon Mechanical Turk. Users were presented with websites for which ad-blocking results in both a significant reduction of PLT and a significant increase of TTFP. We find, surprisingly, that 71.5% of the time users show a clear preference for faster first paint over page load times, suggesting the importance of first impressions on web QoE.

In summary, our main contributions are:

- We report on the first large-scale evaluation of the web QoE impact of ad-blocking with the 5,000 top Alexa sites.
- We show the complex relationship between ad-blocking and quality of experience – while ad-blocking yields clear improvements to PLT in the average case, for the bottom 10 percentile, this improvement comes at the cost of a significant slowdown on the initial responsiveness of websites, with a 19% increase to TTFP.
- We present results from the largest crowd-sourced analysis of ad-blocking impact on QoE today, with 1,000 users in Amazon Mechanical Turk. Our results suggest that user experience is more sensitive to faster first paint than slower page load times.
- To assist open science, we will publicly release our dataset from our controlled experiment with the top 5,000 Alexa websites and the 1,000-user crowd-sourced experiment.[1]

2   Ad-Block Background

Ad-blockers come in a number of formats – as browser extensions, VPN-based solutions and full browsers (e.g., Brave, Cliqz and now Chrome Canary [13]). In this work we focus on the browser-extension format as this is by far the most commonly used option.

---

[1] http://www.aqualab.cs.northwestern.edu/projects/AdQoE.

There is a wide range of browser extensions aimed at avoiding or blocking ads including Ghostery, 1Blocker, NoScript, Adblock, and Adblock Plus [18]. Most web-based ad-blockers rely on the browser's webRequest API to intercept requests from websites for modification [7]. The API allows an extension or plugin to act as a proxy and interact with requests from the website at different points in their life cycle.[2] For example, in the Chrome browser Adblock Plus uses the "onBeforeRequest" callback to receive the URL of a request and determines whether or not to block it.

To decide whether a URL should be blocked or not, ad-blockers use crowd-sourced list of filter rules ("filter lists"). Filter list rules are regular expressions that match HTTP requests and HTML elements. Ad-blockers block HTTP requests and hide HTML elements if they match any of the filter rules. Ad-blockers typically allow users to subscribe to different filter lists and even incorporate custom filter rules. EasyList [32] is the most popular of these list, but there are others such as Fanboy's Enhanced Tracking List [11], Disconnect.me [9] and Blockzilla [14] as well as language-specific ones [3]. Filters lists can include thousands of rules; EasyList alone is over 69K-rules long at the time of submission.

For our analysis we use Adblock Plus (ABP). ABP is by far the most popular ad-blocker holding, according to a recent study by Malloy et al. [19], over 90% of the market for Firefox and Internet Explorer and nearly 50% of Google Chrome's market. Despite or focus on ABP, we believe our finding are generalizable to any of the ad-blockers relying on EasyList or similar filter lists.

3   The Performance Cost of Ad-Blocking

Our analysis aims to identify specifically how ad-blockers impact user QoE. The following paragraphs present our experimental methodology and dataset, and describe our evaluation results.

3.1   Methodology and Dataset

To analyze the impact of ad-blocking on user QoE, we load a range of popular websites in a controlled environment, with and without ABP enabled. For this we use WebPageTest (WPT) [20], an online, open-source web performance diagnostic tool. WPT creates a sandbox with virtual machines in which testers can load websites using various devices and browsers over different network conditions. The tool returns a straightforward report card summarizing the performance results of its tests, including a table of milestones alongside speed metrics, such as PLT and TTFP. WPT performs a similar analysis of web pages as [30] and was used by Netravali et al. for accurate record-and-replay for HTTP [23].

We employ a private instance of WPT using a dedicated virtual machine on a desktop and a web server instantiated on Google Cloud Platform [1]. We

---

[2] https://developer.chrome.com/extensions/webRequest.

use a private instance instead of a public one to avoid polluting our results with traffic from other users' concurrent tests. To load different websites in succession, with and without Adblock Plus enabled, we use the Chrome browser flag `--load-extension` to load the unpacked Adblock Plus extension from the local computer's storage.

For our analysis, we aim to limit overhead or bias from the testbed. As such, we do not add latency and leave the default bandwidth for both upload and download. We use the Google Chrome browser (version 57.0.2979.2[3]) with Adblock Plus browser extension (version 1.12.4). After all of the websites have completely loaded, we collect the results using the WPT REST API hosted on our web server, before parsing the resulting HAR files with Haralyzer [12].

We use the top 5,000 popular sites world-wide according to Alexa [2]. This set includes websites with similar URLs and different country codes, which we opted to keep as the may be hosted by different servers or CDNs and potentially be affected differently by ad-blocking.

3.2   Ad-Blocking, Requested Objects and Web QoE

We begin by measuring the reduction in the number of objects loaded with ad-blocking for the top 5,000 Alexa sites. We focus on two of the metrics, Page Load Time and Time to First Paint.[4]

Impact on Requested Objects. Sites are made up of many different types of objects including HTML, CSS, JavaScript, image, and video files. Butkiewicz et al. [5] highlight the growing complexity of websites and report that loading a base web page requires fetching more than 40 objects in the median case. For a non-trivial fraction (20%) of websites, the number of objects requested is well above 100. Our analysis on the impact of ad-blocker usage on the number of requested objects focuses on three of the five common object types – JavaScript, images, and HTML [22] – as these are most typically associated with ads [25].

When websites are loaded with ABP enabled, we see 19% fewer objects requested on average, and a 75% reduction for the 95pct (220 instead of 900 objects when loading with ABP disabled).

Table 1 shows a set of percentile numbers of requested objects across our collection of web sites, when the sites were loaded with and without ad-blocker. The last column in the table is the ad-block exposure rate, defined as in Malloy et al. [19], as the number of ads shown to ad-block users per ad shown to no-ad-block users. The drop in the number of requested objects is clear; at the 30th percentile there is already a 10% reduction from ad-blocking. At the 90th percentile, the use of ad-blocking yields a 25% reduction in ad-block exposure rate.

In Fig. 1 we focus on the difference in requests for various object types across the 90th percentile of websites. The most blocked type of objects are images,

---

[3] The newest version able to work with WebPageTest.

[4] We excluded SpeedIndex results for space considerations; these results were consistent with other findings.

Table 1. When loaded with ad-block, websites request noticeably fewer objects as soon as the 30th percentile. This is mirrored in the ad-block exposure rate, defined as the number of ads shown to an ad-block user per ad shown to a non-blocking user.

Percentile	Adblock	No adblock	Ad-block exposure rate
10	20.0	20.2	0.99
30	51.0	56.0	0.91
50	79.0	93.0	0.85
70	116.0	140.0	0.83
90	177.0	237.0	0.75

followed by JavaScript and HTML files. We see that, on average, 5 fewer requests were made for images, while 3 fewer JS and 2 fewer requests for HTML objects were made. This is, in many ways, as expected since images make up the core of ads [25], and are typically requested asynchronously by JavaScript or included in HTML pages.

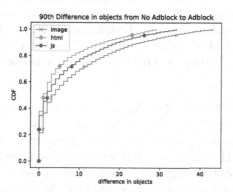

Fig. 1. 90th percentile for the number of requests the types of objects most associated with ads. The most blocked type of objects are images, seen in the right-most line, followed by JavaScript and HTML objects. Java Scripts are used typically for asynchronous loading of ads while HTML objects are used for iFrame ads.

Overall Impact on QoE. In the following paragraphs we focus on the impact that the decreased number of objects requested has on user QoE as captured by TTFP, PLT, and SI.

Page Load Time (PLT). Page load time (PLT), the most ubiquitous QoE metric, is an approximation of the time it takes for all objects on the website to load. PLT is typically measured as the time between when a page is requested and when the *OnLoad* event is fired by the browser. While some studies have explored other estimates of PLT (such as perceived PLT [15]), we use the traditional PLT metric as our proxy for user QoE.

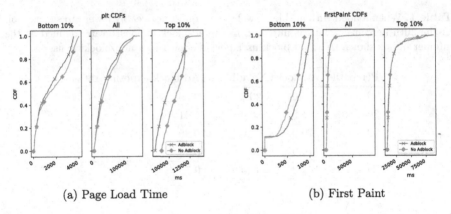

(a) Page Load Time   (b) First Paint

Fig. 2. CDFs of Page Load Time (2a) and First Paint (2b); each set includes the bottom 10% and top 10%.

Figure 2a shows the CDFs of PLT with the complete distribution in the center and the bottom and top 10% of the distribution at the left and right of the figure, respectively. The average PLT is approximately 40 s when loaded without ABP. Using ABP yields and improvement of 5 s, in average. The improvement is even more noticeable in the bottom ten percentile (left-most graph of Fig. 2a), with websites loading 14% faster with ABP enabled, as a consequence of loading fewer objects.

Time to First Paint (TTFP). The impact of ad-blocker usage on Time to First Paint is quite different. TTFP captures the time it takes to begin rendering the first objects of a website [35]. When a user navigates to a website, the browser requests the initial HTML page before requesting and rendering the content. TTFP is a function of the complexity of the webpage and the latency to servers hosting the content and is considered an important factor of web QoE, as a lower TTFP means less time a user must wait before starting to view an active site.

Figure 2b shows the CDF of TTFP in milliseconds. The figure contains a similar set of three graphs as with PLT, with the whole distribution in the center and the bottom and top 10% of the distribution at each side of the figure.

The figure shows the clearly negative impact of ad-blocker usage on first paint time, particularly for the lower 10% of the distribution. This delay results from the time it takes for the ad-blocker to decide whether or not it should block an object. Even if the absolute time to process URLs through the EasyList is small, this small overhead can have a significant impact on TTFP for the fastest sites, many of which finish the painting of the first object in less than a second without ad-blocking.

Summary. The use of ad-blocker introduces a constant processing overhead from checking each URL request with the filter list. For many sites, the reduction in the number of ads' associated objects requested yields clear improvements on

PLT. As most ads are loaded asynchronously with JavaScript, however, these benefits do not offset the processing overhead by the time of painting of the first object (TTFP). The following paragraphs explore this trade-off.

4   Crowd-Sourced Evaluation of Trade-Offs in QoE

The results from the previous section show a clear trade-off in the use of ad-blocker between the *responsiveness* of a website and the total time the user spend waiting on a page to load – for a large number of sites, ad-blocking improves PLT at a significant cost on TTFP.

The relative importance of these two metrics to overall users' QoE, however, is not well understood. To explore this we run a large, crowd-sourced experiment of Web QoE; the following paragraphs describe our experimental methodology and present a summary of our findings.

4.1   Crowd-Sourced Experiment Methodology

Our goal is to capture the impact of the trade-off between PLT and TTFP on users' perception. To this end, we need the ability to present a large random set of users with both version of a website, with and without ad-blocker, under the same or similar network conditions.

Experiment Setting. We conduct a user study with 1,000 users on Amazon Mechanical Turk.[5] In our experiments, we direct workers to a website under our control and present them with two versions (with and without Adblock Plus) for each of a sample of sites.[6] For each Human Intelligence Task (HIT), a user is presented with both versions of 10 sites, loaded with and without ad-blocking, and asked to select the site that "loaded faster."

The websites we use in these experiments were selected, at random, from a subset of 965 websites, from our corpus of 5,000, that show both a significantly slower TTFP and a faster PLT when loaded with Adblock Plus.

As in Varvello et al. [33], rather than using live sites during these experiments, we collect videos of the websites loading through WebPageTest under controlled conditions. Videos recorded with WebPageTest have the time included and end with a gray tinted frame. We modified the server to remove these and make sure the user has no indication of when the website has loaded. We use these videos to provide a consistent experience to all participants, regardless of their network connections and device configurations.

We use two different types of instructions during an experiment to ensure we capture the proper response. The first set of instructions, or *primer*, informs the user as to what they should be looking for during the experiment, asking them to *Immediately select the video they believe loaded first.*

---

[5] https://www.mturk.com.
[6] adblock.aqualab.cs.northwestern.edu.

The second set of instructions, or *directions*, instructs users on how to make their actual selection by asking them: *Once one of the websites finishes loading, immediately click the video.*

Pre- and Post-experiment Survey. Before each experiment, we collect some basic demographic information on users' including gender, age group and country of residence. In addition, we ask two additional questions regarding their familiarity with technology: the range of hours spent online on a typical day, and their own rating of their personal technological expertise. These last questions look to determine the impact a user's perceived level of technical proficiency and experience has on their sensitivity to the performance changes introduced by ad-block.

We also include an exit survey that users must complete before submitting their HIT to Amazon. We ask users whether, in their selection of the page which loaded first, they opted for the page which first showed content or the page which appeared to have loaded everything first. Here we are interested in determining what effect, if any, the user's interpretation of *loaded faster* has on their selection.

Quality Control. We apply a number of common techniques to validate the quality of our crowd-sourced data. First, we restrict our survey to workers that have completed ≥ 50 HITs and have an approval rating $\geq 95\%$. Second, beyond our 10 sites, sampled from a larger set of websites where ad-blocking impact on QoE is ambiguous, we include 2 other websites as control cases. Both cases, placed randomly among the other 10 sites, present an obvious choice of "loading faster" in either the right or left of the screen. We employ this as a form of quality control on all of the HITs. All 1,000 HITs correctly chose the control cases. We received 1,080 experiment results and eliminated 5.6% (52) of them that were partially completed (rated less than 10 sites).

Ethical Considerations. Amazon's conditions of use explicitly prohibit tasks that gather personally identifiable information (PII). The information we did collect is coarse enough that we have no reasonable way to map it to individuals. Our experiments collect data "about what", rather than "about whom", through the relatively innocuous task of selecting videos. Our institution's Institutional Review Board (IRB) did not consider our experiment human subject research.

4.2 Summary of Results

Looking at the set of individual experiments, summarized in Table 2, we see that users chose the website loaded without ad-blocker 71.5% of the time as the one "loading faster". Focusing on users rather than individual page comparisons, we find that 86.7% of them choose the non-ad-blocker option as "loading faster" the majority of the time.

This clear preference for non-ad-blocking appears to be independent of any user attribute, including their age, gender, locale and even their self-reported technical proficiency. As an example, Fig. 3a shows users' majority preference,

Table 2. Experiments and user majority preference for ad-blocking and non-ad-blocking. In 71.5% of tests users selected non-ad-blocking as loaded faster.

Indicator	Non-ad-blocking (%)	Ad-blocking (%)
Experiments (10,000)	71.5	28.5
Users (1,000)	86.7	13.3

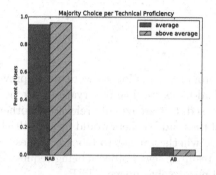
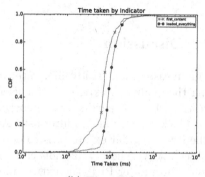

(a) Majority Choice by Technical Proficiency   (b) Time Taken

Fig. 3. On the left is the number of users per majority choice aggregated by technical proficiency. On the right is the time taken per user for users based on what they looked for to indicate the page was done loading.

broken down by technical proficiency. The figure combines users with *below average* and *average* self-reported technical proficiency, as only 3.8% of users selected the former. When examining the results of users' preferences by technical proficiency, there is not significant difference in their preferences, with "average" proficiency and "above average" proficiency choosing the non-ad-blocking option 95% and 93% of the time, respectively.

Interestingly enough, this clear preference is even independent of the user's own understanding of what they consider "loading faster" – the site that show some content first or the one that loaded everything first. When aggregating users based on this, we find that despite 65.1% of users selecting *loaded_everything* as their definition of "loading faster", a large fraction of them opted for the non-ad-blocking option that yields a shorter time to first-content (and longer loading time). Table 3 shows the number of users that selected majority non-ad-blocking ("NAB") or ad-blocking ("AB"), separated by their definition of "loading faster" from the exit survey. Over 96% of users selecting "loading everything" opted for the non-ad-blocking (NAB) version.

For validation, Fig. 3b plots the time users take to make a decision, aggregated by their choice of "loading faster" in the exit survey. As expected, users who are looking for the first content take less time to select a webpage than users who are looking for everything to be loaded.

Table 3. Number of users for "NAB" and "AB" majority choice based on their indicator of page load. We see that users selected *loaded_everything* more often than *first_content*.

Indicator	NAB users	AB users	No majority	Skipped survey
first_content	227	15	209	17
loaded_everything	525	21		

5   Discussion

Our measurement study motivates and provides direction to work on improving the quality of experience for users of ad-blockers. The observations are not restricted to the particular ad-blocker we used, but are equally relevant to other ad-blocker that relies on filter lists. Any of these ad-blockers would need to check the list of regular expressions to determine whether or not to block a requested object. As we show, while this check may result in fewer objects being requested and, thus, lower PLT, the extra time will negatively impact TTFP.

There is a number of possible paths to optimize ad-blockers based on their impact on QoE. One could imagine using historical data to identify when loading a website with ad-blocking results in a significantly degraded TTFP/improved PLT. For these sites, the ad-blocker could delay checking until after reaching the TTFP not to impact a website's initial responsiveness if a potential cost on ad exposure.

Our analysis of ad-blocking's impact on users' web experience is preliminary. Our study focuses on how ad-blocking impacts QoE performance metrics such as PLT and TTFP, but that is only one aspect of the whole web browsing experience. Issues such as *Do ad-blockers make web browsing less distracting for users?*, *Do ad-blockers improve users' data privacy?*, or *Despite their performance overhead, do users prefer browsing with ad-blocking enabled?* are interesting research questions that we leave for future work.

6   Related Work

The rapid proliferation of tools to evade or block ads and their potential impact on the web ecosystem have served as motivation to a number of recent studies.

Pujol et al. [26] examines network-wide advertisement traffic and infers the prevalence of ad-block usage. The authors identify advertisement traffic from passive network measurements in a residential broadband network of a European ISP in order to assess the prevalence of ad-blockers. They found that 18% of the total requests in the traffic they monitored were ad-related traffic.

Malloy et al. [19] studies the global prevalence and impact of ad-blockers. Utilizing a dataset composed of information from 2 million users and more than 20 billion page views across half a million top level domains, the paper examines the pervasiveness of ad-blockers around the world. In addition to studying the geographic, demographic, and publisher trends of ad-blockers, the financial impact of ad-blockers on a small set of publishers is discussed. The paper finds that ad-blockers can significantly impact the revenue of publishers, causing a $3.9M/mo. negative impact on a particular publisher.

A recent study by Walls et al. [34] focuses on Adblock Plus and the Adblock Plus' Acceptable Ads program. This program allows some advertisement providers to pay in order to have their advertisements shown to users. The authors measure the effects of this "whitelist" in order to understand who benefits from it as well as how users perceive "acceptable" advertisements. After running a user study to see how users perceive advertisements, they find that not all advertisements in Adblock Plus' Acceptable Ads program abide by the program's stated policies.

Additionally, different works have analyzed how filter lists work, particularly with respect to anti-adblocking [37]. These works focus on understanding how filter lists identify anti-adblocking functionality on websites. However, they don't examine the time it takes to process the regular expressions present in filter lists.

Other recent work has explored how to effectively defend against JavaScript-based advertisements [10,16]. These studies attempt to define ways to block JavaScript ads without compromising the security of webpages which serve them. They find that a small number of rules is capable of blocking a large majority of ads on the web.

Our work focuses on a so-far ignored potential side effect of ad-blocker usage: their impact on users' QoE. Internet QoE, and web QoE in particular, have received significant attention in recent years. Much of the work has focused on improving Web page loads, with new network protocols [17,31], new Web architectures [22,27,28,36], and developing tools. More recent work, such as Kelton et al. [15] and Butkiewicz et al. [6], present alternative approaches and non-traditional metrics to model users' QoE of experience.

7   Conclusions

The growing prevalence of online advertisements has motivated a number of research efforts to understand their scale, mechanisms, and economics while, concurrently, fueling the adoption of services to block them. We presented the first detailed analysis of ad-blocking's impact on user Web QoE. We used the most popular web-based ad-blocker to capture the impact of ad-blocking on common metrics of QoE for the top Alexa 5,000 websites

We found that, while ad-blocking reduction on the number of objects loaded yields a clear improvement on page load time (PLT), for a significant fraction of sites this PLT improvement comes at a high cost on time to first paint (TTFP). We presented results from a large crowdsourced experiment with 1,000 AMT users to understand the relative importance of these metrics on users' experience. We found that, surprisingly, 71.5% of times users indicated a preference for faster TTFP over shorter PLT, hinting at the importance of first impressions on web quality of experience.

While extensive, our evaluation focused on just one aspect of web quality of experience. The impact of ads or the costs/benefits of ad-blockers are not restricted to the chosen metrics of experience we used in our analysis. Understanding other aspects of experience with ad-blocking is left as future work. We have also started to explore ways to leverage our findings to optimize ad-block users' experience, something that will become increasingly relevant as browsers begin to move towards blocking ads [4, 38].

References

1. Google Cloud Computing, Hosting Services & APIs—Google cloud. https://cloud.google.com/
2. Alexa: The top 500 Sites on the Web (2018). https://www.alexa.com/topsites
3. Barrett, C.: Filter Lists (2018). https://filterlists.com/
4. Brave Software Inc.: Brave Browser: Secure, Fast and Private Web Browser with Adblocker. https://brave.com/
5. Butkiewicz, M., Madhyastha, H.V., Sekar, V.: Measurements, metrics and implications. In: Proceedings of IMC, Understanding Website Complexity (2011)
6. Butkiewicz, M., Wang, D., Wu, Z., Madhyastha, H.V., Sekar, V.: KLOTSKI: reprioritizing web content to improve user experience on mobile devices. In: Proceedings of USENIX NSDI (2015)
7. Chrome: Chrome Webrequest API. https://developer.chrome.com/extensions/webRequest. Accessed 25 May 2018
8. Cortland, M.: 2017 Adblock Report (2017). https://pagefair.com/blog/2017/adblockreport/
9. Disconnect: Disconnect.me. https://disconnect.me/
10. Dong, X., Tran, M., Liang, Z., Jiang, X.: Adsentry: comprehensive and flexible confinement of Javascript-based advertisements. In: Proceedings of ACSAC (2011)
11. Fanboys: Fanboys enhanced tracking list. https://fanboy.co.nz/filters.html. Accessed 24 May 2018
12. Python Software Foundation haralyzer 1.4.11 (2017). https://pypi.org/project/haralyzer/
13. Google: Chrome Canary. https://www.google.com/chrome/browser/canary.html. Accessed 25 May 2018
14. Jimdo: Blockzilla: Ad Blocking List (2018). https://blockzilla.jimdo.com/
15. Kelton, C., Ryoo, J., Balasubramanian, A., Das, S.R.: Improving user perceived page load times using gaze. In: Proceedings of USENIX NSDI (2017)
16. Krammer, V.: An effective defense against intrusive web advertising. In: Proceedings of Conference on Privacy, Security and Trust (2008)
17. Langley, A., et al.: Design and internet-scale deployment. In: Proceedings of ACM SIGCOMM, The QUIC Transport Protocol (2017)
18. Lifehacker: Ad Blocking. https://lifehacker.com/tag/ad-blocking. Accessed 25 May 2018
19. Malloy, M., Matthew, M., Cahn, A., Barford, P.: Ad blockers: global prevalence and impact. In: Proceedings of IMC (2016)
20. Meenan, P.: WebPageTest (2018). http://www.webpagetest.org/. Accessed 24 May 2018
21. Metwalley, H., Traverso, S., Mellia, M., Miskovic, S., Baldi, M.: The online tracking horde: a view from passive measurements. In: Proceedings of TMA (2015)

22. Netravali, R., Goyal, A., Mickens, J., Balakrishnan, H.: Polaris: faster page loads using fine-grained dependency tracking. In: Proceedings of USENIX NSDI (2016)
23. Netravali, R., et al.: Mahimahi: accurate record-and-replay for HTTP
24. Poss, T.: How Does Load Speed Affect Conversion Rate? https://blogs. oracle.com/marketingcloud/how-does-load-speed-affect-conversion-rate. Accessed 14 Jan 2016
25. Post, E.L., Sekharan, C.N.: Comparative study and evaluation of online ad-blockers. In: Proceedings of International Conference on Information Science and Security (2015)
26. Pujol, E., Hohlfeld, O., Feldmann, A.: Annoyed users: ads and ad-block usage in the wild. In: Proceedings of IMC (2015)
27. Ruamviboonsuk, V., Netravali, R., Uluyol, M., Madhyastha, H.V.: Vroom: accelerating the mobile web with server-aided dependency resolution. In: Proceedings of ACM SIGCOMM (2017)
28. Sivakumar, A., Narayanan, S.P., Gopalakrishnan, V., Lee, S., Rao, S., Sen, S.: PARCEL: proxy assisted browsing in cellular networks for energy and latency reduction. In: Proceedings of ACM CoNEXT (2014)
29. Sood, A.K., Enbody, R.J.: Malvertising - exploiting web advertising. Comput. Fraud Secur. 2011(4), 11–16 (2011)
30. Sundaresan, S., Magharei, N., Feamster, N., Teixeira, R., Crawford, S.: Web performance bottlenecks in broadband access networks. In: Proceedings of SIGMETRICS (2013)
31. The Chromium Projects: SPDY: An Experimental Protocol for a Faster Web (2012). https://www.chromium.org/spdy/spdy-whitepaper
32. The EasyList Authors: Easylist (2018). https://easylist.to/
33. Varvello, M., Blackburn, J., Naylor, D., Papagiannaki, K.: Eyeorg: a platform for crowdsourcing web quality of experience measurements. In: Proceedings of ACM CoNEXT (2016)
34. Walls, R., Kilmer, E., Lageman, N., McDaniel, P.D.: Measuring the impact and perception of acceptable advertisements. In: Proceedings of IMC (2015)
35. Walton, P.: User-Centric Performance Metrics (2018). https://developers.google. com/web/fundamentals/performance/user-centric-performance-metrics
36. Wang, X.S., Balasubramanian, A., Wetherall, D.: Speeding Up Web Page Loads with Shandian. In: Proceedings of USENIX NSDI (2016)
37. Wills, C.E., Uzunoglu, D.C.: What ad blockers are (and are not) doing. In: Fourth IEEE Workshop on Hot Topics in Web Systems and Technologies (2016)
38. Wired: The New Chrome and Safari Will Reshape the Web (2017). https://www. wired.com/2017/06/new-chrome-safari-will-reshape-web/
39. Work, S.: How Loading Time Affects Your Bottom Line, 28 April 2011. https:// blog.kissmetrics.com/loading-time/. Accessed 22 May 2018
40. Zarras, A., Kapravelos, A., Stringhini, G., Holz, T., Kruegel, C., Vigna, G.: The dark alleys of Madison avenue: understanding malicious advertisements. In: Proceedings of IMC (2014)

Web Performance Pitfalls

Theresa Enghardt[1]([⊠]), Thomas Zinner[1], and Anja Feldmann[2]

[1] TU Berlin, Berlin, Germany
{theresa,zinner}@inet.tu-berlin.de
[2] Max-Planck Institute for Informatics, Saarbrücken, Germany
anja@mpi-inf.mpg.de

Abstract. Web performance is widely studied in terms of load times, numbers of objects, object sizes, and total page sizes. However, for all these metrics, there are various definitions, data sources, and measurement tools. These often lead to different results and almost all studies do *not* provide sufficient details about the definition of metrics and the data sources they use. This hinders reproducibility as well as comparability of the results. This paper revisits the various definitions and quantifies their impact on performance results. To do so we assess Web metrics across a large variety of Web pages.

Amazingly, even for such "obvious" metrics as load times, differences can be huge. For example, for more than 50% of the pages, the load times vary by more than 19.1% and for 10% by more than 47% depending on the exact definition of load time. Among the main culprits for such difference are the in-/exclusion of initial redirects and the choice of data source, e.g., Resource Timings API or HTTP Archive (HAR) files. Even "simpler" metrics such as the number of objects per page have a huge variance. For the Alexa 1000, we observed a difference of more than 67 objects for 10% of the pages with a median of 7 objects. This highlights the importance of precisely specifying all metrics including how and from which data source they are computed.

Keywords: Web performance · Measurement

1 Introduction

Web browsing is one of the most prevalent applications in today's Internet. Thus, understanding its performance is critical. Hereby, both metrics as well as experiments have to realistically reflect possible performance improvements for actual users. Moreover, they need to be reproducible. However, quantifying Web performance is challenging due to Web page diversity, heterogeneous devices types and browsers, choice of metrics, including network-centric, browser-centric, and user-centric metrics, and the lack of well-established standards. Given this diversity, it is critical that studies provide sufficient details regarding their choice of metrics, data sources, and tools, to (a) understand and interpret the results, (b) to compare results across studies, and (c) to reproduce them independently.

© Springer Nature Switzerland AG 2019
D. Choffnes and M. Barcellos (Eds.): PAM 2019, LNCS 11419, pp. 286–303, 2019.
https://doi.org/10.1007/978-3-030-15986-3_19

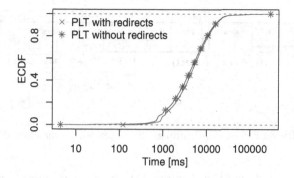

Fig. 1. Page Load Time (PLT) with and without initial redirects.

For instance, Page Load Time (PLT) is a common metric used to estimate user-perceived quality (QoE) and to evaluate mechanisms for improving Web browsing. Thus, inaccuracies can lead to skewed results which may even lead to wrong conclusions. PLT is often defined as "time until onLoad[1] event". A less considered aspect is the *start point* of the measurement. PLT may include initial redirects, e.g., when a browser starts loading http://example.com and is redirected to https://www.example.com—the actual landing page. Such redirects increase PLT. To highlight that the discrepancies are non-negligible Fig. 1 depicts PLTs with and without initial redirects[2]. According to the most recent W3C Navigation Timings specification [3] initial redirects should be included in all browser timings. But, whether redirects actually occur in a page load depends on the web workload, i.e., whether one starts with http://example.com or https://www.example.com. Moreover, even the end point of the measurement is not always well specified (see the Survey section), nor is it obvious how to precisely measure it. We are not aware of any prior work that quantifies the impact of the exact choice of metric on the measurement results.

The main contributions of this paper are as follows. (1) We survey Web performance studies and summarize which measurement tools, methods, and metrics are used. Amazingly, we find that a third of these studies do not provide precise definitions of their metrics and/or data sources. However, it allows us to identify tools which are typically used for evaluating Web performance. (2) We realize a test environment that allows us to compare different tools against a baseline to assess their accuracy. Among our results are that in-/exclusion of initial redirects skews the page load times by up to 47% for 10% of the pages. Moreover, object sizes differ from the packet trace for more than 60% of objects. This is critical as metrics derived from object sizes, e.g., Byte Index of loaded objects over time, differ by more than 50%. (3) We discuss lessons learned regarding Web performance measurements and provide guidance on how to increase the

---

[1] See Fig. 2 for an overview and Appendix A for more explanation.

[2] For details regarding the methodology and the corresponding dataset see Sect. 4.

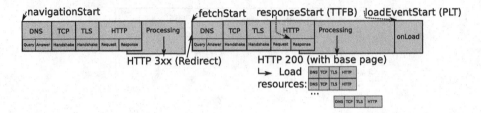

Fig. 2. Browser events and timings. See Appendix A for more details.

accuracy of measured load times and object sizes[3]. Most importantly: (1) HAR files are the most reliable data source for object counts and sizes. Resource timings underestimate these metrics, as they do not include objects in embedded frames, and they often do not provide object sizes for cross-origin objects. (2) As redirects may highly influence load times, make a conscious choice whether to include them.

2   Web Metrics and Tools

Typical Web metrics include load times, object sizes, number of objects, and page sizes. Each of these metrics has various definitions and data sources. Moreover, there are different tools to measure them which we outline in the following.

2.1   Load Times

The time for loading Web pages strongly correlates with user experience [28]. To load a Web page, a browser usually loads the base document, parses it, constructs a Document Object Model (DOM), loads the referenced objects, processes them, and displays the results. Figure 2 shows a detailed view of this process including the browser events which are the basis of several commonly used load times metrics.

Definitions for Load Times: Typically, *Page Load Time (PLT)* is defined as the time until the *onLoad event*. However, in the eye of the user, the actual Web page display is often finished earlier, e.g., when the content is first displayed on the screen. Thus, other timings include *domContentLoaded*, when all objects referenced in the base document have been loaded, *Time To First Paint (TTFP)*, when the first content is rendered, or *Above The Fold Time (AFT)*, when the part of the page visible on the user's screen has been fully rendered. Start times can be the *navigationStart*, the *fetchStart*, or when the first DNS request or TCP connection is opened.

Data Sources for Load Times: Load times based on browser navigation events are available through the standardized Navigation Timings API [2,3].

---

[3] Our tools are publicly available at https://github.com/theri/web-measurement-tools.

Moreover, Time To First Paint (TTFP) is currently being standardized [6]. Being standardized implies that these metrics are available for different browsers based on a "similar" definition. HTTP Archive (HAR) files [7] also include onLoad and domContentLoaded times. However, AFT is not standardized, and estimating it requires not only load time data but also object positions within the Web page [11]. Load times are available through the Resource Timings API from version 1 [4] onward or from HAR files. Object positions are available by querying the DOM, e.g., using JavaScript.

Tools: Most popular browsers[4] implement Navigation Timings and Resource Timings. The standardized version of TTFP is not yet supported by all browsers[5] as of September 2018. AFT is realized via a browser plugin available for Chrome [11]. HAR files can be exported using built-in developer tools.

To automate page loads, both Chrome and Firefox provide remote debugging interfaces, i.e., the Chrome DevTools Protocol[6], and Firefox Marionette[7]. For both interfaces, there is a variety of clients to navigate to a page and interact with it, e.g., to inject JavaScript code to export a timing.

Browser automation frameworks such as Selenium [8] allow more complex Web page interactions using a standardized webdriver interface, which controls Firefox using the Marionette protocol. The authors of Selenium advise against using it for Web performance testing, as its complex setup may incur significant performance overhead [9]. Furthermore, WebPagetest [10] integrates different browser automation frameworks into a single platform. It provides a Web-based User Interface for Navigation Timings, HAR files, load times, and Speed Index.

2.2 Number and Size of Objects

Number and sizes of objects are used to estimate the complexity of Web pages and are needed to compute metrics such as Object Index or Byte Index.

Possible Definition of Object Count, Object Size, and Derived Metrics: Nowadays, Web pages often fetch objects continuously even after the initial page load has completed. Therefore, *object counts* should only include those objects loaded until the onLoad event. This can be done by either observing HTTP request-response pairs or by using the objects in the DOM. With regards to *object size*, networking-related studies usually use the *encoded size*, i.e., the number of bytes transferred over the network. One alternative is the *decoded size*, namely the number of bytes after decompression. However, as objects are transferred over HTTP there is overhead, namely the HTTP headers. Unfortunately, it is often unclear if the object size includes the header or not. The *total page size* is the sum of all object sizes. *Byte Index* is the integral of sizes of objects loaded over time, see [1].

---

[4] See http://gs.statcounter.com/browser-market-share/desktop/worldwide.
[5] Chrome and Opera support it, Firefox is still validating their implementation.
[6] https://chromedevtools.github.io/devtools-protocol/.
[7] https://firefox-source-docs.mozilla.org/testing/marionette/marionette.

Table 1. Survey of Web performance studies: metrics and data sources.

Metrics	Definition	Data source	Used in papers
PLT	Time of onLoad	Navigation timings	6
		HAR file	1
		Unknown	2
	Time to load all objects	HAR file	1
	Unknown	Unknown	3
DOM time	Time of domContentLoaded	Navigation timings	1
AFT	Visible content rendered	Resource timings	2
Object load times	Time until object responseEnd	Resource timings	1
		HAR file	1
Object size	Number of bytes transferred	HAR file	2
		Unknown	2
Number of objects	HTTP request-responses before onLoad	Resource timings	1
	Number of DOM resources	HAR file	4

Data Sources for Object Sizes: One way to derive the number of objects is to count the number of HTTP request-response pairs using the list of entries in a HAR file. The number of objects involved in constructing a page is available via the Resource Timings API. HAR files [7] as well as Resource Timings version 2 [5] provide encoded and decoded body size of each object. In addition, HAR files include HTTP headers, possibly including a Content-Length header, and header size[8], while Resource Timings also includes the transfer sizes of header and body. An alternative is to extract the number of objects from a packet capture trace if it is possible to successfully decrypt all elements. However, exact object sizes can be off due to TLS padding.

3   Survey of Web Studies

Given the variety of metrics definitions, data sources, and tools, we survey Web performance studies published at SIGCOMM, IMC, PAM, NSDI, and CoNEXT during the last 8 years. In total, we include 15 papers [11–25], two of which include links to their code repositories in their papers.

Table 1 summarizes the metrics and data sources of the surveyed papers. Many of them use PLT, as it is well-known and widely used across academia and industry, standardized by W3C, and readily available from various data sources. However, the surveyed papers use diverse definitions and data sources which surprisingly are often not even specified in the paper. We note that only one of the surveyed papers even mentions initial redirects. Several papers compare PLT

---

[8] Note that for HTTP/2, logged header sizes do not correspond to bytes on the wire anymore due to HTTP/2 header compression.

Table 2. Survey of Web performance studies: browsers and automation tools.

Browser	Automation tool	Used in papers
Chrome (desktop)	DevTools	6
	Selenium	1
	Unknown	1
Chrome (mobile)	adb shell	1
Firefox (desktop)	Selenium	1
	Unknown	2
phantomJS	-	1

with other metrics such as AFT, which is more user-centric, but not standardized and, thus, harder to measure. Finally, several papers in the survey (also) measure the number, size, and load times of individual objects to compute integral metrics to quantify the page load process. Such metrics are readily available from the data sources. But many papers fail to precisely specify how they measure or compute these metrics.

Tools Used to Fetch Pages: Table 2 summarizes which browsers and automation tools are used in the surveyed papers. Chrome is most popular, with Firefox in second place. Most studies use the DevTools interface but some use Selenium. To highlight the need for more information we point out that one paper uses a dataset and testbed without stating either the browser or the tools used. Overall, we conclude that a variety of different tools are used, with yet unclear effects on the results.

4 Methodology

So far we have pointed out that many different Web performance studies used different metrics. In this section, we explain our setup to understand the impact of different metrics. To compare the impact of different frameworks[9] and different Web pages we use the following tools[10]: (1) Firefox 61.0.2 with Selenium 3.14.0 and geckodriver 0.21.0, (2) Firefox 61.0.2 with Marionette, and (3) Chrome 69 with Chrome DevTools.

We load pages from a Thinkpad L450 with Debian Stretch. To avoid bandwidth issues, our vantage point is directly connected to a university network. To minimize the effects of DNS caching and delay to the resolver, we use a recursive resolver close[11] to our vantage point instead of popular open resolvers.

---

[9] Our scripts instrument browser automation frameworks directly to give us more control and avoid the overhead of an integrated framework such as WebPagetest.

[10] For realistic browser behavior, which includes the rendering engine, we open Web browsers including the graphical user interface rather than using them in headless mode.

[11] Close in terms of network distance.

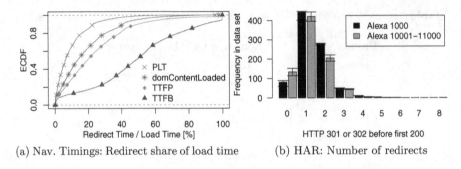

(a) Nav. Timings: Redirect share of load time

(b) HAR: Number of redirects

Fig. 3. Effects of initial redirects.

Since the most commonly used workload are the Alexa Top Lists despite their limitations [26] we also use a snapshot of the global Alexa Top 1000[12], and the Alexa 10001 to 11000 for Marionette and ChromeDevTools. We then repeatedly accessed each page 10 times with the different frameworks. This ensures that all experiments for a single page are done within a reasonable time window. Overall, the experiments were executed between 18. September and 11. October 2018.

For each page, we first initialize a new browser profile with a cold browser cache. We then fetch the page and wait for it to load[13]. As data sources, we export Navigation Timings, Resource Timings, TTFP, and the HAR file using the native HAR export of the browser via har-export-trigger 0.6.1. In parallel, we also run a packet capture to derive our baseline. If one of the data sources does not yield any data, we log an error and exclude the page load attempt from the data set.

5   Results

In this section, we point out various pitfalls with Web performance metrics.

5.1   Pitfall: Redirects

As already pointed out, see Fig. 1, initial redirects can increase PLT substantially, especially for short page loads. Timings excluding redirects may be more representative of page loads by actual users due to browser optimizations, e.g., the user types the first few letters and then clicks on a URL suggested by the browser, or the browser automatically uses HTTPS due to HSTS or adds "www" to domain names the user types[14]. In contrast, load times including redirects are representative of page loads if a user types in the full URL and presses Enter. However, a conscious choice should be made and the web workload adjusted accordingly.

---

[12] 18. September 2018 for Alexa 1000 and 30. September 2018 for Alexa 10001–11000.
[13] We instruct the browser automation tool to wait for the onLoad event.
[14] See, e.g., https://support.mozilla.org/en-US/kb/search-web-address-bar.

Table 3. Object sizes: accuracies for unencrypted objects.

Comparison	Browser	Match	Counted too many bytes			Counted too few bytes		
		Cases [%]	Cases [%]	99%q [KB]	Max [KB]	Cases [%]	99%q [KB]	Max [KB]
Content-length	Firefox	100	0	0	0	0	0	6.8
	Chrome	100	0	0	0	0	0	0
HAR body size	Firefox[a]	72.6	13.4	66.28	2170	14	0.13	852.4
	Chrome	91.9	0.5	0	303.4	7.6	0.3	2925
Res body size	Firefox	39.6	0.8	0	2910	59.6	196.6	5092
	Chrome	46	0.5	0	276.5	53.5	181.5	5092

[a]In HAR files, Firefox logs body size including headers, contradicting [7], see https:// dxr.mozilla.org\mozilla-central/source/devtools/server/actors/network-monitor/network-resp onse-listener.js\#428, accessed 28.09.2018. Thus, we subtract header size from all object sizes.

To assess the impact of redirects we first count the number of server-side redirects[15] for both the Alexa 1000 and 10000–11000, see Fig. 3b. The most common cause for a redirect is that a page is no longer available via HTTP and the browser is redirected to the HTTPS version. Given that many pages have migrated to HTTPS, e.g., 75% of Web pages loaded by Firefox users in September 2018 [27], this is not surprising. Other reasons for redirects include pointers to subdomains, e.g., for localized versions of the content based on the geolocation. Often both occur and lead to two redirects.

Next, we revisit page load times[16]. To quantify their contribution to the load time, we show, in Fig. 3a, the relative percentage of load times of redirects for all Web pages. Redirects account for 6.1% of PLT for 50% of the pages and for 23% of PLT for 10% of pages. This implies that the PLT with or without redirects differs by this amount. The difference is even larger for user-centric load time metrics as these are usually shorter. For instance, Time To First Paint (TTFP) differs by 19.1% for 50% of pages and by 47% for 10% of pages. Indeed, the time for the redirects is about the same as the Time To First Byte after the redirect for about 50% of pages. The reason is that most redirects, typically involve an additional name resolution, TCP connection establishment, TLS handshake[17], and HTTP request.

In summary, we make the following observations: (1) Redirects account for a significant share of PLT and a substantial share of user-centric load time metrics such as TTFP. (2) Studies should make a conscious choice on in-/exclude redirects, see Sect. 6.

---

[15] Server-side redirects use HTTP status 301 or 302. Client-side redirects use status 200 and contain the redirection URL in the response content, which we do not log.

[16] For Navigation Timings, redirects are the time between navigationStart and fetch-Start. For HAR files, we use the time before the first HTTP 200 response.

[17] In September and early October 2018, TLS 1.3 was still not deployed.

5.2   Pitfall: Object Sizes

Next, we take a closer look at object sizes. In particular, we explore if different data sources are consistent with the baseline from the packet capture trace and if they yield similar results.

Comparison with the Baseline for Unencrypted Objects: To validate the object sizes recorded by the different data sources, see Sect. 2.2, we compare them against the baseline which we get via the packet capture trace. This, unfortunately, is only possible for objects loaded over unencrypted HTTP/1.0 or HTTP/1.1. If TLS is used object sizes may be incorrect due to padding. For computing the baseline, we extract HTTP request and response pairs from the packet capture trace and exclude objects with missing bytes. For the remaining object, we separate the TCP payload into the HTTP header and body, and count bytes[18]. Finally, we match the object to the corresponding HAR and Resource Timing (Res) data based on timestamp. Hereby, we exclude ambiguous cases, i.e., where multiple HAR entries match an object from the trace.

The resulting comparison is summarized in Table 3. If the Content-Length header is present its information is mostly consistent with the traces. None of the other data sources is that good. Rather, we find that the accuracy varies widely across data sources and browsers. When manually investigating the most significant mismatches, we find that Resource Timings set object size to 0 for most cross-origin objects[19]. In HAR files, body size is often set to −1 if the browser did not succeed in loading a resource. In several cases, Firefox counted too many bytes if redirects happened. Apparently, it is returning the size of the redirect destination instead of the actual object size.

Comparison of Data Sources for All Objects: Next, we explore the consistency of the results for *all* objects including those that are transferred over an encrypted connection. Figure 4, shows the object size differences for the same object and various data source combinations, i.e., HAR file body size (HAR), Content-Length header taken from HAR file, and Resource Timings encoded body size (Res). Since Content-Length is a close approximation to the baseline for unencrypted objects we use it as a baseline. Res provides the exact same object size as Content-Length in only 42.5% of cases for Firefox and in 43.4% of cases for Chrome. This is consistent with the results for unencrypted objects, see Table 3. For HAR, Firefox provides an object size which matches the Content-Length for 91.3% of cases, see Fig. 4a. Thus, we conclude that HAR's accuracy is better than for unencrypted objects. In contrast, Chrome provides an object size which matches the Content-Length in only 39.4% of cases for all objects. When investigating the difference, we find that Chrome sets HAR body and header size to −1 for all HTTP/2 objects[20].

From this, we conclude: (1) Content-Length provides the most accurate object size but is not always available. (2) Resource Timings are an unreliable

---

[18] See analysis script eval/validate_object_sizes.py in our repository.

[19] Unless the 'Timing-Allow-Origin' header is set, see [5].

[20] In Firefox, only HTTP/2 Server Push objects lack body size and timings.

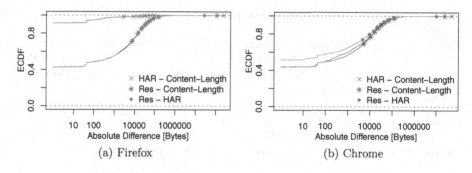

Fig. 4. Object sizes: differences due to metric for all objects.

data source for object sizes, as they do not provide sizes for cross-origin objects, except when explicitly allowed. (3) HAR body size is inaccurate for a significant number of objects, due to bugs in both Firefox and Chrome (whereby Firefox is more accurate than Chrome).

5.3 Pitfall: Object Count and ByteIndex

Amazingly, we find that not only the object sizes differ by data sources but also the object counts (for the same page download)! For the Alexa 1000 dataset, object counts from HAR and Res always differ by at least one object and by 7 or more objects for 50% of cases. For 10% of the cases, they are off by more than 67 objects. Numbers for Alexa 10000 are similar. Among the main contributor to this difference is that Resource Timings do not include objects loaded within commonly embedded HTML Inline Frames (iframes)[21]. Rather, these objects are recorded in the Resource Timeline for the iframe.

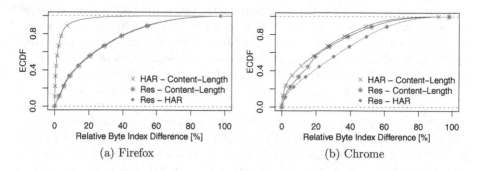

Fig. 5. Byte index: difference due to data source.

Next, we quantify the impact of object size and count differences on the Byte Index [1], which captures page load progress, i.e., loaded bytes over time. In

---
[21] See the examples in Sect. 4.2 of [5].

Table 4. Missing data source: successful page loads vs. errors for Alexa 1000 run

Tools	Success		Before onLoad	No data		No Res	No HAR	No Res and HAR
	Min	Max	Median	Min	Max	Median	Median	Median
Firefox with Selenium	880	898	0	60	76	35	4	3
Firefox with Marionette	915	922	0	37	43	38	3	2
Chrome with DevTools	740	801	100	32	81	14.5	31.5	21.5

Fig. 5, we plot the relative difference between Byte Index for the same page load, calculated from HAR body sizes, Resource Timings body sizes, and Content-Length header (using the HAR body size if the Content-Length header is missing). For Firefox, see Fig. 5a, the Byte Index is almost identical for Content-Length and HAR body size, but differs by 17.1% for Res in 50% of the pages loads, and by 56.4% for 10%. For Chrome, see Fig. 5b, the Byte Index derived from both Res and HAR differs substantially from the Byte Index derived from Content-Length.

Thus, we conclude: (1) Resource Timings do not include all objects of a Web page download. (2) Byte Indexes from Resource Timings vs. HAR files differ by 13.8%/17% in median and by more than 50% for 10% of the pages.

5.4   Pitfall: Data Source Availability

Besides being inaccurate some data sources do not even provide us with any data for some Web page access. More precisely, Table 4 shows the number of successful page loads as well as the errors for the Alexa 1000 for different browsers and automation tools. Firefox with Marionette yields the best results in terms of successful runs that include all data elements. Using Chrome often yields invalid timings, in particular, for the onLoad event. The main culprit is a too early export of the data—the page load has not yet been completed even though Chrome was instructed to wait for the onLoad event[22]. For a non-negligible number of Web pages, we did not get any results for *all* or for *some* of the 10 repeated page loads per browser framework. For most of these page downloads, the browser never invoked the onLoad event, see also Sect. 2.1, and, thus, timed out without exporting any data. Using a different tool would not fix the problem in some cases: Investigating both the error messages logged by the browser automation tool as well as the captured traces we find that common reasons are no DNS response, not being able to establish a TCP connection, or certificate errors. We limit intermittent connectivity issues by spreading out page loads over time. But, we cannot rule out filtering, e.g., due to our vantage point. Still, manual tests for some of the page loads showed that these also fail for

---

[22] Using the Page.frameStoppedLoading event instead did not resolve this problem.

different vantage points. These even involve domains of large application service providers and content distribution networks, which are hosting resources only under subdomains[23].

In summary, our conclusions are: (1) Not all domains in the Alexa Top Lists point to actual Web pages. (2) Firefox with Marionette is more likely to provide complete data than Firefox with Selenium or Chrome.

6   Guidelines for Web Performance Measurement

Next, we derive some guidelines for designing and conducting experiments.

Use HAR Files and Navigation Timings, Not Resource Timings: As shown in Sect. 5.2, Resource timings are an unreliable data source, as they do not include resources of embedded frames and often do not provide sizes for cross-origin objects.

Choose Whether to Exclude Redirects: Redirects significantly contribute to page load times. Yet, they may not be representative for typical end-user Web browsing, recall Sect. 5.1. It is possible to exclude redirects upfront, e.g., by adjusting the hit list to post-redirect URLs. However, post-redirect URLs may change, e.g., due to geolocation or HTTPS migration. Such changes may lead to more page load failures, compared to starting from the "base" URLs of http:// and the top-level domain name. Alternatively, redirects can be excluded in retrospect by computing the timings relative to fetchStart instead of navigationStart for Navigation Timings resp. relative to the start time of the first HTTP 200 object for HAR files.

Choice of Tools: Make a conscious choice whether to use a framework that integrates browser automation tools, such as WebPagetest [10], or write your own scripts. The first has the advantage that it enables comparing multiple browsers out of the box, while the latter gives more explicit control over details. Note, WebPagetest provides Navigation Timings and HAR files. So pitfalls related to Resource Timings do not apply. Moreover, it provides additional metrics such as SpeedIndex. WebPagetest always includes redirects—in line with the W3C definition of load times.

Use Up-to-Date Software: Major Web browsers are updated rather often, typically every 1–2 months. While research projects typically last longer one has to address the trade-off of updating to a newer version during the study: On the one hand, software updates may fix bugs and provide performance optimizations so that the results are more representative of state-of-the-art setups and actual user experience. On the other hand, updating may cause compatibility issues, e.g., with measurement tools that are updated less often and hinder backward compatibility. We recommend to consciously address this trade-off and to include the version numbers of the used tools. See Appendix B for more details.

---

[23] Examples include microsoftonline.com and googleusercontent.com.

Disable Features for a Quiet Browser: Modern browsers do not just load the requested Web page. Rather they often automatically load additional data, e.g., software updates or blocklists, or transmit performance statistics to the browser vendor. This can cause significant performance overhead. We, thus, recommend turning off such features. See Appendix B for more details.

Record and Compare Different Data Sources: Whenever possible multiple data sources should be recorded to enable cross-checks. Data sources include but are not limited to Navigation Timings, Resource Timings, and HAR files. Combining them helps improve accuracy. When choosing metrics it is essential to understand their status with regards to standardization, e.g., published as W3C Recommendation, and to which extent the implementation conforms to the standard.

Mind New Protocols: Deployment of new protocols always has the chance of invalidating existing assumptions about traffic both in general as well as for Web traffic. Moreover, new protocols may require updates to the measurement and evaluation setup or trigger so far unknown bugs in the evaluation. Recent examples include the increased deployment of HTTP/2 and QUIC which use features such as header compression and HTTP/2 Server Push.

7   Conclusion

We show that Web metrics highly depend on which specific metrics, data sources, and/or measurement tools are used. For example, initial redirects can cause Page Load Times (PLTs) to vary by 6.1% in median and by more than 23% for 10% of pages. The impact is even larger for user-centric metrics such as Time To First Paint (TTFP), with 19.1% and 47%, respectively. Furthermore, HAR files and Resource Timings provide widely differing object sizes and numbers of objects which in turn bias derived metrics, e.g., Byte Index varies by 17.1% for 50% of pages and by 54.2% for 10% of pages. However, in almost all Web measurement studies none of the metrics or the data sources are described in sufficient detail. Moreover, they often ignore the bias of the above differences.

Thus, our study clearly highlights the need to (a) improve documentation, (b) choose metrics consciously and with all caveats in mind, (c) double check the results against alternative metrics, and (d) enable qualitative comparisons. To enable this we strongly follow the recommendations of a recent Dagstuhl seminar on reproducibility and suggest that conferences and journals should not count the pages needed to document the precise measurement/simulation setup and the used metrics against the available page limit.

Acknowledgements. Thanks to Dominik Strohmeier for the discussion and the pointers to resources, to our shepherd Jelena Mirkovic, as well as our anonymous reviewers.

A   Web Page Load Explained

In this section, we explain a Web page load in more detail. See also Fig. 2 and the processing models in the Navigation Timings specifications [2,3].

The starting point for a new page load, also called navigation, of a particular URL, is called *navigationStart* in [2]. Initially, *fetchStart* is set to the same value, but if a redirect occurs, *fetchStart* is overwritten before the new URL is loaded.

If another page has been previously loaded by the browser, e.g., in the same browser tab, this document has to be first unloaded. Then, the browser checks its cache to see whether the page is already there. If the page is not in the cache, the browser usually resolves the hostname (resulting in a DNS query and usually answer), establishes a TCP connection, and performs a TLS handshake if the scheme of the URL is `https`. Then, the browser issues an HTTP GET request for the URL. As soon as it receives an HTTP reply, which always contains a status line, headers, and body, the browser processes the reply.

If the reply contains an HTTP status code of 3xx, such as "301 Moved Permanently" or "302 Found", this means that the server redirects the browser to a different URL, which is given in the "Location" header in the HTTP response. This redirect may be a same-origin redirect, which roughly means that both the old and the new URL have the same scheme (`http` or `https`), hostname, and port (see RFC 6454 [29] for details), or it may be a cross-origin redirect. For same-origin redirects, the start and end time of the redirect are recorded as Navigation Timings *redirectStart* and *redirectEnd* [2], while for cross-origin redirects they are not. Unfortunately, nearly all redirects we observed are cross-origin, as the purpose of the redirect is to use a different scheme (HTTPS instead of HTTP) or hostname (www.example.com instead of `example.com`). The same-origin policy is an important security and privacy feature in the Web, so information access is often restricted to, e.g., the same hostname.

Given the new URL to be fetched, the browser records the current time as *fetchStart*, potentially overwriting the old value[24]. It then checks its application cache again, resolves the host name if needed, establishes a new TCP connection, performs a new TLS handshake, and sends an HTTP request for the new URL. If it gets an HTTP reply, this may be another redirect, an error code such as "404 Not Found" or "503 Internal Server Error", or the request may succeed with a "200 OK". In the latter case, the body of the HTTP response usually contains the base document of the Web page in HyperText Markup Language (HTML). As soon as the browser starts receiving this document, it parses it and starts constructing the Document Object Model (DOM) of the page. For example, the document may reference additional resources, such as JavaScript, Cascading Stylesheets (CSS), or images. Typically, for each of these additional resources, the browser has to issue a new HTTP request, unless the resource

---

[24] After a redirect, the browser overwrites the old *fetchStart* value before it fetches the new URL using a GET request. This implies that once the page load is finished, *fetchStart* is the start time of the loading of the final base page, as all previous values related to redirects are overwritten.

is proactively sent by the server using HTTP/2 Server Push. Each new HTTP request may involve an additional name resolution, TCP handshake, and TLS handshake, because resources are often hosted on different servers than the base page. The browser now simultaneously fetches new resources, continues to parse the HTML base page, and processes the CSS and Javascripts, even though these processes may block each other. See Wang et al. [16] for a detailed explanation of this complex process.

At some point, the browser flushes the current state of the DOM to the rendering engine. The time at which this happens corresponds to *Time To First Paint (TTFP)*. The point at which all resources in the DOM have been loaded is called *DOMContentLoaded* and recorded in the Navigation Timings and HAR file. However, processing of the page usually continues, until, eventually, the browser fires the *onLoad* event for the page which is recorded in the Navigation Timings and HAR file. The onLoad Time is usually taken as *Page Load Time (PLT)*. At this point, the page load is considered finished. However, onLoad usually triggers the execution of one or more javascripts, which may result in loading more resources, sending data, e.g., to third parties, or other network traffic. In fact, most modern Web pages load resources continuously long after the onLoad event. Thus, Related Work usually stops counting objects after onLoad.

B   Details of Lessons Learned

Next, we outline additional details regarding our lessons learned, which led to our guidelines for Web performance measurement, recall Sect. 6.

Software Versions: The Debian Linux distribution includes a version of the Firefox browser which is usually quite dated. This can have a major impact on load times. For instance, in Firefox version 61 ("Firefox Quantum"), parts of the code have been rewritten and optimized, which makes the browser much faster than previous versions. Consequently, carrying out Web page loads using an older version results in unrealistically long load times. However, updating Firefox frequently to the newest version can result in incompatibilities with measurement tools. For instance, not every version of the HAR Export Trigger extension works with every version of Firefox, so it has to be updated along with the browser. However, the upside is that in newer versions of Firefox, HAR Export Trigger is supposed to work without having the developer panel open.

Browser Traffic Unrelated to Page Loads: Modern browsers usually issue a significant number of requests that are not directly related to the page load that a user has requested. For instance, Firefox by default loads blocklists for "safe browsing", to protect users from malware or phishing. It also automatically checks for updates and may even automatically download and install these updates for the entire browser or for individual browser extensions. These queries can involve substantial data transfers: For example, we observed the automatic download of a binary related to an H264 media component which we never activated or requested: 500 KB were downloaded in the background. Worse yet, the state of such updates is often stored in the browser profile. This may cause such downloads to be triggered for every fresh browser profile, i.e., each of our page loads. Additionally, the Chrome browser by default issues queries to various Google servers, e.g., it tries to connect each browsing session to a Google account. We provide configurations for Firefox and Chrome to turn off most features that generate such traffic, see our repository https://github.com/theri/web-measurement-tools.

Logging a Trace and Client-Side SSL Keys: To be able to better debug and validate measurement setups and tools, we recommend capturing packet traces that include at least ports 53 (DNS), 80 (HTTP), and 443 (HTTPS). Encrypted traffic can be decrypted after logging the SSL session keys within the browser: Firefox and Chrome log keys into a specified SSLKEYLOGFILE. Note that this option must be compiled into Firefox. It, e.g., does not work with the Firefox binary in the Debian repositories.

C   Artifacts Related to This Paper

The following artifacts are available:

Our Tools, Such as Measurement and Evaluation Scripts: See https://github.com/theri/web-measurement-tools. This repository includes the scripts to automatically load Web pages using Firefox with Selenium and Marionette, and using Chrome with DevTools. Furthermore, it includes the analysis scripts we used to generate our plots.

Data Set of Web Page Loads: See http://dx.doi.org/10.14279/depositonce-8100. This dataset includes data from all of our experiment runs, see Sect. 4. It can be used along with our evaluation scripts to reproduce the plots in this paper, see https://github.com/theri/web-measurement-tools for details.

References

1. Bocchi, E., De Cicco, L., Rossi, D.: Measuring the quality of experience of web users. In: ACM SIGCOMM Computer Communication Review, vol. 46, no. 4, pp. 8–13 (2016)
2. W3C Recommendation: Navigation Timing. Version 17 December 2012. https://www.w3.org/TR/navigation-timing/. Accessed 29 Aug 2018
3. W3C Working Draft: Navigation Timing Level 2. Version 30 November 2018. https://www.w3.org/TR/2018/WD-navigation-timing-2-20181130/. Accessed 17 Dec 2018
4. W3C Candidate Recommendation: Resource Timing Level 1. Version 30 March 2017. https://www.w3.org/TR/resource-timing-1/. Accessed 29 Aug 2018
5. W3C Working Draft: Resource Timing Level 2. Version 11 October 2018. https://www.w3.org/TR/resource-timing-2/. Accessed 13 Oct 2018
6. W3C First Public Working Draft: Paint Timing 1. Version 07 September 2017. https://www.w3.org/TR/paint-timing/. Accessed 10 Oct 2018

7. W3C Editor's Draft: HTTP Archive (HAR) format. Version 14 August 2012. https://w3c.github.io/web-performance/specs/HAR/Overview.html. Accessed 29 Aug 2018
8. Bruns, A., Kornstadt, A., Wichmann, D.: Web application tests with selenium. IEEE Softw. **26**(5), 88–91 (2009)
9. Selenium Documentation: Worst Practices. https://seleniumhq.github.io/docs/worst.html. Accessed 29 Aug 2018
10. Meenan, P.: WebPageTest. https://www.webpagetest.org. Accessed 17 Dec 2018
11. da Hora, D.N., Asrese, A.S., Christophides, V., Teixeira, R., Rossi, D.: Narrowing the gap between QoS metrics and web QoE using above-the-fold metrics. In: Beverly, R., Smaragdakis, G., Feldmann, A. (eds.) PAM 2018. LNCS, vol. 10771, pp. 31–43. Springer, Cham (2018). https://doi.org/10.1007/978-3-319-76481-8_3
12. Goel, U., Steiner, M., Wittie, M.P., Flack, M., Ludin, S.: Measuring what is not ours: a tale of 3rd party performance. In: Kaafar, M.A., Uhlig, S., Amann, J. (eds.) PAM 2017. LNCS, vol. 10176, pp. 142–155. Springer, Cham (2017). https://doi.org/10.1007/978-3-319-54328-4_11
13. Erman, J., Gopalakrishnan, V., Jana, R., Ramakrishnan, K.K.: Towards a SPDY'ier mobile web? IEEE/ACM Trans. Netw. **23**(6), 2010–2023 (2015)
14. Qian, F., Gopalakrishnan, V., Halepovic, E., Sen, S., Spatscheck, O.: TM 3: flexible transport-layer multi-pipe multiplexing middlebox without head-of-line blocking. In: Proceedings of the 11th ACM Conference on Emerging Networking Experiments and Technologies, p. 3. ACM, New York (2015)
15. Wang, X.S., Krishnamurthy, A., Wetherall, D.: Speeding up web page loads with Shandian. In: Proceedings of the 13th USENIX Symposium on Networked Systems Design and Implementation (NSDI 2016), pp. 109–122. USENIX Association (2016)
16. Wang, X.S., Balasubramanian, A., Krishnamurthy, A., Wetherall, D.: Demystifying page load performance with WProf. In: NSDI 2013, pp. 473–485 (2013)
17. Butkiewicz, M., Madhyastha, H.V., Sekar, V.: Understanding website complexity: measurements, metrics, and implications. In: Proceedings of the 2011 ACM SIGCOMM Conference on Internet Measurement Conference, pp. 313–328. ACM, New York (2011)
18. Kelton, C., Ryoo, J., Balasubramanian, A., Das, S.R.: Improving user perceived page load times using gaze. In: Proceedings of the 14th USENIX Symposium on Networked Systems Design and Implementation (NSDI 2017), pp. 545–559. USENIX Association (2017)
19. Varvello, M., Schomp, K., Naylor, D., Blackburn, J., Finamore, A., Papagiannaki, K.: Is the web HTTP/2 yet? In: Karagiannis, T., Dimitropoulos, X. (eds.) PAM 2016. LNCS, vol. 9631, pp. 218–232. Springer, Cham (2016). https://doi.org/10.1007/978-3-319-30505-9_17
20. Netravali, R., Mickens, J.: Prophecy: accelerating mobile page loads using final-state write logs. In: Proceedings of the 15th USENIX Symposium on Networked Systems Design and Implementation (NSDI 2018). USENIX Association (2018)
21. Netravali, R., Nathan, V., Mickens, J., Balakrishnan, H.: Vesper: measuring time-to-interactivity for web pages. In: Proceedings of the 15th USENIX Symposium on Networked Systems Design and Implementation (NSDI 2018). USENIX Association (2018)
22. Netravali, R., Goyal, A., Mickens, J., and Balakrishnan, H.: Polaris: faster page loads using fine-grained dependency tracking. In: Proceedings of the 13th USENIX Symposium on Networked Systems Design and Implementation (NSDI 2016). USENIX Association (2016)

23. Zaki, Y., Chen, J., Pötsch, T., Ahmad, T., Subramanian, L.: Dissecting web latency in Ghana. In: Proceedings of the 2014 Conference on Internet Measurement Conference, pp. 241–248. ACM, New York (2014)
24. Han, B., Qian, F., Hao, S., Ji, L.: An anatomy of mobile web performance over multipath TCP. In: Proceedings of the 11th ACM Conference on Emerging Networking Experiments and Technologies, p. 5. ACM, New York (2015)
25. Naylor, D., et al.: The cost of the S in HTTPS. In: Proceedings of the 10th ACM International on Conference on Emerging Networking Experiments and Technologies, pp. 133–140. ACM, New York (2014)
26. Scheitle, Q., et al.: A long way to the top: significance, structure, and stability of internet top lists. In: Internet Measurement Conference 2018. ACM, New York (2018)
27. Let's Encrypt: Percentage of Web Pages Loaded by Firefox Using HTTPS. https://letsencrypt.org/stats/#percent-pageloads. Accessed 30 Sept 2018
28. Egger, S., Hossfeld, T., Schatz, R., Fiedler, M.: Waiting times in quality of experience for web based services. In: 2012 Fourth International Workshop on Quality of Multimedia Experience (QoMEX), pp. 86–96. IEEE (2012)
29. Barth, A.: The web origin concept. RFC 6454 (2011)

Characterizing Web Pornography
Consumption from Passive Measurements

Andrea Morichetta, Martino Trevisan, and Luca Vassio$^{(\boxtimes)}$

Politecnico di Torino, Turin, Italy
{andrea.morichetta,martino.trevisan,luca.vassio}@polito.it

Abstract. Web pornography represents a large fraction of the Internet traffic, with thousands of websites and millions of users. Studying web pornography consumption allows understanding human behaviors and it is crucial for medical and psychological research. However, given the lack of public data, these works typically build on surveys, limited by different factors, e.g., unreliable answers that volunteers may (involuntarily) provide.

In this work, we collect anonymized accesses to pornography websites using HTTP-level passive traces. Our dataset includes about 15 000 broadband subscribers over a period of 3 years. We use it to provide quantitative information about the interactions of users with pornographic websites, focusing on time and frequency of use, habits, and trends. We distribute our anonymized dataset to the community to ease reproducibility and allow further studies.

Keywords: Passive measurements · Web pornography ·
Adult content · User behaviour · Network monitoring

1 Introduction

Pornography and technology have enjoyed a close relationship in the last decades, with technology hugely increasing the capabilities of the porn industry. From the limited market reachable through public theatres, the introduction of the video-cassette recorder in the 1970s abruptly changed the way of accessing pornography, allowing to access pornography in the privacy and comfort of each individual home. Then, the birth of cable networks and specialty channels in the 1990s, allowed a further step towards accessibility and privacy, giving the possibility to retrieve content directly from home. Finally, the Internet revolutionized again the market, guaranteeing direct desktop delivery to every individual with a connection, interactivity through forums and webcams, free content and, at the same time, anonymity. In 2017, the most used pornographic platform in the

The research leading to these results has been funded by the Vienna Science and Technology Fund (WWTF) through project ICT15-129 (BigDAMA) and the Smart-Data@PoliTO center for Big Data technologies.

world (Pornhub, according to Alexa ranking)[1], claims 80 million daily accesses to its website.[2] The importance of Internet pornography as a prevalent component of popular culture and the need of its study has been recognized for a long time [6].

In this work we do not attempt to classify Internet pornography. Rather, we refer to the term web pornography (WP) to any online material that, directly or indirectly, *seeks to bring about sexual stimulation* [4]. Therefore, the term *pornographic website* is here used to describe services that provide actual pornographic videos, sell sex related merchandise, help in arranging sexual encounters, etc. We refer only to adult pornography websites and we do not advocate the inclusion of child pornography websites in our research, thus this paper has no application whatsoever to child pornography. The word pornography, in the context of this article, refers exclusively to legal content in the territories of EU and USA.

Through the years, WP has been the subject of many studies, that aimed at describing how people make use of it, or pinpointing eventual pathological situation correlated to an excessive use. However, such works typically come from the medical and psychology communities, and are based on surveys that cover a very small number of volunteers. Moreover, previous studies [10,12] report that people tend to lie, either consciously or unconsciously, when answering to private-life concerning surveys, especially about sexuality; there are people who declare more accesses than real (e.g., to show to be uninhibited) and others who understate the actual consumption, fearing social blame. Both these behaviours, called social desirability biases, and egosyntonic/egodystonic feelings (i.e., being or not in accordance with their self-image) make surveys less reliable with respect to other sources of information.

In contrast to previous works, in this study we investigate WP by means of passive network measurements, collected from about 15 000 broadband subscribers over a period of 3 years. MindGeek, a company operating many popular pornographic websites, switched to encryption only in April 2017, being the first big player of WP industry to adopt HTTPS.[3] As such, the vast majority of WP portals used plain-text HTTP up to March 2017, allowing us to leverage HTTP-level measurements, and obtain detailed results of WP consumption. Using recent advances in data science, we extract only user actions to WP portals from a deluge of HTTP data.

The main contributions of this paper are:

- We provide a thorough characterization of WP consumption leveraging measurements from 15 000 broadband subscribers over a period of 3 years.
- We show how users moved to mobile devices through the years, even if the time spent onWP remains constant.

---

[1] As of October 17th, 2018 www.alexa.com/topsites.

[2] www.pornhub.com/insights/2017-year-in-review.

[3] www.washingtonpost.com/news/the-switch/wp/2017/03/30/porn-websites-beef-up-privacy-protections-days-after-congress-voted-to-let-isps-share-your-web-history.

- We show that typical WP sessions last less than 15 min, with users rarely accessing more than one website. Less than 10% of users consume WP more than 15 days in a month, and repeated use within a single day is very sporadic.
- We release our dataset to the community in anonymized form for further investigation [1]. To the best of our knowledge, this is the only public datasets that includes WP accesses from regular Internet users.

The employed metrics are taken from the surveys reported in medical literature and from WP portal reports that we use throughout the paper. We restrict our analysis only to those that we were able to verify given our data. Our results enhance the visibility and understanding of those topics, and give a less mediated overview of users behaviors, mostly confirming what emerges from medical surveys.

The remainder of the paper is organized as follows: Sect. 2 summarizes related work. Section 3 describes data collection, processing and privacy issues, while Sect. 4 presents the results. Finally, Sect. 5 concludes the paper.

2   Related Work

Most previous works that investigate the interaction between users and WP leverage the information contained in surveys proposed to groups of volunteers. Vaillancourt-Morel et al. [18] examine the potential presence of different profiles of pornography users and their relation with sexual satisfaction and sexual dysfunction. The investigation is conducted over a poll that involved 830 adults, and they group users' behavior in three clusters. Daspe et al. [5] investigate the relationship between frequency of WP consumption and the personal perception of this behavior, pointing out that often there are strong discrepancies. Another analysis of the phenomenon is provided by Grubbs et al. [9], where the analysis is conducted over two participants sets, divided in students and adults, showing that moral scruples can infect the self-impression over their consumption. Wetterneck et al. [14] propose a critical analysis of WP, showing the various limitations of the state of the art of studies that assessed online pornography usage, concerning its definition, consumption, and the variability of its measurements.

Fewer works used network measurements to study WP. Tyson et al. [17] extract trends and characteristics in a major adult video portal (YouPorn) by analyzing almost 200k videos, together with meta-data such as page content, ratings and tags. In a similar direction, Maziéres et al. [11] produce and analyze a semantic network of WP categories, extracted from the portal xHamster, in order to find which are the most dominants and if they are actually meaningful. Ortiz et al. [13] study a Chilean websites containing human images and classify them in normal, porno and nude, with the objective of automatically discovering WP websites. Finally, Coletto et al. [3] study users' activity in social networks related to WP, in order to extract information about the seclusion of those communities with respect to the rest of the population and their characteristics in terms of age and habits and gender. To the best of our knowledge, we are the first to use passive measurements to study the behavior of users accessing web pornography.

3   Measurements

3.1   Data Collection

In this work, we rely on network measurements coming from passive monitoring of a population of broadband subscribers over a period of 3 years (from March 2014 to March 2017). We have instrumented a Point-of-Presence (PoP) of a European ISP, where $\approx 10\,000$ ADSL and $\approx 5\,000$ FTTH customers are aggregated. ADSL downlink capacity is 4–20 Mbit/s, with uplink limited to 1 Mb/s. FTTH users enjoy 100 Mb/s downlink, and 10 Mbit/s uplink. Each subscription refers to an installation, where users' devices (PCs, smartphones, etc.) connect via WiFi or Ethernet through a home gateway. Important to our analysis, the ISP provides each customer a fixed IP address, allowing us to track her over time. Nevertheless, a small fraction of customers abandoned the ISP during the observation period, and few new ones joined. All ADSL customers are residential customers (i.e., households), while a small number of business customers exist among the FTTH customers.

To gather measurements we use Tstat [15], a passive meter that collects rich per-flow summaries, with hundreds of statistics regarding TCP/UDP connections issued by clients. Beside, Tstat includes a DPI module that creates log files containing details about observed HTTP transactions. For each transaction, it records the URL, a client identifier as well as other HTTP headers of requests and responses. Our measurements are based on the inspection of HTTP headers, and, as such, neglect all encrypted traffic. However, no big WP portal used encryption at the time our dataset was collected. Generated log files are copied to our back-end servers with a daily frequency. Data is stored on a medium-sized Hadoop cluster to allow scalable processing. All processing is done using Apache Spark and Python. The stored data covers 3 years of measurements, totaling 20.5 TB of compressed and anonymized flow logs (around 138 billion records).

3.2   Definition of User and Its Limitations

Our PoP is located at the Broadband Remote Access Server (BRAS) level. Each subscription is identified by a unique and fixed IP address. However, subscriptions typically refer to households where potentially more than one person surf the Internet sharing the same public IP address. As such, relying on the client IP to identify a user would not be precise enough to study habits and behavior. Thus, in our work we define a *user* as the concatenation of the client IP address and the user-agent as extracted from the corresponding HTTP header. Note that with this definition a single person may appear multiple times with different identifiers if she uses multiple devices or her device incurs software updates that modify the user agent string. Analyses are thus performed on a per-browser fashion – i.e., each user-agent string observed in a household. Privacy requirements limit any finer granularity.

The evaluated dataset includes only a regional sample of households in a single country. Users in other regions may have diverse browsing habits. Equally, mobile devices have been monitored only while connected to home WiFi networks. As such, our quantification of browsing on mobile terminals is actually a lower-bound, since visits while connected on mobile networks are not captured.

3.3 Data Filtering and Session Definition

Starting from a HTTP-level dataset, we need to filter only entries referring to WP websites. Studying innovative methodologies to automatically isolate traffic towards particular services is out of the scope of this work. We employ a blacklist based approach to perform classification. We build on public available lists, achieving robustness by combining three different sources.[4] These three lists provide a set of domain names that offer different WP content (ranging from video streaming to thematic forums). To avoid false positives, we consider only those domain names contained in at least two over three lists. We come up with 310 252 unique entries, arranged over 460 top-level domains.

After filtering entries referring to WP websites, we perform a further step to identify *sessions* of continuous activity. To this end, we group data by user, and process HTTP transactions by start time. We then identify session as follows: when a user accesses a pornographic website we open a new session and account to this all subsequent entries to WP websites. We terminate a session if we do not observe any entry to WP for a period of 30 min. While defining a browsing session is complicated [8], we simply consider a time larger than 30 min as an indication of the session end as it is often seen in previous works (e.g., [2]), and in applications like Google Analytics.[5]

3.4 User Actions Extraction

Subsequently, we further filter the dataset to isolate only those HTTP requests containing an explicit user action by the user. This step aims at isolating users' behavior discarding all HTTP traffic related to inner objects of webpages such as images, style-sheets, and scripts To this end, we implement the methodology described in our previous work [19] that builds a machine-learning model to pinpoint intentionally visited URLs (i.e., webpages) from raw HTTP traces. The followed strategy has as core module a supervised classifier, which is able to correctly recognize user actions in HTTP traces. It results to reach an accuracy of over 98%, and it can be successfully applied to different scenarios, including smartphone apps [20].

In total, after the extraction, we have 58 million user actions/visited webpages towards 59 989 different adult domains. We observe an average of 13 261 different WP users per month. For each user, we determine information about used OS, browser, and if the device was a PC, a smartphone, or a tablet. These information are extracted from the user-agent of the original HTTP request at

---

[4] www.shallalist.de/categories.html, www.similarweb.com, and dsi.ut-capitole.fr/blacklists/index_en.php.

[5] support.google.com/analytics/answer/2731565?.

the time of the capture, using the Universal Device Detection library.[6] We made these data available to the community in anonymized form to guarantee reproducibility of our results and further investigations [1]. In the remainder of the paper, we only take into account user actions, to which we simply refer with the term *visited webpages*.

3.5 Privacy and Ethical Concerns

Passive measurements potentially expose information which may threaten users' privacy. As such, our data collection program has been approved by the partner ISP and by the ethical board of our University. Moreover, this specific data analysis project was also subject to a privacy impact assessment that was done with the data protection officer of our institution.

We undertake several countermeasures to avoid recording any personally identifiable information. Before any storage, all client identifiers are anonymized using Crypto-PAn algorithm [7], and URLs are truncated to avoid recording URL-encoded parameters. Encryption keys are varied on a monthly basis, to avoid persistent users tracking. Sensitive information such as cookies and Post data are not monitored at all. Logs are stored in a secured data center in an encrypted format. We emphasize again that in our research we only refer to adult pornography websites, obtained through open datasets, referring exclusively to legal content in the territories of EU and USA.

4 Results

In this section, we report the most significant results emerging from our dataset. We first focus on the time dimension, showing the evolution of WP consumption from 2014 to 2017 in terms of quantity and device type. We then focus on users, characterizing duration and frequency of their WP use. Finally, we provide some figures about the popularity of services.

4.1 Usage Trends

Our first analysis aims at describing WP consumption trends from 2014 to 2017. In Fig. 1a, we focus on the time spent on WP by monitored users. The blue (solid), red (dash-dot) and green (dashed) curves report, respectively, the 25th, 50th and 75th percentiles of the total per-user daily time spent on WP, i.e., the sum of the duration of all the WP sessions. Curves are calculated only for active users, i.e., users visiting at least one WP website during one day. Curves are not continuous, for the lack of data due to outages in out PoP. The outcome shows a rather stable trend over the observation period, with half of the users spending less than 18 min per day on WP; however almost 25% of users reaches 40 min of daily activity. These are day-wise statistics, and do not provide figures

---

[6] github.com/piwik/device-detector

about the repeated use of WP across multiple days by the same user, as we will see later. Measuring the overall share of users accessing WP portals is not easy using our data, as a single identifier – the client IP address – identifies a broadband subscription, potentially shared by multiple users. However, we notice that every day 12% of subscribers access WP websites, and this value is constant across years. A further analysis on WP pervasiveness is given in Sect. 4.2.

Those results can be used as a comparison with surveys statistics, fortifying or confuting what the participants declare. Vaillancourt-Morel *et al.* [18] study the characteristics of WP consumers. The majority of the chosen sample uses WP for recreation only, on average 24 min per week, a value consistent but slightly higher compared to our data.

Then, we investigate the evolution in device categories use (PCs, tablets and smartphones). We compute, for each device category, its share in terms of number of sessions. Figure 1b shows the results. We notice that smartphones (blue surface), have largely increased their share from 27% to 42% at the expense of PCs. Tablets pervasiveness, reported in green, is instead rather constant. Not shown, the evolution of daily time spent with different devices did not changed too much throughout the years (see Sect. 4.2 for more details).

4.2 Usage Frequency, Duration and Habits

For detailed analyses, we restrict to the last month of our dataset that does not include nor public holidays nor measurement outages, i.e., October 2016. We first characterize WP sessions in terms of duration. Figure 2a shows the empirical cumulative distribution function (CDF) of session duration, expressed in minutes. The duration is larger for PCs than for tablet and smartphones. While most of the sessions are rather short, i.e., less than 15 min for PCs and 10 for smartphones, we observe sporadic longer sessions up to more than one hour. We now draw the attention on the number of webpages accessed during WP sessions, whose CDF is reported in Fig. 2b. Here the difference among devices is limited, with users accessing in median 5 or 6 webpages in a session, with 28% of them limited to one or two. However, in some cases tens of webpages are accessed. Similarly, in Fig. 2c we report the distribution of the number of *unique* websites accessed during a WP session. Results show that smartphone users tend to focus on a single WP website at a time (78% of sessions), while PC users are more prone to visit more websites. For all the devices, very few sessions include visits to 4 or more different websites. Finally, Fig. 2d reports the number of daily sessions for an active user. The figure shows that users hardly make repeated use of WP within a day, without differences among devices.

We next focus on the frequency of WP consumption by users over the month. In Fig. 3 we report the CDF of number of days of activity for WP users in the dataset. The figure indicates that the monthly frequency is generally low, with 76% of the users visiting WP 5 or less days in a month. Still, there are some users with a reiterate usage, with 8% of them consuming WP more than 15 days. These results confirm what is found by Daspe *et al.* [5], who show that the 73% of the participants to a survey access pornography no more than once or twice

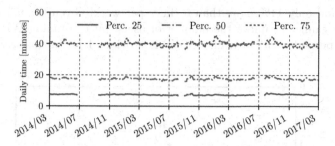

(a) Per-user daily time spent on WP. 25th, 50th, and 75th percentiles are shown.

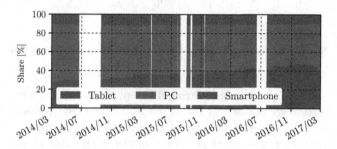

(b) Device category share for accessing WP.

Fig. 1. Usage trends from March 2014 to March 2017. (Color figure online)

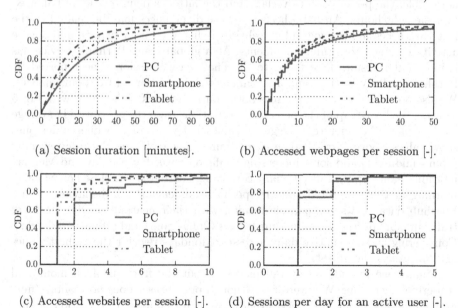

(a) Session duration [minutes].

(b) Accessed webpages per session [-].

(c) Accessed websites per session [-].   (d) Sessions per day for an active user [-].

Fig. 2. CDF of WP session characteristics, divided by device type.

per week, and only 11% more than 5 times per week. Given the nature of our dataset, we cannot estimate the number of users *not* consuming WP. Still, an analysis of per-*subscription* traffic to WP is provided later in this section.

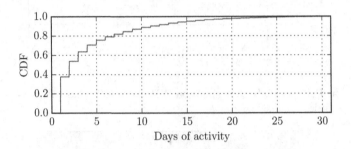

Fig. 3. Number of distinct days in which users consumed WP in a month.

WP consumption also changes during different time of day. Figure 4 provides the average percentage of sessions across the 24 h of the day (red solid line). For ease of visualization, we start the x-axis from 4am, correspondent to the lowest value of the day. The two higher peaks are immediately after lunch time (2pm - 4pm) and after dinner (9pm - midnight). In addition to WP traffic, the figure also reports the overall trend considering all HTTP transactions, regardless their nature (dashed blue line). Comparing WP to total traffic, some differences are noticeable; the peaks do not overlap, and the latter is definitely more balanced over daylight hours. An hypothesis for those divergences may be related to the fact that accessing pornographic websites is likely to be a private and leisure activity confined to intimate moments. At a global scale, Pornhub service has found similar results (See footnote 2). The average session time reported by Pornhub for Italy is 9 min and 30 s, similar to what observed from our analysis. We also provide a breakdown across both hours and days of the week, with Fig. 5 showing the heat-map of the percentage variations from the gross weekly average (white color). Warmer tones register values below average, while colder ones show values above. Notice some clear diminishing traffic on Saturday evening (7pm - midnight) and some increasing traffic on Saturday, Sunday and Monday morning (9am - 1pm). Indeed, many commercial activities are closed on Monday morning in the monitored country, perhaps influencing this behavior. Again, Pornhub data shows comparable results, with their heatmap having peaks of traffic in more or less the same time frames (2pm - 5pm) and (10pm - midnight). Considering the cumulative daily accesses, Mondays register the highest values and Saturdays the lowest.

Finally, we provide an overall picture about the fraction of all monitored subscribers accessing WP website. Although our dataset does not contain fine-grained details about WP pervasiveness, we can still show the fraction of subscriptions where at least one user accessed WP during our period of observation. In Fig. 6, the x-axis represents the 31 days of our reference month (being

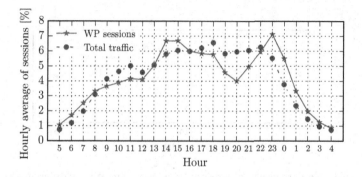

Fig. 4. Average hourly percentage of number of WP sessions and total traffic. (Color figure online)

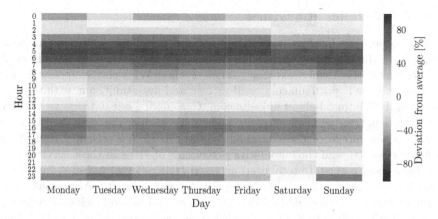

Fig. 5. Weekly breakdown of hourly WP usage. Heat-map of deviation from hourly average.

day 1 October 1st, 2016 and day 31 October 31st, 2016), while y-axis reports the cumulative fraction of subscriptions that accessed at least one WP website. Considering a single day, less than 12% of subscriptions accessed WP, but this fraction raises to 27% after a week. At the end of the month it reaches 38%, meaning that more than one subscription over three generated traffic toward WP websites at least once in a month. For comparison, YouTube and Netflix are daily accessed by 45% and 3% of subscribers respectively. Considering social networks, 60% and 25% of subscribers contact Facebook and Instagram on a daily basis, respectively.[7]

---

[7] A deeper analysis can be found in our previous work [16].

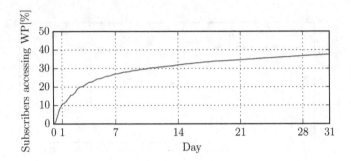

Fig. 6. Cumulative percentage of subscriptions accessing WP at different time in the trace.

4.3   WP Websites at a Glance

In this section, we briefly describe WP website popularity and pervasiveness. Similarly to the Internet global trend, the market is dominated by few big players. Looking at the Alexa rank, (See footnote 1) three WP websites appear among the top-50, namely pornhub.com, xvideos.com and livejasmin.com, with the first one ranked 29th, just behind linkedin.com. Considering our dataset, we observe a similar situation, with over-the-top companies leading the rank. In Fig. 7 we show the percentage of users reached by the top-15 WP websites using bars (left-most y-axis), and the cumulative percentage of visits to these services (red line, right-most y-axis). In total users accessed 7 048 different websites during the entire month. The top-3 websites in our dataset match exactly Alexa rank, with pornhub.com being accessed by 34% of the users. Global tendencies are reflected in our top-15, with only 2 *omitted* websites as local representative of the monitored country. Considering the percentage of visited webpages, pornhub.com alone accounts for 14% of them, and the top-15 together approximately 63% of all WP visits. The percentage reaches 90% considering the top-204 websites, confirming the concentration of users around top services. Interestingly, very similar numbers hold for the overall traffic (including also non-WP websites), with top-15 accounting for 61% of traffic and 90% due to 195 websites.

Finally, we notice that 3 out of 15 WP websites of Fig. 7 belong to MindGeek, a company owning pornhub.com, redtube.com, youporn.com, and dozens of other websites.[8] MindGeek websites account for more than 20% of accesses in our dataset, making it a market leader. For comparison, the second website in terms of users and visits is xvideos.com (owned by WGCZ Holding), with less than half the users of MindGeek services, according to our data, suggesting a scenario where the ecosystem is lead by few big players in a dominant position.

---

[8] https://goo.gl/UgLqAj.

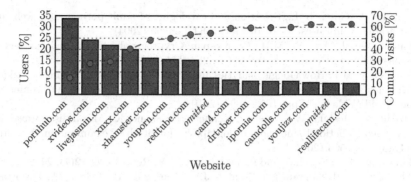

Fig. 7. Top-15 WP websites ranked according to percentage of users accessing them. Cumulative percentages of their visits with respect to all WP visits are also shown. (Color figure online)

5 Conclusion

In this paper we offered a quantitative analysis concerning web pornography consumption. To the best of our knowledge, we are the first to use network passive measurements to study the interactions of users with these services. We followed an exploratory approach on data, focusing on questions, topics and metrics typically analyzed in previous surveys and research works, e.g., frequency of fruition and the time spent on WP. We found interesting results, some typical of the observed population and others capable of confirming global trends.

Our results draw the attention to a large and active group of users, and may be helpful for researchers that study web services consumption and human behavior at large. The obtained outcomes can be checked and verified, thanks to the fact that we release our anonymized dataset. Furthermore, the chosen metrics allowed a comparison with outcomes of previously conducted surveys, and mostly confirmed their results.

References

1. Anonymized datasaset of visits to webpages belonging to web pornographic domains, obtained from network passive measurements (2018). https://smartdata. polito.it/adult-clickstreams/
2. Catledge, L.D., Pitkow, J.E.: Characterizing browsing strategies in the world-wide web. Elsevier Comput. Netw. ISDN Syst. **27**(6), 1065–1073 (1995)
3. Coletto, M., Aiello, L.M., Lucchese, C., Silvestri, F.: Adult content consumption in online social networks. Soc. Netw. Anal. Min. **7**(1), 28:1–28:21 (2017)
4. Cornog, M.: Libraries, erotica, pornography. Libr. Q.: Inf. Community Policy **61**(4), 457–459 (1991)
5. Daspe, M.E., Vaillancourt-Morel, M.P., Lussier, Y., Sabourin, S., Ferron, A.: When pornography use feels out of control: the moderation effect of relationship and sexual satisfaction. J. Sex Marital Ther. **44**(4), 343–353 (2018)

6. Dilevko, J., Gottlieb, L.: Selection and cataloging of adult pornography web sites for academic libraries. J. Acad. Libr. **30**(1), 36–50 (2004)
7. Fan, J., Xu, J., Ammar, M.H.: Crypto-pan: Cryptography-based prefix-preserving anonymization. Comput. Netw. **46**(2), 253–272 (2004)
8. Fomitchev, M.I.: How Google analytics and conventional cookie tracking techniques overestimate unique visitors. In: Proceedings of the 19th International Conference on World Wide Web, pp. 1093–1094 (2010)
9. Joshua, G., Joshua, W., Julie, E., Kenneth, P., Shane, K.: Moral disapproval and perceived addiction to internet pornography: a longitudinal examination. Addiction **113**(3), 496–506 (2014)
10. Lewontin, R.C.: Sex, lies, and social science. N. Y. Rev. Books **42**(7), 24–29 (1995)
11. Mazières, A., Trachman, M., Cointet, J.P., Coulmont, B., Prieur, C.: Deep tags: toward a quantitative analysis of online pornography. Porn Studies **1**(2), 80–95 (2014)
12. Ochs, E.P., Binik, Y.M.: The use of couple data to determine the reliability of self-reported sexual behavior. J. Sex Res. **36**(4), 374–384 (1999)
13. Ortiz, F., Castañeda, V., Baeza-Yates, R., Verschae, R., del Solar, J.R.: Characterizing objectionable image content (pornography and nude images) of specific web segments: Chile as a case study. In: Web Congress, Latin American(LA-WEB), pp. 269–278 (2005)
14. Short, M.B., Black, L., Smith, A.H., Wetterneck, C.T., Wells, D.E.: A review of internet pornography use research: methodology and content from the past 10 years. Cyberpsychology Behav. Soc. Netw. **15**(1), 13–23 (2012)
15. Trevisan, M., Finamore, A., Mellia, M., Munafo, M., Rossi, D.: Traffic analysis with off-the-shelf hardware: challenges and lessons learned. IEEE Commun. Mag. **55**(3), 163–169 (2017)
16. Trevisan, M., Giordano, D., Drago, I., Mellia, M., Munafo, M.: Five years at the edge: watching internet from the ISP network. In: Proceedings of the 14th International Conference on Emerging Networking EXperiments and Technologies, pp. 1–12. CoNEXT 2018. ACM, New York (2018). https://doi.org/10.1145/3281411.3281433
17. Tyson, G., Elkhatib, Y., Sastry, N., Uhlig, S.: Measurements and analysis of a major adult video portal. ACM Trans. Multimedia Comput. Commun. Appl. **12**(2), 35:1–35:25 (2016)
18. Vaillancourt-Morel, M.P., Blais-Lecours, S., Labadie, C., Bergeron, S., Sabourin, S., Godbout, N.: Profiles of cyberpornography use and sexual well-being in adults. J. Sex. Med. **14**(1), 78–85 (2017)
19. Vassio, L., Drago, I., Mellia, M.: Detecting user actions from HTTP traces: toward an automatic approach. In: 2016 International Wireless Communications and Mobile Computing Conference (IWCMC), pp. 50–55 (2016)
20. Vassio, L., Drago, I., Mellia, M., Houidi, Z.B., Lamali, M.L.: You, the web, and your device: longitudinal characterization of browsing habits. ACM Trans. Web **12**(4), 24:1–24:30 (2018)

Author Index

Printed in the United States
By Bookmasters